Fodor's 95 Paris

Fodor's Travel Publications, Inc.
New York • London • Toronto • Sydney • Auckland

Fodor's Paris

Editor: Kristen D. Perrault
Editorial Contributors: Steven K. Amsterdam, William Echikson, Janet Foley, Echo Garrett, Elva Harding, Corinne LaBalme, Baty Landis, Bevin McLaughlin, Mary Ellen Schultz, Alexandra Siegel, Nancy van Itallie
Creative Director: Fabrizio La Rocca
Cartographer: David Lindroth
Illustrator: Karl Tanner
Cover Photograph: Nicholas Devore III/Photographers/Aspen

Design: Vignelli Associates

Special Sales

Contents

Maps and Plans

Foreword

While every care has been taken to ensure the accuracy of the information in this guide, the passage of time will always bring change, and consequently, the publisher cannot accept responsibility for errors that may occur.

All prices and opening times quoted here are based on information supplied to us at press time. Hours and admission fees may change, however, and the prudent traveler will avoid inconvenience by calling ahead.

Fodor's wants to hear about your travel experiences, both pleasant and unpleasant. When a hotel or restaurant fails to live up to its billing, let us know and we will investigate the complaint and revise our entries where the facts warrant it.

Send your letters to the editors of Fodor's Travel Publications, 201 East 50th Street, New York, NY 10022.

Highlights'95 and Fodor's Choice

Highlights '95

Visitors to Paris have even more reasons to head straight for the Louvre—about twice as many, in fact. By the time the **Grand Louvre** project is completed in 1996, the museum (now officially named the Grand Louvre, though it's doubtful anyone will call it that) will have doubled its exhibition space. The renovation of the Richelieu wing has already added 165 exhibition rooms. Most of the facades have been cleaned, and dozens of paintings have been restored. Other additions include the underground Carrousel du Louvre concourse, housing scores of glossy showcases for French luxury-goods manufacturers and a permanent space for the presentation of French fashion collections, and an underground garage.

As François Mitterand's presidency draws toward its close in 1995, the ambitious building campaign that included the Louvre project (with I.M. Pei's dazzling pyramid), as well as the Opéra Bastille, the Arche de la Défense, and the science museum at La Villette, enters its final phase. His (personal and political) health permitting, Mitterand will inaugurate the **Bibliothèque de France,** the last major monument of his mandate, shortly before his term ends. The controversial library's four transparent towers—shaped like open books—soar upward, taking their considerable place in the Paris skyline.

The TGB (*Très Grande Bibliothèque*), as it is called, anchors the city's burgeoning southeast. Though not a tourist attraction in the usual sense, this area (the Quai de la Gare on the Left Bank in the 13th arrondissement and the Quai de Bercy on the Right Bank in the 12th arrondissement) will soon be a must-see for visitors interested in urban planning. By 1996, this far-flung sector—known as **Seine Rive Gauche**—will be linked to central Paris and points west by the express **Météor** métro line; the area is already being touted as the "Latin Quarter of the next millennium." Covering nearly half a mile of riverfront, it will include, along with the TGB, a university, a graphic-arts center, student housing, artists' studios, and cultural facilities.

The **Centre National d'Art et de Culture Georges-Pompidou,** better known as the **Beaubourg,** is benefitting from a much-needed brushup. Since 1977 more than 20,000 visitors a day have tramped through the museum, straining the already fragile structure and facilities. Architect Renzo Piano, who with Richard Rogers designed the center, ordered a fresh coat of paint for the museum's skeletal shell, and is supervising the current full-scale renovation of the interior.

More from the face-lift department: A year-long restoration completed in December 1992 left the regal **place Vendôme** with a sparkling granite pavement and twice its previous number of Second Empire–style street lamps (they create a magic glow on misty nights). Better still, motor traffic is now confined to two lanes, and parking (even for the privileged patrons of the Ritz, Chanel, and Cartier's) is restricted to an underground lot.

On the economic front, a recession within France has kept prices down, and U.S. visitors will find their money goes further in Paris stores and restaurants than it has in recent years. Dining can be particularly affordable, as the trend toward budget bistros shows no signs of abating. Parisians are flocking to these informal eateries for traditional dishes such as pot au feu, mashed potatoes, and crème brûlée—comfort foods for an uncertain *fin de siècle*.

Outside Paris, the much-ballyhooed **Euro Disney Resort** was struggling at press time with slack attendance and less-than-enthusiastic crowds. Europeans, it seems, are balking at the high restaurant and hotel prices, especially since 1992's devaluation of the lira, the peseta, and the pound. Additional hotel rooms at the resort, as well as film studios, a second theme park, and another golf course, have been postponed until 1996 at the earliest.

Fodor's Choice

No two people will agree on what makes a perfect vacation, but it's fun and helpful to know what others think. We hope you'll have a chance to experience some of Fodor's Choices yourself while visiting the City of Light. For detailed information about each entry, refer to the appropriate chapters within this guidebook.

Views

The Champs-Elysées from place de la Concorde

The Eiffel Tower from Trocadéro across the Seine River

Paris spread out beneath the Sacré-Coeur at Montmartre

Notre Dame from the Square Jean XXIII

Walks

Along the banks of the Seine between the Pont Neuf and the Ile St-Louis

From place St-Germain-des-Prés to the Panthéon and place de la Contrescarpe via boulevard St-Germain, the Latin Quarter, and the Sorbonne

From the Eiffel Tower to the place des Invalides and the National Assembly via rue St-Dominique

From the Arc de Triomphe to the Louvre, via the Champs-Elysées, place de la Concorde, and the Tuileries Gardens

Monuments

Arc de Triomphe

Eiffel Tower

Louvre's glass pyramids

The bronze column on place Vendôme

Works of Art

The *Lady and the Unicorn* tapestries at the Musée National du Moyen-Age (formerly the Musée de Cluny)

Manet's *Déjeuner sur l'Herbe* in the Musée d'Orsay

Monet's *Water Lilies* at the Musée de l'Orangerie

The Rubens room in the renovated Louvre, displaying 21 murals describing the life of Marie de Médicis

The royal tombs in the basilica of St-Denis

Museums

Musée d'Orsay

Musée Rodin

Musée Marmottan

Musée Picasso

The Louvre

Churches

Notre Dame Cathedral

St-Germain-des-Prés

Sainte-Chapelle

St-Eustache

Dôme Church at the Invalides

Times to Treasure

Coffee and croissants outside a café on a sunny morning

Fête de la Musique: impromptu street concerts (June 21)

The French Open Tennis Championships at Roland Garros in May

An early evening aperitif at Café Beaubourg, admiring the street performers in front of the Pompidou Center

Bastille Day (July 14)

Restaurants

Jamin/Robuchon, 16e (*$$$$*)

Ledoyen, 8e (*$$$$*)

Les Ambassadeurs, 8e (*$$$$*)

Lucas Carton, 8e (*$$$$*)

Miravile, 4e (*$$$*)

Chez Pauline, 1er (*$$–$$$*)

La Timonerie, 5e (*$$–$$$*)

Campagne et Provence, 5e (*$$*)

Casa Olympe, 9e (*$$*)

La Régalade, 14e (*$*)

Thoumieux, 7e (*$*)

Hotels

Crillon, 8e (*$$$$*)

Ritz, 1er (*$$$$*)

Deux-Iles, 4e (*$$$*)

Hôtel d'Angleterre, 6e (*$$$*)

Grandes Ecoles, 5e (*$$*)

Marronniers, 6e (*$$*)

Place des Vosges, 4e (*$$*)

Argenson, 8e (*$*)

Castex, 4e (*$*)

Shopping

Rue du Faubourg St-Honoré and avenue Montaigne (designer clothes)

The Marais and place des Victoire (avant-garde designer clothes)

Place Vendôme (jewelry)

Trocadéro–Victor Hugo area (second-hand shops)

Au Printemps (department store)

Louvre des Antiquaires complex (antiques)

Rue Lepic, rue de Buci, and rue Mouffetard (street markets)

Open-air bookstalls along the Seine

Bastille area (trendy boutiques)

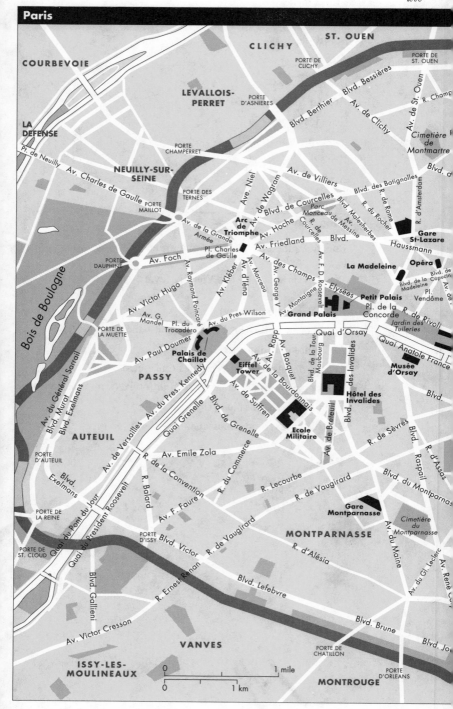

Paris

COURBEVOIE

CLICHY

ST. OUEN

PORTE DE
CLICHY

PORTE DE
ST. OUEN

LEVALLOIS-
PERRET

PORTE
D'ASNIERES

Blvd. Berthier

Blvd. Bessières

Av. de Clichy

Av. de St. Ouen

R. Champ

Cimetière
de
Montmartre

LA
DEFENSE

Pt. de Neuilly

PORTE
CHAMPERRET

Blvd. d'

NEUILLY-SUR-
SEINE

Av. Charles de Gaulle

PORTE
MAILLOT

PORTE DES
TERNES

Av. de Villiers

Ave. Niel

Av. de Wagram

Blvd. de Courcelles

Blvd. des Batignolles

R. de Rome

R. du Rocher

Av. d'Amsterdam

Gare
St-Lazare

Av.
Hoche

Parc
Monceau

Blvd. Malesherbes

R. de
Courcelles

Av. de Messine

Arc
de
Triomphe

PORTE
DAUPHINE

Av. Foch

Av. de la Grande
Armée

Pl. Charles
de Gaulle

Av. Friedland

Blvd.

Haussmann

Av. Kléber

Av. d'Iéna

Av. Marceau

Av. des Champs

Av. George V

Bois de Boulogne

Av. Victor Hugo

Av. Raymond Poincaré

PORTE DE
LA MUETTE

Av. G.
Mandel

Pl. du
Trocadéro

Av. Paul Doumer

Av. du Pres.-Wilson

La Madeleine

Opéra

Blvd. de la
Madeleine

Blvd.
Capucin

PL.
Vendôme

Av.

Petit Palais

Elysées

Av. Montaigne

Av. F. D. Roosevelt

Grand Palais

Pl. de la
Concorde

R. de Rivoli

Jardin des
Tuileries

Quai d'Orsay

Quai Anatole France

Palais de
Chaillot

Eiffel
Tower

PASSY

Av. du Pres. Kennedy

Av. de Suffren

Av. de la Bourdonnais

Av. Rapp

Av. Bosquet

Blvd. de la Tour Maubourg

des Invalides

Musée
d'Orsay

Hôtel des
Invalides

Blvd.

AUTEUIL

Av. Murat

Blvd. Exelmans

Quai Grenelle

Blvd. de Grenelle

Ecole
Militaire

Av. de Breteuil

R. de Sèvres

Blvd.
Raspail

R. d'Assas

Av. du Général Sarrail

PORTE
D'AUTEUIL

Blvd.
Exelmans

Av. de Versailles

R. de la Convention

Av. Emile Zola

R. du Commerce

R. Lecourbe

R. de Vaugirard

Blvd. du Montparnasse

PORTE DE
LA REINE

Quai du Pont du Jour

R. Balard

PORTE
D'ISSY

Blvd. Victor

R. de Vaugirard

Gare
Montparnasse

Cimetière
du
Montparnasse

Av. du Maine

PORTE DE
ST. CLOUD

Quai du Président Roosevelt

Blvd. Gallieni

R. Ernest Renan

Av. F. Faure

R. d'Alésia

MONTPARNASSE

Av. du Gl. Leclerc

Av. René Co

Blvd. Lefebvre

Blvd. Brune

Blvd. Jo

Av. Victor Cresson

VANVES

PORTE DE
CHATILLON

PORTE
D'ORLEANS

MONTROUGE

ISSY-LES-
MOULINEAUX

0 _____ 1 mile

0 _____ 1 km

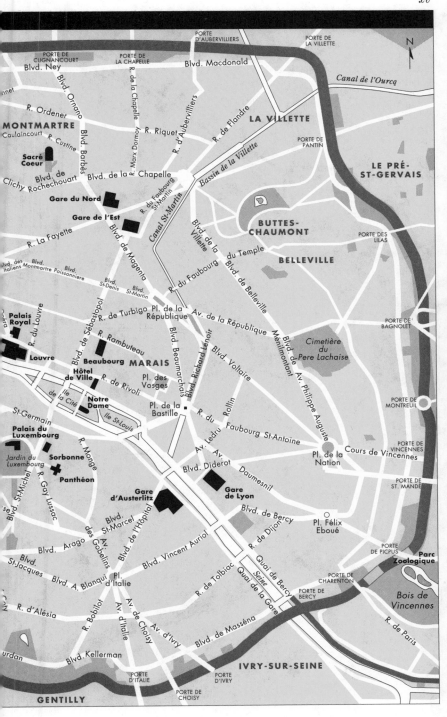

Paris Arrondissements

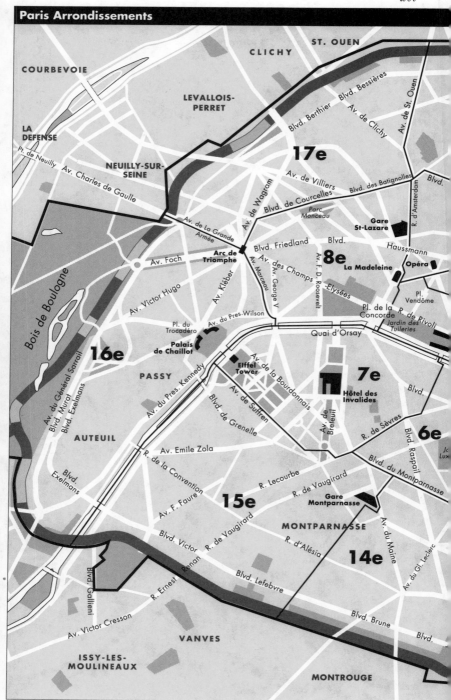

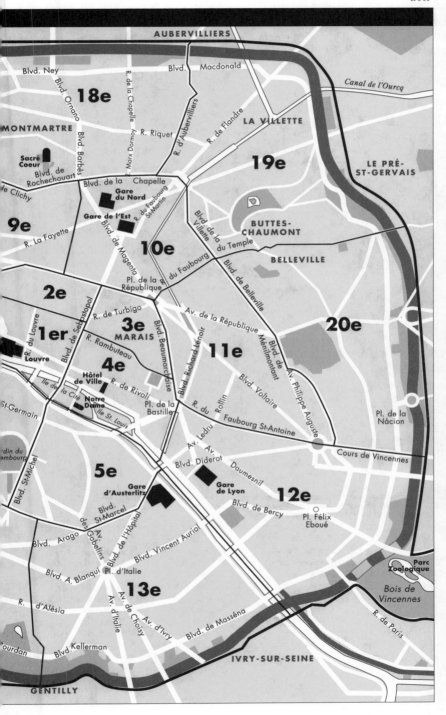

World Time Zones

Numbers below vertical bands relate each zone to Greenwich Mean Time (0 hrs.).
Local times frequently differ from these general indications,
as indicated by light-face numbers on map.

Algiers, **29**	Berlin, **34**	Delhi, **48**	Istanbul, **40**
Anchorage, **3**	Bogotá, **19**	Denver, **8**	Jerusalem, **42**
Athens, **41**	Budapest, **37**	Djakarta, **53**	Johannesburg, **44**
Auckland, **1**	Buenos Aires, **24**	Dublin, **26**	Lima, **20**
Baghdad, **46**	Caracas, **22**	Edmonton, **7**	Lisbon, **28**
Bangkok, **50**	Chicago, **9**	Hong Kong, **56**	London (Greenwich), **27**
Beijing, **54**	Copenhagen, **33**	Honolulu, **2**	Los Angeles, **6**
	Dallas, **10**		Madrid, **38**
			Manila, **57**

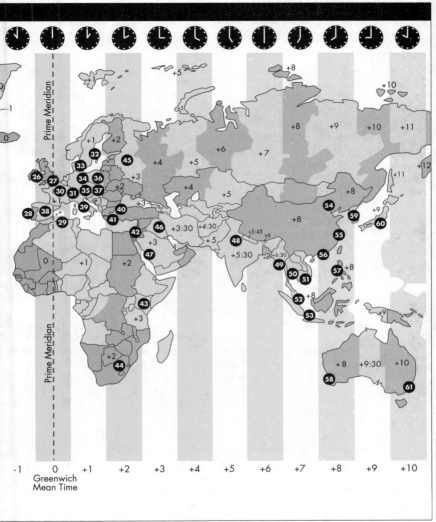

-1   0   +1   +2   +3   +4   +5   +6   +7   +8   +9   +10

Greenwich
Mean Time

Introduction

By John G. Morris

John G. Morris has worked as a journalist for major American newspapers and magazines—the Washington Post, *the* New York Times, Life, Ladies' Home Journal, *and* National Geographic. *He now contributes regularly to the* International Herald Tribune.

It is often said that Paris isn't what it used to be. Of course not. When I first came to Paris in 1944, there was still shooting in the streets. I looked out on the sleepy city from a balcony of the Hôtel Scribe, early on a September morning, and the air was heavy with suspense. Paris had just emerged from 50 months of German occupation. There was an ominous, audible rumble of war to the north and east. During the night there had been occasional small-arms fire, as the *résistance* rounded up German soldiers still in hiding—and settled scores with their collaborators.

I had checked into the Scribe, headquarters for Allied war correspondents, in the middle of the night, after hitching rides in jeeps and command cars all the way from Normandy. My mission was to help *Life* magazine reestablish a Paris bureau. I had never been in Paris before, and my French was strictly from high school. How was I to manage in the vast, unfamiliar, and malfunctioning city? *Life* photographer Robert Capa, with whom I had shared both perilous and frivolous moments in Normandy, came to my rescue. At breakfast he said, "I have a French friend who will show you around, a photographer named Henri Cartier-Bresson. He's been living underground in Paris ever since he escaped from a German prison camp. He went to Oxford, so I think you'll understand him." At the door of the Scribe, I was introduced to a slight, blue-eyed young man, shy but friendly. He held a bicycle with one hand, his pants clipped to avoid the gears; with the other he greeted me. Certainly, Paris isn't what it used to be.

These days I can sit in a café with a *crème* or a *thé au citron*, reading the paper to the tinkling musical background of the pinball machine. I can sit there for hours, in the sun or shade, and the waiter will not even fidget. I look up and watch the people around me. Just to my left a couple is making love across the table, elbows firmly planted and hands clasped together, faces virtually invisible. The young man over there is obviously waiting for someone. He alternates coffee and cigarettes. Finally she comes, hands him a little note, and leaves without a word. What has happened between them? The old man on the right orders tea with milk. He unwraps the sugar cube, touches it to his tongue, wraps it again, and puts it in his pocket. How long will it last him? A strolling *accordéoniste* comes by, plays just enough not to become a nuisance, passes the hat, and quietly goes on . . . followed by a girl selling red roses and, a bit later, by a bare-chested black man who swallows flaming swords.

You have heard it said that "Paris would be great if it weren't for the Parisians." If a Frenchman says it, it means that he is determined to be provincial. But if it comes from a foreigner, it probably means that he or she has had an unfortunate linguistic encounter. It takes a certain nerve to try out one's French, no matter one's level. A former *New York Times* Paris bureau chief told me he got by only because his French was "audacious." Many foreigners, and I am one, are afraid of being laughed at. The cure for this is to make a faux pas so ridiculous that you can tell it on yourself. A young photographer friend of mine, for example, was trying to tell some French friends about his first date with a girl of good family and prim reputation. He thought he was telling them that he had kissed her good night—the polite peck. Instead, he was saying that he had bedded her the first night. They were impressed but incredulous.

My own greatest blooper came in our local mom-and-pop produce store. We had noticed that it was possible to order a spit-roasted chicken, and one Sunday morning I was dispatched to place such an order. After rehearsing my speech, I pushed my way past the line of fruit-and-vegetable customers to the rear of the shop and said, *"Madame, je voudrais commander un chien rôti"* (I should like to order a roast dog). With perfect *politesse* she replied, *"Un chien rôti?"* Immediately realizing what I had said, I broke up—as did the entire line of customers. If only I had had the presence to continue, *"Mais oui, madame, vous savez bien que les Américains aiment les hot dogs"* (Of course, madame, you know very well that we Americans love hot dogs!).

Paris is the city where, once you are known, shopkeepers greet you coming and going and proprietors shake your hand as you leave their restaurants. It is the city where bus drivers may reopen the door for you if you come on the run, and where bellmen are sometimes too proud to linger for a tip.

Not that Parisians are perfect. There are the usual shady characters who populate our urbanized world. There are pickpockets, just to make you feel at home. *En garde!* Weapons are not often used in Paris crime, but thieves can be ingenious. A friend from Manhattan was the victim of a classic ploy. Sensing that his wallet had been lifted while he was standing in awe of Notre Dame, he whirled on the probable thief, a girl of about 12. To attest her innocence, she lifted her dress, revealing a totally naked brown body. Our friend was too flustered to pursue the matter further.

Paris is not France, but France would be unimaginable without Paris. Here, past and present coexist, sometimes comfortably, sometimes uneasily. Children play house in the playground of the Cluny museum, on the spot where Romans took their leisure in baths 100 meters long.

Called Lutetia by the Romans but renamed for the Parisii, a Celtic tribe, Paris has been a settlement on the Seine for more than two millennia. Blood has flowed here as constantly as the river. Crossing the place de la Concorde, one still shivers at the thought of the 1,344 persons beheaded there by the guillotine, including King Louis XVI and Marie Antoinette. Tourists flock to the Sacré-Coeur, at once the ugliest and boldest church in

Paris. It stands on a hill named Montmartre, for the Christian martyrs; one of them, Saint Denis, is said to have carried his severed head in his hands as he walked north out of the city in the third century. Joan of Arc was wounded in Paris in 1429, but it was another woman, Geneviève, a shepherdess from Nanterre, who became the special saint of Paris, having rallied the city against Attila the Hun. Today, students at the Sorbonne study in a reading room as long as a football field and high enough for a dropkick, in the library of her name. A department store, La Samaritaine, backs up against the church of St-Germain l'Auxerrois, from whose tower bells rang on the night of August 24, 1572, to signal the prearranged massacre of 3,000 Huguenots. A short walk away, at a Jewish restaurant called Goldenberg's in the heart of the Marais district, a mini-massacre, on August 9, 1982, took the lives of six people at lunchtime.

If the French have a knack of putting the past into perspective (they take their time about naming streets for statesmen; artists and scientists have a better chance), they nevertheless have a problem with the turbulent present. In Paris, the tourist may have an opportunity not only to observe history but also to participate in it. Scarcely a month goes by without a *manifestation* (demonstration) of some kind, and sometimes they get out of hand. The city, too, has its share of terrorist activities—the occasional bomb or an Algerian remembering past wrongs, the normal *va-et-vient* of European life.

For those of us who lived through World War II, Paris is full of poignancy. Around the corner from where I used to live on the Ile St-Louis, there is a large apartment house. A plaque near the front door says: *"A la mémoire des 112 habitants de cette maison dont 40 petits enfants deportés et morts dans les camps allemands en 1942"* (To the memory of 112 residents of this building, of whom 40 were little children, deported to and died in German camps in 1942). On April 28, the National Day of the Deportation, a silent little parade forms at the synagogue just across from here, in the Marais. With bared heads, muffled drums, and tricolored sashes, the marchers—no doubt including relatives of those 112 residents—file across to the Ile de la Cité, on whose point, facing up the Seine, is the Memorial to the Deported. There the Unknown Deportee sleeps in a bed of stone as the river flows silently by on both sides. It is a moving and little-visited shrine, only a stone's throw from the gardens of Notre Dame.

Only London and Rome can even come close to holding such treasures of the past as does Paris. Hitler, furious with the retreat of his forces in World War II, ordered the city burned, but his own commander failed him and Allied forces swept in. To sense the grandeur that would have been lost, try sitting on a bench above the Seine on the pedestrian Pont des Arts, which offers a kind of gracious scaffolding over the river. Face downstream and set your watch by the clock of the Institut Français on the Left Bank as the rays of the sun, setting into the muddy green river, gild the towers of the Louvre on your right. Or look upstream at the Pont Neuf as it crosses the prow of the Ile de la Cité. Beyond but out of sight is the Ile St-Louis, perhaps the world's most perfect village, standing almost exactly as it began—a real estate development built on pastures of the 17th century.

Paris has a museum for every period and taste. Parisians argue museums as Americans fight over baseball teams. They tend either to loathe or love the Beaubourg, its red and blue insides exposed like an oil refinery. And unlike almost any other city, Paris's artistic life is closely tied to its political realities. The battle royal between Jacques Chirac (in his role as mayor) and President François Mitterrand's cultural impresario of the early 1980s, Jack Lang, raged up and down the avenues and boulevards, and the evidence of their struggle is still around, notably in the Buren Pillars at the Palais-Royal. The exciting Musée d'Orsay is dedicated to the art of the period 1848–1914 and houses the great collection of Impressionists that was formerly in the Jeu de Paume.

I first entered the Louvre in 1944, only to find it virtually empty. The foresighted French had evacuated and hidden most of the great masterpieces at the onset of war. All that remained of the *Mona Lisa* was a chalk scrawl to indicate its normal hanging place. Nevertheless, the Grande Galérie of the Louvre was just as staggering a spectacle as it is today. The Louvre is a palace so vast that one can make a fresh discovery on every visit.

Great exhibitions are not limited to museums. The Grand Palais, a marvel of turn-of-the-century iron and glass construction, and its little neighbor of the same vintage, the Petit Palais, occasionally attract lines that stretch far down avenue Winston Churchill. As if those are not enough, the city has built another huge complex, a kind of fairground of halls, playgrounds, and theaters (one of which is enclosed in a shining sphere) on the site of the former slaughterhouses of La Villette, on the city's outskirts.

There are another dozen or so art museums. The Musée Guimet has Oriental art; the Marmottan is a mansion containing Monets and others. Museums have been created in the studios of Rodin, Delacroix, and Brancusi. Paris has major museums of anthropology, natural history, history, and science, and smaller ones dealing with everything from advertising and bread to urban transport and wine. The Musée Grévin, the waxworks museum on the boulevard Montmartre and in the Forum des Halles, is perhaps the most amusing of all.

If you're a nosy type, one who loves to poke and peek, a certain amount of respectful audacity will take you far in Paris. Instead of taking the guided tour at the Bourse, or stock exchange, you can try to talk your way into a look at the trading floor. Nearby, at the Bibliothèque Nationale, without a reader's card, you can look into the main reading room or the equally impressive periodicals room. For lawyers, a place of interest is the Palais de Justice, with courtrooms where black-robed judges and *avocats* hear and plead cases all day long. Just walking the halls there is a spectacle; one can tiptoe into courts in session. In the waiting rooms of the nearby Préfecture de Police, you will find scenes of poverty and desperation reminiscent of Daumier.

Notre Dame is just a bit farther; for your first visit, try entering through the north portal instead of through the nave, as most tourists do. You will then immediately confront the most glorious of the three rose windows. Stay for a mass or an organ concert.

Finally, if you are fascinated by the celebration of life eternal, as are the Catholic French, you can quietly visit Père Lachaise, one of the world's most famous cemeteries and well worth seeing for its exotic and nostalgic monuments to the *célèbres*.

Some come to Paris just to eat. They come laden with research, with starred lists, credit cards, and calculated appetites. Many have done their homework well, with one or more of the useful books that devote themselves to mouth-watering descriptions of Parisian delicacies. My own approach is more casual; to my way of thinking, it's rather difficult to get a *bad* meal in Paris.

The sheer profusion of places to eat in Paris is staggering. There are thousands of places where one can get a cup of tea or coffee—*or* a glass of wine or beer—a convenience that is one of the finer attributes of French civilization. I go sometimes by hearsay, sometimes by looks, often by ambience. The *carte* posted at the door offers further clues, especially as to price. The same rules apply in Paris as elsewhere: One tends to pay for name and fame. Some places seem so cheap that one gets suspicious, but there is often more fun in a bistro than in an elegant two-star.

The French Government Tourist Office, that most helpful, over-worked institution on the Champs-Elysées near the Arc de Triomphe, offers an extensive listing of Paris restaurants. Like many of the good things in Paris, it is free—and in English. In a line or two, it charts the attributes of each place. The least snobbish of restaurant guides, it gives equal linage to the most expensive restaurants and the cheapest. Among specialties, you will find not only pig's feet béarnaise but also milkshakes, macrobiotic food, stuffed carp, "60 kinds of crêpe," and "exotic sherbets," not to mention the conventional gourmet dishes. As for ambience, you can dine in a cellar or in a high rise, in a former stable or in a former monastery. You may have the elegant surroundings of Louis XV or the Second Empire, the bustle of a railroad station, or the calm of a farmhouse. You may look out on the Louvre, on the Tour Eiffel, or on Notre Dame. Or you may look up at them as you glide along aboard a Bateau Mouche *au restaurant*. For entertainment with dinner, you can have flamenco or karaoke, polkas or cancan. For music, it can be violins, accordions, or oompah bands. The listed restaurants represent only a small fraction of what Paris has to offer when it comes to food and drink. In addition, there are the thousands of wine bars, bistros, and cafés. It's fun to make your own discoveries.

At cafés and wine bars, and at most brasseries, no reservations are required. If the table has no tablecloth, you can normally just sit down. Your best chance of getting a table, if you have not called ahead, is to go early, but not before 7:30 PM or you will find the staff eating. Go a little before 8, when the first diners arrive. Some restaurants take credit cards, and almost any business establishment in Paris will take a Eurocheck in francs. Don't hurry, and when you leave, shake hands with the proprietor.

Next to dining, entertainment is the most appealing industry of Paris. The week begins on Wednesday with the appearance of *Pariscope*, one of the three weekly bibles for those who go out often. A typical issue will list the hundreds of films that play the cinemas in Paris and environs in an average week. It also lists revivals, film festivals, as well as free screenings at the film libraries of the subsidized Beaubourg and Palais de Chaillot.

Not to be outdone by the film industry, the theater stages works at publicly supported theaters (Comédie Française, the Opéra, etc.), as well as on commercial stages, including works by Shakespeare, Strindberg, Brecht, Aristophanes, Chekhov, Sartre, Neil Simon, and Sam Shepard—most, but not all, in French. Cafés, cabarets, music halls, discos, and nightclubs offer programs ranging from political satire to striptease, New Orleans jazz, and the traditional cancan. Churches often offer chamber music. In this typical week, 96 concerts and 13 ballets are performed.

There is an easy informality about attending Paris theaters. Many are small and intimate. One can normally get tickets at the last minute, except for hit shows, and prices are low. Take one night at the Opéra. Early one New Year's Eve, Nureyev was dancing. We didn't bother to call; we simply went to the box office 10 minutes before curtain time. "What do you have?" I asked. "Standing room, no view, 20 francs," was the quick reply. We bought two, and climbed the onyx and marble staircase under the chandeliered dome with its ceiling painted by Chagall. Checking our coats, we rented opera glasses and were ushered to a box right over the stage. For the first act, we stood, looking down over the shoulders of those in the first row. At the interval, hoping to do better, we climbed to the Opéra's top circle. There we found a series of little pie-shaped loges; one was open and empty—save for one chair. My wife planted herself there while I scavenged for another. Then, after a quick trip to the bar for a demi of champagne and two glasses, we enjoyed the second and third acts with a full view of the stage. The *soirée* in our little aerie had cost the equivalent of $12 for the evening. "Paris is a moveable feast."

Paris is the home of the exile. It is here that Chopin came to compose, Picasso to paint, Joyce to write *Ulysses*. In Paris, even more than in London and New York, it is possible to live as a citizen of the world. It is almost possible to forget one's race, one's religion, almost possible to believe all men are brothers. Burnoose and sari, blue jeans and haute couture walk side by side.

Gallic cynicism and *la vie en rose* go together. Victor Hugo aptly stated the message of Paris:

Cities are bibles of stone. This city possesses no single dome, roof, or pavement that does not convey some message of alliance and of union, and that does not offer some lesson, example, or advice. Let the people of all the world come to this prodigious alphabet of monuments, of tombs, and of trophies to learn peace and to unlearn the meaning of hatred. Let them be confident. For Paris has proven itself. To have once been Lutèce and to have become Paris—what could be a more magnificent symbol! To have been mud and to have become spirit!

1 Essential Information

Before You Go

Government Tourist Offices

Contact the French Government Tourist Office for free information.

In the U.S. 610 5th Ave., New York, NY 10020, tel. 212/315–0888 or 212/757–1125; 676 N. Michigan Ave., Chicago, IL 60611, tel. 312/751–7800; 750 North St. Paul, Dallas, TX 75201, tel. 214/720–4011.

In Canada 1981 McGill College Ave., Suite 490, Montreal, Québec H3A 2W9, tel. 514/288–4264; 30 St. Patrick St., Suite 700, Toronto, Ontario M5G 3A3, tel. 416/593–4723.

In the U.K. 178 Piccadilly, London W1V 0AL, tel. 089/244–1234 between 9 AM and 10 PM Mon.–Fri. and 9 AM–5 PM Sat. There is a charge for this call.

U.S. Government Travel Briefings The U.S. Department of State's **Overseas Citizens Emergency Center** (Room 4811, Washington, DC 20520; enclose S.A.S.E.) issues Consular Information Sheets, which cover crime, security, political climate, and health risks as well as embassy locations, entry requirements, currency regulations, and other routine matters. For the latest information, stop in at any U.S. passport office, consulate, or embassy; call the interactive hotline (tel. 202/647–5225; fax 202/647–3000); or, with your PC's modem, tap into the Bureau of Consular Affairs' computer bulletin board (tel. 202/647–9225).

Tours and Packages

Should you buy your travel arrangements packaged or do it yourself? There are advantages either way. Buying packaged arrangements saves you money, particularly if you can find a program that includes exactly the features you want. You also get a pretty good idea of what your trip will cost from the outset. Generally, two types of packaged travel arrangements are available. Escorted tours are one option if you don't mind having limited free time and traveling with strangers. Escorted tours are most often via motorcoach, with a tour director in charge. Your baggage is handled, your time rigorously scheduled, and most meals planned. Escorted tours are therefore the most hassle-free way to see a destination, as well as generally the least expensive. Independent packages allow plenty of flexibility. They generally include airline travel and hotels, with certain options available, such as sightseeing, car rental, and excursions. Independent packages are usually more expensive than escorted tours, but your time is your own.

While you can book directly through tour operators, you will pay no more to go through a travel agent, who will be able to tell you about tours and packages from a number of operators. Whatever program you ultimately choose, be sure to find out exactly what is included: taxes, tips, transfers, meals, baggage handling, ground transportation, entertainment, excursions, sports or recreation (and rental equipment if necessary). Ask about the level of hotel used, its location, the size of its rooms, the kind of beds, and its facilities and amenities, such as pool, room service, or programs for children. Find out the operator's cancellation penalties. Nearly everyone charges them, and the only way to avoid them is to buy trip-cancellation insurance (*see* Insurance, *below*). Also ask about the single supplement, a surcharge assessed to solo travelers. Some operators do not make you pay it if you agree to be matched up with a roommate of the same sex, even if one is not found by departure time. Remember that a program that has features you won't use may not be the most cost-wise choice.

Fully Escorted Tours Escorted tours are usually sold in three categories: deluxe, first-class, and tourist or budget class. The most important differences are the price, of course, and the level of accommodations. Some operators specialize in one category, while others offer a range. Programs that include Paris generally spend two nights and only one full day in Paris; most are first-class, among them **Caravan** (401 N. Michigan Ave., Chicago, IL 60611, tel. 800/227–2862), **Certified Vacations** (Box 1525, Ft. Lauderdale, FL 33302, tel. 305/522–1414 or 800/233–7260), **DER Tours** (Box 1606, Des Plaines, IL 60017, tel. 800/782–2424), **Globus** (5301 S. Federal Circle, Littleton, CO 80123, tel. 303/797–2800 or 800/221–0090), **Olson-Travelworld** (Box 10066, Manhattan Beach, CA 90226, tel. 310/546–8400 or 800/421–5785), and **Trafalgar Tours** (21 E. 26th St., New York, NY 10010, tel. 212/689–8977 or 800/854–0103). Budget offerings include programs by **Cosmos Tourama,** a sister company of **Globus** (*see above*), and the "Cost Savers" of **Trafalgar Tours** (*see above*).

Most itineraries are jam-packed with sightseeing, so you see a lot in a short amount of time (usually one place per day). To judge just how fast-paced the tour is, review the itinerary carefully. If you are in a different hotel each night, you will be getting up early each day to head out, travel to your next destination, do some sightseeing, have dinner, and go to bed, then you'll start all over again. If you want some free time, make sure it's mentioned in the tour brochure; if you want to be escorted to every meal, confirm that any tour you consider does that. Also, when comparing programs, be sure to find out if the motorcoach is air-conditioned and has a restroom on board. Make your selection based on price and stops on the itinerary.

Independent Packages Independent packages, which travel agents call FITs (for foreign independent travel), are offered by airlines, tour operators who may also do escorted programs, and any number of other companies from large, established firms to small, new entrepreneurs. Their programs come in a wide range of prices based on levels of luxury and options—in addition to hotel and airfare, sightseeing, car rental, transfers, admission to local attractions, and other extras. **European Holidays** (137 S. Pugh St., State College, PA 16801, tel. 814/238–3557 or 800/752–9578) has a "Paris Stay Put" package with city tours and countryside excursions. The **French Experience** (370 Lexington Ave., New York, NY 10017, tel. 212/986–1115), has a wide selection of Paris programs. Airline packages, typically including hotel, round-trip airfare, and limited sightseeing, are available through **Air France** (tel. 800/237–2747), **American Airlines Fly AAway Vacations** (tel. 800/321–2121), **Continental Airlines' Grand Destinations** (tel. 800/634–5555), **Delta Dream Vacations** (tel. 800/328–6877), and **TWA Getaway Vacations** (tel. 800/438–2929). **Globus** and **Trafalgar Tours** (*see above*) offer Paris and London–Paris programs with accommodations, airfare, and some sightseeing.

When to Go

The major tourist season in France stretches from Easter to mid-September, but Paris has much to offer at every season. Paris in the early spring can be disappointingly damp; June is delightful, with good weather and plenty of cultural and other attractions. July and August can be sultry and dusty. Moreover, many restaurants, theaters, and small shops close for at least four weeks in summer.

September is ideal. Cultural life revives after the summer break and sunny weather often continues through the first half of October. The ballet and theater are in full swing in November, but the weather is part wet-and-cold, part bright-and-sunny.

December is dominated by the *fêtes de fin d'année* (end-of-year festivities), with splendid displays in food shops and restaurants and a busy theater, ballet, and opera season into January. February and March are the worst months, weatherwise, but with the coming of Easter, Paris starts looking beautiful again.

Climate What follow are the average daily maximum and minimum temperatures for Paris.

Jan.	43F	6C	May	68F	20C	Sept.	70F	21C
	34	1		49	10		53	12
Feb.	45F	7C	June	73F	23C	Oct.	60F	16C
	34	1		55	13		46	8
Mar.	54F	12C	July	76F	25C	Nov.	50F	10C
	39	4		58	14		40	5
Apr.	60F	16C	Aug.	75F	24C	Dec.	44F	7C
	43	6		58	14		36	2

Information Sources For current weather conditions and forecasts for cities in the United States and abroad, plus the local time and helpful travel tips, call the **Weather Channel Connection** (tel. 900/932–8437; 95¢ per minute) from a touch-tone phone.

National Holidays (1995) With 11 national holidays (*jours feriés*) and five weeks of paid vacation, the French have their share of repose. In May there is a holiday nearly every week, so be prepared for stores, banks, and museums to shut their doors for days at a time. Bastille Day (July 14) is observed in true French form, with an annual military parade down the Champs-Elysées and a fireworks display, usually at the Tuileries.

January 1 (New Year's Day); April 3 (Easter Monday); May 1 (Labor Day); May 8 (VE Day); May 12 (Ascension); May 23 (Pentecost Monday); July 14 (Bastille Day); August 15 (Assumption); November 1 (All Saints); November 11 (Armistice); December 25 (Christmas).

Festivals and Seasonal Events

Top seasonal events in Paris include the French Open Tennis Championships in May, the Fête de la Musique on June 21, July's Bastille Day, the Festival Estival musical event in the summer, and the Autumn Festival from September through December.

Feb. **Foire à la Feraille de Paris** is an antiques and bric-a-brac fair held in the Parc Floral de Paris and the Bois de Vincennes in the 12th arrondissement.

Mar. **Salon du Livre,** the international book exposition, is held annually at the Grand Palais at the end of the month.

Late Mar.– Apr. The **Prix du Président de la République** takes place at the Auteuil Racecourse.

May– late Sept. **Grandes Eaux Musicales** is a fountain display at the Château de Versailles. Sundays only.

Mid-May **International Marathon of Paris** leaves from the Champs-Elysées and ends at the Arc de Triomphe.

Late May– early June	**Festival de Jazz de Boulogne-Billancourt** attracts big names and varied styles of jazz in the suburbs of Boulogne-Billancourt. Some jazz movies, too.
Late May– early June	**French Open Tennis Championships** take place at Roland Garros Stadium.
Mid-June– mid-July	**Festival du Marais** features everything from music to dance to theater in the churches and historic mansions of the Marais.(Tickets: 44 rue François-Miron, 4e, tel. 48–87–60–08.)
June	**Paris Air Show,** which takes place in odd-numbered years only, is a display of old and new planes and an update on worldwide technological developments in the aeronautical industry, at Le Bourget Airport.
Mid-June	**Grand Steeplechase de Paris** is a popular horse race at Auteuil Racecourse. The **Course des Garçons de Café** is an entertaining race through the streets of Paris by waiters bearing full trays of drinks. It begins and ends at the Hôtel de Ville.
June 21	**Fête de la Musique de Paris** celebrates the summer solstice with parades, street theater, and live bands throughout the city.
Late June	**Grand Prix de Paris,** a major test for three-year-old horses, is held at Longchamp Racecourse.
July 14	**Bastille Day** celebrates the storming of the Bastille prison in 1789. This national holiday is commemorated throughout France. In Paris, there's a military parade along the Champs-Elysées in the morning, fireworks at night in the Tuileries, and local firemen's balls that spill into the streets of every arrondissement.
Mid-July– late Sept.	**Festival Estival of Paris** features classical music concerts in churches, museums, and concert halls throughout the city. (Tickets: 20 rue Geoffroy-l'Asnier, 4e, tel. 48–04–98–01.)
Late July	**Tour de France,** the world's leading bicycle race, finishes on the Champs-Elysées.
Late July– end Aug.	**Musique en l'Ile** is a series of concerts held in the picturesque 17th-century Eglise St-Louis on the Ile St-Louis. (Tel. 45–23–18–25 for details.)
Mid-Sept.– end Dec.	**Festival d'Automne,** with concerts, plays, dance, and exhibitions throughout Paris. (Tickets: 156 rue de Rivoli, 1er, tel. 42–96–96–94.)
Early Oct.	**Prix de l'Arc de Triomphe,** one of Europe's top horse races, takes place at Longchamp Racecourse. The **Fêtes des Vendanges,** held the first Saturday of the month, marks the grape harvest in the Montmartre Vineyard, at the corner of rue des Saules and rue St-Vincent.
Oct.	**Paris Motor Show** (even-numbered years only) features the latest developments in the international automobile industry.
Mid-Oct.– early Nov.	**Festival de Jazz de Paris** is a two-week celebration that includes lots of big-name jazz artists. (Tel. 47–83–33–58 for information.)
Oct.–Nov.	**Festival d'Art Sacré** features concerts and exhibitions held in churches throughout the city. (Tel. 42–77–92–26 for information.)
Nov. 11	**Armistice Day** ceremonies at the Arc de Triomphe include a military parade down the Champs-Elysées.

Third Thursday in Nov.	**Beaujolais Nouveau,** a light, fruity wine from the Beaujolais region of France, is officially "released" at midnight on Wednesday; its arrival is celebrated in true Dyonisian form in cafés and restaurants around the city.
Dec.	**Christmas** in Paris is highlighted by illuminations throughout the city, particularly on the Champs-Elysées, avenue Montaigne, and boulevard Haussmann.

What to Pack

Clothing
Pack light: Baggage carts are scarce at airports, and luggage restrictions on international flights are tight. What you pack depends more on the time of year than on any particular dress code. It can rain a fair amount in Paris, even in the summer, so consider bringing a raincoat and umbrella. Otherwise, pack as you would for a major American city: formal clothes for formal restaurants and nightclubs, casual clothes elsewhere. Jeans are as popular in Paris as anywhere and are perfectly acceptable for sightseeing and informal dining. However, a jeans-and-sneakers outfit will raise eyebrows at the theater, at expensive restaurants, and when visiting French families.

Wear sturdy walking shoes for sightseeing: Paris is full of cobblestone streets, and many historic buildings are surrounded by gravel paths. To protect yourself against purse snatchers and pickpockets, take a handbag with long straps that you can sling across your body, bandolier-style, with a zippered compartment for your money and passport—French law requires that you carry identification at all times.

Miscellaneous
Bring an extra pair of eyeglasses or contact lenses in your carry-on luggage. If you have a health problem that requires a prescription drug, pack enough to last the duration of the trip or have your doctor write a prescription using the drug's generic name, because brand names vary from country to country. Always carry prescription drugs in their original packaging to avoid problems with customs officials. Don't pack them in luggage that you plan to check in case your bags go astray. Pack a list of the offices that supply refunds for lost or stolen traveler's checks.

Electricity
The electrical current in Paris is 220 volts, 50 cycles alternating current (AC); the United States runs on 110-volt, 60-cycle AC current. Unlike wall outlets in the United States, which accept plugs with two flat prongs, outlets in France take plugs with two round prongs.

Adapters, Converters, Transformers
To use U.S.-made electric appliances abroad, you'll need an adapter plug. Unless the appliance is dual-voltage and made for travel, you'll also need a converter. Hotels sometimes have 110-volt outlets for low-wattage appliances marked "For Shavers Only" near the sink; don't use them for a high-wattage appliance like a blowdryer. If you're traveling with an older laptop computer, carry a transformer. New laptop computers are auto-sensing, operating equally well on 110 and 220 volts, so you need only the appropriate adapter plug. For a copy of the free brochure "Foreign Electricity is No Deep Dark Secret," send a stamped, self-addressed envelope to adapter-converter manufacturer Franzus Company (Customer Service, Dept. B50, Murtha Industrial Park, Box 142, Beacon Falls, CT 06403, tel. 203/723–6664).

Luggage Regulations
Free airline baggage allowances depend on the airline, the route, and the class of your ticket; ask in advance. In general, on domestic flights and on international flights between the United States and foreign destinations, you are entitled to check two bags—neither

exceeding 62 inches, or 158 centimeters (length + width + height), or weighing more than 70 pounds (32 kilograms). A third piece may be brought aboard as a carryon; its total dimensions are generally limited to less than 45 inches (114 centimeters), so it will fit easily under the seat in front of you or in the overhead compartment. In the United States the Federal Aviation Administration gives airlines broad latitude to limit carry-on allowances and tailor them to different aircraft and operational conditions. Charges for excess, over-size, or overweight pieces vary.

If you are flying between two foreign destinations, note that bag-gage allowances may be determined not by piece but by weight method, which generally allows 88 pounds (40 kilograms) of luggage in first class, 66 pounds (30 kilograms) in business class, and 44 pounds (20 kilograms) in economy. If your flight between two cities abroad *connects* with your transatlantic or transpacific flight, the piece method still applies.

Safeguarding Before leaving home, itemize your bags' contents and their worth in
Your Luggage case they go astray. To minimize that risk, tag them inside and out with your name, address, and phone number. (If you use your home address, cover it so that potential thieves can't see it.) Put a copy of your itinerary inside each bag, so that you can easily be tracked. At check-in, make sure that the tag attached by baggage handlers bears the correct three-letter code for your destination. If your bags do not arrive with you, or if you detect damage, immediately file a written report with the airline before you leave the airport.

Taking Money Abroad

Traveler's Traveler's checks are preferable in metropolitan centers, although
Checks you'll need cash in rural areas and small towns. The most widely rec-ognized are **American Express, Citicorp, Diners Club, Thomas Cook,** and **Visa,** which are sold by major commercial banks. Both American Express and Thomas Cook issue checks that can be counter-signed and used by you or your traveling companion. Typically the issuing company or the bank at which you make your purchase charges 1%–3% of the checks' face value as a fee. Some foreign banks charge as much as 20% of the face value as the fee for cashing travelers' checks in a foreign currency. Buy a few checks in small denomina-tions to cash toward the end of your trip, so you won't be left with excess foreign currency. Record the numbers of checks as you spend them, and keep this list separate from the checks.

Currency Banks are good standbys for changing money, though they'll usually
Exchange slap you with a commission (1%, or 25 francs minimum). Privately run *bureaux de change* generally offer the most favorable exchange rates, without commission. If you use currency exchange booths at airports, rail and bus stations, hotels, or stores, you'll typically get less favorable rates, but you may find the hours more convenient.

You can get good rates and avoid long lines at airport currency-exchange booths by getting a small amount of currency at **Thomas Cook Currency Services** (630 5th Ave., New York, NY 10111, tel. 212/757–6915 or 800/223–7373 for locations in major metropolitan areas throughout the U.S.) or **Ruesch International** (tel. 800/424–2923 for locations) before you depart. Check with your travel agent to be sure that the currency of the country you will be visiting can be imported.

Getting Money from Home

Cash Machines Many automated-teller machines (ATMs) are tied to international networks such as **Cirrus** and **Plus.** You can use your bank card at ATMs away from home to withdraw money from your account and get cash advances on a credit-card account if your card has been programmed with a personal identification number, or PIN. Check in advance on limits on withdrawals and cash advances within specified periods. Ask whether your bank-card or credit-card PIN will need to be reprogrammed for use in the area you'll be visiting. Four digits are commonly used overseas. Note that Discover is accepted only in the United States. On cash advances you are charged interest from the day you receive the money from ATMs as well as from tellers. Although transaction fees for ATM withdrawals abroad may be higher than fees for withdrawals at home, Cirrus and Plus exchange rates are excellent, because they are based on wholesale rates only offered by major banks.

Plan ahead. Though ATMs in Paris work pretty much the same way as in the United States, not all have English prompts. Learn the French equivalents for key words, such as *withdraw, how much?, amount, transaction, okay,* and *clear* before you go. Also obtain ATM locations and the names of affiliated cash-machine networks before departure. For specific foreign Cirrus locations, call 800/424–7787; for foreign Plus locations, consult the Plus directory at your local bank.

Wiring Money You don't have to be a cardholder to send or receive a **MoneyGram from American Express** for up to $10,000. Go to a MoneyGram agent in retail and convenience stores and American Express travel offices, pay up to $1,000 with a credit card and anything over that in cash. You are allowed a free long-distance call to give the transaction code to your intended recipient, who needs only present identification and the reference number to the nearest MoneyGram agent to pick up the cash. MoneyGram agents are in more than 70 countries (call 800/926–9400 for locations). Fees range from 3% to 10%, depending on the amount and how you pay.

You can also use **Western Union.** To wire money, take either cash or a cashier's check to the nearest office or call and use your MasterCard or Visa. Money sent from the United States or Canada will be available for pick up at agent locations in France within minutes. Once the money is in the system it can be picked up at *any* one of 22,000 locations (call 800/325–6000 for the one nearest you).

French Currency

The unit of currency in France is the franc, which is divided into 100 centimes. The bills are 500, 200, 100, and 50 francs. Coins are 20, 10, 5, 2, and 1 francs and 50, 20, 10, and 5 centimes. At press time (mid-1994), the exchange rate was 5.8 francs to the dollar and 8.6 francs to the pound.

What It Will Cost

Inflation in France has continued to average a modest annual 3%–3½% increase in recent years.

As in most capital cities, life in Paris is more expensive than anywhere else in the country (except the Riviera). Yet, unlike, say, central London, Paris is a place where people live as well as work; Parisians, who shop and lunch locally, are not prepared to pay extravagant rates, and visitors who avoid the obvious tourist traps will not have to pay those rates, either.

Prices tend to reflect the standing of an area in the eyes of Parisians; much sought-after residential arrondissements such as the 7th, 16th, and 17th—of limited tourist interest—are far more expensive than the student-oriented, much-visited Latin Quarter. The tourist area where value for money is most difficult to find is the 8th arrondissement, on and around the Champs-Elysées. Places where you can be virtually certain to shop, eat, and stay without overpaying include the streets surrounding Montmartre (not the Butte, or hilltop, itself); the St-Michel/Sorbonne area on the Left Bank; the mazelike streets around the Halles and Marais in central Paris; and Bastille and eastern Paris.

Taxes All taxes must be included in affixed prices in France. Restaurant and hotel prices must by law include taxes and service charges: If these appear as additional items on your bill, you should complain. VAT (value added tax, known in France as TVA), at a standard rate of 18.6%, is included in the price of many goods, but foreigners are often entitled to a refund (*see* Shopping, Chapter 4).

Sample Costs A cup of coffee, standing at a bar, costs from 5 francs; if you sit, it will cost from 10 francs. A glass of beer costs from 7 francs standing at the bar and from 12 francs if you're seated; a soft drink costs between 7 francs and 14 francs. A ham sandwich will cost between 12 francs and 15 francs. Expect to pay 30–35 francs for a short taxi ride.

Long-Distance Calling

AT&T, MCI, and Sprint have several services that make calling home or the office more affordable and convenient when you're on the road. Use one of them to avoid pricey hotel surcharges. **AT&T** Calling Card (tel. 800/225–5288) and the AT&T Universal Card (tel. 800/662–7759) give you access to the service. With AT&T's USADirect (tel. 800/874–4000 for codes in the countries you'll be visiting) you can reach an AT&T operator with a local or toll-free call. **MCI**'s Call USA (MCI Customer Service, tel. 800/444–4444) allows that service from 85 countries or from country to country via MCI WorldReach. **Sprint** Express (tel. 800/793–1153) has a toll-free number travelers abroad can dial to reach a Sprint operator in the United States.

Passports and Visas

If your passport is lost or stolen abroad, report it immediately to the nearest embassy or consulate and to the local police. If you can provide the consular officer with the information contained in the passport, he or she will usually be able to issue you a new passport. For this reason, keep a photocopy of the data page of your passport separate from your money and traveler's checks. Also leave a photocopy with a relative or friend at home.

U.S. Citizens All U.S. citizens, even infants, need a valid passport to enter France for stays of up to 90 days.

You can pick up new and renewal application forms at any of the 13 U.S. Passport Agency offices and at some post offices and courthouses. Although passports are usually mailed within four weeks of your application's receipt, allow five weeks or more from April through summer. Call the Department of State Office of Passport

Services' information line (1425 K St. NW, Washington, DC 20522, tel. 202/647–0518) for fees, documentation requirements, and other details.

Canadian Citizens Canadian citizens need a valid passport to enter France for stays of up to 90 days. Application forms are available at 23 regional passport offices as well as post offices and travel agencies. Whether for a first or subsequent passport, you must apply in person. Children under 16 may be included on a parent's passport but must have their own to travel alone. Passports are valid for five years and are usually mailed within two weeks of an application's receipt. For fees, documentation requirements, and other details in English or French, call the passport office (tel. 514/283–2152 or 800/567–6868).

U.K. Citizens Citizens of the United Kingdom need a valid passport to enter France for stays of up to 90 days. Applications for new and renewal passports are available from main post offices as well as at the six passport offices, located in Belfast, Glasgow, Liverpool, London, Newport, and Peterborough. You may apply in person at all passport offices, or by mail to all except the London office. Children under 16 may travel on an accompanying parent's passport. All passports are valid for 10 years. Allow a month for processing.

A British Visitor's Passport is valid for holidays and some business trips of up to three months to France. It can include both partners of a married couple. A British Visitor's Passport is valid for one year and will be issued on the same day that you apply. An Excursion Document is valid for trips to France of up to 72 hours. You must apply in person at a main post office.

Customs and Duties

On Arrival If you're coming from outside the European Union, you may import duty free: (1) 200 cigarettes or 100 cigarillos or 50 cigars or 250 grams of tobacco (twice that if you live outside of Europe); (2) 2 liters of wine and, in addition, (a) 1 liter of alcohol over 22% volume (most spirits) or (b) 2 liters of alcohol under 22% volume (fortified or sparkling wine) or (c) 2 more liters of table wine; (3) 50 milliliters of perfume and 250 milliliters of toilet water; (4) 200 grams of coffee, 100 grams of tea; and (5) other goods to the value of 300 francs (100 francs for those under 15).

If you're arriving from an EU country, you may be required to declare all goods and prove that anything over the standard limit is for personal consumption. As of January 1993, however, there is no longer any limit or customs tariff imposed on goods carried within the EU.

Any amount of French or foreign currency may be brought into France, but foreign currencies converted into francs may be reconverted into a foreign currency only up to the equivalent of 5,000 francs.

Returning Home **U.S. Customs** If you've been out of the country for at least 48 hours and haven't already used the exemption, or any part of it, in the past 30 days, you may bring home $400 worth of foreign goods duty free. So can each member of your family, regardless of age; and your exemptions may be pooled, so one of you can bring in more if another brings in less. A flat 10% duty applies to the next $1,000 of goods; above $1,400, the rate varies with the merchandise. (If the 48-hour or 30-day limits apply, your duty-free allowance drops to $25, which may not be pooled.) Please note that these are the *general* rules, applicable to most countries, including France.

Travelers 21 or older may bring back 1 liter of alcohol duty-free, provided the beverage laws of the state through which they reenter the United States allow it. In addition, 100 non-Cuban cigars and 200 cigarettes are allowed, regardless of your age. Antiques and works of art more than 100 years old are duty free.

Gifts valued at less than $50 may be mailed to the United States duty free, with a limit of one package per day per addressee, and do not count as part of your exemption (do not send alcohol or tobacco products or perfume valued at more than $5); mark the package "Unsolicited Gift" and write the nature of the gift and its retail value on the outside. Most reputable stores will handle the mailing for you.

For a copy of "Know Before You Go," a free brochure detailing what you may and may not bring back to the United States, rates of duty, and other pointers, contact the **U.S. Customs Service** (Box 7407, Washington, DC 20044, tel. 202/927–6724).

Canadian Customs Once per calendar year, when you've been out of Canada for at least seven days, you may bring in C$300 worth of goods duty-free. If you've been away less than seven days but more than 48 hours, the duty-free exemption drops to C$100 but can be claimed any number of times (as can a C$20 duty-free exemption for absences of 24 hours or more). You cannot combine the yearly and 48-hour exemptions, use the C$300 exemption only partially (to save the balance for a later trip), or pool exemptions with family members. Goods claimed under the C$300 exemption may follow you by mail; those claimed under the lesser exemptions must accompany you on your return.

Alcohol and tobacco products may be included in the yearly and 48-hour exemptions but not in the 24-hour exemption. If you meet the age requirements of the province through which you reenter Canada, you may bring in, duty free, 1.14 liters (40 imperial ounces) of wine or liquor *or* two dozen 12-ounce cans or bottles of beer or ale. If you are 16 or older, you may bring in, duty free, 200 cigarettes, 50 cigars or cigarillos, and 400 tobacco sticks or 400 grams of manufactured tobacco. Alcohol and tobacco must accompany you on your return.

An unlimited number of gifts valued up to C$60 each may be mailed to Canada duty free. These do not count as part of your exemption. Label the package "Unsolicited Gift—Value under $60." Alcohol and tobacco are excluded.

For more information, including details of duties on items that exceed your duty-free limit, ask the Revenue Canada Customs and Excise Department (2265 St. Laurent Blvd. S, Ottawa, Ont. K1G 4K3, tel. 613/957–0275) for a copy of the free brochure "I Declare/Je Déclare."

U.K. Customs If your journey was wholly within EU countries, you no longer need to pass through customs when you return to the United Kingdom. According to EU guidelines, you may bring in 800 cigarettes, 400 cigarillos, 200 cigars, and 1 kilogram of smoking tobacco, plus 10 liters of spirits, 20 liters of fortified wine, 90 liters of wine, and 110 liters of beer. If you exceed these limits, you may be required to prove that the goods are for your personal use or are gifts.

For further information or a copy of "A Guide for Travellers," which details standard customs procedures as well as what you may bring into the United Kingdom from abroad, contact HM Customs and Excise (Dorset House, Stamford St., London SE1 9PY, tel. 071/928–3344).

Traveling with Cameras, Camcorders, and Laptops

About Film and Cameras If your camera is new or if you haven't used it for a while, shoot and develop a few test rolls of film before you leave. Store film in a cool, dry place—never in the car's glove compartment or on the shelf under the rear window.

Airport security X-rays generally aren't harmful to film with ISO below 400. To protect your film, carry it with you in a clear plastic bag and ask for a hand inspection. Such requests are honored at U.S. airports, up to the inspector abroad. Don't depend on a lead-lined bag to protect film in checked luggage—the airline may increase the radiation to see what's inside. Call the Kodak Information Center (tel. 800/242–2424) for details.

About Camcorders Before your trip, put camcorders through their paces, invest in a skylight filter to protect the lens, and check all the batteries. Most newer camcorders are equipped with batteries that can be recharged with a universal or worldwide AC adapter charger (or multivoltage converter) usable whether the voltage is 110 or 220. All that's needed is the appropriate plug.

About Videotape Videotape is not damaged by X-rays, but it may be harmed by the magnetic field of a walk-through metal detector, so ask for a hand-check. Airport security personnel may ask you to turn on the camcorder to prove that it's what it appears to be, so make sure the battery is charged. Note that rather than the National Television System Committee video standard (NTSC) used in the United States and Canada, France uses SECAM technology. You will not be able to view your tapes through the local TV set or view movies bought there in your home VCR. Blank tapes bought in France can be used for NTSC camcorder taping, but they are pricey.

About Laptops Security X-rays do not harm hard-disk or floppy-disk storage, but you may request a hand-check, at which point you may be asked to turn on the computer to prove that it is what it appears to be. (Check your battery before departure.) Most airlines allow you to use your laptop aloft except during takeoff and landing (so as not to interfere with navigation equipment). For international travel, register your foreign-made laptop with U.S. Customs as you leave the country. If your laptop is U.S.-made, call the consulate of the country you'll be visiting to find out whether it should be registered with customs upon arrival. Before departure, find out about repair facilities at your destination, and don't forget any transformer or adapter plug you may need (*see* Electricity, *above*).

Staying Healthy

Finding a Doctor The **International Association for Medical Assistance to Travellers** (IAMAT, 417 Center St., Lewiston, NY 14092, tel. 716/754–4883; 40 Regal Rd., Guelph, Ont. N1K 1B5; 57 Voirets, 1212 Grand-Lancy, Geneva, Switzerland) publishes a worldwide directory of English-speaking physicians whose qualifications meet IAMAT standards and who have agreed to treat members for a set fee. Membership is free.

Assistance Companies Pretrip medical referrals, emergency evacuation or repatriation, 24-hour telephone hot lines for medical consultation, dispatch of medical personnel, relay of medical records, up-front cash for emergencies, and other personal and legal assistance are among the services provided by several membership organizations specializing in medical assistance to travelers. Among them are **International SOS**

Assistance (Box 11568, Philadelphia, PA 19116, tel. 215/244–1500 or 800/523–8930; Box 466, Pl. Bonaventure, Montréal, Qué. H5A 1C1, tel. 514/874–7674 or 800/363–0263), **Medex Assistance Corporation** (Box 10623, Baltimore, MD 21285, tel. 410/296–2530 or 800/874–9125), **Near Services** (450 Prairie Ave., Suite 101, Calumet City, IL 60409, tel. 708/868–6700 or 800/654–6700), and **Travel Assistance International** (1133 15th St. NW, Suite 400, Washington, DC 20005, tel. 202/331–1609 or 800/821–2828), part of Europ Assistance Worldwide Services, Inc. Because these companies will also sell you death-and-dismemberment, trip-cancellation, and other insurance coverage, there is some overlap with the travel-insurance policies discussed under Insurance, *below.*

Publications   *The Safe Travel Book* by Peter Savage ($12.95, Lexington Books, 866 Third Ave., New York, NY 10022, tel. 212/702–4771 or 800/257–5755, fax 800/562–1272) is packed with handy lists and phone numbers to make your trip smooth. *Traveler's Medical Resource* by William W. Forgey ($19.95, ICS Books, Inc., 1 Tower Plaza, 107 E. 89th Ave., Merrillville, IN 45410, tel. 800/541–7323) is also a good, authoritative guide to medical care overseas.

Insurance

For U.S. Residents   Most tour operators, travel agents, and insurance agents sell specialized health-and-accident, flight, trip-cancellation, and luggage insurance as well as comprehensive policies with some or all of these features. Before you make any purchase, review your existing health and homeowner policies to find out whether they cover expenses incurred while traveling.

Health-and-Accident Insurance   Specific policy provisions of supplemental health-and-accident insurance for travelers include reimbursement for from $1,000 to $150,000 worth of medical and/or dental expenses caused by an accident or illness during a trip. The personal-accident, or death-and-dismemberment, provision pays a lump sum to your beneficiaries if you die or to you if you lose one or more limbs or your eyesight; the lump sum awarded can range from $15,000 to $500,000. The medical-assistance provision may reimburse you for the cost of referrals, evacuation, or repatriation and other services, or it may automatically enroll you as a member of a particular medical-assistance company (*see* Assistance Companies, *above*).

Flight Insurance   Often bought as a last-minute impulse at the airport, flight insurance pays a lump sum when a plane crashes either to a beneficiary if the insured dies or sometimes to a surviving passenger who loses eyesight or a limb. Like most impulse buys, flight insurance is expensive and basically unnecessary. It supplements the airlines' coverage described in the limits-of-liability paragraphs on your ticket. Charging an airline ticket to a major credit card often automatically entitles you to coverage and may also embrace travel by bus, train, and ship.

Baggage Insurance   In the event of loss, damage, or theft on international flights, airlines' liability is $20 per kilogram for checked baggage (about $640 per 70-pound bag) and $400 per passenger for unchecked baggage. On domestic flights, the ceiling is $1,250 per passenger. Excess-valuation insurance can be bought directly from the airline at check-in for about $10 per $1,000 worth of coverage. However, you cannot buy it at any price for the rather extensive list of excluded items shown on your airline ticket.

Trip Insurance **Trip-cancellation-and-interruption insurance** protects you in the event you are unable to undertake or finish your trip, especially if your airline ticket, cruise, or package tour does not allow changes or cancellations. The amount of coverage you purchase should equal the cost of your trip should you, a traveling companion, or a family member fall ill, forcing you to stay home, plus the nondiscounted one-way airline ticket you would need to buy if you had to return home early. Read the fine print carefully, especially sections defining "family member" and "preexisting medical conditions." **Default** or **bankruptcy insurance** protects you against a supplier's failure to deliver. Such policies often do not cover default by a travel agency, tour operator, airline, or cruise line if you bought your tour and the coverage directly from the firm in question. Tours packaged by one of the 33 members of the United States Tour Operators Association (USTOA, 211 E. 51st St., Suite 12B, New York, NY 10022; tel. 212/750–7371), which requires members to maintain $1 million each in an account to reimburse clients in case of default, are likely to present the fewest difficulties. Even better, pay for travel arrangements with a major credit card, so that you can refuse to pay the bill if services have not been rendered—and let the card company fight your battles.

Comprehensive Policies Companies supplying comprehensive policies with some or all of the above features include **Access America, Inc.** (Box 90315, Richmond, VA 23230, tel. 800/284–8300); **Carefree Travel Insurance** (Box 310, 120 Mineola Blvd., Mineola, NY 11501, tel. 516/294–0220 or 800/323–3149); **Tele-Trip** (Mutual of Omaha Plaza, Box 31762, Omaha, NE 68131, tel. 800/228–9792); **The Travelers Companies** (1 Tower Sq., Hartford, CT 06183, tel. 203/277–0111 or 800/243–3174); **Travel Guard International** (1145 Clark St., Stevens Point, WI 54481, tel. 715/345–0505 or 800/782–5151); and **Wallach and Company, Inc.** (107 W. Federal St., Box 480, Middleburg, VA 22117, tel. 703/687–3166 or 800/237–6615).

U.K. Residents Most tour operators, travel agents, and insurance agents sell specialized policies covering accident, medical expenses, personal liability, trip cancellation, and loss or theft of personal property. You can also buy an annual travel-insurance policy valid for every trip (usually of less than 90 days) you make during the year in which it's purchased. Make sure you will be covered if you have a preexisting medical condition or are pregnant.

For advice by phone or a free booklet, "Holiday Insurance," that sets out what to expect from a holiday-insurance policy and gives price guidelines, contact the **Association of British Insurers** (51 Gresham St., London EC2V 7HQ, tel. 071/600–3333; 30 Gordon St., Glasgow G1 3PU, tel. 041/226–3905; Scottish Providence Bldg., Donegall Sq. W, Belfast BT1 6JE, tel. 0232/249176; call for other locations).

Car Rentals

There's no reason to rent a car if you plan to stay in the Paris area. Traffic is almost always heavy, parking is impossible, and unpleasant confrontations with Parisian drivers will not contribute to a favorable impression of the city. On the other hand, taxis are a relatively good deal, and public transportation is generally fast and efficient; RER trains go directly to Versailles and Euro Disney, and other trains depart frequently for Fontainebleau and Giverny. For more information on other transportation options, *see* Getting Around Paris, *below*.

All major car-rental companies are represented in Paris, including **Alamo** (tel. 800/327–9633); **Avis** (tel. 800/331–1212, 800/879–2847 in Canada, 45–50–32–31 in Paris); **Budget** (tel. 800/527–0700, 42–25–79–89 in Paris); **Eurodollar Rent A Car Ltd.** (tel. 800/800–6000); **Hertz** (tel. 800/654–3131, 800/263-0600 in Canada, 45–74–97–39 in Paris); **National** (tel. 800/227–7368), known internationally as InterRent and Europcar (tel. 800/227–7368, 45–63–04–27 in Paris). Rates range from $40 per day for an economy car to $80 for a mid-size car with automatic transmission, weekly unlimited-mileage rates range from $200 to $430. This does not include VAT tax, which in France is among the highest in Europe, 18.6%.

Requirements Your own driver's license is acceptable. An International Driver's Permit, available from the American or Canadian Automobile Association, is a good idea.

Extra Charges Picking up the car in one city or country and leaving it in another may entail substantial drop-off charges or one-way service fees. The cost of a collision or loss-damage waiver (*see below*) can be high, also. Some rental agencies will charge you extra if you return the car *before* the time specified on your contract. Ask before making unscheduled drop-offs. Fill the tank when you turn in the vehicle to avoid being charged for refueling at what you'll swear is the most expensive pump in town. Automatic transmissions and air-conditioning are not universally available abroad; ask for them when you book if you want them, and check the cost before you commit yourself to the rental.

Cutting Costs If you know you will want a car for more than a day or two, you can save by planning ahead. Major international companies have programs that discount their standard rates by 15%–30% if you make the reservation before departure (anywhere from 24 hours to 14 days), rent for a minimum number of days (typically three or four), and prepay the rental. Ask about these advance-purchase schemes when you call for information. More economical rentals may come as part of fly/drive or other packages, even bare-bones deals that combine only the rental plus an airline ticket (*see* Tours and Packages, *above*).

Budget companies with offices in town may cost less than major companies with an airport outlet; but you could waste time trying to locate it in return for only a small savings. If you're arriving and departing from different airports, look for a one-way car rental with no return fees.

Several companies that operate as wholesalers—they do not own their own fleets but rent in bulk from those that do and offer advantageous rates to their customers. Rentals through such companies must be arranged and paid for before you leave the United States. Among them are **Auto Europe** (Box 1097, Camden, ME 04843, tel. 207/236–8235 or 800/223–5555, 800/458–9503 in Canada), **Connex International** (23 N. Division St., Peekskill, NY 10566, tel. 914/739-0066, 800/333–3949, 800/843–5416 in Canada), **Europe by Car** (mailing address, 1 Rockefeller Plaza, New York, NY 10020; walk-in address, 14 W. 49th St., New York, NY 10020, tel. 212/581–3040 or 212/245–1713; 9000 Sunset Blvd., Los Angeles, CA 90069, tel. 213/252–9401 or 800/223–1516 in CA), **The Kemwel Group** (106 Calvert St., Harrison, NY 10528, tel. 914/835–5555 or 800/678–0678), and **Foremost Euro-Car** (5430 Van Nuys Blvd., Suite 306, Van Nuys, CA 91401, tel. 818/786–1960 or 800/272–3299). Always ask whether the prices are guaranteed in U.S. dollars or foreign currency and if unlimited mileage is available. Find out about any required deposits, cancellation penalties, and drop-off charges, and confirm the cost of any required insurance coverage.

Insurance and Collision Damage Waiver Before you rent a car, find out exactly what coverage, if any, is provided by your personal auto insurer and the rental company. Don't assume that you are covered. If you do want insurance from the rental company, secondary coverage may be the only type offered. You may already have secondary coverage if you charge the rental to a credit card.

In general, if you have an accident, you are responsible for the automobile. Car rental companies may offer a collision damage waiver (CDW), which ranges from $4 to $14 a day. You should decline the CDW only if you are certain you are covered through your personal insurer or credit card company.

Rail Passes

The **French Flexipass** (formerly the France-Vacances Rail Pass) is a good value for those planning to do a lot of traveling by train. The pass allows you to stagger your train travel time instead of having to use it all at once. For example, the four-day pass ($180 in first class, $125 in second) may be used on any four days within a one-month period. Travelers may also add on up to five days of travel for $40 a day in first class and $29 in second class. Air-and-rail passes, rail-and-car rental passes, and air-rail-car rental passes are also available. All must be purchased before leaving for France, and are sold by travel agents and by **Rail Europe** (226–230 Westchester Ave., White Plains, NY 10604, tel. 914/682–5172 or 800/848–7245).

Many travelers with rail passes do not realize that on some trains, such as the high-speed TGVs, seat reservations are required. Getting them in advance through Rail Europe costs $10, more than in France, but assures you of a seat. On most other trains, while you don't need a seat reservation, you may want to get one anyway if you want to be guaranteed a seat. Reservations are always required for overnight sleeping accommodations.

Student and Youth Travel

Students are a noticeable presence in the capital, where intellectuals are the French equivalent of American movie stars. The area surrounding the Sorbonne in the bohemian Latin Quarter is filled with students discoursing in smoke-filled cafés, or browsing in crowded bookshops. Visiting students should have no trouble meeting their Parisian counterparts.

In keeping with a tradition of subsidizing education, Paris offers a variety of student discounts. Most museums and movie theaters offer students a **tarif réduit** of 20%–50%. An International Student Identity Card (*see below*) entitles you to significant discounts on train and airplane travel, theater, and youth hostels. For a detailed listing of deals for students in Paris, ask for the brochure *Jeunes à Paris* from the main tourist office (127 av. des Champs-Elysées, tel. 49–52–53–54). Also try **Usit Voyages** (12 rue Vivienne, 2e, tel. 42–96–15–88), a travel agency specializing in youth travel, for current information.

Travel Agencies **Council Travel Services (CTS),** a subsidiary of the nonprofit Council on International Educational Exchange, specializes in low-cost travel arrangements abroad for students and is the exclusive U.S. agent for several discount cards. Also newly available from CTS are domestic air passes for bargain travel within the United States. CIEE's twice-yearly *Student Travels* magazine is available at the CTS office at CIEE headquarters (205 E. 42nd St., 16th Floor, New York, NY 10017, tel. 212/661–1450) and in Boston (tel. 617/266–1926), Miami (tel. 305/670–9261), Los Angeles (tel. 310/208–3551), and at 43 branches in college towns nationwide (free in person, $1 by mail). **Campus Connections** (1100 East Marlton Pike, Cherry Hill, NJ 08034, tel. 800/428–3235) specializes in discounted accommodations and airline fares for students. The **Educational Travel Centre** (438 N. Frances St., Madison, WI 53703, tel. 608/256–5551) offers low-cost domestic and international airline tickets, mostly for flights departing from Chicago, and rail passes. Other travel agencies catering to students include **TMI Student Travel** (1146 Pleasant St., Watertown, MA 02172, tel. 617/661–8187 or 800/245–3672), and **Travel Cuts** (187 College St., Toronto, Ont. M5T 1P7, tel. 416/979–2406).

Discount Cards For discounts on transportation and on museum and attractions admissions, buy the **International Student Identity Card** (ISIC) if you're a bona fide student, or the **International Youth Card** (IYC) if you're under 26. In the United States the ISIC and IYC cards cost $16 each and include basic travel accident and sickness coverage. Apply to **CIEE** (*see* address *above*, tel. 212/661–1414; the application is in *Student Travels*). In Canada the cards are available for $15 each from **Travel Cuts** (*see above*). In the United Kingdom they cost £5 and £4 respectively at student unions and student travel companies, including Council Travel's London office (28A Poland St., London W1V 3DB, tel. 071/437–7767).

Hosteling A **Hostelling International** (HI) membership card is the key to more than 6,000 hostels in 70 countries; the sex-segregated, dormitory-style sleeping quarters, including some for families, go for $7 to $20 a night per person. Membership is available in the United States through **Hostelling International/American Youth Hostels** (HI/AYH, 733 15th St. NW, Suite 840, Washington, DC 20005, tel. 202/783–6161), and costs $25 for adults 18–54, $10 for those under 18, $15 for those 55 and over, and $35 for families. Volume 1 of the two-volume *Guide to Budget Accommodation* lists hostels in Europe and the Mediterranean ($13.95, including postage). HI membership is available in Canada through the **Hostelling International-Canada** (205 Catherine St., Suite 400, Ottawa, Ont. K2P 1C3, tel. 613/748–5638) for $26.75, and in the United Kingdom through the Youth Hostel Association of England and Wales (Trevelyan House, 8 St. Stephen's Hill, St. Albans, Herts. AL1 2DY, tel. 0727/855215) for £9.

Tour Operators **Aesu Travel** (2 Hamill Rd., Suite 248, Baltimore, MD 21210, tel. 410/323–4416) and **Contiki** (300 Plaza Alicante, No. 900, Garden Grove, CA 92640, tel. 714/740–0808 or 800/266–8454) specialize in package tours for travelers 18 to 35.

Traveling with Children

Despite their reputed chilliness, most Parisians regard children warmly. Many restaurants serve children's portions and have high chairs, and larger hotels will provide cribs free to guests with young children. (This is often not the case in *pensions* and smaller hotels.) Paris has plenty of diversions for the young (*see* What to See and Do with Children in Chapter 3), and almost all museums and movie theaters offer discounted rates to children.

Getting around Paris with a stroller can be a challenge. Not all métro stations have escalators, and many museums will require you to check the stroller at the entry. Buses are a better bet, since they are often not as crowded as the métro and have adequate space for strollers and carriages. You won't have a problem finding items such as diapers (*couches à jeter*) or baby food. Supermarkets carry several major brands of each, and after-hours pharmacies provide the essentials.

Publications *Family Travel Times*, published 10 times a year by **Travel With Your**
Newsletter **Children** (TWYCH, 45 W. 18th St., 7th Floor Tower, New York, NY 10011, tel. 212/206–0688; annual subscription $55), covers destinations, types of vacations, and modes of travel.

Books *Traveling with Children—And Enjoying It*, by Arlene K. Butler ($11.95 plus $3 shipping; Globe Pequot Press, Box 833, Old Saybrook, CT 06475, tel. 800/243–0495, or 800/962–0973 in CT), helps you plan your trip with children, from toddlers to teens. *Innocents Abroad: Traveling with Kids in Europe*, by Valerie Wolf Deutsch and Laura Sutherland ($15.95 or $4.95 paperback, Penguin USA, 120 Woodbine St., Bergenfield, NJ 07621, tel. 800/253–6476), covers child and teen-friendly activities, food, and transportation.

Tour **Grandtravel** (6900 Wisconsin Ave., Suite 706, Chevy Chase, MD
Operators 20815, tel. 301/986–0790 or 800/247–7651) offers international and domestic tours for people traveling with their grandchildren. The catalogue, as charmingly written and illustrated as a children's book, positively invites armchair traveling with lap-sitters aboard. **Families Welcome!** (21 W. Colony Pl., Suite 140, Durham, NC 27705, tel. 919/489–2555 or 800/326–0724) packages and sells family tours to Europe. Another family travel arranger that can even set up short-term rentals is **The French Experience** (370 Lexington Ave., New York, NY 10017, tel. 212/986–3800).

Hotels The **Novotel** chain (international reservations, tel. 800/221–4542) allows up to two children under 15 to stay free in their parents' room, and many properties have playgrounds. **Sofitel** hotels (international reservations, tel. 800/221–4542) offer a free second room for children during July and August and over the Christmas period.

Getting There On international flights, the fare for infants under age 2 not occupy-
Air Fares ing a seat is generally either free or 10% of the accompanying adult's fare; children ages 2–11 usually pay half to two-thirds of the adult fare.

Baggage In general, infants paying 10% of the adult fare are allowed one carry-on bag, not to exceed 70 pounds or 45 inches (length + width + height) and a collapsible stroller; check with the airline before departure, because you may be allowed less if the flight is full. The adult baggage allowance applies for children paying half or more of the adult fare.

Safety Seats The FAA recommends the use of safety seats aloft and details approved models in the free leaflet **"Child/Infant Safety Seats Recommended for Use in Aircraft"** (available from the Federal Aviation Administration, APA–200, 800 Independence Ave. SW, Washington, DC 20591, tel. 202/267–3479). Airline policy varies. U.S. carriers allow FAA-approved models bearing a sticker declaring their FAA approval. Because these seats are strapped into a regular passenger seat, they may require that parents buy a ticket even for an infant under 2 who would otherwise ride free. Foreign carriers may not allow infant seats, may charge the child's rather than the infant's fare for their use, or may require you to hold your baby during take-off and landing, thus defeating the seat's purpose.

Facilities Aloft Some airlines provide other services for children, such as children's meals and freestanding bassinets (only to those with seats at the bulkhead, where there's enough legroom). Make your request when reserving. The annual February/March issue of *Family Travel Times* gives details of the children's services of dozens of airlines (*see above*). "Kids and Teens in Flight" (free from the U.S. Department of Transportation, tel. 202/366–2220) offers tips for children flying alone.

Baby-sitting Services First check with the hotel concierge for recommended child-care arrangements. Local agencies include: **Ababa,** 8 av. du Maine, 15e, tel. 45–49–46–46; **Allô Service Maman,** 21 rue de Brey, 17e, tel. 42–67–99–37; **Allo Maman Poule,** 4 rue Greffulhe, Levallois, tel. 47–48–01–01; and **Baby Sitting Service,** 18 rue Tronchet, 8e, tel. 46–37–51–24. All can provide English-speaking baby-sitters with just a few hours notice. *L'Officiel des Spectacles* lists babysitting agencies under "Gardes d' Enfants." Expect to pay between 30 and 40 francs per hour, plus an additional 50-franc agency fee.

Miscellaneous Contact the **CIDJ** (Centre d'Information et de Documentation pour la Jeunesse, 101 quai Branly, 75015 Paris, tel. 44–49–12–00) for information about activities and events for youngsters in Paris.

Hints for Travelers with Disabilities

Though it has a long way to go, Paris ranks above many European cities in its ability to accommodate travelers with mobility impairments. Most sidewalks now have low curbs, and most arrondissements have public restrooms and telephone boxes that are wheelchair-accessible. Taxi drivers are required by law to assist travelers with disabilities in and out of their vehicles. In addition, most métro stations are wheelchair-accessible; an RER and métro access guide is available from the Paris Transit Authority (RATP) kiosk (Pl. de la Madeleine, 8e, tel. 40–46–42–17). Ask for the free brochure *Touristes Quand Même* at the main tourist office (127 av. des Champs-Elysées) for detailed information about wheelchair accessibility.

Organizations Several organizations provide travel information for people with disabilities, usually for a membership fee, and some publish newsletters and bulletins. Among them are the **Information Center for Individuals with Disabilities** (Fort Point Pl., 27–43 Wormwood St., Boston, MA 02210, tel. 617/727–5540 or 800/462–5015 in MA between 11 and 4, or leave message; TDD 617/345–9743); **Mobility International USA** (Box 3551, Eugene, OR 97403, tel. and TDD 503/343–1284, fax 503/343–6812), is the U.S. branch of an international organization based in Britain and present in 30 countries; **MossRehab Hospital Travel Information Service** (tel. 215/456–9603, TDD 215/456–9602); the **Travel Industry and Disabled Exchange** (TIDE, 5435 Donna Ave., Tarzana, CA 91356, tel. 818/368–5648, fax 818/344–0078); and **Travelin' Talk** (Box 3534, Clarksville, TN 37043, tel. 615/552–6670, fax 615/552–1182).

In the U.K. Main sources include the **Royal Association for Disability and Rehabilitation** (RADAR, 25 Mortimer St., London W1N 8AB, tel. 071/637–5400), which publishes travel information for the disabled in Britain, and **Mobility International** (228 Borough High St., London SE1 1JX, tel. 071/403–5688), the headquarters of an international membership organization that serves as a clearinghouse of travel information for people with disabilities.

Travel Agencies **Flying Wheels Travel** (143 W. Bridge St., Box 382, Owatonna, MN 55060, tel. 507/451–5005 or 800/535–6790) is a travel agency specializing in domestic and worldwide cruises, tours, and independent travel itineraries for people with mobility problems.

Publications Several free publications are available from the Consumer Information Center (Pueblo, CO 81009): "New Horizons for the Air Traveler with a Disability," a U.S. Department of Transportation booklet describing changes resulting from the 1986 Air Carrier Access Act and those still to come from the 1990 Americans with Disabilities Act (include Dept. 608Y in the address), and the Airport Operators Council's *Access Travel: Airports* (Dept. 5804), which describes facilities and services for the disabled at more than 500 airports worldwide.

Travelin' Talk Directory (*see* Organizations, *above*) was published in 1993. This 500-page resource book ($35) is packed with information for travelers with disabilities. Twin Peaks Press (Box 129, Vancouver, WA 98666, tel. 206/694–2462 or 800/637–2256) publishes the *Directory of Travel Agencies for the Disabled* ($19.95), listing more than 370 agencies worldwide and *Wheelchair Vagabond* ($14.95), a collection of personal travel tips. Add $2 per book for shipping.

Hints for Older Travelers

Older travelers to Paris enjoy most of the same discounts offered students. Museums and movie theaters offer a 20%–50% discount for people over 60. Seniors traveling outside Paris can take advantage of the French rail system's 30%–50% reduced fare (*Carte Vermeil*) when making at least four train trips within either France or Europe.

Organizations The **American Association of Retired Persons** (AARP, 601 E St. NW, Washington, DC 20049, tel. 202/434–2277) provides independent travelers who are members of the AARP (open to those age 50 or older; $8 per person or couple annually) with the Purchase Privilege Program, which offers discounts on hotels, car rentals, and sightseeing, and arranges group tours, cruises, and apartment living through AARP Travel Experience from American Express (400 Pinnacle Way, Suite 450, Norcross, GA 30071, tel. 800/927–0111 or 800/745–4567).

Two other organizations offer discounts on lodgings, car rentals, and other travel products, along with such nontravel perks as magazines and newsletters: the **National Council of Senior Citizens** (1331 F St. NW, Washington, DC 20004, tel. 202/347–8800; membership $12 annually) and **Mature Outlook** (6001 N. Clark St., Chicago, IL 60660, tel. 800/336–6330; $9.95 annually).

Note: Mention your senior-citizen identification card when booking hotel reservations for reduced rates, not when checking out. At restaurants, show your card before you're seated; discounts may be limited to certain menus, days, or hours. If you are renting a car, ask about promotional rates that might improve on your senior-citizen discount.

Educational Travel The nonprofit **Elderhostel** (75 Federal St., 3rd Floor, Boston, MA 02110, tel. 617/426–7788) has offered inexpensive study programs for people 60 and older since 1975. Held at more than 1,800 educational and cultural institutions, courses cover everything from marine science to Greek myths and cowboy poetry. Participants usually attend lectures in the morning and spend the afternoon sightseeing or on field trips; they live in dormitory-type lodging.

Fees for two- to three-week international trips—including room, board, and transportation from the United States—range from $1,800 to $4,500.

Interhostel (University of New Hampshire, 6 Garrison Ave., Durham, NH 03824, tel. 603/862–1147 or 800/733–9753) caters to a slightly younger clientele—50 and over—and runs programs in some 25 countries. The idea is similar: Lectures and field trips mix with sightseeing, and participants stay in dormitories at cooperating educational institutions or in modest hotels. Programs usually last two weeks and cost $1,500–$2,100, excluding airfare.

Tour Operators The following tour operators specialize in older travelers: **Evergreen Travel Service** (4114 198th St. SW, Suite 3, Lynnwood, WA 98036, tel. 206/776–1184 or 800/435–2288) has introduced the "Lazy Bones" tours for those who like a slower pace. **Saga International Holidays** (222 Berkeley St., Boston, MA 02116, tel. 800/343–0273) caters to those over age 60 who like to travel in groups. If you want to take your grandchildren, look into **Grandtravel** (*see* Traveling with Children, *above*).

Publications *The 50+ Traveler's Guidebook: Where to Go, Where to Stay, What to Do* by Anita Williams and Merrimac Dillon ($12.95; St. Martin's Press, 175 Fifth Ave., New York, NY 10010) is available in bookstores and offers many useful tips. "The Mature Traveler" (Box 50820, Reno, NV 89513, tel. 702/786–7419; $29.95), a monthly newsletter, contains many deals for older travelers.

Hints for Gay and Lesbian Travelers

Organizations
United States The **International Gay Travel Association** (Box 4974, Key West, FL 33041, tel. 305/292–0217 or 800/999–7925 or 800/448–8550), which has 700 members, will provide you with names of travel agents and tour operators who specialize in gay travel. The **Gay & Lesbian Visitors Center of New York Inc.** (135 West 20th St., 3rd Floor, New York, NY 10011, tel. 212/463–9030 or 800/395–2315; $100 annually) mails a monthly newsletter, valuable coupons, and more to its members.

Paris **FAACTS** (Free Anglo-American Counseling Treatment Support) at the American Church (65 quai d'Orsay, 7e, Métro: Alma Marceau) has weekly meetings for people infected or affected by the HIV virus. **Agora** (92 bis rue Picpus, 12e, tel. 43–42–09–49), a federation of several gay organizations, provides information on events, meetings, and rallies. The **Centre du Christ Liberateur** (3 bis rue Clairaut, 17e, tel. 46–27–49–36) provides gays and lesbians with medical care and counseling. The **Centre Gai et Lesbien** (25 rue Michel Le Comte, 3e, tel. 42–77–72–77) offers a wide range of information on events in Paris. Call the **Association des Médecins Gais** (tel. 48–05–81–71) or **Ecoute Gaie** (tel. 48–06–19–11 after 6 PM) for advice and information over the phone.

Travel Agencies and Tour Operators
United States The dominant travel agency in the market is **Above and Beyond** (3568 Sacramento St., San Francisco, CA 94118, tel. 415/922–2683 or 800/397–2681). Tour operator **Olympus Vacations** (8424 Santa Monica Blvd., Suite 721, West Hollywood, CA 90069; tel. 310/657–2220 or 800/965–9678) offers gay and lesbian resort holidays. **Skylink Women's Travel** (746 Ashland Ave., Santa Monica, CA 90405, tel. 310/452–0506 or 800/225–5759) handles individual travel for lesbians all over the world and conducts two international and five domestic group trips annually.

Paris   **Gays Randonneurs & Voyageurs** (BP 68 75462, Paris Cedex 10) and **Rando's** (BP 419 75870, Paris Cedex 18, tel. 42–26–08–04) plan weekend hikes and trips.

Publications   The premiere international travel magazine for gays and lesbians is
United States   *Our World* (1104 North Nova Rd., Suite 251, Daytona Beach, FL 32117, tel. 904/441–5367; $35 for 10 issues). "Out & About" (tel. 203/789–8518 or 800/929–2268; $49 for 10 issues) is a 16-page monthly newsletter with extensive information on resorts, hotels, and airlines that are gay-friendly.

Paris   A number of informative newspapers and magazines that cover the gay/lesbian scene are available at kiosks and newsagents. *Paris Exit* is a well-rounded newspaper that discusses issues of interest; publishes an up-to-date calendar of events; regularly reviews new clubs, bars, restaurants, and cultural events; and lists services from travel agents to saunas. The *Gai Guide* lists gay bars, parties, and other events. The popular *Gai Pied Hebdo*, a weekly magazine, produces a summer guidebook (about 50 francs). *Lesbia*, a monthly magazine, has a wide range of listings, reviews, and contacts.

Further Reading

For a look at the American expatriates in Paris between the wars, read *Sylvia Beach and the Lost Generation* by Noel R. Fitch, or *A Moveable Feast* by Ernest Hemingway. Flaubert's *Sentimental Education* includes excellent descriptions of Paris and its environs, as do many Zola novels. Other recommended titles include Charles Dickens's *A Tale of Two Cities*, Henry James's *The Ambassadors*, Colette's *The Complete Claudine*, and Hemingway's *The Sun Also Rises*. George Orwell's *Down and Out in Paris and London* gives a stirring account of life on a shoestring in these two European capitals between the world wars. For those who like it hot, try Henry Miller's *Tropic of Cancer* or *The Diary of Anaïs Nin*, by Miller's errant lover. For a racy read about three generations of women in Paris, take along *Mistral's Daughter* by Judith Krantz. Helen MacInnes's *The Venetian Affair* is a well-known spy thriller that winds through Paris.

Arriving and Departing

From North America by Plane

Flights are either nonstop, direct, or connecting. A **nonstop** flight requires no change of plane and makes no stops. A **direct** flight stops at least once and can involve a change of plane, although the flight number remains the same; if the first leg is late, the second waits. This is not the case with a **connecting** flight, which involves a different plane and a different flight number.

Airlines   The airlines that serve Paris from various major U.S. cities include **Air France** (tel. 800/237–2747), **TWA** (tel. 800/892–4141), **American Airlines** (tel. 800/433–7300), **Delta** (tel. 800/241–4141), **United** (tel. 800/538–2929), **Continental** (tel. 800/231–0856), **Northwest** (tel. 800/225–2525) and **USAir** (tel. 800/428–4322). Most local reservations offices close their phone lines after 10 PM and on Sundays.

Flying Time   From New York: 7 hours. From Chicago: 9½ hours. From Los Angeles: 11 hours.

Cutting Flight Costs The Sunday travel section of most newspapers is a good source of deals. When booking, particularly through an unfamiliar company, call the Better Business Bureau and your local or state Consumer Protection Bureau to find out whether any complaints have been registered against the company, pay with a credit card if you can, and consider trip-cancellation and default insurance (*see* Insurance, *above*).

Promotional Airfares Less expensive fares, called promotional or discount fares, are round-trip and involve restrictions, which vary according to the route and season. You must usually buy the ticket—commonly called an APEX (advance purchase excursion) when it's for international travel—in advance (seven, 14, or 21 days are usual), although some of the major airlines have added no-frills, cheap flights to compete with new bargain airlines on certain routes.

With the major airlines the cheaper fares generally require minimum- and maximum-stays (for instance, over a Saturday night or at least seven and no more than 30 days). Airlines generally allow some return-date changes for a $25 to $50 fee, but most low-fare tickets are nonrefundable. Only a death in the family would prompt the airline to return any of your money if you cancel a nonrefundable ticket. However, you can apply an unused nonrefundable ticket toward a new ticket, again with a small fee. The lowest fare is subject to availability, and only a small percentage of the plane's total seats will be sold at that price. Contact the U.S. Department of Transportation's Office of Consumer Affairs (I–25, Washington, DC 20590, tel. 202/366–2220) for a copy of "Fly-Rights: A Guide to Air Travel in the U.S." *The Official Frequent Flyer Guidebook* by Randy Petersen ($14.99 plus $3 shipping; 4715-C Town Center Drive, Colorado Springs, CO 80916, tel. 719/597–8899 or 800/487–8893 or 800/485–8893) yields valuable hints on getting the most for your air travel dollars.

Consolidators Consolidators or bulk-fare operators—"bucket shops"—buy blocks of seats on scheduled flights that airlines anticipate they won't be able to sell. They pay wholesale prices, add a markup, and resell the seats to travel agents or directly to the public at prices that still undercut the airline's promotional or discount fares (higher than a charter ticket but lower than an APEX ticket, and usually without the advance-purchase restriction). Moreover, some consolidators sometimes give you your money back. Carefully read the fine print detailing penalties for changes and cancellations. If you doubt the reliability of a company, call the airline once you've made your booking and confirm that you do, indeed, have a reservation on the flight.

The biggest U.S. consolidator, C. L. Thomson Express, sells only to travel agents. Well-established consolidators selling to the public include **UniTravel** (Box 12485, St. Louis, MO 63132, tel. 314/569–0900 or 800/325–2222), **Council Charter** (205 E. 42nd St., New York, NY 10017, tel. 212/661–0311 or 800/800–8222), and **Travac** (989 6th Ave., New York, NY 10018, tel. 212/563–3303 or 800/872–8800).

Charter Flights Charters usually have the lowest fares and the most restrictions. Departures are limited and seldom on time, and you can lose all or most of your money if you cancel. (The closer to departure you cancel, the more you lose.) The charterer, on the other hand, may legally cancel the flight for any reason up to 10 days before departure; within 10 days of departure, the flight may be canceled only if it becomes physically impossible to operate it. The charterer may also revise the itinerary or increase the price after you have bought the ticket, but if the new arrangement constitutes a "major change," you have the right to a refund. Before buying a charter ticket, read the fine print for the company's refund policy and details on major changes. Money for charter flights is usually paid into a bank escrow account, the name of which should be on the contract. If you don't pay by credit card, make your check payable to the escrow account (unless you're dealing with a travel agent, in which case, his or her check should be payable to the escrow account). The U.S. Department of Transportation's Office of Consumer Affairs (I–25, Washington, DC 20590, tel. 202/366–2220) can answer questions on charters and send you its "Plane Talk: Public Charter Flights" information sheet.

Charter operators may offer flights alone or with ground arrangements that constitute a charter package. You typically must book charters through your travel agent. One good source is **Charterlink** (988 Sing Sing Rd., Horseheads, NY 14845, tel. 607/739–7148 or 800/221–1802), a no-fee charter broker that operates 24 hours a day.

Discount Travel Clubs Travel clubs offer members unsold space on airplanes, cruise ships, and package tours at as much as 50% below regular prices. Membership may include a regular bulletin or access to a toll-free hot line giving details of available trips departing from three or four days to several months in the future. Most also offer 50% discounts off hotel rack rates, but double check with the hotel to make sure it isn't offering a better promotional rate independent of the club. Clubs include **Discount Travel International** (114 Forrest Ave., Suite 203, Narberth, PA 19072, tel. 215/668–7184; $45 annually, single or family), **Entertainment Travel Editions** (Box 1014, Trumbull, CT 06611, tel. 800/445–4137; $28–$48 annually), **Great American Traveler** (Box 27965, Salt Lake City, UT 84127, tel. 800/548–2812; $29.95 annually), **Moment's Notice Discount Travel Club** (425 Madison Ave., New York, NY 10017, tel. 212/486–0503; $45 annually, single or family), **Privilege Card** (3391 Peachtree Rd. NE, Suite 110, Atlanta, GA 30326, tel. 404/262–0222 or 800/236–9732; domestic annual membership $49.95, international, $74.95), **Travelers Advantage** (CUC Travel Service, 49 Music Sq. W, Nashville, TN 37203, tel. 800/548–1116; $49 annually, single or family), and **Worldwide Discount Travel Club** (1674 Meridian Ave., Miami Beach, FL 33139, tel. 305/534–2082; $50 annually for family, $40 single).

Enjoying the Flight Because the air aloft is dry, drink plenty of beverages while on board; remember that drinking alcohol contributes to jet lag, as do heavy meals. Sleepers usually prefer window seats to curl up against; restless passengers ask to be on the aisle. Bulkhead seats, in the front row of each cabin, have more legroom, but since there's no seat ahead, trays attach awkwardly to the arms of your seat, and you must stow all possessions overhead. Bulkhead seats are usually reserved for people with disabilities, the elderly, and people traveling with babies.

Smoking Since February 1990, smoking has been banned on all domestic flights of less than six hours duration; the ban also applies to domestic segments of international flights aboard U.S. and foreign carriers. On U.S. carriers flying to Paris and other destinations abroad, a seat in a no-smoking section must be provided for every passenger who requests one, and the section must be enlarged to accommodate such passengers if necessary as long as they have complied with the airline's deadline for check-in and seat assignment. If smoking bothers you, request a seat far from the smoking section.

Foreign airlines are exempt from these rules but do provide no-smoking sections, and some nations have gone as far as to ban smoking on all domestic flights; other countries may ban smoking on flights of less than a specified duration. The International Civil Aviation Organization has set July 1, 1996, as the date to ban smoking aboard airlines worldwide, but the body has no power to enforce its decisions.

Between the Airports and Downtown *Charles de Gaulle (Roissy)* The easiest way to get into Paris is on the **RER-B** line, the suburban express train. A free shuttle bus—look for the word *navette*—runs between the two terminal buildings and the train station; it takes about 10 minutes. Trains to central Paris (Les Halles, St-Michel, Luxembourg) leave every 15 minutes. The fare (including métro connection) is 33 francs, and journey time is about 30 minutes. **Buses** operated by **Air France** run every 20 minutes between Charles de Gaulle airport and the Arc de Triomphe, with a stop at the Air France air terminal at Porte Maillot. The fare is 48 francs, and journey time is about 40 minutes. The **Roissybus,** operated by the Paris Transit Authority, has buses every 15 minutes to rue Scribe at the Opéra; cost is 30 francs. Rush-hour traffic can make this trip slow and frustrating. **Taxis** are readily available. Journey time is around 30 minutes, depending on the traffic, and the fare is around 200 francs.

Orly Airport There are two simple ways of getting to Paris from Orly by train. The most economical is to take the free shuttle bus from the terminal to the train station, where you can pick up the **RER-C** line, the suburban express train. Trains to Paris leave every 15 minutes. The fare is 42 francs, and journey time is about 25 minutes. Or you can take the new shuttle-train service, **Orlyval,** which runs between the Antony **RER-B** station and Orly airport every 7 minutes. The fare to downtown Paris is 45 francs during peak periods, or 35 francs daily 11 AM–3 PM and after 9 PM, and Saturday noon–Sunday noon. **Air France buses** run every 12 minutes between Orly airport and the Air France air terminal at Les Invalides on the Left Bank. The fare is 32 francs, and journey time is between 30 and 60 minutes, depending on traffic. The Paris Transit Authority's **Orlybus** leaves every 15 minutes for the Denfert-Rochereau métro station; cost is 25 francs. **Taxis** take around 25 minutes in light traffic; the fare will be about 160 francs.

From the United Kingdom

By Plane **Air France** (tel. 081/742–6600) and **British Airways** (tel. 081/897–4000) together offer service from London's Heathrow Airport to Paris every hour to two hours. The cost of round-trip tickets is almost halved if you purchase them 14 days in advance and stay over on a Saturday night. There are three **British Airways** and up to five **Air France** flights daily, except weekends, to Paris from London's most central airport, London City, in the Docklands area.

Other airlines with regular scheduled flights from London to Paris include **British Midland** (tel. 081/754-7321) and **TAT European** (tel. 0293–567955). Except on Sunday, there are several daily flights (mostly Air France and BA) direct to Paris from Manchester, Bristol, and Birmingham, and up to four from Glasgow, Edinburgh, Aberdeen, Cardiff, Belfast, Newcastle, and Southampton.

The Paris Travel Service (115 Buckingham Palace Rd., London SW1 V9SJ, tel. 071/2337892) operates a good-value weekly Paris Express from Gatwick to Beauvais (a 40-minute flight and a one-hour bus ride into central Paris). Departure is on Friday, and return is the following Monday.

By Car There are a number of different driving routes to Paris. The Dover–Calais route includes the shortest Channel crossing; the Newhaven–Dieppe route requires a longer Channel crossing but a shorter drive through France.

Dover–Calais Ticket prices for ferries vary widely depending on the number of passengers in a group, the size of the car, the season and time of day, and the length of your trip. Call one of the ferry service reservation offices for more exact information. **P&O European Ferries** (Channel House, Channel View Rd., Dover, Kent CT17 9TJ, tel. 081/575–8555) has up to 20 sailings a day; the crossing takes about 75 minutes. **Sealink** (Charter House, Park St., Ashford, Kent TN24 8EX, tel. 0233/646801) operates up to 18 sailings a day; the crossing takes about 90 minutes. **Hoverspeed** (Maybrook House, Queens Gardens, Dover, Kent CT17 9UQ, tel. 0304/240241) operates up to 23 crossings a day, and the crossing (by Hovercraft) takes 35 minutes.

Dover–Boulogne **Hoverspeed** is the sole operator on this route, with six 40-minute crossings a day. The fares are the same as for the Dover–Calais route.

Ramsgate–Dunkerque **Sally Line** (Argyle Centre, York St., Ramsgate, Kent CT11 9DS, tel. 084/3595522) has up to five 2½-hour crossings a day.

Newhaven–Dieppe **Sealink** has as many as four sailings a day, and the crossing takes four hours.

Portsmouth–Le Havre **P&O European Ferries** has up to three sailings a day, and the crossing takes 5¾ hours by day, 7 by night.

Driving distances from the French ports to Paris are as follows: **from Calais,** 290 kilometers (180 miles); **from Boulogne,** 243 kilometers (151 miles); **from Dieppe,** 193 kilometers (120 miles); **from Dunkerque,** 257 kilometers (160 miles). The fastest routes to Paris from each port are via the N43, A26, and A1 from Calais; via the N1 from Boulogne; via the N15 from Le Havre; via the D915 and N1 from Dieppe; and via the A25 and A1 from Dunkerque.

The Channel Tunnel The **Channel Tunnel** opened in May 1994, providing the fastest route across the Channel—35 minutes from Folkestone to Calais, or 60 minutes from motorway to motorway. It consists of two large 50-kilometer-long (31-mile-long) tunnels for trains, one in each direction, linked by a smaller service tunnel running between them. **Le Shuttle** (tel. 0345/353535 in the U.K., 800/388–3876 in the U.S.), a special car, bus, and truck train, which was scheduled to begin service in June 1994, operates a continuous loop, with trains departing every 15 minutes at peak times and at least once an hour through the night. No reservations are necessary, although tickets may be purchased in advance from travel agents. Most passengers travel in their own car, staying with the vehicle throughout the "crossing," with progress updates via radio and display screens. Motorcyclists park their bikes in a separate section with its own passenger compartment, while foot passengers must book passage by coach (*see* By Train, *below*).

The Tunnel is reached from exit 11a of the M20/A20. Drivers purchase tickets from toll booths, then pass through frontier control before loading onto the next available service. Unloading at Calais takes 8 minutes. Ticket prices start at £130 for a low-season 5-day round trip in a small car and are based on season, time of day, length of stay, and car size regardless of the number of passengers. Peak season fares are not always competitive with ferry prices.

By Train **British Rail** has four departures a day from London's Victoria Station, all linking with the Dover–Calais/Boulogne ferry services through to Paris. There is also an overnight service using the Newhaven–Dieppe ferry. Journey time is about eight hours. Round-trip fare is around £65 (five-day excursion). Credit-card bookings are accepted by phone (tel. 071/834–2345) or in person at a British Rail Travel Centre.

The Channel **Eurostar** high-speed train service was scheduled to begin in July
Tunnel 1994, with passenger-only trains whisking riders between new stations in Paris (Gare du Nord) and London (Waterloo) in 3 hours and between London and Brussels (Midi) in 3¼ hours. The service of five trains daily each way was scheduled to increase in January 1995 to 15 trains daily in each direction. At press time, ticket prices had not been set. Tickets are available in the United Kingdom through **Intercity Europe,** the international wing of BritRail (London/Victoria Station, tel. 071/834–2345 or 071/828–8092 for credit-card bookings), and in the United States through **Rail Europe** (tel. 800/942–4866) and **BritRail Travel** (1500 Broadway, New York, NY 10036, tel. 800/677–8585).

Train Stations Paris has six international rail stations: **Gare du Nord** (northern France, northern Europe, and England via Calais or Boulogne); **Gare St-Lazare** (Normandy, England via Dieppe); **Gare de l'Est** (Strasbourg, Luxembourg, Basle, and central Europe); **Gare de Lyon** (Lyon, Marseille, the Riviera, Geneva, Italy); and **Gare d'Austerlitz** (Loire Valley, southwest France, Spain). Note that **Gare Montparnasse** has taken over as the main terminus for trains bound for southwest France since the introduction of the new TGV-Atlantique service. For train information from any station, call 45–82–50–50. You can reserve tickets in any Paris station, irrespective of destination. Go to the **Grandes Lignes** counter for travel within France and to the **Billets Internationaux** desk if you're heading out of France.

By Bus **Eurolines** (52 Grosvenor Gardens, London SW1W 0AU, tel. 071/730–0202) operates a nightly service from London's Victoria Coach Station, via the Dover–Calais ferry, to Paris. Departures are at 9 AM, arriving at 6:15 PM; 12 noon, arriving at 9:45 PM; and 9 PM, arriving at 7:15 AM. Fares are £52 round-trip (under-25 youth pass £49), £31 one-way.

Hoverspeed (Maybrook House, Queen's Gardens, Dover, Kent CT17 9UQ, tel. 0304/240241) offers a faster journey time with up to five daily departures from Victoria Coach Station. The fares are £49 round-trip, £30 one-way.

Both the Eurolines and Hoverspeed services are bookable in person at any **National Express** office or at the **Coach Travel Centre,** 13 Regent Street, London SW1 4LR. Credit-card reservations can be made by calling 071/824–8657.

Staying in Paris

Important Addresses and Numbers

Tourist The main **Paris Tourist Office** (127 av. des Champs-Elysées, 75008
Information Paris, tel. 49–52–53–54) is open daily 9–8. There are also offices at all main train stations, except Gare St-Lazare. Dial 49–52–53–56 for recorded information in English. All of these offices—and certain métro stations—sell museum passes (*Carte Musées et Monuments*),

which offer unlimited access to more than 60 museums and monuments in Paris over a one-, three-, or five-day period; cost, respectively, is 60, 120, or 170 francs.

Embassies   **U.S. Embassy** (2 av. Gabriel, 8e, tel. 42–96–12–02). **Canadian Embassy** (35 av. Montaigne, 8e, tel. 44–43–32–00). **British Embassy** (35 rue du Fbg St-Honoré, 8e, tel. 42–66–91–42).

Emergencies   **Police** (tel. 17). **Ambulance** (tel. 15 or 45–67–50–50). **Doctor** (tel. 47–07–77–77). **Dentist** (tel. 43–37–51–00).

Hospitals   **The American Hospital** (63 blvd. Victor Hugo, Neuilly, tel. 46–41–25–25) has a 24-hour emergency service. **The Hertford British Hospital** (3 rue Barbès, Levallois-Perret, tel. 47–58–13–12) also offers a 24-hour service.

Pharmacies   **Dhéry** (Galerie des Champs, 84 av. des Champs-Elysées, 8e, tel. 45–62–02–41) is open 24 hours. **Drugstore Publicis** (corner of blvd. St-Germain and rue de Rennes, 6e) is open daily till 2 AM. **Pharmacie des Arts** (106 blvd. Montparnasse, 14e) is open daily till midnight.

Tour Operators   **American Express** (11 rue Scribe, 9e, tel. 47–77–70–00). **Air France** (119 av. des Champs-Elysées, 8e, tel. 44–08–24–24). **Wagons-Lits** (8 rue Auber, 9e, tel. 42–66–57–33).

Telephones

To call Paris from the United States, dial 011–33–1 and then the local eight-digit number.

Local Calls   The French telephone system is modern and efficient. A local call costs 73 centimes for the first six minutes plus 12 centimes for every additional minute. Call-boxes are plentiful; they're found at post offices and often in cafés.

Most French pay phones are now operated by cards *(télécartes)*, which you can buy from post offices and some *tabacs* (the cost is 40 francs for 50 units; 96 francs for 120 units). These cards will save you money and hassle. In cafés you can still find pay phones that operate with 1-, 2-, and 5-franc coins (1 franc for local calls). Lift the receiver, place your coin(s) in the appropriate slots, and dial. Unused coins are returned when you hang up. All French phone numbers have eight digits; a code is required only when calling Paris from outside the city (add 16–1 for Paris) and when calling outside the city from Paris (add 16, then the number). Note that the number system was changed in 1985, so you may come across some seven-figure numbers in Paris and some six-figure ones elsewhere. Add 4 to the start of such Paris numbers, and add the former two-figure area code to the provincial numbers.

International Calls   Dial 19 and wait for the tone, then dial the country code (1 for the United States and Canada, 44 for the United Kingdom) and the area code (minus any initial 0) and number. Expect to be overcharged if you make calls from your hotel. Approximate daytime rates, per minute, are 7 francs to the United States and Canada; 4 francs to the United Kingdom; reduced rates, per minute, are 5 francs (2 AM–noon) to the United States and Canada or 6 francs (8 PM–2 AM weekdays, noon–2 AM Sun. and public holidays); and 3 francs to the United Kingdom (before 8 AM and after 2 PM).

Operators and Information   To find a number within France or to request information, dial 12. For international inquiries, dial 19–33 plus the country code.

Mail

Post offices, or PTT, are scattered throughout every arrondissement, and are recognizable by a yellow sign. They are usually open weekdays 8 AM–noon and 2:30–7 PM, Sat. 8 AM–noon. The main office, 52 rue du Louvre, 1er, is open 24 hours.

Rates Airmail letters to the United States and Canada cost 4.30 francs for 20 grams, 7.90 francs for 40 grams, and 12.50 francs for 60 grams. Letters to the United Kingdom cost 2.80 francs for up to 20 grams, as they do within France. Postcards cost 2.80 francs within France and EU. countries, and 4.30 francs to the United States and Canada. Stamps can be bought in post offices and cafés sporting a red TABAC sign.

Receiving Mail If you're uncertain where you'll be staying, have mail sent to **American Express** (if you're a card member), or to **Poste Restante** at any post office.

Getting Around Paris

Paris is relatively small as capital cities go, and most of its prize monuments and museums are within easy walking distance of one another. Walking also lets you participate in the French national sport of people-watching, and gives you an appetite (and an excuse) for that next memorable meal. The most convenient form of public transportation is the métro, with stops every few hundred yards. Buses are a slower alternative, though you do see more of the city. Taxis are relatively inexpensive and convenient, but not always easy to hail. Private car travel within Paris is best avoided; parking is extremely difficult.

Maps of the métro/RER network are available free from any métro station and in many hotels. They are also posted on every platform, as are maps of the bus network. Bus routes are also marked at bus stops and on buses. To help you find your way around Paris, we suggest you buy a *Plan de Paris par arrondissement* (about 20 francs), a city guide with separate maps of each district, including the whereabouts of métro stations and an index of street names. They're on sale in newsstands, bookstores, stationers, and drugstores. Hint: The last two digits of Paris zip codes tell you the arrondissement of the address; for example, the zip code 75005 indicates that this address is located in the 5th arrondissement, 75011 is in the 11th, etc.

By Métro Métro stations are recognizable either by a large yellow M within a circle or by the distinctive curly green Art Nouveau railings and archway bearing the full title (Métropolitain). The métro is the most efficient way to get around Paris and is so clearly marked at all points that it's easy to find your way around without having to ask directions.

There are 13 métro lines crisscrossing Paris and the suburbs, and you are seldom more than 500 yards from the nearest station. It is essential to know the name of the last station on the line you take, as this name appears on all signs. A connection (you can make as many as you like on one ticket) is called a *correspondance*. At junction stations, illuminated orange signs bearing the name of the line terminus appear over the correct corridors for each *correspondance*. Illuminated blue signs marked *sortie* indicate the station exit.

The métro service starts at 5:30 AM and continues until 1:15 AM, when the last train on each line reaches its terminus. Some lines and stations in the less salubrious parts of Paris are a bit risky at night; in particular

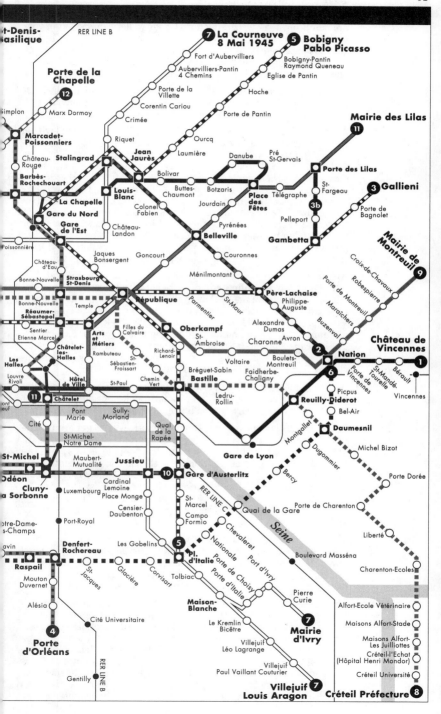

Lines 2 and 13. But in general, the métro is relatively safe throughout, providing you don't walk around with your wallet hanging out of your back pocket or (especially women) travel alone late at night. The biggest nuisances you're likely to come across will be the wine-swigging *clochards* (tramps) blurting out drunken songs as they bed down on platform benches.

The métro network connects at several points in Paris with the **RER** network. RER trains, which race across Paris from suburb to suburb, are a sort of supersonic métro and can be great time-savers.

All métro tickets and passes are valid for RER *and* bus travel within Paris. Métro tickets cost 6.50 francs each, though a carnet (10 tickets for 39 francs) is better value. If you're staying for a week or more and plan to use the métro frequently, the best deal is the weekly *(coupon jaune)* or monthly *(carte orange)* ticket, sold according to zone. Zones 1 and 2 cover the entire métro network; tickets cost 59 francs a week or 208 francs a month. If you plan to take suburban trains to visit places in the Ile-de-France, we suggest you consider a four-zone (Versailles, St-Germain-en-Laye; 109 francs a week) or six-zone (Rambouillet, Fontainebleau; 142 francs a week) ticket. For these weekly/monthly tickets, you will need a pass (available from rail and major métro stations) and a passport-size photograph.

Alternatively, there are one-day *(Formule 1)* and three- and five-day *(Paris Visite)* unlimited travel tickets for the métro, bus, and RER. Their advantage is that, unlike the *coupon jaune*, which is good from Monday morning to Sunday evening, *Formule 1* and *Paris Visite* passes are valid starting any day of the week and also give you discounts on a limited number of museums and tourist attractions. The price is 36 (one-day), 90 (three-day), and 145 (five-day) francs for Paris only; 85, 200, and 275 francs, respectively, for suburbs including Versailles, St-Germain-en-Laye, and Euro Disney.

Access to métro and RER platforms is through an automatic ticket barrier. Slide your ticket in and pick it up as it pops out. Keep your ticket during your journey; you'll need it to leave the RER system.

By Bus Travel by bus is a convenient, though slower, way to get around the city. Paris buses are green single-deckers; route number and destination are marked in front and with major stopping-places along the sides. Most routes operate from 6 AM to 8:30 PM; some continue to midnight. Ten *Noctambus,* or night buses, operate hourly (1:30–5:30 AM) between Châtelet and various nearby suburbs; they can be stopped by hailing them at any point on their route. The brown bus shelters, topped by red and yellow circular signs, contain timetables and route maps.

The bus accepts métro tickets, or you can buy a single ticket on board. You need to show (but not punch) weekly, monthly, and *Paris-Visite/ Formule 1* tickets to the driver as you get on. If you have individual tickets, you should state your destination and be prepared to punch one or more tickets in the red and gray machines on board the bus.

By Taxi Paris taxis may not have the charm of their London counterparts— there is no standard vehicle or color—but they're cheaper. Daytime rates (7 AM till 7 PM) within Paris are around 2.80 francs per kilometer, and nighttime rates are around 4.50 francs. There is a basic hire charge of 11 francs for all rides, and a 5-franc supplement per piece of luggage. Rates outside the city limits are about 40% higher. Waiting time is charged at roughly 100 francs per hour. You are best off asking your hotel or restaurant to ring for a taxi, or going to the nearest taxi station (you can find one every couple of blocks); cabs with their signs lit can be hailed, but are annoyingly difficult to spot. Note that taxis seldom take more than three people at a time. Tip the driver about 10%.

By Bike You can hire bikes in the Bois de Boulogne (Jardin d'Acclimatation), Bois de Vincennes, some RER stations, and from the Bateaux-Mouches embarkation point by place de l'Alma. Or try **Paris-Vélo** (2 rue du Fer à Moulin, 5e, tel. 43–37–59–22). Rental rates vary from about 90 to 140 francs per day, 160 to 220 francs per weekend, and 420 to 500 francs per week, depending on the type of bike. There is about a 1,000-franc deposit for rental, which can be put on a charge card.

Guided Tours

Orientation Tours
Bus tours of Paris offer a good introduction to the city, though complaints of dull and confusing narration are not infrequent. The two largest operators are **Cityrama** (4 pl. des Pyramides, 1er, tel. 44–55–61–00) and **Paris Vision** (214 rue de Rivoli, 1er, tel. 42–60–31–25). Their tours start from the place des Pyramides, across from the Louvre end of the Tuileries Gardens. Tours are generally in double-decker buses with either a live or tape-recorded commentary (English, of course, is available) and last three hours. Expect to pay about 150 francs.

For a more intimate—albeit expensive—tour of the city, **Citirama** also runs several minibus excursions per day. The bus has a maximum capacity of eight people, and can pick up or drop off at hotels. The cost is 210 francs for a 2-hour tour, 350 francs for 3 hours. Reservations are necessary.

The **RATP** (Paris Transport Authority, tel. 40–46–42–17) has many guide-accompanied excursions in and around Paris. Inquire at its Tourist Service on the place de la Madeleine, 8e (to the right of the church as you face it) or at the office at 53 bis quai des Grands-Augustins, 6e. Both are open daily 9–5.

For those who prefer to sightsee at their own pace, **Parisbus,** a red double decker with nine pick-up and drop-off points around Paris, allows you to discover the city's main tourist sites independently. Tours start from Trocadéro at 10:20 AM and depart every 50 minutes until 5. Tickets are good for two days and cost 80 francs for adults, 40 francs for children under 12.

Special-Interest Tours
Cityrama and **Paris Vision** (*see* Orientation Tours, *above*) offer a variety of thematic tours ("Historic Paris," "Modern Paris," "Paris-by-Night") lasting from 2½ hours to all day and costing between 150 and 300 francs (more if admission to a cabaret show is included).

Bike Tours **Paris by Cycle** (99 rue de la Jonquiere, 17e, tel. 42–63–36–63) organizes daily bike tours around Paris and its environs (Versailles, Chantilly, and Fontainebleau) for about 200 francs (including lunch and insurance, with an additional 120 francs for bike rental).

Boat Trips Boat trips along the Seine, usually lasting about an hour, are a must for the first-time visitor. Many boats have powerful floodlights to illuminate riverbank buildings; on some, you can also lunch or wine and dine—book ahead. The following services operate regularly throughout the day and in the evening.

Bateaux-Mouches has departures from Pont de l'Alma (Right Bank), 8e, tel. 42–25–96–10. Boats depart 10–noon, 2–7, and 8:30–10:30. The price is 40 francs, 20 francs for children under 14. Lunch is served on the 1 PM boat and costs 300 francs (150 francs children under 12). Dinner on the 8:30 service costs 500 francs (reservations required;

no children). Wine and service are included in the lunch and dinner prices.

Vedettes du Pont Neuf has departures from Square du Vert Galant (Ile de la Cité), 1er, tel. 46–33–98–38. Boats depart 10–noon, 1:30–6:30, and 9–10:30 every half hour. The price is 40 francs during the day (20 francs children under 10).

Bateaux Parisiens–Tour Eiffel has departures from Pont d'Iéna (Left Bank), 7e, tel. 44–11–33–44. Boats depart every half-hour in summer and every hour in winter, starting at 10 AM. Last tour boat leaves at 6 PM. The price is 40 francs during the day (20 francs children under 12). Lunch service costs 300 francs (200 francs children under 12). Dinner cruises on the 8 PM service cost 550 francs. Wine and service are included in the lunch and dinner prices.

Canauxrama (tel. 42–39–15–00) organizes leisurely half-day canal tours in flat-bottom barges along the picturesque but relatively unknown St-Martin and Ourcq Canals in East Paris. Departures are from 5 bis quai de la Loire, 19e (9:15 and 2:45), or from Bassin de l'Arsenal, 12e (9:45 and 2:30), opposite 50 boulevard de la Bastille. The price is 75 francs (60 francs for students and senior citizens and on weekend afternoons; 45 francs children under 12).

Bat-O-Bus, a trip along the Seine without commentary, has the advantage of allowing you to get on and off at any one of five stops along the river, including Trocadero, Musée d'Orsay, the Louvre, Notre Dame, and Hôtel de Ville. Take it one stop for 12 francs, or pay 60 francs for a full-day ticket. Operating from April to September only, the Bat-O-Bus departs every half hour between 9 and 6.

Walking Tours There are plenty of guided tours of specific areas of Paris, often concentrating on a historical or architectural topic—"Restored Mansions of the Marais," "Private Walled Gardens in St-Germain," or "Secret Parts of the Invalides." Tours are often restricted to 30 people and are popular with Parisians as well as tourists. They are accompanied by guides whose enthusiasm and dedication is invariably exemplary, though most are French and may not be able to communicate their enthusiasm to you in English. These potential linguistic problems are more than outweighed by the chance to see Paris in a new light and to visit buildings and monuments that are not usually open to the public. Charges vary between 35 and 50 francs, depending on fees that may be needed to visit certain buildings. Tours last around two hours and are generally held in the afternoons, starting at 2:30 or 3. Details are published in the weekly magazines *Pariscope* and *L'Officiel des Spectacles* under the heading "Conférences." In most cases, you must simply turn up at the meeting point (usually listed as "RV" or "rendezvous"), but it's best to get there early in case of restriction on numbers. You can get information on walking tours by contacting the **Caisse Nationale des Monuments Historiques** (Bureau des Visites/Conférences, Hôtel de Sully, 62 rue St-Antoine, 4e, tel. 44–61–20–00), which publishes a small booklet every two months listing all upcoming tours. For visits to some private mansions, you may be asked to show identification, so be sure to have your passport with you.

Personal Guides **Espaces Limousine** (18 rue Vignon, 9e, tel. 42–65–63–16) and **Executive Car** (25 rue d'Astorg, 8e, tel. 42–65–54–20) have limousines and minibuses (taking up to seven passengers) that will take you around Paris and environs for a minimum of three hours. Reservations are required. The cost is about 250 francs per hour.

Opening and Closing Times

Banks are open weekdays, but there's no strict pattern to their hours of business. Generally, they're open from 9:30 to 4:30 or 5. Some banks close for lunch between 12:30 and 2.

Most Paris **museums** close one day a week—usually either Monday or Tuesday—and on national holidays. Usually, they're open from 10 to 5 or 6. A few museums close for lunch (12 to 2) and are open Sundays only in the afternoon.

Large **shops** are open from 9 or 9:30 to 6 or 7 and don't close at lunchtime. Smaller shops often open earlier (8 AM) but take a lengthy lunch break (1 to 3); small food shops are often open Sunday mornings, 9 to 1. Some corner grocery stores will stay open until about 10 PM. Most shops close all day Sunday, except in the Marais, where shops are closed Monday.

Tipping

Bills in bars and restaurants must, by law, include service, but it is customary to leave some small change unless you're dissatisfied. The amount of this varies—from 30 centimes for a beer to a few francs after a meal. In expensive restaurants, it's common to leave an additional 5% of the bill on the table.

Tip **taxi drivers** and **hairdressers** about 10% of the bill. Give theater and cinema **ushers** a couple of francs. In some theaters and hotels, **cloakroom attendants** may expect nothing (*pourboire interdit*—no tip); otherwise, give them 5 francs. **Washroom attendants** usually get 2–5 francs, though the sum is often posted.

If you stay more than two or three days in a hotel, it is customary to leave something for the **chambermaid**—about 10 francs per day. Expect to pay about 10 francs (5 francs in a moderately priced hotel) to the person who carries your bags or who hails you a taxi. In hotels providing room service, give 5 francs to the waiter (this does not apply if breakfast is routinely served in your room). If the chambermaid does some pressing or laundering for you, give her 5–10 francs on top of the bill.

Service station attendants get nothing for gas or oil, but 5 or 10 francs for checking tires. Train and airport **porters** get a fixed sum (6–10 francs) per bag. **Museum guides** should get 5–10 francs after a guided tour. It is standard practice to tip **bus drivers** about 10 francs after an excursion.

Participant Sports

Biking   The Bois de Boulogne and the Bois de Vincennes, with their wide leafy avenues, are good places for biking. Bikes can be rented from **Paris Vélo** (2 rue du Fer à Moulin, 5e, tel. 43–37–59–22) for around 90 francs a day or 160 francs a weekend.

Boules   The rules of this classic French game involving metal balls thrown at a wooden sphere (also called *pétanque*), are fairly fundamental; The elderly blue- and brown-clad men who gather each day for matches in the Arènes de Lutèce (a restored Roman amphitheater on rue Navarre in the 5th arrondissement) and in the Bois de Vincennes near the Château might let you have a go if you demonstrate some enthusiasm. Otherwise, a set of your own costs very little.

Hotel Fitness Centers Paris's classic hostelries have the edge in ambience, but the best fitness facilities are in the newer hotels on the edges of the city center. The Vitatop Club on the top floors of the **Sofitel Paris** (8 rue Louis-Armand, 15e, tel. 45–54–79–00) offers a 15-meter pool, a sauna, a steam room, and a Jacuzzi, plus a stunning view of the Paris skyline; the club is free to hotel guests. Next door lies the **Parc Suzanne Lenglen,** with plenty of room for running, plus indoor and outdoor tennis courts. The **Nikko** hotel (61 quai de Grenelle, 15e, tel. 45–75–25–45) has a 17-meter pool, health club, and weight room. The facilities are open to the public for 100 francs (20 francs for pool only). The **Bristol** (112 rue du Fbg. St-Honoré, 8e, tel. 42–66–91–45) provides its guests with a large, elegant pool, plus a sauna.

Jogging The best inner-city running is in the **Champs de Mars,** next to the Eiffel Tower, measuring 1½ miles around the perimeter. Shorter and more crowded routes are found in the **Luxembourg Gardens,** with a 1-mile loop just inside the park's fence; in the **Tuileries,** again measuring about 1 mile; and in the **Parc Monceau,** which has a loop of two-thirds of a mile. The **Bois de Boulogne,** on the western edge of Paris, offers miles of trails through woods, around lakes, and across grassy meadows. The equally bucolic **Bois de Vincennes,** on the eastern side of the city, offers a 9-mile circuit or a 1-mile loop around the Château de Vincennes itself.

Physical Fitness Several gyms and clubs in Paris offer one-day or short-term memberships. Facilities are generally less up-to-date than in American gyms, but nonetheless provide a satisfactory way to work off croissants. **Espace Vit'Halles** in the 1st arrondissement offers a broad range of aerobics classes (80 francs per class, 800 francs for 12), exercise machines, sauna, and steam room (60 francs a day, 10-franc towel rental). *Place Beaubourg, 48 rue Rambuteau, 1er, tel. 42–77–21–71. Open weekdays 8 AM–10 PM; Sat. 10–7, Sun. 11–3.*

Club Quartier Latin boasts a 30-meter skylighted pool, a climbing wall, squash courts, and exercise equipment. Sixty francs per day entitles you to use of the gym and pool; add another 75 francs per hour for squash (raquets, 15-franc rental). *19 rue de Pontoise, 5e, tel. 43–54–82–45. Open Mon.–Thurs. 10 AM–midnight, Fri. 10–10, weekends 9:30–7:30.*

One of the oldest health clubs in Paris, **Club Jean de Beauvais** is also one of the best. An entire floor is devoted to cardiovascular and strength-training equipment, and the range of programs includes low-impact aerobics and special back-care classes. Cost is 180 francs for a one-day pass; 550 francs per week. The club also rents gymwear for a small fee. *5 rue Jean-de-Beauvais, 5e, tel. 46–33–16–80. Open weekdays 7 AM–10:30 PM; Sat. 8:30–7, Sun. 9:30–5.*

Tennis Tennis courts within Paris are few and far between. Your best bet is to try the public courts in the **Luxembourg Gardens.** There is also a large complex of courts at the "Polygone" sports ground in the **Bois de Vincennes.** It's a 20-minute walk down route de la Pyramide from Château de Vincennes métro, so you might want to take a taxi.

Spectator Sports

The **Palais Omnisports de Paris-Bercy** at 8 boulevard de Bercy in the 12th arrondissement (Métro: Bercy, tel. 40–02–60–60) hosts a wide range of sporting events, including handball, show jumping, ice skating, motorcross, and gymnastics. Look for listings in the weekly **Pariscope,** available at kiosks for 3 francs.

Cricket There are cricket grounds in the **Bois de Boulogne** (Bagatelle), **Bois de Vincennes** (Belle Etoile), and at **Château de Thoiry,** with games most weekends during summer. Admission is free.

Horse Racing Paris and its suburbs are remarkably well-endowed with racetracks. The most beautiful is **Longchamp** in the Bois de Boulogne, stage for the prestigious (and glamorous) Prix de l'Arc de Triomphe in October. Also in the Bois de Boulogne, and easier to get to (by métro to Porte d'Auteuil) is **Auteuil** racetrack. Other grass tracks *(hippodromes)* close to Paris are at **St-Cloud, Chantilly,** and **Enghien-les-Bains.** Vincennes has a cinder track for trotting races. Admission is usually between 35 and 50 francs. Details can be found in the daily press.

Rugby The Racing Club de France, one of France's leading teams, plays Saturday afternoons in winter at **Colombes,** just north of Paris (trains from St-Lazare to Le Stade station).

Soccer As in most European countries, soccer is the sport that pulls in the biggest crowds. The main Paris club is Paris St-Germain, which plays at the **Parc des Princes** stadium in southwest Paris; take the métro to Porte de St-Cloud. Matches are usually on Saturday evenings with an 8:30 kickoff. Admission prices vary from 25 to 200 francs.

Tennis The highlight of the season—in fact the second most important European tennis tournament after Wimbledon—is the **French Open,** held during the last two weeks in May at the **Roland Garros Stadium** on the eastern edge of the Bois de Boulogne. (Take the métro to Porte d'Auteuil.) Center-court tickets are difficult to obtain; try your hotel or turn up early in the morning (play starts at 11) and buy a general ground ticket. Tickets range from 90 to 350 francs. The Bercy Indoor Tournament in November is one of the richest in the world and attracts most of the top players.

2 Portraits of Paris

Paris at a Glance:
A Chronology

c 200 BC The Parisii—Celtic fishermen—live on the Ile de la Cité.

52 Romans establish a colony, Lutetia, on the Ile de la Cité, which soon spreads to both Seine banks. Under the Romans, Paris becomes a major administrative and commercial center, its situation on a low, defensible crossing point on the Seine making it a natural communications nexus.

c AD 250 St-Denis, first bishop of Paris and France's patron saint, is martyred in Christian persecutions.

451 The hordes of Attila the Hun are said to have been halted before reaching Paris by the prayers of Saint Geneviève (died 512); in fact they are halted by an army of Romans and mercenaries. Few traces of the Roman era in Paris remain. Most of those that do are from the late empire, including the catacombs of Montparnasse and the baths that form part of the Cluny Museum.

486–751 The Merovingian Dynasty

507 Clovis, king of the Franks and founder of the Merovingian dynasty, makes Paris his capital. Many churches are built, including the abbey that will become St-Germain-des-Prés. Commerce is active; Jewish and Oriental colonies are founded along the Seine.

751–987 The Carolingian Dynasty

Under the Carolingians, Paris ceases to be the capital of France and sinks into political insignificance, but it remains a major administrative, commercial, and ecclesiastical center—and, as a result of the latter, one of the foremost centers of culture and learning west of Constantinople.

845–887 Parisians restore the fortifications of the city, which are repeatedly sacked by the Vikings (up to 877).

987–1328 The Capetian Dynasty

987 Hugh Capet, Count of Paris, becomes king. Paris, once more the capital, grows in importance. The Ile de la Cité is the seat of government, commerce makes its place on the Right Bank, and the university develops on the Left Bank.

1140–63 The Gothic style of architecture appears at St-Denis: Notre Dame, begun in 1163, sees the style come to maturity. In the late 12th century, the streets are paved.

1200 Philippe-Auguste charters the university, builds walls around Paris, and constructs a fortress, the first Louvre.

1243–46 The Sainte-Chapelle is built to house the reputed Crown of Thorns brought by Louis IX (St. Louis) from Constantinople.

1253 The Sorbonne is founded, to become a major theological center.

1328–1589 The Valois Dynasty

1348–49 The Black Death and the beginning of the Hundred Years War bring misery and strife to Paris.

1364–80 Charles V works to restore prosperity to Paris. The Bastille is built to defend new city walls. The Louvre is converted into a royal palace.

1420–37 After the battle of Agincourt, Henry V of England enters Paris. Joan of Arc leads an attempt to recapture the city (1429). Charles VII of France drives out the English (1437).

1469 The first printing house in France is established at the Sorbonne.

1515–47 François I imports Italian artists, including Leonardo da Vinci, to work on his new palace at Fontainebleau, bringing the Renaissance to France. François resumes work on the Louvre and builds the Hôtel de Ville in the new style. The St. Jacques (Bell) Tower is completed (all that now remains of the church of St-Jacques-de-la-Boucherie).

1562–98 In the Wars of Religion, Paris remains a Catholic stronghold. On August 24, 1572, Protestant leaders are killed in the St. Bartholomew's Day Massacre.

1589–1789 The Bourbon Dynasty

1598–1610 Henri IV begins his reign after converting to Catholicism: "Paris is worth a mass." He embellishes Paris, laying out the Renaissance place des Vosges, first in a new Parisian style of town planning that will last till the 19th century. In 1610, Henri is assassinated. His widow, Marie de Médicis, begins the Luxembourg Palace and Gardens.

1624 Cardinal Richelieu is appointed Minister to Louis XIII and concludes the ongoing religious persecution by strictly imposing Catholicism on the country. In 1629 he begins construction of the Palais-Royal.

1635 The Académie Française is founded.

1643–1715 Reign of Louis XIV, the Sun King. Paris rebels against him in the Fronde risings (1648–52). During most of his reign, he creates a new palace at Versailles, away from the Paris mobs. It is the largest royal complex in Europe, the symbolic center of a centralized French state. His minister of finance, Colbert, establishes the Gobelins factory/school for tapestries and furniture (1667). André Le Nôtre transforms the Tuileries Gardens and lays out the Champs-Elysées (1660s). Louis founds the Hôtel des Invalides (1670). Ile St-Louis is created out of the merger of two islands in the Seine.

1715–89 During the reigns of Louis XV and Louis XVI, Paris becomes the European center of culture and style. Aristocrats build town houses in new fashionable quarters (Faubourg St-Honoré). The Rococo style gains popularity.

1783 New outer walls of Paris are begun, incorporating customs gatehouses to control the flow of commerce into the city. The walls, which include new parks, triple the area of Paris.

1789–1814 The Revolution and the First Empire

1789–99 The French Revolution begins as the Bastille is stormed on July 14, 1789. The First Republic is established. Louis XVI and his queen,

Marie Antoinette, are guillotined in the place de la Concorde. Almost 2,600 others perish in the same way during the Terror (1793–94). The transformation of St-Geneviève's church into the Panthéon is completed.

1799–1814 Napoléon begins to convert Paris into a neo-Classical city—the Empire style. The Arc de Triomphe and the first iron bridges across the Seine are built. In 1805, he orders the completion of the Louvre Museum.

1815 The Congress of Vienna ensures the restoration of the Bourbon dynasty following the fall of Napoléon.

1828–42 Urban and political discontent causes riots and demonstrations in the streets. Yet another uprising replaces Charles X with Louis-Philippe's liberal monarchy in 1830. Napoléon's remains are returned to Paris in 1840.

1848 Europe's "Year of Revolutions" brings more turmoil to the Paris streets.

1852–70 **The Second Empire**

In 1852, further additions to the Louvre are made. Under Napoléon III, the Alsatian town planner, Baron Haussmann, guts large areas of medieval Paris to lay out broad boulevards linking important squares. Railroad stations and the vast covered markets at Les Halles are built.

1862 Victor Hugo's *Les Miserables* is published in Paris while the liberal author remains in exile by order of Napoléon III.

1870–71 Franco-Prussian War; Paris is besieged by Prussian troops; starvation is rampant—each week during the winter, 5,000 people die. The Paris Commune, an attempt by the citizens to take power in 1871, results in bloody suppression and much property damage. Hugo returns to Paris.

1875 The Paris Opera, Paris's first permanent theater, is inaugurated after 15 years of construction.

1889 The Eiffel Tower is built for the Paris World Exhibition.

1900 The International Exhibition in Paris popularizes the curving forms of Art Nouveau with the entrance for the newly opened Paris Métro.

1910 Sacré-Coeur (Montmartre) is completed.

1914–18 World War I. The Germans come within nine miles of Paris (so close that Paris taxis are used to carry troops to the front).

1919 The Treaty of Versailles is signed, formally ending World War I.

1918–39 Between the wars, Paris attracts artists and writers, including Americans Ernest Hemingway and Gertrude Stein. Paris nourishes Existentialism, a philosophical movement, and major modern art movements—Constructivism, Dadaism, Surrealism.

1939–45 World War II. Paris falls to the Germans in 1940. The French government moves to Vichy and collaborates with the Nazis. The Resistance movement uses Paris as a base. The Free French Army, under Charles de Gaulle, joins with the Allies to liberate Paris after D-Day, August 1944.

1944–46 De Gaulle moves the provisional government to Paris.

1958–69 De Gaulle is President of the Fifth Republic.

1960s–70s Paris undergoes physical changes: Dirty buildings are cleaned, beltways are built around the city, and expressways are driven through the heart of the city, even beside the Seine, in an attempt to solve traffic problems. Major new building projects (especially La Défense) are banished to the outskirts.

1962 De Gaulle grants Algeria independence; growth of immigrant worker problem in Paris and other cities.

1968 Parisian students declare the Sorbonne a commune in riots that lead to de Gaulle's resignation.

1969 Les Halles market is moved and its buildings demolished.

1970s Paris, with other Western capitals, becomes the focus of extreme leftist and Arab terrorist bomb outrages.

1977 The Beaubourg (Centre Pompidou) opens to controversy, marking a high point in modern political intervention in the arts and public architecture.

1981 François Mitterrand is elected President. Embarks on a major building program throughout the city.

1986 Musée d'Orsay opens in the former Gare d'Orsay train station, housing hitherto scattered collections of 19th-century art and design.

1988 President Mitterrand is elected to a second term.

1989 Paris celebrates the bicentennial of the French Revolution. Grande Arche (La Défense) and Opéra Bastille completed. Louvre's glass pyramid completed in the first phase of major renovations designed by architect I. M. Pei.

1990 Cognacq-Jay museum reopens in the Marais.

1991 Edith Cresson becomes France's first female Prime Minister.

1992 Euro Disney opens in Marne-la-Vallée near Paris.

1993 After nine years of painstaking renovations by Pei, the Richelieu wing of the Louvre is opened to the public, doubling the museum's exhibition space and allowing 25% more works to be displayed. The completion of the Channel Tunnel between England and France is announced. The stock yards of La Villette are transformed into La Villette Park, a public center for outdoor activities and concerts, and home to the new Museum of Science, Technology, and Industry and the National Conservatory of Music and Dance.

Why Paris Works

By Steven
Greenhouse

Steven
Greenhouse
was a
correspondent
in the New
York Times
Paris bureau
for five
years.
This article
originally
appeared in
the July 19,
1992, issue of
the New York
Times
Magazine.

In a hidden, walled-off area, just west of the Boulevard St.-Michel, Paul Rissel looks like a figure borrowed from the 19th century as he opens the door to the lush greenhouse. Wearing a rough brown tweed sport coat and a long camel-colored scarf, he pushes past some ficus and stops next to a dozen unobtrusive black trays. These trays, he points out, are one of the secrets behind the ageless beauty of Paris's ornate Jardin du Luxembourg, which was built for Queen Marie de Médicis some 370 years ago. Rissel, one of the two chief gardeners, explains that the trays produce seedlings for the tens of thousands of geraniums, dahlias and petunias that the Jardin's 80 gardeners meticulously replant each May around the majestic central fountain.

The resplendent array of flowers gives the garden the idyllic air of a Renoir painting. During the gentle rains of spring, lovers stroll hand in hand, and when the sun breaks through, 5-year-olds scamper around the fountain to chase after their toy sailboats.

"People just love this garden," says Rissel, with a pride nurtured by 38 years of working at the Jardin. "In most big cities, the natives lack contact with nature, and that's what we're trying to give them."

A soft-spoken man with soft hands and long gray sideburns, Rissel heads a small army of gardeners. Each year they plant or transplant 350,000 flowers, and each spring they cart out 150 palm and orange trees, some of them 200 years old, that were lovingly sheltered from the winter cold.

At a time when cities from Lagos to Los Angeles are afflicted by homelessness, crime and budget traumas, Paris's famed garden is an oasis from urban turmoil. Mayors around the world may be screaming for cash, but the Jardin du Luxembourg is awash in money. It boasts more than one gardener per acre, which allows for an attention to detail and beauty that is rare in modern cities. One gardener devoted two full months to scooping out the rot from the trunk of a beech tree that the gardeners were eager to save because it stood eloquently alongside a small Bartholdi Statue of Liberty. "We function like the gardeners of an old house of the bourgeoisie," Rissel says. "We do much more by hand."

Rissel and the garden he nurses are just one gilded strand in the tapestry of cobbled streets, quaint quays and medieval churches that make Paris one of the world's most beautiful, best-run cities. Although many cities appear to be breaking down from poverty and decaying infrastructure, Paris seems to be improving with age.

For many of the city's 2.2 million residents and many of the 20 million tourists who visit each year, Paris remains a magical, even transcendent, place. While many Americans shun their own cities as if they were places suffering from the plague, Paris is a city with which countless people still have a passionate love affair.

The people who run Paris know that if their city relied on just the charms of its past, it would lose its magic. Thus, they have sought to superimpose a smoothly running, modern metropolis on the city bequeathed them by medieval kings and 18th-century revolutionaries. And they have succeeded royally.

Garbage is picked up seven days a week, mail is delivered three times a day and all of Paris's 800 miles of streets are swept by hand each day. At rush hour, the subways come once every 80 seconds, and many Métro stops are decorated with mosaics and murals. Affluent families are rushing not to flee for the suburbs, but to buy apartments in Paris's choicest neighborhoods and to send their children to public schools.

There is no single explanation for why Paris works so well. Rather, Paris has become a shining model for urban planners thanks to numerous ingredients lacking in many other cities: ample financing, sound administration, farsighted planning, technological ingenuity, a flair for design and an ambition to always improve.

It would be wrong to single out Paris from other French cities as a success story, because Toulouse, Lyons, Nice, Bordeaux and Strasbourg have worked just as hard to keep their beauty, build a vibrant cultural life and remain attractive for families. Nonetheless, Paris, whose metropolitan area includes 10.5 million people (one-fifth of France's population), is undeniably the Olympus of French cities.

Parisians have two major complaints. Traffic congestion has created a miasma of noise, pollution and stress, helping to make Paris's high-strung population even more irritable. The other is that crime is growing, although the roughest parts of Paris seem no more dangerous than the safest parts of many American cities. Paris had 80 murders last year, compared with 482 in Washington, which has about one-fourth the population.

Homelessness is another problem, although it does not seem one of the Parisians' main concerns, perhaps because the city has long romanticized the *clochards* who sleep along the Seine. The homeless, estimated at between 6,000 and 15,000, can stay for up to six months in 60 government-run or private shelters where they receive free room, board, medical care and job training. Most go to these shelters voluntarily, but the police often round up sleeping drunks to protect them from the cold.

"Paris's streets are cleaner than American cities, its garbage is picked up more regularly, its streets are paved more often and its bureaucracy is more efficient," says Michel Rousseau, an economics professor who studies urban problems. "But all this costs a lot of money."

Fortunately for Paris, the national Government contributes more than half the city's revenues. Because the state pays so much, Paris's affluent families do not shoulder a huge fiscal burden of caring for the immigrants and poor living in the city. This is one reason Paris has not suffered from the middle-class flight that has hurt so many American cities.

As one urban planner puts it: "One reason Paris has so few problems is that the type of people who make problems can't afford to live in Paris." Economic realities force the poor to live in suburbs ringing Paris, but even there, in the *banlieue*, the levels of poverty, violence and drugs are a fraction of those in American cities.

"Because of France's republican traditions, there is a real sense of solidarity, a real desire to help the less-well-off," says Roland Castro, director of the national Government's efforts to help the suburbs. "People often point to American cities as a model to avoid. They say, 'That can happen to us if we let things slide.'"

At one of the 50 mahogany tables under the gaze of two austere Chinese statues, François Dupin is scribbling on a napkin to explain why his cafe, Les Deux Magots, remains a mecca for Paris's beau monde. "The Chamber of Deputies is over there," says the short, dapper cafe manager, drawing a short black arrow to the west. "The students come from over there," he says, aiming an arrow to the east. "And all the artists and antique dealers come from down there." His last arrow points north to the Seine.

On the cream-colored wall behind him is a photograph of Simone de Beauvoir hunched over a table, writing at the famed cafe on the Boulevard St.-Germain. Nearby is a photo of a debonair, mustached young Ernest Hemingway, reading a newspaper at the cafe. Partly to imbibe the legend of such famous writers, partly to taste its flavorful coffee and atmosphere, camera-toting Japanese tourists, chain-smoking French intellectuals and lanky American Hemingway-wannabes crowd into Les Deux Magots each day. Many rush to the sidewalk tables, next to artists selling lithographs and in the shadow of the 12th-century towers of the church of St.-Germain-des-Prés.

"We're in a privileged neighborhood," Mr. Dupin says.

In one way or another all of Paris's 20 *arrondissements*, or districts, are privileged. The first arrondissement has the Palais Royal and Louvre; the fourth has the Place des Vosges and the Île St.-Louis; the fifth has the Sorbonne; the sixth, the Jardin du Luxembourg and École des Beaux-Arts; the seventh, the Invalides and the Eiffel Tower. The eighth is known for the Champs-Élysées, the Élysée Palace and world-famous shops like Hermès and Christian Lacroix. The ninth has the grandiose 19th-century Palais Garnier opera house, and the plush 16th is renowned for its opulent fin-de-siècle mansions.

Everyone wants to live in these neighborhoods, but only the privileged few need apply. One reason is that Paris is small, about half the size of Brooklyn. Rents have been pushed sky-high by limits on building heights and a shortage of land for new housing, caused in part by all the space used for parks, businesses and government. Not wanting Paris to become Manhattan-sur-Seine, the city's planners have generally limited building heights to seven stories in the historic center and relegated skyscrapers to the outskirts.

A two-bedroom apartment in central Paris often costs $2,500 a month, about the same as in Manhattan and some 60 percent more than in Chicago. Parking a car costs about $250 a month, roughly the same as in Manhattan. Cleaning a suit is around $15 and a good chicken runs $2.30 a pound. About the only things cheaper in Paris than in America are baguettes, Beaujolais and Christian Dior gowns.

"I love to live in Paris—I love the possibilities it offers," says Françoise Romand, a 36-year-old film maker. "The Métro is great, the buses are great and the city's very safe. If you get lost anywhere, there's hardly any risk."

In her view, there is nowhere else to live in France for people in film. Paris gives her the cultural fix she needs day after day. She recently went to a dance concert by Dominique Bagouet's French troupe, an experimental farce about a restaurant, "Lapin Chasseur," and a rock concert at the Cigalle, one of Paris's hottest nightclubs. She also visited Sophie Calle's photography exhibit at the Museum of Modern Art and Nicholas Garnier's avant-garde show at an art gallery near the Boulevard Montparnasse.

And that's not to mention exhibitions at the Grand Palais, Louvre, Picasso Museum and Musée d'Orsay. The money the national and city governments spend on Paris's cultural life is probably equal to the overall budgets of some third world nations.

"The French remain very attached to the idea of culture and education," says Françoise Cachin, director of the Musée d'Orsay. She says that both the left and the right agree it is important to finance museums generously to improve Paris's cultural life and to keep the tourists coming.

"There is a rivalry between the national and city governments about who can sponsor the best shows," Cachin says. "It's very positive for the museums and museumgoers."

Notwithstanding the impressive array of museums and municipal services, Parisians' local taxes are not astronomical. The reason: L'État, the national Government, pays 40 percent of the city's $23 billion operating budget. The national Government also pays half of most large projects, like schools, sewers and day-care centers. In addition, the state finances Paris's public hospitals, covers almost all welfare costs and pays the salaries of Paris's 24,650 teachers and 26,000 police officers and firefighters.

"In almost every European country, the central Government plays an important role in supporting the cities," says Leo van den Berg, director of the European Institute for Comparative Urban Research at the University of Rotterdam. "Europe's cities are very dependent on central money, and not so much on local fiscal circumstances."

That the cost of running Paris is spread throughout France means the city's residents are not socked with exorbitant taxes, although overall the French pay a greater share of their income for national taxes than Americans do. Indeed, the main taxes in Paris—the apartment tax and the business tax—are lower than in many country towns, causing some provincial politicians to complain that they are subsidizing Paris's elite.

Paris is probably far more spoiled by the state than are other European cities because it is the seat of Government and the capital of French finance, industry, entertainment and mass communication. Not only that, it is the cradle of French culture and history, the city of Voltaire, Napoleon, Pasteur, Hugo, Proust, de Gaulle and Sartre.

No one will ever see a headline like "Mitterrand to Paris: Drop Dead," because one of President François Mitterrand's preoccupations is adding new baubles to the capital. The French press has dubbed him Mitterramses I because of the huge monuments he has built, including the $400 million Bastille Opera, the I. M. Pei glass pyramid at the Louvre, the gigantic new finance ministry and the 350-foot-tall Grande Arche de la Défense. And that doesn't include the $1.3 billion Bibliothèque de France that Mitterrand has commissioned, which is slated to be the world's largest library.

Mitterrand's presidential projects, with a price tag of $3 billion, follow similarly grandiose schemes by his predecessors: Valéry Giscard d'Estaing masterminded the Musée d'Orsay and the Cité des Sciences museum, while Georges Pompidou fathered the Pompidou Center, the hugely popular art museum.

Although many critics deride these buildings as monuments to presidential egos, these projects have undeniably increased Paris's stature as a city of art, culture and architecture. The Musée d'Orsay, for instance, attracts almost four million visitors a year, and art critics from around the world have hailed its recent exhibitions on Seurat, Munch and Gauguin. The museum, which used to be a train station, was slated for demolition until President Giscard d'Estaing moved to save it. "It was a project that couldn't be done without the will of the State," says Cachin, the museum's director. "I can only rejoice."

Tourists strolling along Quai de Montebello near Notre Dame often pass a man in a green uniform who is intently sweeping the street with what looks like a large twig broom. Street cleaners like him are ubiquitous in Paris—of the city's 38,000 employees, 4,500 are sweepers, most of them Arab or African immigrants.

They sweep each of Paris's streets daily, and heavily trafficked business and tourist streets are swept twice.

All this work by hand shows Paris's efficiency, obsession with detail and willingness to spend money to achieve its goals. Each year Paris spends 10 percent of its budget, or about $2.2 billion, on cleanliness, which translates to $1,000 for every resident.

"The broom remains irreplaceable," says Alain Le Troquet, technical director for Paris's department of sanitation and the environment. "You can't do everything with a machine."

Astute observers will notice a curious thing. The brooms no longer have crude brown branches, but instead bright green plastic fingers. Engineers in Paris's sanitation department had long appreciated how efficiently peasants' twig brooms swept debris along, but they were frustrated by how much the brooms cost and how often the twigs broke.

So Paris's sanitation department, considered Europe's most innovative, asked manufacturers to develop a broom that used sturdy plastic fingers rather than wood. The new plastic brooms cost one-fifth as much as the wooden ones and last seven times as long.

This is just one way Paris's administrators have demonstrated their technological ingenuity. The city's water system churns out a foot-wide stream that runs alongside the city's curbs to wash away litter. Paris has worked with industry to develop a vehicle to clean up the animal oil left from all the poultry, rabbit and beef sold at open-air markets. *Voilà*, the Gyrolave squirts steaming, swirling soapy water onto the pavement and then sweeps the street.

Another truck shoots compressed water under cars to remove the litter beneath them, while a second vehicle has long arms with five joints to pick up leaves. The newest vehicle has an elephantlike trunk that vacuums up sidewalk litter. The city soon hopes to introduce a robotic, unmanned version of this contraption.

"You have to give the French credit for being innovative," says van den Berg, the urban expert in Rotterdam.

Parisians say the city has become much cleaner since 1977 when Jacques Chirac became their first democratically elected mayor in a century. Previously Paris had been run by a prefect appointed by the Interior Minister, but residents often argued that a mayor held accountable in regular elections would be more attentive to their needs. (The prefect still runs the police department.)

When Parisians talk about cleanliness, their main complaint is canine excrement, notwithstanding the city's vaunted new motor scooters that vacuum up dog droppings. Not wanting to alienate dog owners, who represent a powerful voting bloc, the city for years refused to fine owners who did not clean up after their poodles. But with complaints growing, Philippe Galy, director of the department of sanitation and the environment, started ordering fines in May: $110 for the first offense and $230 for the second. "It's absurd," he says. "With all the serious environmental problems, like global warming, the ozone layer, Chernobyl and nuclear waste, it's unbelievable that the No. 1 subject of conversation at every Paris dinner party is dog doo."

A public high school like Lycée Janson-de-Sailly, built with busts of Pascal, Hugo and other luminaries along its majestic 200-yard facade, simply does not exist in an American city. The 109-year-old institution is in the 16th arrondissement, the Paris equivalent of Park Avenue, and the bankers, diplomats and high government officials who live there scurry to send their children to Janson.

Janson has 3,200 students, a lengthy waiting list and a substantial number of students from Paris's rich western suburbs, who are attracted by the school's reputation. The school has 250 teachers, several of them accomplished novelists and historians. Janson's alumni include former President Giscard d'Estaing, former Prime Minister Laurent Fabius and the Attali twins—Jacques, president of the European Bank for Reconstruction and Development, and Bernard, chairman of Air France.

Its paint may be peeling, its long, primitive desks may be gnarled from decades of use and abuse, but its student body continues to excel. About 95 percent of Janson's graduates pass the forbidding, all-important *baccalauréat* examination that is the ticket to a university.

"The school is excellent in many ways," says Françoise Rietsch, who heads one of Janson's parent associations. "There is a lot of discipline, self-discipline, among the students."

Sitting behind the old wooden desk in her tidy office, Yvonne Cluzet, the school's earnest principal, makes clear that her main concern is academics and not the woes often associated with urban schools.

"Drugs just aren't a problem here," she says. "And we don't have problems with teen-age pregnancy. Our students are mature." The biggest problem she could think of was that two years ago bands of teen-agers from the suburbs stole pocketbooks, wallets and expensive coats from Janson students as they left school. The police quickly stopped it.

Janson and other Parisian schools do not suffer from a vicious cycle in which the middle class pulls its children out of public schools, tilting the balance toward poorer immigrant children and causing more middle-class families to send their children elsewhere.

Jean-Marie Demade, manager at a metallurgy company, moved his family from Rueil-Malmaison, a suburb, back to Paris so his son Julien could attend Janson. "I returned because of the quality of the education," he says. "And life for children is more interesting and lively in Paris, with the movies, museums, theaters and concerts, than it is in the suburbs."

Twenty-four percent of Paris's high-school students go to private schools. Parents choose those schools because they want their children to receive a religious education or because they have underachieving children and think that private schools will be stricter. The overachievers are sent to public schools like Janson, which, good as it is, doesn't even rank at the top of Paris's public lycées. Most teachers rate Louis-le-Grand and Henri IV even higher.

"The middle class flocking to private schools just isn't a problem here," says Michèle Gendreau-Massalou, the rector of Paris's school system. "In terms of passing the *baccalauréat*, public schools produce better results than private schools."

Schools are just one of the quality services that keep families in Paris. The city has begun building moderately priced three-bedroom apartments because many couples have complained that once they have two or three children they can no longer afford Parisian rents. The city issues a "Paris-Famille" card to parents of three or more children entitling them to $400 in annual discounts on a range of activities, including transport, school meals and college tuition.

Another magnet for families is the city-run day-care system, which cares for 20,000 children a day, attracting rich and poor alike. The day-care center at 54 rue St.-Maur is typical of the 250 city-run centers except for its bold architecture: it has a spiraling concrete facade that resembles the Guggenheim Museum. Its front is windowless to keep out street noise and pollution, while its back is filled with sun-drenched floor-to-ceiling windows.

The center on the rue St.-Maur has a staff of 25 to watch over 87 children, aged 3 months to 3 years. Each of its three floors has a glass-enclosed nap area, and the staff has painted pink and blue rabbits and stars on the see-through walls. Each week, one of the center's aides stages a marionette show; the city offers special courses to teach day-care workers how to do such shows.

"I can afford my own au pair, but I much prefer the day-care center," says Patricia Fayet, a radiologist, as she watches her 1-year-old son, Yann, play in a bright blue plastic tub filled with hundreds of striped balls. "At the day-care center, the children get professional care and learn how to live with others."

Each center has a director who lives on the site and is trained as a licensed nurse and specialist in early child development. All the day-care workers must have spent a year in college studying care of children under age 3. A doctor visits each center once a week.

At the center on the rue St.-Maur, parents can leave their children from 7:30 A.M. to 6:30 P.M., but France Galas, the director, chides parents who leave a child for more than eight hours. Payments are on a sliding scale, ranging from $30 to $400 a month per child, with the city picking up half the cost of running the centers.

The centers are so successful that there is a waiting list of thousands of children, and the city is struggling to keep up by building one new daycare center a month.

"A few years ago mothers thought it was bad to put their children in a public day-care center because they felt guilty they weren't doing enough for their kids," says Elisabeth Allaire, director of social services, children and health for Paris. "Now mothers have heard so many good things about our day-care centers that they think they are bad mothers if they *don't* send their kids to our centers."

In many ways, Paris is a tale of two cities. There is the Paris of the travel guides: the city of three-star restaurants and Yves Saint Laurent boutiques, the city of the 2.2 million privileged souls who live within the 22-mile ring road, the Boulevard Périphérique.

Then there is the other Paris, the outer ring where the working classes live, often in anonymous 1960's tower blocks. These are the suburbs where gangs of immigrant teen-agers clash with the police, where the sons of Algerian and Moroccan workers have a 25 percent jobless rate and where the native French tilt heavily toward Jean-Marie Le Pen, the far-right, anti-immigrant leader. These suburbs include Sartrouville, Montfermeil, Mantes-la-Jolie and Gennevilliers.

"One important reason why Paris is successful is that it's a fantastically elitist city," says Christopher Brooks, an economist specializing in urban issues at the Organization for Economic Cooperation and Development in Paris. "While a lot of people would like to live there, lots of people can't afford to. The social composition is skewed as a result. The poor are forced to live in the outskirts."

The Quartier du Luth in Gennevilliers is neither the worst nor the best of the banlieue. It is a United Nations of immigrants from Algeria, the Antilles, the Ivory Coast, Morocco, Tunisia, Turkey, Zaire and a dozen other countries. About 40 percent of its 10,000 residents are immigrants, and fewer than half the children finish high school. Teachers complain that they find syringes near the school gates.

"This isn't the greatest neighborhood," says Ahmet Ersoy, a 30-year-old unemployed refugee from Turkey. "We'd like to move on to another neighborhood eventually." Ersoy lives in a nondescript, 14-story, 500-yard-long block that could have won a Stalinist design contest. Its graffiti-splattered walls say "Momo" and "Chaka Chaoui." Social agencies steer immigrants to districts like the Luth, four miles northwest of Paris, because they have the cheapest housing in the region. A modest two-bedroom apartment is $350, about one-seventh the cost in central Paris.

In the Luth, France's activist Government works hard to improve living conditions. There are playgrounds with bright red swings and slides, and an office has been set up where four social workers counsel the Luth's residents.

The district has been designated a "Priority Education Zone." This means its schools receive extra money and teachers to help integrate immigrant children and provide special help to the laggards. At Guy Moquet Middle School, Claude Naveau, the principal, is proud that his school, filled with Botticelli and Manet posters, has a computer room and its own radio station.

"We have a lot of children who don't have a good family environment, who don't have someone asking them, 'Are you doing your homework?'" says Naveau, whose heavy glasses and thick beard make him look like an archetypal intellectual. "Children love our school because it's an oasis from the chaos outside."

To be sure, Paris proper also has its less chic neighborhoods, most notably the 18th, 19th and 20th arrondissements in the north and east. These have a large North African population, much of it second generation, many of whom work in small businesses, especially textiles.

The epicenter of Arab Paris is Barbès-Rochechouart, the intersection of two bustling avenues, which seems a cross between a Moroccan souk and Manhattan's 14th Street. Elevated trains rumble by as people squeeze past a 200-yard line of sidewalk stalls. Nearby, young toughs wait until sundown to begin their purse snatchings.

"A lot of young kids come up from the Maghreb, can't find jobs and start creating trouble," says Youssef Karoui, who runs the Eslem restaurant.

The problem in these neighborhoods, residents say, is not violent crime, but purse-snatchings, burglaries and car thefts. Fortunately for Paris, crack has not made inroads and drug addiction is far less prevalent than in American cities.

The entrance to the concrete, 1960's building on the Boulevard Bourdon, 250 yards south of the Bastille, could not be more nondescript. There isn't even a nameplate. But deep inside, behind the security guards, is a cavernous room filled with display panels and flashing lights that looks like the Pentagon's war room.

Welcome to the central command post for Paris's subway system, an intricate web with 434 stations, 686 escalators and 1.6 billion riders a year.

At rush hour, 560 trains snake through the city, and on the command center's 13 display panels, each as long as a baseball scoreboard, orange lights show the location and progress of every single train. If there is a subway fire or someone jumps in front of a train—there are about 150 such suicides each year—a subway line manager leaps up from his console and runs to his display panel to switch off power for his line.

"We have already extended this display panel to include some new stations that we still haven't opened," says Jean-Pierre Renard, a longtime manager at the command center. The panel shows two stations to be added when line No. 1 is extended under the Seine to La Défense, the ultramodern office district west of Paris.

Probably better than anything else, the Métro demonstrates Paris's devotion to constant improvement: to improve through planning, bold engineering and a willingness to spend money. The Métro recently added a conductorless train that connects Orly Airport with the main subway line. The express suburban rail system, known as the R.E.R., has been extended east to Euro-Disneyland, which opened in April. There are plans for a six-mile-long tramway that will connect blue-collar suburbs north of Paris and for an express subway connecting the southernmost part of Paris to the St.-Lazare train station on the right bank.

The budget for these and other transit projects—which are selected by a regional transportation board—will total $3 billion over the next five years. The financing comes from ticket revenues and from the city, regional and national governments.

Thanks to a solid flow of funds, the subway cars undergo maintenance once a week, and as a result mechanical failures are responsible for less than a third of line shutdowns. Usually the problem is human failures, like fights between passengers or pranksters pulling the emergency cord.

"If our trains ran without passengers, we'd hardly have any problems," jokes Renard, a short, dapper man in a blue bow tie and charcoal-striped suit.

Like many Parisian civil servants, Renard exudes an extreme pride in his work and his city. He boasts about a new varnish that helps keep the Métro graffiti-free. He brags about the system's safety record, saying he cannot remember the last time there was a fatal accident.

"I'm a modest man, so don't expect me to say that our Métro is the best in the world," he says, with a twinkle in his eye. "Let's just say it's one of the best.

"We plan to keep it that way."

3 Exploring Paris

*Updated by
Alexandra
Siegel*

Paris is a city of vast, noble perspectives and winding, hidden streets. This combination of the pompous and the intimate is a particularly striking and alluring feature of Paris. The French capital is also, for the tourist, a practical city: It is relatively small as capitals go, with many of its major sites and museums within walking distance of one another.

In fact, the best method of getting to know Paris is on foot, although public transportation—particularly the métro subway system—is excellent. Buy a *Plan de Paris* booklet: a city map-guide with a street-name index that also shows métro stations. Note that all métro stations have a detailed neighborhood map just inside the entrance.

Paris owes both its development and much of its visual appeal to the river Seine, which weaves through its heart. Each bank of the Seine has its own personality; the Rive Droite (Right Bank), with its spacious boulevards and haughty buildings, generally has a more sober and genteel feeling to it than the more carefree and bohemian Rive Gauche (Left Bank) to the south.

Paris's historical and geographical heart is Notre Dame Cathedral on the Ile de la Cité, the larger of the Seine's two islands (the other is the Ile St-Louis). The city's principal tourist axis is less than 4 miles long, running parallel to the north bank of the Seine from the Arc de Triomphe to the Bastille.

Monuments and museums are sometimes closed for lunch, usually between 12 and 2, and one day a week, usually Monday or Tuesday. Check before you set off. And don't forget that cafés in Paris are open all day long. They are a great boon to foot-weary tourists in need of a coffee, a beer, or a sandwich. *Boulangeries* (bakeries) are another reliable source of sustenance.

We've divided our coverage of Paris into six tours, but there are several "musts" that any first-time visitor to Paris is loath to miss: the Eiffel Tower, the Champs-Elysées, the Louvre, and Notre Dame. It would be a shame, however, not to explore the various *quartiers*, or districts, each with its own personality and charm.

The Historic Heart

Numbers in the margin correspond to points of interest on the Historic Heart map.

Of the two islands in the Seine—the Ile St-Louis (*see* The Marais and Ile St-Louis, *below*) and Ile de la Cité—it is the Ile de la Cité that forms the historic heart of Paris. It was here, for obvious reasons of defense, and in the hope of controlling the trade that passed along the Seine, that the earliest inhabitants of Paris, the Gaulish tribe of the Parisii, settled in about 250 BC. They called their little home Lutetia, meaning "settlement surrounded by water." Whereas the Ile St-Louis is today largely residential, the Ile de la Cité remains deeply historic, the result not just of more than 2,000 years of habitation, but of the fact that this is the site of the most important and one of the most beautiful churches in France—the great brooding cathedral of Notre Dame. Few of the island's other medieval buildings have survived to the present, most having fallen victim to town planner Baron Haussmann's ambitious rebuilding of the city in the mid-19th century. But among the rare survivors are the jewel-like Sainte-Chapelle, a vision of shimmering stained glass, and the Conciergerie, the grim former city prison.

Another major attraction on this tour—the Louvre, recently renovated—came into existence in the mid-13th century, when Philippe-Auguste built it as a fortress to protect the city's western flank. It was not until pleasure-loving François I began a partial rebuilding of this original rude fortress in the early 16th century that today's Louvre began gradually to take shape. A succession of French rulers was responsible for this immense, symmetrical structure, now the largest museum in the world, as well as the easiest to get lost in.

If Notre Dame and the Louvre represent Church and State, respectively, the third major attraction we cover—Les Halles (pronounced *lay al*)—stands for the common man. For centuries, this was Paris's central market, replenished by an army of wagons and later, trucks, which caused astounding traffic jams in the city's already congested streets. The market was closed in 1969 and replaced by a striking shopping mall, the Forum. The surrounding streets have since undergone a transformation, much like the neighboring Marais, with shops, cafés, restaurants, and chic apartment buildings. However, the vast public spaces here have attracted a large vagrant population to the area, and general shabbiness has emerged.

Old and new blend and clash in Paris, contrasts that are hard to escape as you follow this tour. The brash modernity of the Forum, for example, stands in contrast to the august church of St-Eustache nearby. The Louvre itself has not been spared controversy: While Louis XIV's harmoniously imposing Cour Carrée, one of the supreme architectural achievements of his reign, has been painstakingly restored and thousands of cobblestones have been laid in place of tarmac, a mixture of awe and outrage has greeted the glass pyramid on the opposite side of the complex. Similarly, the incongruous black-and-white columns in the classical courtyard of Richelieu's neighboring Palais Royal present a further case of architectural vandalism—or daring modernity, depending on your point of view. The Parisians take seriously their role as custodians of a glorious heritage, but they are not content to remain mere guardians of the past. If the city is to remain in the forefront of urban change, it is imperative that present generations bequeath something to the future. Well, so some say.

Toward the Louvre

The tour begins at the western tip of the Ile de la Cité, at the sedate
❶ **Square du Vert Galant.** Nothing is controversial here, not even the statue of the Vert Galant himself, literally the vigorous—by which was really meant the amorous—adventurer, Henri IV, sitting four-square on his horse. Henri, King of France from 1589 until his assassination in 1610, was something of a dashing figure, by turns ruthless and charming, a stern upholder of the absolute rights of monarchy, and a notorious womanizer. He is probably best remembered for his cynical remark that *Paris vaut bien une messe* ("Paris is worth a mass"), a reference to his readiness to renounce his Protestantism as a condition of gaining the throne of predominantly Catholic France, and indeed of being allowed to enter the city. A measure of his canny statesmanship was provided by his enactment of the Edict of Nantes in 1598, by which French Protestants were accorded (almost) equal rights with their Catholic counterparts. It was Louis XIV's renunciation of the Edict nearly 100 years later that led to the massive Huguenot exodus from France, greatly to the economic disadvantage of the country. The square itself is a fine spot to linger on a sunny afternoon. It is also the departure point for the glass-topped *vedette* tour boats on the Seine.

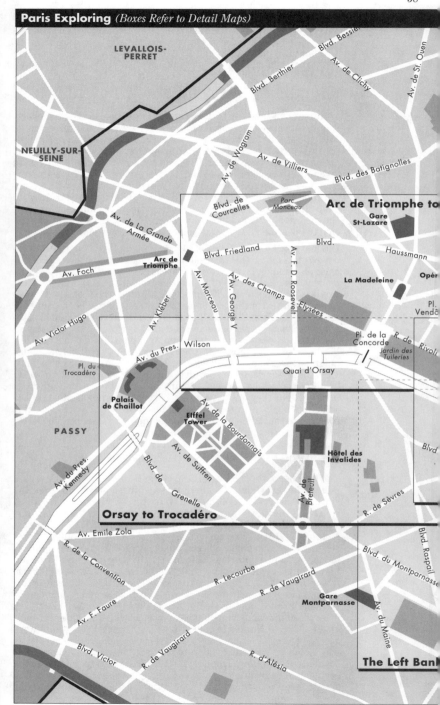

Paris Exploring *(Boxes Refer to Detail Maps)*

LEVALLOIS-PERRET

NEUILLY-SUR-SEINE

Blvd. Bessières

Av. de St. Ouen

Blvd. Berthier

Av. de Clichy

Av. de Wagram

Av. de Villiers

Blvd. des Batignolles

Av. de La Grande Armée

Blvd. de Courcelles

Parc Monceau

Arc de Triomphe to

Gare St-Lazare

Blvd.

Haussmann

Av. Foch

Arc de Triomphe

Blvd. Friedland

Av. F. D. Roosevelt

La Madeleine

Opér

Av. Victor Hugo

Av. Kléber

Av. Marceau

Av. George V

Av. des Champs

Elysées

Pl. Vendô

Av. Victor Hugo

Wilson

Pl. de la Concorde

R. de Rivoli

Pl. du Trocadéro

Av. du Pres. Wilson

Quai d'Orsay

Jardin des Tuileries

Palais de Chaillot

Eiffel Tower

Av. de la Bourdonnais

PASSY

Av. du Pres. Kennedy

Blvd. de

Av. de Suffren

Grenelle

Av. de Breteuil

Hôtel des Invalides

Blvd

Orsay to Trocadéro

R. de Sèvres

Av. Emile Zola

R. de la Convention

R. Lecourbe

R. de Vaugirard

Blvd. du Montparnasse

Blvd. Raspail

Av. F. Faure

Gare Montparnasse

Av. du Maine

Blvd. Victor

R. de Vaugirard

R. d'Alésia

The Left Bank

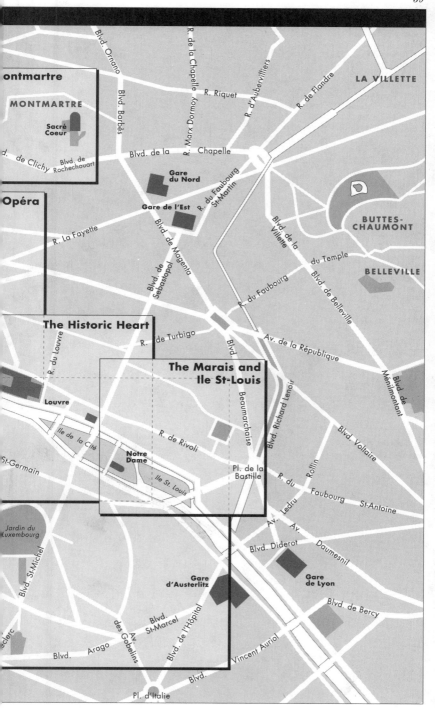

Montmartre

MONTMARTRE

Sacré
Coeur

Blvd. Ornano

Blvd. Barbès

R. de la Chapelle

Marx Dormoy

R. Riquet

R. d'Aubervilliers

R. de Flandre

LA VILLETTE

Blvd. de Clichy

Blvd. de Rochechouart

Blvd. de la Chapelle

Gare
du Nord

Gare de l'Est

BUTTES-
CHAUMONT

BELLEVILLE

Opéra

R. La Fayette

Blvd. de Sebastopol

Blvd. de Magenta

R. du Faubourg St-Martin

Blvd. de la Villette

du Temple

Blvd. de Belleville

R. du Faubourg

The Historic Heart

R. du Louvre

R. de Turbigo

Blvd.

Av. de la République

Blvd. de Ménilmontant

Louvre

Ile de la Cité

**The Marais and
Ile St-Louis**

R. de Rivoli

Beaumarchaise

Blvd. Richard Lenoir

Blvd. Voltaire

St-Germain

Notre
Dame

Ile St. Louis

Pl. de la
Bastille

R. du

Rollin

Faubourg

St-Antoine

Jardin du
Luxembourg

Av. Ledru

Av.

Daumesnil

Blvd. St-Michel

Blvd. Diderot

Gare
de Lyon

Gare
d'Austerlitz

Blvd. de Bercy

leclerc

Blvd.

Arago

Av. des Gobelins

Blvd. St-Marcel

Blvd. de l'Hôpital

Vincent Auriol

Blvd.

Pl. d'Italie

The Historic Heart

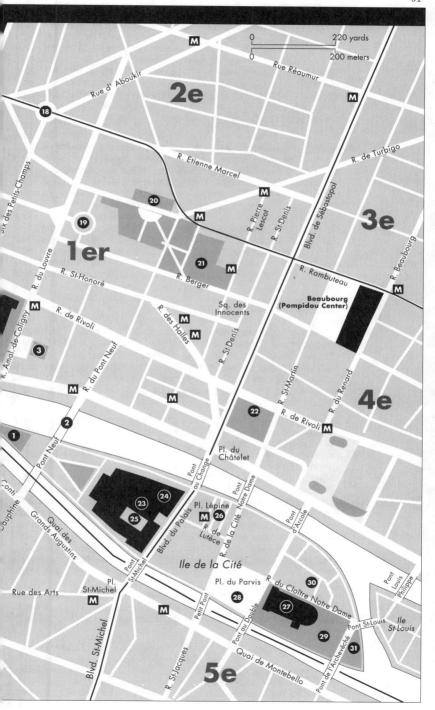

Crossing the Ile de la Cité, just behind the Vert Galant, is the oldest bridge in Paris, confusingly called the **Pont Neuf,** or New Bridge. It was completed in the early 17th century and was the first bridge in the city to be built without houses lining either side. Turn left onto it. Visible to the north of the river is the large-windowed **Samaritaine** department store. Once across the river, turn left again and walk down to rue Amiral-de-Coligny. Opposite you is the massive eastern facade of the Louvre. It is Baroque dignity and coherence with no frills, a suitably imposing entrance to the rigorous classicism of the Cour Carrée beyond.

However, before heading for the Louvre, stay on the right-hand sidewalk and duck into the church of **St-Germain l'Auxerrois.** This was the French royal family's Paris church, used by them right up to 1789, in the days before the Revolution, when the Louvre was a palace rather than a museum. The fluid stonework of the facade reveals the influence of 15th-century Flamboyant Gothic, the final, exuberant fling of the Gothic before the classical takeover of the Renaissance. Notice the unusually wide windows in the nave, light flooding through them, and the equally unusual double aisles. The triumph of classicism is evident, however, in the fluted columns around the choir, the area surrounding the altar. These were added in the 18th century and are characteristic of the desire of 18th-century clerics to dress up medieval buildings in the architectural raiment of their day.

The Louvre

The Louvre colonnade across the road from St-Germain l'Auxerrois screens one of Europe's most dazzling courtyards, the **Cour Carrée,** a monumental, harmonious, and superbly rhythmical ensemble. It has something of the assured feel of an Oxford or Cambridge quadrangle, though on a much grander scale. In the **crypt** under it, excavated in 1984, sections of the defensive towers of the original, 13th-century fortress can be seen.

If you enter the museum via the quai du Louvre entrance, saunter through the courtyard and pass under the **Pavillon de l'Horloge**—the Clock Tower—and you come face to face with the Louvre's most controversial development, I. M. Pei's notorious **Great Pyramid,** surrounded by three smaller pyramids in the Cour Napoléon. Unveiled in March of 1989, it's more than just a grandiloquent gesture, a desire on the part of President François Mitterrand, who commissioned it, to make his mark on the city. First, the pyramid provides a new, and much needed, entrance to the Louvre; it also houses a large museum shop, café, and restaurant. Second, it acts as the terminal point for the most celebrated city view in Europe, a majestic vista stretching through the Arc du Carrousel, the Tuileries Gardens, across place de la Concorde, up the Champs-Elysées to the towering Arc de Triomphe, and ending at the giant modern arch at La Défense, 2½ miles more to the east. Needless to say, the architectural collision between classical stone blocks and pseudo-Egyptian glass panels has caused a furor. Adding insult to injury, at least as far as many Parisians are concerned, is the shocking fact that Pei isn't even a Frenchman!

The pyramids mark only the first phase of the **Grand Louvre project,** a plan for the restoration of the museum launched by Mitterand in 1981, projected to reach a total cost of $1.3 billion by its completion in 1996. In November 1993, exactly 200 years since the Louvre first opened its doors to the public, Mitterand cut the ribbon on the sec-

Louvre

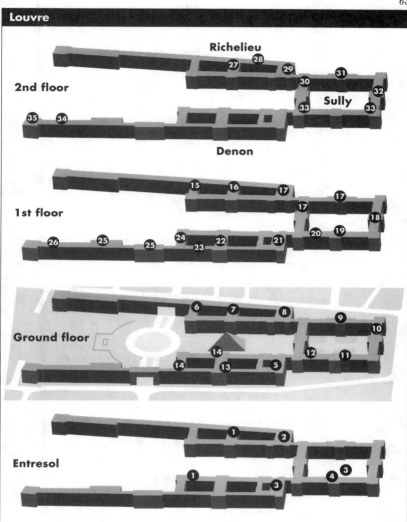

2nd floor · Richelieu · Sully · Denon

1st floor

Ground floor

Entresol

Bronzes and Precious Objects, **20**

Ceramics and Terracotta, **19**

Crypt of the Sphinx, **4**

Documentation Rooms, **15**

Documentation and Reference, **26**

Egyptian Antiquities (Pharaonic Egypt, Christian Egypt), **11**

French Paintings:
16th–17th Cent., **31**
18th–19th Cent., **33**
19th Cent., **22**

French Sculptures:
17th–18th Cent., **1**
17th–19th Cent., **7**
Middle Ages and Renaissance, **6**

Galerie d'Apollon (Crown Jewels), **21**

Greek, Etruscan, and Roman Antiquities, **5**

Gudéa, **8**

Information Center, **29**

Italian Paintings, **23**

Italian School, **24**

Italian Sculptures (16th–19th Cent.), **14**

Islamic Art, **2**

Medieval Louvre (History of the Louvre), **3**

Mona Lisa, **22**

Napoléon III Apartments, **15**

Northern Sculptures (17th–19th Cent.), **14**

Objets d'Art:
17th–18th Cent., **17**
19th Cent., **15**
Middle Ages and Renaissance, **16**

Oriental Antiquities:
Mesopotamia, Iran, **9**
Near East, **10**

Paintings: Holland, Flanders, Germany, **27**

Pharaonic Egypt, **18**

Prints and Drawings:
French School,
17th Cent., **30**
18th Cent., **32**
Northern Schools, **28**

Seated Scribe, **11**

Salle du Manège (copies of antiques), **13**

Spanish Paintings, **25**

Temporary Exhibitions, **17**

Thematic Exhibits, **34**

Venus de Milo, **12**

ond phase of construction. This includes first of all the renovation of the **Richelieu wing** on the north side of the Cour Napoléon. Built between 1852 and 1857 by Napoléon III and grudgingly vacated in 1989 by the Ministry of Finance, the wing was gutted and reconstructed by Pei and his French associates and reopened to house over 12,000 artworks, nearly a third of them brought out from storage. The wing contains principally the Islamic and Mesopotamian art collections, French sculpture and painting, and Napoléon III's sumptuous apartments lovingly restored to their full ostentatious glory. Second is the opening of the **Carrousel du Louvre,** a subterranean shopping complex centered around an inverted glass pyramid, containing a wide range of stores, a food court, spaces for fashion shows, an auditorium, and a huge parking garage. The third and final phase of the Grand Louvre project is slated to be finished in 1996, which means the ubiquitous construction crews will be around for a few months yet. This leg of the renovations includes a much-needed improvement of lighting and air conditioning throughout the museum, while on the exterior the remaining facades will be restored and cleaned. In addition, the Tuileries Gardens are being redesigned and a pedestrian bridge built to connect the Louvre with the Musée d'Orsay.

Though it may seem a coherent, unified structure, today's Louvre is the product of many generations of work. The earliest parts of the building date from the reign of François I at the beginning of the 16th century. Down the years, Henri IV (1589–1610), Louis XIII (1610–1643), Louis XIV (1643–1715), Napoléon (1804–1814), and Napoléon III (1852–1870) have all contributed to the construction. Before rampaging revolutionaries burned part of it down during the bloody Paris Commune of 1871, the building was even larger. The open section facing the Tuileries Gardens was originally the Palais des Tuileries, the main Paris residence of the royal family.

The uses to which the building has been put have been almost equally varied. Though Charles V (1364–1380) made the Louvre his residence, later French kings preferred to live elsewhere, mainly in the Loire Valley. Even after François I decided to make the Louvre his permanent home, and accordingly embarked on an ambitious rebuilding program (most of which came to nothing), the Louvre never became more than a secondary palace. When, in 1682, Louis XIV decided to move the French court out of the city to Versailles, despite having previously initiated a major program of rebuilding at the Louvre, it seemed that the Louvre would never be more than a home for minor courtiers. Indeed, during the remainder of Louis's reign, the palace underwent a rapid decline. Its empty apartments were taken over by a rabble of artists; little shacklike shops were set up against the walls; and chimneys projected higgledy-piggledy from the severe lines of the facades. Louis XV (1715–1774), thanks in large measure to the financial shrewdness of his chief minister, Marigny, then inaugurated long-overdue renovations, though he, too, preferred to live at Versailles. The Louvre's association with the French crown was not to last much longer. It was from the Tuileries Palace that Louis XVI and Marie Antoinette fled in 1791, two years after the start of the Revolution, only to be arrested and returned to Paris for their executions. The palace was taken over by the Revolutionary leaders—the Convention first, then the Directory. At the very end of the century, Napoléon, initially as first consul, subsequently as emperor, initiated a further program of renovation and rebuilding and established the Louvre, first and foremost, as a museum rather than as a palace. This did not, however, prevent the three remaining French kings—Louis XVIII (1814–1824), who has the dubious distinction of having been the only French monarch to have died in the Louvre; Charles X (1824–1830); and Louis-Philippe (1830–1848)—from making the Louvre their home. The latter pair suffered the indignity of expulsion at the hands of the dreaded Paris mob in the uprisings of 1830 and 1848, respectively.

Today, of course, you'll want to see the Louvre not just to walk through a central part of French history, or even to marvel at the French gift for creating buildings that convey the pomp and prestige they consider their nation's due; rather, you'll be drawn here to see the extraordinary collections assembled under its roofs. Paintings, drawings, antiquities, sculpture, furniture, coins, jewelry—the quality and the sheer variety are intimidating. The number-one attraction for most is Leonardo da Vinci's enigmatic *Mona Lisa,* "La Joconde" to the French. But there are numerous other works of equal quality. The collections are divided into seven sections: Oriental antiquities; Egyptian antiquities; Greek and Roman antiquities; sculpture; paintings, prints, and drawings; furniture; and objets d'art. What follows is no more than a selection of favorites, chosen to act as key points for your exploration. If you have time for only one visit, they will give some idea of the riches of the museum. But try to make repeat visits—the Louvre is half-price on Sundays. Study the plans at the entrance to get your bearings, and pick up a map to take with you.

Paintings: French paintings dominate the picture collection. Here are the highlights, in chronological order:

Shepherds in Arcadia, by Poussin (1594–1665), is a sturdy example of the Rome-based painter's fascination with the classical world and of the precision of his draftsmanship. The coloring, by contrast, is surprisingly vivid, almost Venetian.

Cleopatra Landing, by Claude (1600–1682), presents an altogether more poetic vision of the ancient world, delicately atmospheric, with the emphasis on light and space rather than on the nominal subject matter.

The Embarkation for the Island of Cythera, by Watteau (1684–1721), concentrates on creating an equally poetic mood, but there is an extra layer of emotion: The gallant gentlemen and their courtly women seem drugged by the pleasures about to be enjoyed, but disturbingly aware of their transitory nature, too.

The Oath of the Horatii, by David (1748–1825), takes a much sterner view of classical Rome; this is neo-Classicism—severe, uncompromising, and austere. The moral content of the painting takes precedence over purely painterly qualities; it also held an important political message for contemporaries, championing the cause of Republicanism.

La Grande Odalisque, by Ingres (1780–1867), is the supreme achievement by this habitually staid "academic" artist; sensuous yet remote and controlled. Here, exoticism and the French classical tradition gel to produce a strikingly elegant image.

The Raft of the Medusa, by Gericault (1791–1824), presages a much more gloomily Romantic view of the human state, nightmarish despite its heroism and grand scale.

Liberty Guiding the People, by Delacroix (1798–1863), in sharp contrast to the conservative classical paintings of the 19th century, celebrates the courageous spirit of revolutionary idealism. While Liberty evokes a classical reference, she symbolizes the heroism of the bloody uprising on July 27–29, 1830.

Among works by non-French painters, pride of place must go to the *Mona Lisa,* if only by virtue of its fame. The picture is smaller than you might expect and kept behind protective glass; it is invariably surrounded by a crowd of worshipers. The Italian Renaissance is also strongly represented by Fra Angelico, Mantegna, Raphael, Titian, and Veronese. Holbein, Van Eyck, Rembrandt, Hals, Brueghel, and Rubens underline the achievements of northern European painting. The Spanish painters El Greco, Murillo, Velázquez, and Goya are also well represented.

Sculpture: Three-dimensional attractions start with marvels of ancient Greek sculpture such as the soaring *Venus of Samothrace,* from the 3rd century BC, and the *Venus de Milo,* from the 2nd century BC. The strikingly realistic *Seated Scribe* dates from around 2000 BC. Probably the best-loved exhibit is Michelangelo's pair of *Slaves,* intended for the unfinished tomb of Pope Julius II.

Furniture and Objets d'Art: The number-one attraction is the **French crown jewels,** a glittering display of extravagant jewelry, including the 186-karat Regent diamond. Among the collections of French furniture, don't miss the grandiose 17th- and 18th-century productions of Boulle and Riesener, marvels of intricate craftsmanship and typical of the elegant luxury of the best French furniture. The series of immense Gobelins tapestries may well be more to the taste of those with a fondness for opulent decoration. *Tel. 40–20–50–50. Palais du Louvre. Admission: 35 frs adults, 20 frs 18–25 years, over 60, and Sun.; children under 18 free. Open Thurs.–Sun. 9–6, Mon. and Wed. 9 AM–9:45 PM. Some sections open limited days.*

Time Out The recently opened **Carrousel du Louvre,** the subterranean shopping complex on the west side of the museum, features a mall–style food court with a selection of 13 food counters ranging from brasserie–style to Italian to Chinese food. For something more refined, if you can make it to the Tuileries, stop at **Angelina** (226 rue de Rivoli). Founded in 1903, this elegant salon de thé is famous for its "L'Africain"—a cup of hot chocolate so thick you'll need a fork to eat it (irresistible even in the summer). Non-chocoholics can select from a dizzying assortment of pastries and other goodies.

North of the Louvre

Stretching westward from the main entrance to the Louvre and the Great Pyramid is an expanse of stately, formal gardens. These are the **Tuileries Gardens** (*see* From the Arc de Triomphe to the Opéra, *below*), currently undergoing a renovation which will restore the fountains, statues, and shady groves to their condition under Louis-Philippe and Napoléon III by the end of 1996. Leading to them is the ➐ **Arc du Carrousel,** a small relation of the distant Arc de Triomphe and, like its big brother, put up by Napoléon. To the north, in the Pavillon de Marsan, the northernmost wing of the Louvre, is the ➑ **Musée des Arts Décoratifs,** which houses over 50,000 objects charting the course of French furniture and applied arts through the centuries. The Musée de la Publicité, with its collection of 50,000 posters, stages temporary exhibits. *107 rue de Rivoli. Admission: 25 frs. Open Wed.–Sat. 12:30–6, Sun. 12–6.*

Running the length of the Louvre's northern side is Napoléon's elegant, arcaded **rue de Rivoli,** a street whose generally dull tourist ➒ ➓ shops add little to their surroundings. Cross it and you're in **place des Pyramides** and face-to-face with its gilded statue of Joan of Arc on horseback. The square is a focal point for city tour buses.

⑪ Walk up rue des Pyramides and take the first left, rue St-Honoré, to the Baroque church of **St-Roch.** The church was begun in 1653 but completed only in the 1730s, the decade of the coolly classical facade. Classical playwright Corneille (1606–1684) is buried here; a commemorative plaque honoring him is located at the left of the entrance. It's worth having a look inside the church to see the bombastically baroque altarpiece in the circular Lady Chapel at the far end.

⑫ Double back along rue St-Honoré to place du Palais-Royal. On the far side of the square, opposite the Louvre, is the **Louvre des Antiquaires,** a chic shopping mall housing upscale antiques shops. It's a minimuseum in itself. Its stylish, glass-walled corridors deserve a browse whether you intend to buy or not.

⑬ Retrace your steps to place André-Malraux, with its exuberant fountains. The Opéra building is visible down the avenue of the same name, while, on one corner of the square, at rue de Richelieu, is the **Comédie Française.** This theater is the time-honored setting for performances of classical French drama, with tragedies by Racine and Corneille and comedies by Molière regularly on the bill. The building itself dates from 1790, but the Comédie Française company was created by that most theatrical of French monarchs, Louis XIV, back in 1680. Those who understand French and who have a taste for the mannered, declamatory style of French acting—it's a far cry from method acting—will appreciate an evening here. (*See* The Arts and Nightlife, Chapter 7, for details on how to get tickets.)

⑭ To the right of the theater is the unobtrusive entrance to the gardens of the **Palais-Royal.** The buildings of this former palace —royal only in that all-powerful Cardinal Richelieu (1585–1642) magnanimously bequeathed them to Louis XIII—date from the 1630s. In his early days as king, Louis XIV preferred the relative intimacy of the Palais-Royal to the intimidating splendor of the Louvre. He soon decided, though, that his own intimidating splendor warranted a more majestic setting; hence, of course, that final word in un-intimacy, Versailles.

⑮ Today, the Palais-Royal is home to the French Ministry of Culture and is not open to the public. But don't miss the **Jardin du Palais-Royal,** gardens bordered by arcades harboring discreet boutiques and divided by rows of perfectly trimmed little trees. They are a surprisingly little-known oasis in the gray heart of the city. It's hard to imagine anywhere more delightful for dozing in the afternoon sun. As you walk into the gardens, there's not much chance that you'll miss the black-and-white striped columns in the courtyard or the revolving silver spheres that slither around in the two fountains at either end, the controversial work of architect Daniel Buren. Everyone will muse on the days when this dignified spot was the haunt of prostitutes and gamblers, a veritable sink of vice, in fact. It's hard to imagine anywhere much more respectable these days. Walk up to the end, away from the main palace, and peek into the
⑯ opulent, Belle Epoque, glass-lined interior of **Le Grand Véfour.** This is more than just one of the swankiest restaurants in the city; it's probably the most sumptuously appointed, too (*see* Chapter 5).

⑰ Around the corner from here, on rue de Richelieu, stands France's national library, the **Bibliothèque Nationale.** It contains over 7 million printed volumes. A copy of every book and periodical printed in France must, by law, be sent here. Visitors can admire Robert de Cotte's 18th-century courtyard and peep into the 19th-century reading room. The library galleries stage exhibits from time to time from the collections. *58 rue de Richelieu. Open daily 9–8.*

From the library, walk southeast along rue des Petits-Champs to the circular **place des Victoires.** It was laid out in 1685 by Mansart, a leading proponent of 17th-century French classicism, in honor of the military victories of Louis XIV, that indefatigible warrior whose near-continuous battles may have brought much prestige to his country but came perilously close to bringing it to bankruptcy, too. Louis is shown prancing on a plunging steed in the center of the square; it's a copy, put up in 1822 to replace the original one destroyed in the Revolution. You'll find some of the city's most upscale fashion shops here and on the surrounding streets.

Head south down rue Croix des Petits-Champs. You'll pass the undistinguished bulk of the Banque de France on your right. The second street on the left leads to the circular, 18th-century **Bourse du Commerce,** or Commercial Exchange. Alongside it is a 100-foot-high fluted column, all that remains of a mansion built here in 1572 for Catherine de Médicis. The column is said to have been used as a platform for stargazing by Catherine's astrologer, Ruggieri.

You don't need to scale Ruggieri's column to be able to spot the bulky outline of the church of **St-Eustache,** away to the left. Since the demolition of the 19th-century iron and glass market halls at the beginning of the '70s, an act that has since come to be seen as little short of vandalism, St-Eustache has re-emerged as a dominant element on the central Paris skyline. It is a huge church, the "cathedral" of Les Halles, built as the market people's Right Bank reply to Notre Dame on the Ile de la Cité. St-Eustache dates from a couple of hundred years later than Notre Dame. With the exception of the feeble west front, added between 1754 and 1788, construction lasted from 1532 to 1637, spanning the twilight of Gothic and the rise of the Renaissance. As a consequence, the church is a curious architectural hybrid. Its exterior flying buttresses, for example, are solidly Gothic. Its column orders, rounded arches, and comparatively simple and thick window tracery are unmistakably classical. Few buildings bear such eloquent witness to stylistic transition. St-Eustache also features occasional organ concerts. *2 rue du Jour, tel. 46–27–89–21, for concert information. Open daily.*

Nothing now remains of either the market halls or the rumbustious atmosphere that led 19th-century novelist Emile Zola to dub Les Halles *le ventre de Paris* ("the belly of Paris"). Today, the vast site is part shopping mall and part garden. The latter, which starts by the provocative, king-size sculpture *Hand* in front of St-Eustache, is geared for children. They'll also love the bush shaped like a rhinoceros.

The once-grimy facades of the buildings facing Les Halles have been expensively spruced up to reflect the mood of the shiny new **Forum des Halles,** the multilevel mall. Just how long the plastic, concrete, glass, and mock-marble of this gaudy mall will stay shiny is anyone's guess. Much of the complex is already showing signs of wear and tear, a state of affairs not much helped by the hordes of down-and-outs who invade it toward dusk. Nonetheless, the multitude of shops gathered at the Forum makes it somewhere no serious shopper will want to miss. The sweeping white staircase and glass reflections of the central courtyard have a certain photogenic appeal.

Leave by square des Innocents to the southeast; its 16th-century Renaissance fountain has recently been restored. As you make your way toward boulevard de Sébastopol, you can see the futuristic funnels of the Beaubourg jutting above the surrounding buildings (*see* The Marais and Ile St-Louis, *below*). Head right, toward the Seine. Just before you reach place du Châtelet on the river, you'll see the **Tour St-Jacques** to your left. This richly worked, 170-foot stump, now used for meteorological purposes and not open to the public, is all that remains of a 16th-century church destroyed in 1797.

Time Out   Just north of place du Châtelet, at 4 rue St-Denis, is **Le Trappiste.** Twenty different international beers are available on draft here, as well as more than 180 in bottles. Mussels and french fries are the traditional accompaniment, although various other snacks (hot dogs, sandwiches) are also available. There are tables upstairs and on the pavement.

The Ile de la Cité

From place du Châtelet, cross back over the Seine on the Pont au Change to the Ile de la Cité. To your right looms the imposing **Palais de Justice,** the Law Courts, built by Baron Haussmann in his characteristically weighty classical style about 1860. You can wander around the building, watching the bustle of the lawyers, or attend a court hearing. But the real interest here is the medieval part of the complex, spared by Haussmann in his otherwise wholesale destruction of the lesser medieval buildings of the Ile de la Cité. There are two buildings you'll want to see: the Conciergerie and the Sainte-Chapelle.

The **Conciergerie,** the northernmost part of the complex, was originally part of the royal palace on the island. Most people know it, however, as a prison, the grim place of confinement for Danton, Robespierre, and, most famously, Marie Antoinette during the French Revolution. From here, all three, and countless others who fell foul of the Revolutionary leaders, were taken off to place de la Concorde and the guillotine. The name of the building is derived from the governor, or *concierge*, of the palace, whose considerable income was swollen by the privilege he enjoyed of renting out shops and workshops. Inside, you'll see the guardroom, complete with hefty Gothic vaulting and intricately carved columns, and the Salle des Gens d'Armes, an even more striking example of Gothic monumentality. From there, a short corridor leads to the kitchen, with its four vast fireplaces. Those with a yen to throw a really memorable party can rent the room. The cells, including that in which Marie Antoinette was held, and the chapel, where objects connected with the ill-fated queen are displayed, complete the tour. *Admission: 30 frs adults, 15 frs students and senior citizens. Joint ticket with Sainte-Chapelle: 40 frs. Open daily 9:30–6:30, 10–5:30 in winter.*

The other perennial crowd puller in the Palais de Justice is the **Sainte-Chapelle,** the Holy Chapel. It was built by the genial and pious Louis IX (1226–1270), whose good works ensured his subsequent canonization. He constructed it to house what he took to be the Crown of Thorns from Christ's crucifixion and fragments of the True Cross, all of which he had bought from the impoverished Emperor Baldwin of Constantinople at phenomenal expense. Architecturally, for all its delicate and ornate exterior decoration—notice the open latticework of the pencil-like *flèche*, or spire, on the roof— the design of the building is simplicity itself. In essence, it's no more than a thin, rectangular box, much taller than it is wide. But think of it first and foremost as an oversize reliquary, an ornate medieval casket designed to house holy relics.

The building is actually two chapels in one. The plainer, first-floor chapel, made gloomy by insensitive mid-19th-century restorations (which could do with restoration themselves), was for servants and lowly members of the court. The upper chapel, infinitely more spectacular, was for the king and more important members of the court. This is what you come to see. You reach it up a dark spiral staircase. Here, again, some clumsy 19th-century work has added a deadening touch, but the glory of the chapel—the stained glass—is spectacularly intact. The chapel is airy and diaphanous, the walls glowing and sparkling as light plays on the windows. Notice how the walls, in fact, consist of at least twice as much glass as masonry: The entire aim of the architects was to provide the maximum amount of window space. The Sainte-Chapelle is one of the supreme achievements of the Middle Ages and will be a highlight of your visit to Paris. Come early in the day to avoid the dutiful crowds that trudge around it. Better still, try to attend one of the regular, candle-lit concerts given here. *Tel. 43-54-30-09, for concert information. Admission: 26 frs adults, 17 frs students and senior citizens. Joint ticket with Conciergerie: 40 frs. Open daily 9:30–6:30; winter, daily 10–5.*

❷❻ Take rue de Lutèce opposite the Palais de Justice down to place Louis-Lépine and the bustling **Marché aux Fleurs,** the flower market. There's an astoundingly wide range of flowers on sale and, on Sundays, there are birds, too—everything from sparrows to swans. *Open daily 9–7.*

Notre Dame

Around the corner, looming above the large, traffic-free place du Parvis (*kilometre zéro* to the French, the spot from which all distances to and from the city are officially measured), is the most enduring symbol of Paris, its historic and geographic heart, the ❷❼ **Cathédrale Notre Dame.** The building was started in 1163, with an army of stonemasons, carpenters, and sculptors working on a site that had previously seen a Roman temple, an early Christian basilica, and a Romanesque church. The chancel and altar were consecrated in 1182, but the magnificent sculptures surrounding the main doors were not put into position until 1240. The north tower was finished 10 years later. Despite various changes in the 17th century, principally the removal of the rose windows, the cathedral remained substantially unaltered until the French Revolution. Then, the statues of the kings of Israel were hacked down by the mob, chiefly because they were thought to represent the despised royal line of France, and everything inside and out that was deemed "anti-Republican" was stripped away. An interesting postscript to this destruction occurred in 1977, when some of the heads of these statues were discovered salted away in a bank vault on boulevard Haussmann. They'd apparently been hidden there by an ardent royalist who owned the small mansion that now forms part of the bank. The restored heads are now on display in the Musée National du Moyen-Age (*see* The Left Bank, *below*). *Admission free.*

By the early 19th century, the excesses of the Revolution were over, and the cathedral went back to fulfilling its religious functions again. Napoléon crowned himself emperor here in May 1804. (David's heroic painting of this lavish ceremony can be seen in the Louvre.) Full-scale restoration started in the middle of the century, the most conspicuous result of which was the construction of the spire, the *flèche*, over the roof. It was then, too, that Haussmann demolished the warren of little buildings in front of the cathedral, ❷❽ creating the place du Parvis. The **Crypte Archéologique,** the archae-

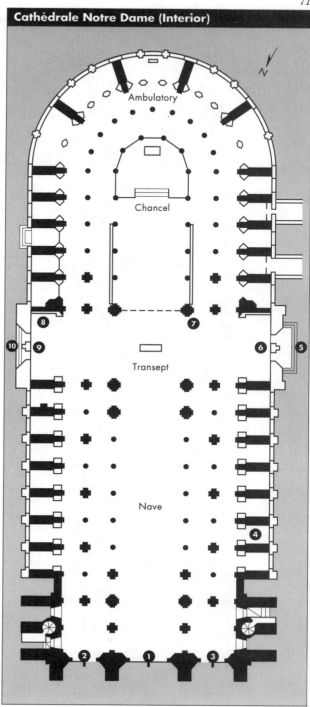

Cathédrale Notre Dame (Interior)

Portal of the Last
Judgment, **1**
Portal to the Virgin, **2**
Portal of St. Anne, **3**
Le Brun, **4**
St. Stephen's Portal, **5**
South Rose Window, **6**
Our Lady of Paris, **7**
Le Sueur, **8**
North Rose Window, **9**
Cloister Portal, **10**

Ambulatory

Chancel

Transept

Nave

ological museum under the square, contains remains unearthed during excavations here in the 1960s. Slides and models detail the history of the Ile de la Cité. The foundations of the 3rd-century Gallo-Roman rampart and of the 6th-century Merovingian church can also be seen. *Place du Parvis. Admission: 25 frs adults (40 frs including tower of Notre Dame), 14 frs age 18–24 and over 60, 6 frs age 7–17. Open daily 10–6:30, 10–5 in winter.*

Place du Parvis provides the perfect place from which to gaze at the facade, divided neatly into three levels. At the first-floor level are the three main entrances, or portals: the Portal of the Virgin on the left, the Portal of the Last Judgment in the center, and the Portal of Ste-Anne on the right. All three are surmounted by magnificent carvings—most of them 19th-century copies of the originals—of figures, foliage, and biblical scenes. Above this level are the restored statues of the kings of Israel, the Galerie des Rois. Above the gallery is the great rose window, and, above that, the Grand Galerie, at the base of the twin towers. Between them, you can glimpse the flèche. The south tower houses the great bell of Notre Dame, as tolled by Quasimodo, Victor Hugo's fictional hunchback. The interior of the cathedral, with its vast proportions, soaring nave, and gentle, multicolored light filtering through the stained-glass windows, inspires awe, despite the inevitable throngs of tourists. Visit early in the morning, when the cathedral is at its lightest and least crowded. You come first to the massive, 12th-century columns supporting the twin towers. Look down the nave to the transepts—the arms of the church—where, at the south (right) entrance to the chancel, you'll glimpse the haunting, 12th-century statue of Notre Dame de Paris, Our Lady of Paris. The chancel itself owes parts of its decoration to a vow taken by Louis XIII in 1638. Still without an heir after 23 years of marriage, he promised to dedicate the entire country to the Virgin Mary if his queen produced a son. When the longed-for event came to pass, Louis set about redecorating the chancel and choir.

On the south side of the chancel is the **Treasury**, with a collection of garments, reliquaries, and silver and gold plate. *Admission: 15 frs adults, 10 frs students and senior citizens, 5 frs children. Open daily 10–5:45.*

The 387-step climb to the top of the **towers** is worth the effort for the close-up view of the famous gargoyles—most of them added in the 19th century—and the expansive view over the city. *Entrance via north tower. Admission: 30 frs adults, 16 frs students and senior citizens. Open daily 9:30–12:15 and 2–6 (5 in winter).*

29 On the subject of views, no visit to Notre Dame is complete without a walk behind the cathedral to **Square Jean XXIII,** located between the river and the building. It offers a breathtaking sight of the east end of the cathedral, ringed by flying buttresses, surmounted by the spire. From here, the building seems to float above the Seine like some vast, stone ship.

30 If your interest in the cathedral is not yet sated, duck into the **Musée Notre Dame.** It displays paintings, engravings, medallions, and other objects and documents, all of which trace the cathedral's history. *10 rue du Cloître-Notre-Dame. Admission: 10 frs, 6 frs students and senior citizens, 4 frs children under 14. Open Wed. and weekends only, 2:30–6.*

31 There's a final pilgrimage you may like to make on the Ile de la Cité to the **Mémorial de la Déportation,** located at square de l'Ile-de-France, at the eastern tip of the island. Here, in what was once the city morgue, you'll find the modern crypt, dedicated to those French men and women who died in Nazi concentration camps. You may wish to visit the quiet garden above it. *Admission free. Open daily 9–6, 9–dusk in winter.*

The Marais and Ile St-Louis

Numbers in the margin correspond to points of interest on the Marais and Ile St-Louis map.

This tour includes two of the oldest and most historic neighborhoods in Paris: the Marais—once a marshy area north of the Seine, today about the most sought-after residential and business district of the city—and the Ile St-Louis, the smaller of the two islands in the Seine. It also includes a side trip to the Bastille, site of the infamous prison stormed on July 14, 1789, an event that came to symbolize the beginning of the French Revolution. Largely in commemoration of the bicentennial of the Revolution in 1989, the Bastille area has been renovated.

Renovation is one of the key notes of this tour, especially around the Marais; the word *marais*, incidentally, means marsh or swamp. Well into the '70s, this was one of the city's poorest areas, filled with dilapidated tenement buildings and squalid courtyards. Today, most of the Marais's spectacular *hôtels particuliers*—loosely, "mansions," one-time residences of aristocratic families—have been restored and transformed into museums. Even the formerly run-down streets of the Jewish quarter, around the rue des Rosiers, are showing signs of gentrification with the displacement of kosher butchers and family storefronts by trendy clothing stores and cafés. The area's regeneration was sparked by the building of the Beaubourg, arguably Europe's most vibrant—and architecturally whimsical—cultural center. The gracious architecture of the 17th and early 18th centuries, however, sets the tone for the rest of the Marais. Try to visit during the Festival du Marais, held every June and July, when concerts, theater, and ballet are performed.

The history of the Marais began when Charles V, king of France in the 14th century, moved the French court from the Ile de la Cité. However, it wasn't until Henri IV laid out the place Royale, today the place des Vosges, in the early 17th century, that the Marais became *the* place to live. Aristocratic dwellings began to dot the neighborhood, and their salons filled with the *beau monde*. But following the French Revolution, the Marais rapidly became one of the most deprived, dissolute areas in Paris. It was spared the attentions of Baron Haussmann, the man who rebuilt so much of Paris in the mid-19th century, so that, though crumbling, its ancient golden-hued buildings and squares remained intact.

Hôtel de Ville to Beaubourg

❶ Begin your tour at the **Hôtel de Ville,** the city hall, overlooking the Seine. The building is something of a symbol for the regeneration of the Marais, since much of the finance and direction for the restoration of the area has been provided by the Parisian municipal authorities. As the area has been successfully redeveloped, so the prestige of the mayor of Paris has grown with it. In fact, until 1977, Paris was the only city in France without a mayor; with the creation of the post and the election to it of Jacques Chirac, leader of the right-of-center

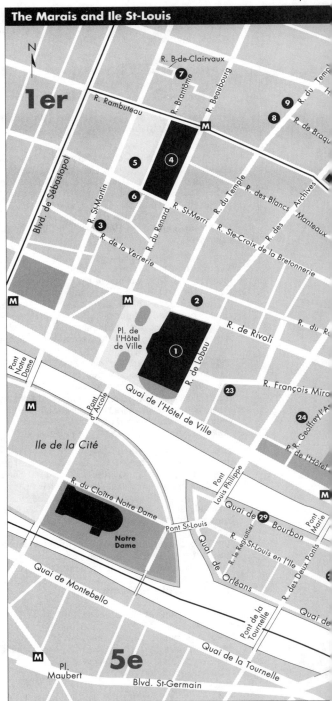

The Marais and Ile St-Louis

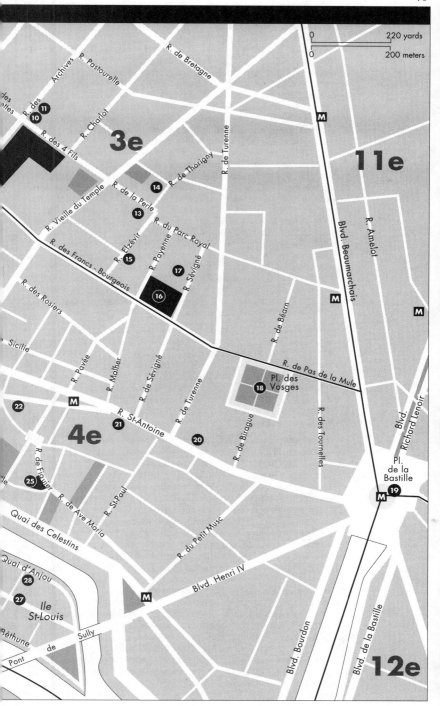

0 — 220 yards
0 — 200 meters

R. Pastourelle
Archives
R. de Bretagne
R. des
11
10
R. Charlot
R. des 4 Fils
3e
11e
R. de Thorigny
R. de Turenne
R. Vieille du Temple
R. de la Perle
14
R. du Parc Royal
13
Blvd. Beaumarchais
R. Elzévir
R. Payenne
R. Amelot
R. des Francs - Bourgeois
15
17
R. Sévigné
M
R. des Rosiers
16
M
Sicilie
R. de Béarn
R. de Pas de la Mule
R. Pavée
R. Malher
R. de Sévigné
Pl. des Vosges
18
R. des Tournelles
22
M
R. de Turenne
R. St-Antoine
Blvd. Richard Lenoir
21
4e
R. de Birague
20
R. de Fauter
R. St-Paul
Pl. de la Bastille
25
R. de Ave Maria
M **19**
Quai des Celestins
R. du Petit Musc
Quai d'Anjou
28
27 Ile St-Louis
Blvd. Henri IV
M
Béthune
de
Sully
Pont
Blvd. Bourdon
Blvd. de la Bastille
12e

Gaullist party, the position has become pivotal in both Parisian and French politics. It comes as no surprise, therefore, that Chirac has overseen a thorough-going restoration of the Hôtel de Ville, both inside and out. You can't go inside, but stand in the traffic-free square in front of it and ponder the vicissitudes that have plagued the Parisian municipal authorities down the years and the dramas that have been played out here. It was here, in 1357, that Etienne Marcel, cloth merchant and prominent city father, attempted to exploit the chaos of the Hundred Years War—the titanic struggle between France and England for control of France—by increasing the power of what he hoped would be an independent Paris. And it was just one year later that his supporters had him assassinated here, believing that his ambitions had outstripped their common interests. There's a statue of Marcel in the little garden on the south side of the building overlooking the Seine. The square was also used for numerous public executions. Most victims were hanged, drawn, and quartered; the lucky ones were burned at the stake. It was also here, during the Revolution, that Robespierre, fanatical leader of the Terror, came to suffer the fate of his many victims when a furious mob sent him to the guillotine in 1794. Following the short-lived restoration of the Bourbon monarchy in 1830, the building became the seat of the French government, a role that came to a sudden end with the uprisings in 1848. In the Commune of 1871, the Hôtel de Ville was burned to the ground. Today's exuberant building, based closely on the Renaissance original, went up between 1874 and 1884. In 1944, following the liberation of Paris from Nazi rule, General de Gaulle took over the leadership of France here.

From the Hôtel de Ville, head north across rue de Rivoli and up rue du Temple. On your right, you'll pass one of the city's most popular ② department stores, the **Bazar de l'Hôtel de Ville,** or BHV, as it's known. The first street on your left, rue de la Verrerie, will take you ③ down to rue St-Martin and the church of **St-Merri,** an ornate mid-16th-century structure. Its dark late-Gothic–style interior can be fun to explore, though it contains nothing of outstanding interest. You may find the upscale stores, restaurants, and galleries of rue St-Martin more diverting.

④ The **Beaubourg/Pompidou Center** or, to give it its full name, the Centre National d'Art et de Culture Georges-Pompidou, is next. Georges Pompidou (1911–1974) was the president of France who inaugurated the project. If nothing else, the Beaubourg is an exuberant melting pot of culture, which casts its net far and wide: Anything goes here. The center hosts an innovative and challenging series of exhibits, in addition to housing the largest collection of modern art in the world. It boasts an avowedly open-door policy toward the public—witness the long hours—and a determination to bring in the crowds by whatever means possible. On the other hand, there's little getting away from the fact that the building itself has been the target of much unfavorable rhetoric. Unveiled in 1977, the Beaubourg is by far the most popular museum in the world, attracting upward of 8 million visitors a year; but it has begun to show its age in no uncertain terms. The much-vaunted, gaudily painted service pipes that snake up the exterior—painted the same colors that were used to identify them on the architects' plans—need continual repainting. The plastic tubing that encloses the exterior escalators is cracked and grimy. In essence, the massive solemnity of a building like the Louvre makes the brashness of the Beaubourg seem cheap, many now maintain. Does the Beaubourg display gross architectural bad manners, contemptuously ignoring the elegant proportions of the surrounding streets? Or is it a bold and potent architectural statement, feeling no need to apologize for its uncompromising nature?

5 You'll approach the center across **plateau Beaubourg,** a substantial square that slopes gently down toward the main entrance. In summer, it's thronged with musicians, mime artists, dancers, fire-eaters, acrobats, and other performers. Probably the single most popular thing to do at the Beaubourg is to ride the escalator up to the roof, with the Parisian skyline unfolding as you are carried through its clear plastic piping. There is a sizable restaurant and café on the roof. The major highlight inside is the modern art collection on the fourth floor. The emphasis is largely on French artists; American painters and sculptors are conspicuous by their absence. Movie buffs will want to take in the cinémathèque, a movie theater showing near-continuous programs of classic films from the world over. There are also magnificent reference facilities, among them a language laboratory, an extensive collection of tapes, videos, and slides, an industrial design center, and an acoustics and musical research center. The bookshops on the first, third, and fourth floors stock a wide range of art books, many in English, plus postcards and posters. *Beaubourg, plateau Beaubourg, tel. 42–77–12–33. Admission free. Admission to art museum: 28 frs, 20–30 frs for special exhibitions. Open Wed.–Mon. noon–10 PM, weekends 10 AM–10 PM; closed Tues. Guided tours in English weekdays 3:30, weekends 11 during summer and Christmas seasons only.*

Time Out Don't leave the plateau without stopping for coffee at the **Café Beaubourg** on the corner of rue St-Merri. A staircase takes you up from the first floor to a *passerelle,* or footbridge, linking the two sides of a mezzanine. The severe high-tech design is lightened by the little glass-top tables, which are gradually being covered with artists' paintings.

On the right side of the Pompidou Center (as you're facing it) is a large digital clock, dubbed the "Genitron." Inaugurated by president François Mitterand in 1987, it counts down the seconds to the year 2000 at what seems like an apocalyptic pace. From here you can

6 turn right into the café-lined **square Igor Stravinsky,** backed by the church of St-Merri—you'll delight in the lively, eponymous fountain animated by the colorful and imaginative sculptures of French artist Niki de Saint-Phalle, together with the aquatic mechanisms of Jean Tinguely.

You can leave plateau Beaubourg by its southeastern corner—to your right as you face the building—and head down rue St-Merri, which becomes rue Ste-Croix de la Bretonnerie to visit the Marais's Jewish quarter; it represents an intriguing element of Parisian ethnic history but, especially since some relatively recent bomb attacks, is a rather cloistered quarter of the Marais.

You'll see the more obvious of the area's historical highlights if you take rue Rambuteau, which runs along the north side of the center

7 (to your left as you face the building). The **Quartier de l'Horloge,** the Clock Quarter, opens off the plateau here. An entire city block has been rebuilt, and, though its shops and cafés make a brave attempt to bring it to life, it retains a resolutely artificial quality. The mechanical clock around the corner on rue Bernard de Clairvaux will amuse kids, however. Saint George defends Time against a dragon, an eagle-beaked bird, or a monstrous crab (symbolizing earth, air, and water, respectively) every hour, on the hour. At noon, 6 PM, and 10 PM, he takes on all three at once.

Around the Marais

You are now poised to plunge into the elegant heart of the Marais. You won't be able to get into many of the historic homes here—the private hôtels particuliers—but this won't stop you from admiring their stately facades. And don't be afraid to push through the heavy formal doors—or *porte-cochères*—to glimpse the discreet courtyards that lurk behind them.

From the Clock Quarter, continue down rue Rambuteau and take a ⑧ left at rue du Temple, to the **Hôtel de Saint-Aignan** at No. 71, built in 1640. The immense entrance is decorated with the sculpted heads of what, in 17th-century France, passed for savages. A few doors up, ⑨ at No. 79, is the **Hôtel de Montmor,** dating from the same period. It was once the scene of an influential literary salon—a part-social and part-literary group—that met here on an impromptu basis and included the philosopher Descartes (1596–1650) and the playwright Molière (1622–1673). Note the intricate ironwork on the second-floor balcony.

⑩ Head east on rue des Haudriettes to the little-known **Musée de la Chasse et de la Nature,** housed in one of the Marais's most stately mansions, the Hôtel de Guénégaud. The collections include a series of immense 17th- and 18th-century pictures of dead animals, artfully arranged, as well as a wide variety of guns and stuffed animals. *60 rue des Archives, tel. 42–72–86–43. Admission: 25 frs adults, 5 frs children under 16. Open Wed.–Mon. 10–12:30 and 1:30–5:30.*

Next door, at 58 rue des Archives, two fairytale towers stand on ei- ⑪ ther side of the Gothic entrance (1380) to the **Hôtel de Clisson.** In the mid-15th century this was the Paris base of the Duke of Bedford, regent of France after Henry V's demise, during the English occupation of Paris, a phase of the Hundred Years War that lasted from 1420 to 1435. At the end of the 17th century, it was bought by the glamorous princess of Soubise, a grande dame of Parisian literary society. She later moved into the neighboring Hôtel de Soubise, now ⑫ the **Archives Nationales.** Its collections today form part of the **Musée de l'Histoire de France,** whose entrance is at the far end of the courtyard. Serious history buffs will be fascinated by the thousands of intricate historical documents dating from the Merovingian period to the 20th century. The highlights are the Edict of Nantes (1598), the Treaty of Westphalia (1648), the wills of Louis XIV and Napoléon, and the Declaration of Human Rights (1789). Louis XVI's diary is also in the collection, containing his sadly ignorant entry for July 14, 1789, the day the Bastille was stormed and, for all intents and purposes, the day the French Revolution can be said to have begun: *Rien* ("nothing"), he wrote. You can also visit the apartments of the prince and princess de Soubise; don't miss them if you have any interest in the lifestyles of 18th-century French aristocrats. *60 rue des Francs-Bourgeois, tel. 40–27–62–18. Admission: 15 frs adults, children under 18 free. Open Wed.–Mon. 1:45–5:45.*

Continue east on rue des Francs-Bourgeois, turning left onto rue Vielle du Temple and passing the Hôtel de Rohan (on your left, on the corner), built for the archbishop of Strasbourg in 1705. Turn ⑬ right onto rue de la Perle and walk down to the **Musée de la Serrure,** the Lock Museum. It's sometimes also called the **Musée Bricard,** a name you'll recognize on many French locks and keys. The sumptuous building in which the collections are housed is perhaps more interesting than the assembled locks and keys within; it was built in 1685 by Bruand, the architect of Les Invalides *(see* From Orsay to Trocadéro, *below).* But those with a taste for fine craftsmanship will appreciate the intricacy and ingenuity of many of the older locks. One represents an early security system—it would shoot anyone who tried to open it with the wrong key. Another was made in the 17th century by a master locksmith who was himself held under lock and key while he labored over it—the task took him four years. *1 rue de la Perle, tel. 42–77–79–62. Admission: 20 frs, under 18 free. Open Mon.–Fri. 2–5; closed Sat. and Sun.*

⑭ From here it is but a step to the Hôtel Salé, today the **Musée Picasso,** opened in the fall of 1985 and so far showing no signs of losing its immense popularity. Be prepared for long lines at any time of year. The building itself, put up between 1656 and 1660 for financier Aubert de Fontenay, quickly became known as the Hôtel Salé—*sal* meaning salt, and *salé* meaning salted—as a result of the enormous profits made by de Fontenay as the sole appointed collector of the salt tax. The building was restored by the French government at phenomenal expense as a permanent home for the pictures, sculptures, drawings, prints, ceramics, and assorted works of art given to the government by Picasso's heirs after the painter's death in 1973 in lieu of death duties. What's notable about the collection—other than the fact that it's the largest collection of works by Picasso in the world—is that these were works that Picasso himself owned; works, in other words, that he especially valued. There are pictures from every period of his life, adding up to a grand total of 230 paintings, 1,500 drawings, and nearly 1,700 prints, as well as works by Cézanne, Miró, Renoir, Braque, Degas, Matisse, and others. If you have any serious interest in Picasso, this is not a place you'd want to miss. The positively palatial surroundings of the Hôtel Salé add greatly to the pleasures of a visit. *5 rue de Thorigny, tel. 42–71–25–21. Admission: 26 frs, 17 frs 18–25, under 18 free; Sun. 17 frs for everyone. Open Thurs.–Mon. 9:30–6.*

Head back down rue de Thorigny and cross to rue Elzévir, opposite.
⑮ Halfway down on the left is the **Musée Cognacq-Jay,** opened here in 1990 after being transferred from its original home on boulevard des Capucines near the Opéra. The museum is devoted to the arts of the 18th century and contains outstanding furniture, porcelain, and paintings (notably by Watteau, Boucher, and Tiepolo). *8 rue Elzévir, tel. 40–27–07–21. Admission: 17 frs, 9 frs students and children. Open Tues.–Sun. 10–5:30.*

Continue down rue Elzévir to **rue des Francs-Bourgeois.** Its name— Street of the Free Citizens—comes from the homes for the poor, or almshouses, built here in the 14th century, whose inhabitants were so impoverished that they were allowed to be "free" of taxes. In marked contrast to the street's earlier poverty, the substantial
⑯ **Hôtel Carnavalet** became the scene, in the late 17th century, of the most brilliant salon in Paris, presided over by Madame de Sévigné. She is best known for the hundreds of letters she wrote to her daughter during her life; they've become one of the most enduring chronicles of French high society in the 17th century, and the Carnavalet was her home for the last 20 years of her life. In 1880, the hotel was transformed into the **Musée Carnavalet,** or Musée Historique de la Ville de Paris. As part of the mammoth celebrations for the bicentennial of the French Revolution, in July 1989, the mu-
⑰ seum annexed the neighboring **Hôtel Peletier St-Fargeau.** Together the two museums chronicle the entire history of the city of Paris, with material dating from the city's origins until 1789 housed in the Hôtel Carnavalet, and objects from that time to the present in the Hôtel Peletier St-Fargeau. Parts of the older collections are quite interesting, albeit repetitive. There are large numbers of maps and

plans, quantities of furniture, and a substantial assemblage of busts and portraits of Parisian worthies down the ages. The sections on the Revolution, on the other hand, are extraordinary and include some riveting models of guillotines and a number of objects associated with the royal family's final days, including the chess set that the prisoners used to pass the time, and the king's razor. *23 rue de Sévigné, tel. 42–72–21–13. Admission: 40 frs adults, 30 frs students and senior citizens. Open Tues.–Sun. 10–5:30; closed Mon.*

Time Out **Marais Plus,** on the corner of rue Elzévir and rue des Francs-Bourgeois, is a delightful, artsy giftshop with a cozy **salon de thé** at the rear. Tarts—*salé* and *sucré* (salty and sweet)—will not disappoint.

Now walk a minute or two farther along rue des Francs-Bourgeois ⑱ to **place des Vosges.** Place des Vosges, or place Royale as it was originally known, is the oldest square in Paris. Laid out by Henri IV at the beginning of the 17th century, it is the model on which all later city squares are based. It stands on the site of a former royal palace, the Palais des Tournelles, which was abandoned by the French Queen, Italian-born Catherine de Médicis, when her husband, Henri II, was killed in a tournament here in 1559. The square achieves a harmony and a balance that make it deeply satisfying. The buildings have been softened by time, their pale pink stones crumbling slightly in the harsh Parisian air, their darker stone facings pitted with age. The combination of symmetrical town houses and the trim green square, bisected in the center by gravel paths and edged with plane trees, makes place des Vosges one of the more pleasant places to spend a hot summer's afternoon in the city. Sit in the garden to take in your surroundings—usually filled with children and dogs—or stroll around the square's covered arcades to browse through antiques shops and art galleries.

Place des Vosges was always a highly desirable address, reaching a peak of glamour in the early years of Louis XIV's reign, when the nobility were falling over themselves for the privilege of living here. Notice the two larger buildings in the center of the north and south sides. The one on the south side was the king's pavilion; the one on the north was the queen's pavilion. The statue in the center is of Louis XIII. It's not the original; that was melted down in the Revolution, the same period when the square's name was changed in honor of the French district of the Vosges, the first area of the country to pay the new revolutionary taxes. You can tour the **Maison de Victor Hugo** at No. 6 (admission 15 frs, 6.50 frs students; open Tues.–Sun. 10–5:40), where the French author lived between 1832 and 1848. The collections here may appeal only to those with a specialized knowledge of the workaholic French writer.

Around the Bastille

From place des Vosges, follow rue de Pas de la Mule and turn right ⑲ down boulevard Beaumarchais until you reach **place de la Bastille,** site of the infamous prison destroyed at the beginning of the French Revolution. Until 1988, there was little more to see at place de la Bastille than a huge traffic circle and the **Colonne de Juillet,** the July Column. As part of the country-wide celebrations for July 1989, the bicentennial of the French Revolution, an **opera house** (Opéra de la Bastille) was put up on the south side of the square. Designed by Argentinian-born Carlos Ott, it seats more than 3,000 and boasts five moving stages. This ambitious project has inspired substantial redevelopment on the surrounding streets, especially along rue de

Lappe—once a haunt of Edith Piaf—and rue de la Roquette. What was formerly a humdrum neighborhood is rapidly becoming one of the most sparkling and attractive in the city. Streamlined art galleries, funky jazz clubs, Spanish-style *tapas* bars—*very* chic in Paris these days—and classy restaurants set the tone. For a taste of the new Bastille-style nightlife, try **Balajo** (9 rue de Lappe); it's the liveliest place here, with music (either salsa, techno, or live) nightly. Don't expect things to get too lively before 11 PM, however.

The Bastille, or, more properly, the Bastille St-Antoine, was a massive building, protected by eight immense towers and a wide moat (its ground plan is marked by paving stones set into the modern square). It was built by Charles V in the late 14th century. He intended it not as a prison but as a fortress to guard the eastern entrance to the city. By the reign of Louis XIII (1610–1643), however, the Bastille was used almost exclusively to house political prisoners. Voltaire, the Marquis de Sade, and the mysterious Man in the Iron Mask were all incarcerated here, along with many other unfortunates. It was this obviously political role—specifically, the fact that the prisoners were nearly always held by order of the king—that led to the formation of the "furious mob" (in all probability no more than a largely unarmed rabble) to break into the prison on July 14, 1789, to kill the governor, steal what firearms they could find, and set free the seven remaining prisoners.

Later in 1789, the prison was knocked down. A number of the original stones were carved into facsimiles of the Bastille and sent to each of the provinces as a memento of royal oppression. The key to the prison was given by Lafayette to George Washington, and it has remained at Mt. Vernon ever since. Nonetheless, the power of legend being what it is, what soon became known as the "storming of the Bastille" was elevated to the status of a pivotal event in the course of the French Revolution, one that demonstrated decisively the newfound power of a long-suffering population. Thus it was that July 14 became the French national day, an event celebrated with great nationalistic fervor throughout the country. Needless to say, the place to be, especially in the evening, is place de la Bastille.

The July Column commemorates a more substantial political event: the July uprising of 1830, which saw the overthrow of the repressive Charles X, the Bourbon king about whom it was said only too truthfully that "the Bourbons learnt nothing, and forgot nothing." It's sometimes hard to imagine the turmoil that was a feature of French political life from the Revolution of 1789 right through the 19th century (and, arguably, well into the 20th). After the fall of Napoléon in 1815, the restoration of a boneheaded monarchy, personified first by Louis XVIII, then by Charles X, virtually guaranteed that further trouble was in store. Matters came to a head in July 1830 with the Ordinances of St-Cloud, the most contentious of which was to restrict the franchise—the right to vote—to a handful of landowners. Charles was duly toppled in three days of fighting at the end of the month—the Three Glorious Days—and a new, constitutionally elected monarch, Louis-Philippe, took the throne. His reign was hardly more distinguished, despite attempts to curry favor among the populace. Nor was it noticeably more liberal. Louis-Philippe did, nonetheless, have the July Column built as a memorial, stipulating that 500 of those killed in the fighting of 1830 were to be buried under it. When, in 1848, Louis-Philippe himself was ousted, the names of a handful of the Parisians killed in the fighting of 1848 were then added to those already on the column. (Louis-Philippe and his wife, disguised as Mr. and Mrs. William Smith, fled to Britain and threw themselves on the mercy of the young Queen Victoria.)

Toward the Ile St-Louis

There's more of the Marais to be visited between place de la Bastille and the Ile St-Louis, the last leg of this tour. Take wide rue St-An-

㉔ toine to the **Hôtel de Sully,** site of the **Caisse Nationale des Monuments Historiques,** the principal office for the administration of French historic monuments. Guided visits to sites and buildings all across the city begin here, though all are conducted in French. Still, it's worth stopping here to look at the stately, 17th-century court-yard with its richly carved windows and lavish ornamentation. The bookshop just inside the gate has a wide range of publications on Paris, many of them in English (open daily 10–12:45 and 1:45–6). You can also wander around the gardens.

Those with a fondness for the Baroque should duck into the early

㉑ 17th-century church of **St-Paul-St-Louis,** a few blocks west on rue St-Antoine. Its abundant decoration, which would be easier to appreciate if the church were cleaned, is typical of the Baroque taste for opulent detail.

㉒ The **Hôtel de Beauvais,** located on rue François Miron, is a Renaissance-era hôtel particulier dating from 1655. It was built for one Pierre de Beauvais and financed largely by a series of discreet payments from the king, Louis XIV. These surprisingly generous payments—the Sun King was normally parsimonious toward courtiers—were de Beauvais's reward for having turned a blind eye to the activities of his wife, Catherine-Henriette Bellier, in educating the young monarch in matters sexual. Louis, who came to the throne in 1643 at the age of 4, was 14 at the time Catherine-Henriette gave him the benefit of her wide experience; she was 40.

Continue down rue François Miron. Just before the Hôtel de Ville is

㉓ the site of one of the first churches in Paris, **St-Gervais-St-Protais,** named after two Roman soldiers martyred by the Emperor Nero in the 1st century AD. The original church—no trace remains of it now—was built in the 7th century. The present church, a riot of Flamboyant-style decoration, went up between 1494 and 1598, making it one of the last Gothic constructions in the country. Pause before you go in, to look at the facade, put up between 1616 and 1621. Where the interior is late Gothic, the exterior is one of the earliest examples of classical, or Renaissance, style in France. It's also the earliest example of French architects' use of the classical orders of decoration on the capitals (topmost sections) of the columns. Those on the first floor are plain and sturdy Doric; the more elaborate Ionic is used on the second floor; while the most ornate of all—Corinthian—is used on the third floor. The church hosts occasional organ and choral concerts. *Tel. 47–26–78–38 for concert information. Open Tues.–Sun. 6:30 AM–8 PM; closed Mon.*

Don't cross the Seine to Ile St-Louis yet: Take rue de l'Hôtel de Ville

㉔ and turn left on rue Geoffroy l'Asnier. At No. 17 is the **Memorial of the Unknown Jewish Martyr,** erected in March, 1992—50 years after the first convoy of deportees left France—to honor the memory of the six million Jews who died "without graves." The monument is part of the **Center for Contemporary Jewish Documentation (CDJC);** its archives, library, and gallery which hosts temporary exhibitions, are open to the public. In the basement of the building is a dramatic underground crypt where a huge black marble star of David contains the ashes of victims from death camps in Poland and Austria. *17 rue Geoffroy l'Asnier, 4e, tel. 42–77–44–72. Admission: 12 frs. Open daily 2–6, Sun 9–6.*

Continue along rue de l'Hôtel de Ville to where it meets rue de
Figuier. The painstakingly restored **Hôtel de Sens** (1474) on the corner is one of a handful of Parisian homes to have survived since the
Middle Ages. With its pointed corner towers, Gothic porch, and
richly carved decorative details, it is a strange mixture, half defensive stronghold, half fairytale château. It was built at the end of the
15th century for the archbishop of Sens. Later, its best-known occupants were Henri IV and his queen, Marguérite, philanderers both.
While Henri dallied with his mistresses—he is said to have had 56—
at a series of royal palaces, Marguérite entertained her almost
equally large number of lovers here. Today the building houses a fine
arts library, the **Bibliothéque Forney** (admission free; open Tues.–
Fri. 1:30–8:30, Sat. 10–8:30).

The Ile St-Louis

Cross pont Marie to the **Ile St-Louis,** the smaller of the two islands in
the heart of Paris, linked to the Ile de la Cité by pont St-Louis. The
contrast between the islands is striking, considering how close they
are. Whereas the Ile de la Cité, the oldest continuously inhabited
part of the city, is steeped in history and dotted with dignified, old
buildings, the Ile St-Louis is a discreet residential district, something of an extension of the Marais. Once thought to be an unimpor-
tant backwater and an area curiously out-of-sync with the rest of the
city, Ile St-Louis is now a highly desirable address; a little old-fashioned perhaps, certainly rather stuffy, but with its own touch of
class. There are no great sights here, but for idle strolling, window-
shopping, or simply sitting on one of the little quays and drinking in
the views while you watch the river swirl by, the Ile St-Louis exudes
a quintessentially Parisian air.

The most striking feature of the island is its architectural unity,
which stems from the efforts of a group of early 17th-century property speculators. At that time, there were two islands here, the Ile
Notre Dame and Ile aux Vaches—the cows' island, a reference to its
use as grazing land. The speculators, led by an energetic engineer
named Christophe Marie (after whom the pont Marie was named),
bought the two islands, joined them together, and divided the newly
formed Ile St-Louis into building plots. Louis Le Vau (1612–1670),
the leading Baroque architect in France, was commissioned to put
up a series of imposing town houses, and by 1664 the project was
largely complete.

There are three things you'll want to do here. One is to walk along
rue St-Louis en l'Ile, which runs the length of the island. People still
talk about its quaint, village-street feel, although this village street
is now lined with a high-powered array of designer boutiques and a
constant throng of tourists patroling its length.

Time Out **Berthillon** has become a byword for amazing ice cream. Cafés all
over Ile St-Louis sell its glamorous products, but the place to come is
still the little shop on rue St-Louis en l'Ile. Expect to wait in line. *31
rue St-Louis en l'Ile. Closed Mon. and Tues.*

The second place to visit is the **Hôtel de Lauzun.** It was built in about
1650 for Charles Gruyn, who accumulated an immense fortune as a
supplier of goods to the French army, but who landed in jail before
the house was even completed. In the 19th century, the revolutionary critic and visionary poet Charles Baudelaire (1821–1867) had an
apartment here, where he kept a personal cache of stuffed snakes
and crocodiles. In 1848, the poet Théophile Gautier (1811–1872)

moved in, making it the meeting place of the Club des Haschisch-
ines, the Hashish-Eaters' Club; novelist Alexander Dumas and
painter Eugène Delacroix were both members. The club came to
represent more than just a den of drug-takers and gossip, for these
men believed passionately in the purity of art and the crucial role of
the artist as sole interpreter of the chaos of life. Art for art's sake—
the more exotic and refined the better—was their creed. Anything
that helped the artist reach heightened states of perception was ap-
plauded by them. Now the building is used for receptions by the
mayor of Paris. *17 quai d'Anjou, tel. 43–54–27–14. Admission: 22
frs. Open Easter–Oct., weekends only 10–5:30.*

The third and most popular attraction is a walk along the quays. The
㉙ most lively, **quai de Bourbon,** is at the western end, facing the Ile de
la Cité. There are views of Notre Dame from here and of the Hôtel de
Ville and church of St-Gervais-St-Protais on the Right Bank. It can
be an almost eerie spot in the winter, when it becomes deserted. In
the summer, rows of baking bodies attest to its enduring popularity
as the city's favorite sunbathing spot. **No. 19** marks the former atelier of female sculptor and Rodin contemporary Camille Claudel, who
worked here from 1899 to 1913.

Time Out The **Brasserie de l'Ile St-Louis** remains the most noisy and bustling of
the little island's eating spots. Food from the French Alsace region,
on the German border, with beer to wash it down, is the draw.
Scores of tourists can nearly always be found on the terrace, but
good value is guaranteed. *55 quai de Bourbon, tel. 43–54–02–59.
Closed Wed. and Thurs. lunch and Aug.*

From the Arc de Triomphe to the Opéra

*Numbers in the margin correspond to points of interest on the Arc de
Triomphe to the Opéra map.*

This tour takes in grand, opulent Paris: the Paris of imposing vistas,
long, arrow-straight streets, and plush hotels and jewelers. It
begins at the Arc de Triomphe, standing foursquare at the top of the
most famous street in the city, the Champs-Elysées. You'll want to
explore both its commercial upper half and its verdant lower section.
The hinterland of the Champs-Elysées, made up of the imposing
streets leading off it, is equally stylish. You're within striking distance of the Seine here (and a ride on a Bateau Mouche) to the south,
and the cheerful, crowded Faubourg St-Honoré to the north. This is
not so much an area for museums as for window-shopping and monument-gazing. Dazzling vistas open up from place de la Concorde,
place de la Madeleine, and L'Etoile. Fashion shops, jewelers, art
galleries, and deluxe hotels proliferate. This is also where the
French president resides in his "palace" (not a very Republican
term, but then French presidents enjoy regal lifestyles) just off the
Champs-Elysées.

Local charm is not, however, a feature of this exclusive sector of
western Paris, occupying principally the 8th Arrondissement. It's
beautiful and rich—and a little impersonal. The French moan that
it's losing its character, and, as you notice the number of fast-food
joints along the Champs-Elysées, you'll know what they mean. In

short: Visit during the day, and head elsewhere in search of Parisian *ambience* and an affordable meal in the evening.

The Arc de Triomphe and Champs-Elysées

Place Charles de Gaulle is known by Parisians as **L'Etoile,** the star—a reference to the streets that fan out from it. It is one of Europe's most chaotic traffic circles, and short of a death-defying dash, your only way of getting to the Arc de Triomphe in the middle is to take an underground passage from the Champs-Elysées or avenue de la Grande Armée.

1 The colossal, 164-foot **Arc de Triomphe** was planned by Napoléon— who believed himself to be the direct heir to the Roman emperors— to celebrate his military successes. Unfortunately, Napoléon's strategic and architectural visions were not entirely on the same plane, and the Arc de Triomphe proved something of a white elephant. When it was required for the triumphal entry of his new empress, Marie-Louise, into Paris in 1810, it was still only a few feet high. To save face, a dummy arch of painted canvas was put up.

Empires come and go, and Napoléon's had been gone for over 20 years before the Arc de Triomphe was finally finished in 1836. It boasts some magnificent sculpture by François Rude, such as the *Departure of the Volunteers,* better known as *La Marseillaise,* situated to the right of the arch when viewed from the Champs-Elysées. After showing alarming signs of decay, the structure received a thorough overhaul in 1989 and is now back to its original neo-Napoléonic splendor. The view from the top illustrates the star effect of the 12 radiating avenues and enables you to admire the vista down the Champs-Elysées toward place de la Concorde and the distant Louvre. In the other direction, you can see down avenue de la Grande Armée toward La Défense and its severe modern arch, surrounded by imposing glass and concrete towers. There is a small museum halfway up the arch devoted to its history. France's Unknown Soldier is buried beneath the archway; the flame is rekindled every evening at 6:30. *Pl. Charles-de-Gaulle. Admission: 31 frs adults, 20 frs students and senior citizens, 6 frs children. Open daily 10–5:30, 10–5 in winter. Closed public holidays.*

The cosmopolitan pulse of Paris beats strongest on the gracefully sloping, 1¼-mile-long **Champs-Elysées.** It was originally laid out in the 1660s by the landscape gardener Le Nôtre as a garden sweeping away from the Tuileries, but you will see few signs of these pastoral origins as you stroll past the cafés, restaurants, airline offices, car showrooms, movie theaters, and chic arcades that occupy its upper half. The City of Paris has launched an ambitious reconstruction program to reestablish this once glorious thoroughfare as one of the world's most beautiful avenues. Plans, which should be complete by early 1995, include underground parking to alleviate congestion, tree-lined walkways, and stricter regulations for businesses on the garishness of their storefronts.

2 Start off by stopping in at the main **Paris Tourist Office** at No. 127. It's at the Arc de Triomphe end of the Champs-Elysées, on the right-hand side as you arrive from Etoile. It is an invaluable source of information on accommodations, places to visit, and entertainment—both in Paris and in the surrounding Ile-de-France region. *Open daily 9–8, 9–9 on weekdays in summer, 9–6 on Sun. out of season.*

The Arc de Triomphe to the Opéra

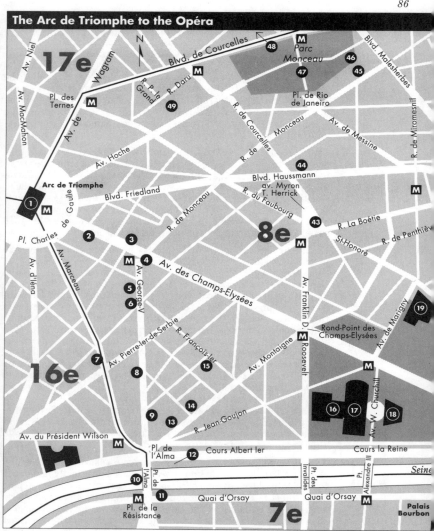

American Cathedral of the Holy Trinity, **8**
Arc de Triomphe, **1**
Atelier de Gustave Moreau, **39**
Bateaux Mouches, **12**
Crazy Horse Saloon, **9**
Crillon, **27**
Eglise de la Madeleine, **21**

Fauchon, **23**
Fouquet's, **4**
Galeries Lafayette, **35**
Gare St-Lazare, **40**
George V, **6**
Grand Palais, **17**
Hédiard, **24**
Les Egouts, **11**
Lido, **3**

Maison de la Vigne et du Vin de France, **15**
Marks & Spencer, **37**
Maxim's, **25**
Musée Cernuschi, **46**
Musée de l'Orangerie, **29**
Musée du Jeu de Paume, **28**
Musée du Parfum, **33**

Musée Jacquemart-André, **44**
Musée Jean-Jacques Henner, **48**
Musée Nissim de Camondo, **45**
Olympia, **32**
Opéra, **34**
Palais de la Découverte, **16**

Palais de l'Elysée, **19**
Parc Monceau, **47**
Paris Tourist Office, **2**
Petit Palais, **18**
Place de la
Concorde, **26**
Place Vendôme, **31**
Plaza Athénée, **14**
Pont de l'Alma, **10**

Prince de Galles, **5**
Printemps, **36**
St-Alexandre
Nevsky, **49**
St-Augustin, **42**
St. Michael's English
Church, **20**
St-Philippe du
Roule, **43**

St-Pierre de
Chaillot, **7**
Square Louis XVI, **41**
Théâtre des Champs-
Elysées, **13**
Ticket kiosk, **22**
Trinité, **38**
Tuileries Gardens, **30**

The Champs-Elysées occupies a central role in French national celebrations. It witnesses the finish of the Tour de France bicycle race on the last Sunday of July. It is also the site of vast ceremonies on July 14, France's national, or Bastille, day, and November 11, Armistice Day. Its trees are often decked with the French *tricolore* and foreign flags to mark visits from heads of state.

❸ Three hundred yards down on the left, at 116b, is the famous **Lido** nightclub: Foot-stomping melodies in French and English and champagne-soaked, topless razzmatazz pack in the crowds every night. In
❹ contrast is the nearby **Fouquet's** café, an 1899 landmark café which still caters to a highbrow clientele (though the outdoor café is thronged with tourists in the summertime). Inside look for the bronze plaques which line the booths, honoring faithful patrons past and present, including François Truffaut, Marcel Pagnol, and Orson
❺ Welles. Swing by the red-awninged **Prince de Galles** (Prince of
❻ Wales) and the blue-awninged **George V,** two of the city's top hotels on avenue George-V, a right-hand turn off the Champs-Elysées. Continue down avenue George-V, and turn right down Pierre Ier-
❼ de-Serbie to the church of **St-Pierre de Chaillot** on avenue Marceau. The monumental frieze above the entrance, depicting scenes from the life of St. Peter, is the work of Henri Bouchard and dates from 1937.

Returning to avenue George-V, continue toward the slender spire of
❽ the **American Cathedral of the Holy Trinity,** built by G. S. Street between 1885 and 1888. *Open weekdays 9–12:30 and 2–5, Sat. 9–noon. Services: weekdays 9 AM, Sun. 9 AM and 11 AM; Sun. school and nursery. Guided tours Sun. and Wed. 12:30.*

❾ Continue down to the bottom of the avenue, passing the **Crazy Horse Saloon** at No. 12, one of Paris's most enduring and spectacular nightspots, to place de l'Alma and the Seine.

❿ The **pont de l'Alma** (Alma bridge) is best known for the chunky stone "Zouave" statue carved into one of the pillars. Zouaves were Algerian infantrymen recruited into the French army who were famous for their bravura and colorful uniforms. (The term came to be used for volunteers in the Union Army during the American Civil War.) There is nothing quite so glamorous, or colorful, about the Alma Zouave, however, whose hour of glory comes in times of watery distress: Parisians use him to judge the level of the Seine during heavy rains. As recently as the winter of 1993, the Zouave was submerged up to his chest, and the roads running along the riverbanks were under several feet of water.

⓫ Just across the Alma bridge, on the left, is the entrance to **Les Egouts,** the Paris sewers (admission: 25 frs adults, 20 frs students and senior citizens; open Sat.–Wed. 11–5). Brave the unpleasant— though tolerable—smell and follow the underground passages and footbridges along the sewers' banks. Signs note the streets above you, and detailed panels and displays illuminate the history of waste disposal in Paris, which boasts the second largest sewer system in the world (after Chicago's). If you prefer a less malodorous tour of the city, stay on the Right Bank and head down the sloping side road
⓬ to the left of the bridge, for the embarkation point of the **Bateaux Mouches.** These popular motorboats set off every half hour, heading east to the Ile St-Louis and then back west, past the Eiffel Tower, as far as the Allée des Cygnes and its miniature version of the Statue of Liberty. *Bateau Mouche* translates, misleadingly, as "fly boat"; but the name Mouche actually refers to a district of Lyon where the boats were originally manufactured.

(13) Stylish avenue Montaigne leads from the Seine back toward the Champs-Elysées. The newly cleaned facade of the **Théâtre des Champs-Elysées** is a forerunner of the Art Deco style. The theater dates from 1913 and was the first major building in France to be constructed in reinforced concrete. *15 av. Montaigne.*

Time Out Although power brokers and fashion models make up half the clientele at the **Bar des Théâtres** (opposite the Théâtre des Champs-Elysées at 6 av. Montaigne), its blasé waiters refuse to bat an eyelid. This is a fine place for an aperitif or a swift, more affordable lunch than around the corner at the luxury restaurants on place de l'Alma.

(14) A few buildings along is the **Plaza Athénée** hotel (the "Plaza"), a favorite hangout for the *beau monde* who frequent the neighboring haute couture houses. Around the corner on the rue François-Ier is

(15) the **Maison de la Vigne et du Vin de France.** This is the classy central headquarters of the French wine industry and a useful source of information about wine regions. Bottles and maps are on display, a boutique sells books and wine-tasting tools, and wine tastings are offered. *21 rue François-Ier, tel. 47–20–20–76. Admission free. Open weekdays 9:30–12:30 and 1:30–6:30.*

Double back on rue François-Ier as far as Place François-Ier, then turn left onto rue Jean-Goujon, which leads to avenue Franklin D. Roosevelt, another spacious boulevard between Champs-Elysées
(16) and the river. Halfway down it is the entrance to the **Palais de la Découverte** (Palace of Discovery), whose scientific and technological exhibits include working models and a planetarium. *Av. Franklin-D-Roosevelt. Admission: 22 frs adults, 11 frs children under 18 (15 frs/10 frs extra for planetarium). Open Tues.–Sat. 9:30–6, Sun. 10–7.*

(17) This "Palace of Discovery" occupies the rear half of the **Grand Palais.** With its curved glass roof, the Grand Palais is unmistakable when approached from either the Seine or the Champs-Elysées and forms an attractive duo with the **Petit Palais** on the other side of avenue Winston Churchill. Both these stone buildings, adorned with mosaics and sculpted friezes, seem robust and venerable. In fact, they were erected with indecent haste prior to the Paris World Fair of 1900. As with the Eiffel Tower, there was never any intention that they would be anything other than temporary additions to the city. But once they were up, no one seemed inclined to take them down. Together with the exuberant, lamp-lit Alexandre III bridge nearby, they recapture the opulence and frivolity of the Belle Epoque—the *fin de siècle* overripeness with which Paris is still so strongly associated. Today, the atmospheric iron and glass interior of the Grand Palais plays host to major exhibitions. Admire the view from the palaces across the Alexandre III bridge toward the Hôtel des Invalides. *Av. Winston Churchill. Admission varies according to exhibition. Usually open daily 10:30–6:30, and often until 10 PM Wed.*

(18) The **Petit Palais** has a beautifully presented permanent collection of French painting and furniture, with splendid canvases by Courbet and Bouguereau. Temporary exhibits are often held here, too. The sprawling entrance gallery contains several enormous turn-of-the-century paintings on its walls and ceilings. *Av. Winston Churchill. Admission: 26 frs adults, 14 frs children. Open Tues.–Sun. 10–5:30.*

Head up Avenue Winston Churchill, cross the Champs-Elysées, and continue on avenue de Marigny to rue du Faubourg St-Honoré, a prestigious address in the world of luxury fashion and art galleries. You'll soon spot plenty of both, but may be perplexed at the presence of crash barriers and stern policemen. Their mission: to protect the French president in the **Palais de l'Elysée.** This "palace," where the head of state lives, works, and receives official visitors, was originally constructed as a private mansion in 1718. Although you catch a glimpse of the palace forecourt and facade through the Faubourg St-Honoré gateway, it is difficult to get much idea of the building's size or of the extensive gardens that stretch back to the Champs-Elysées. (Incidentally, when Parisians talk about "l'Elysée," they mean the President's palace; the Champs-Elysées is known simply as "les Champs," the fields.) The Elysée has known presidential occupants only since 1873; before then, Madame de Pompadour (Louis XV's influential mistress), Napoléon, Josephine, the Duke of Wellington, and Queen Victoria all stayed here. President Félix Faure died here in 1899 in the arms of his mistress. The French government—the Conseil des Ministres—attends to more public affairs when it meets here each Wednesday morning. *Not open to the public.*

Toward place de la Concorde

St. Michael's English Church, close to the British Embassy on rue du Faubourg St-Honoré, is a modern building whose ugliness is redeemed by the warmth of the welcome afforded to all visitors, English-speaking ones in particular. *5 rue d'Aguesseau, tel. 47–42–70–88. Services Thurs. 12:45 and Sun. 10:30 (with Sunday school) and 6:30; supervised nursery for younger children in the morning.*

Continue down rue du Faubourg St-Honoré to rue Royale. This classy street, lined with jewelry stores, links place de la Concorde to the **Eglise de la Madeleine** a sturdy neo-classical edifice that was nearly selected as Paris's first train station (the site of what is now the Gare St-Lazare, just up the road, was eventually chosen). With its rows of uncompromising columns, the Madeleine looks more like a Greek temple than a Christian church. Inside, the only natural light comes from three shallow domes. The walls are richly and harmoniously decorated, and gold glints through the murk. The church was designed in 1814 but not consecrated until 1842. The portico's majestic Corinthian colonnade supports a gigantic pediment with a sculptured frieze of the Last Judgment. From the top of the steps, you can admire the view down rue Royale across place de la Concorde to the Palais Bourbon. From the bottom of the steps, another view leads up boulevard Malesherbes to the dome of the church of St-Augustin. *Open Mon.–Sat. 7:30–7; Sun. 8–7.*

Time Out **L'Ecluse,** on the square to the west of the church, is a cozy wine bar that specializes in stylish snacks, such as foie gras and carpaccio, and offers a range of Bordeaux wines served by the glass. *15 pl. de la Madeleine. Open daily noon–2 AM.*

Alongside the Madeleine, between the church and L'Ecluse, is a **ticket kiosk** (open Tues.–Sat. 12:30–8) selling tickets for same-day theater performances at greatly reduced prices. Behind the church are **Fauchon** and **Hédiard,** two stylish delicatessens that are the ultimate in posh nosh. At the end of the rue Royale, just before place de la Concorde, is the legendary **Maxim's** restaurant. Unless you choose to eat here—an expensive and not always rewarding experience—you won't be able to see the interior decor, a riot of crimson velvets and florid Art Nouveau furniture.

There is a striking contrast between the sunless, locked-in feel of **②** the high-walled rue Royale and the broad, airy **place de la Concorde.** This huge square is best approached from the Champs-Elysées: The flower beds, chestnut trees, and sandy sidewalks of the avenue's lower section are reminders of its original leafy elegance. Place de la Concorde was built in the 1770s, but there was nothing in the way of peace or concord about its early years. Between 1793 and 1795, it was the scene of over a thousand deaths by guillotine; victims included Louis XVI, Marie Antoinette, Danton, and Robespierre. The obelisk, a present from the viceroy of Egypt, was erected in 1833. The handsome, symmetrical, 18th-century buildings facing **②** the square include the deluxe hotel **Crillon,** though there's nothing so vulgar as a sign to identify it—just an inscribed marble plaque above the doorway.

Facing one side of place de la Concorde are the **Tuileries Gardens.** Two smallish buildings stand sentinel here. To the left, nearer rue **②** de Rivoli, is the **Musée du Jeu de Paume,** fondly known to many as the former home of the Impressionists (now in the Musée d'Orsay). After extensive renovation, the Jeu de Paume reopened in 1991 as a home to brash temporary exhibits of contemporary art. *Admission: 35 frs adults, 25 frs students and senior citizens. Open Tues. noon–9:30, Wed.–Fri. 12–7, weekends 10–7.* The other, identical building, **②** nearer the Seine, is the recently restored **Musée de l'Orangerie,** containing some early 20th-century paintings by Monet (including his vast, eight-paneled *Water Lilies*), Renoir, and other Impressionists. *Place de la Concorde. Admission: 26 frs adults, 14 frs students and senior citizens. Open Wed.–Mon. 9:45–5:15; closed Tues.*

③ As gardens go, the newly renovated **Tuileries Gardens** is typically French: formal and neatly patterned, with statues, rows of trees, and gravel paths. It is a charming place to stroll and survey the surrounding cityscape; you may see a string quartet or jugglers entertaining large crowds on weekends. To the north is the disciplined, arcaded rue de Rivoli; to the south, the Seine and the gold-hued Musée d'Orsay with its enormous clocks; to the west, the Champs-Elysées and Arc de Triomphe; to the east, the Arc du Carrousel and the Louvre, with its glass pyramid.

Place Vendôme and the Opéra

③ **Place Vendôme,** north of the Jardin des Tuileries, one of the world's most opulent squares, recently benefitted from a face-lift which included new granite pavement, Second Empire–style street lamps, and an underground garage. Mansart's rhythmic, perfectly proportioned example of 17th-century urban architecture has shone in all its golden-stoned splendor since being cleaned a few years ago. Many other things shine here, too—in jewelers' display windows and on the dresses of guests of the top-ranking **Ritz** hotel. Napoléon had the square's central column made from the melted bronze of 1,200 cannons captured at the battle of Austerlitz in 1805. That's him standing vigilantly at the top. Painter Gustave Courbet headed the Revolutionary hooligans who, in 1871, toppled the column and shattered it into thousands of metallic pieces.

Cross the square and take rue des Capucines on your left to boule- **③** vard des Capucines. The **Olympia** music hall is still going strong, though it has lost some of the luster it acquired as the stage for such great postwar singers as Edith Piaf and Jacques Brel. On the oppo- **③** site side of the boulevard at No. 39, duck into the small **Musée du Parfum** created by the French perfume manufacturer Fragonard (named for the 18th-century painter). The museum exhibits traditional methods for extracting raw materials in the production of perfume; the aromatic results can be purchased at wholesale prices. *Admission free; open daily 9–6.*

Time Out There are few grander cafés in Paris than the **Café de la Paix,** on the corner of place de l'Opéra. This is a good place to people-watch, or just to slow down; but expect the prices to be as grand as the setting.

❸❹ The **Opéra,** begun in 1862 by Charles Garnier at the behest of Napoléon III, was not completed until 1875, five years after the emperor's political demise. It is often said to typify the Second Empire–style of architecture, which is to say that it is a pompous hodgepodge of styles, imbued with as much subtlety as a Wagnerian cymbal crash. After paying the entry fee, you can stroll around at leisure. The monumental foyer and staircase are boisterously impressive, a stage in their own right, where, on first nights, celebrities preen and prance. If the lavishly upholstered auditorium (ceiling painted by Marc Chagall in 1964) seems small, it is only because the stage is the largest in the world—over 11,000 square yards, with room for up to 450 performers. The **Musée de l'Opéra** (Opéra museum), containing a few paintings and theatrical mementos, is unremarkable. *Admission: 30 frs, 15 frs children. Open daily 10–4:30, but closed occasionally for rehearsals; call 47–42–57–50 to check.*

Around the Opéra

❸❺❸❻❸❼ Behind the Opéra are the *grands magasins,* Paris's most renowned department stores. The nearer of the two, the **Galeries Lafayette,** is the most outstanding, if only because of its vast, shimmering, turn-of-the-century glass dome. The domes at the corners of **Printemps,** farther along boulevard Haussmann, to the left, can be best appreciated from the outside; there is a splendid view from the store's roof-top cafeteria. **Marks & Spencer,** across the road, provides a brave outpost for British goods, such as ginger biscuits, bacon rashers, and Cheddar cheese.

❸❽ The **Trinité** church, several blocks north of the Opéra, is not an unworthy 19th-century effort at neo-Renaissance style. Its central tower is of dubious aesthetic merit but is a recognizable feature in the Paris skyline (especially since its cleaning in 1986). The church was built in the 1860s and is fronted by a pleasant garden.

❸❾ The nearby **Atelier de Gustave Moreau** was the town house and studio of painter Gustave Moreau (1826–1898), doyen of the Symbolist movement that strove to convey ideas through images. Many of the ideas Moreau was trying to express remain obscure to the general public, however, even though the artist provided explanatory texts. But most onlookers will be content admiring his extravagant colors and flights of fantasy, which reveal the influence of Persian and Indian miniatures. Fantastic details cover every inch of his canvases, and his canvases cover every inch of wall space, making a trip to the museum one of the strangest artistic experiences in Paris. Go on a sunny day, if possible; the low lighting can strain the eyes even more than Moreau's paintings can. *14 rue de la Rochefoucauld. Admission: 17 frs adults, 10 frs children and senior citizens. Open Thurs.–Sun. 10–12:45 and 2–5:15, Mon. and Wed. 11–5:15.*

❹⓿ Rue St-Lazare leads from Trinité to the **Gare St-Lazare,** whose imposing 19th-century facade has been restored. In the days of steam and smoke, the station was an inspiration to several Impressionist painters, notably Monet. Note an eccentric sculpture to the right of the facade—a higgledy-piggledy accumulation of clocks.

④ The leafy, intimate **Square Louis XVI,** off boulevard Haussmann between St-Lazare and St-Augustin, is perhaps the nearest Paris gets to a verdant, London-style square—if you discount the bombastic mausoleum in the middle. The unkempt chapel marks the initial burial site of Louis XVI and Marie Antoinette after their turns at the guillotine on place de la Concorde. Two stone tablets are inscribed with the last missives of the doomed royals—touching pleas for their Revolutionary enemies to be forgiven. When compared to the pomp and glory of Napoléon's memorial at the Invalides, this tribute to royalty (France was ruled by kings until 1792 and again from 1815 to 1848) seems trite. *Open daily 10–noon and 2–6, 10–4 in winter.*

Before leaving the square, take a look at the gleaming 1930s-style facade of the bank at the lower corner of rue Pasquier. It has some amusing stone carvings halfway up, representing various exotic animals.

A mighty dome is the most striking feature of the innovative iron-
④ and-stone church of **St-Augustin,** dexterously constructed in the 1860s within the confines of an awkward, V-shaped site. The use of metal girders obviated the need for exterior buttressing. The dome is bulky but well-proportioned and contains some grimy but competent frescoes by the popular 19th-century French artist William Bouguereau.

④ Rue La Boétie leads to another church, **St-Philippe du Roule,** built by Chalgrin between 1769 and 1784. Its austere classical portico dominates a busy square. The best thing inside this dimly lit church is the 19th-century fresco above the altar by Théodore Chassériau, featuring the Descent from the Cross.

Make your way back to boulevard Haussmann via avenue Myron T.
④ Herrick. The **Musée Jacquemart-André** features Italian Renaissance and 18th-century art in a dazzlingly furnished, late 19th-century mansion. *158 blvd. Haussmann, tel. 42–89–04–91. Admission: 18 frs. Open Wed.–Sun. 1–6.*

Rue de Courcelles and a right on rue de Monceau will lead to place de Rio de Janeiro. Before venturing into the Parc Monceau at the far end of avenue Ruysdaël, continue along rue de Monceau to the
④ **Musée Nissim de Camondo.** Inside, you will find the stylish interior of an aristocratic Parisian mansion in the style of Louis XVI, dating from the last days of the regal Ancien Régime. *63 rue de Monceau. Admission: 20 frs adults, 14 frs students and senior citizens. Open Wed.–Sun. 10–noon and 2–5.*

④ Rue de Monceau and boulevard Malesherbes lead to the **Musée Cernuschi,** whose collection of Chinese art ranges from neolithic pottery (3rd century BC) to funeral statuary, painted 8th-century silks, and contemporary paintings. *7 av. Velasquez. Admission: 15 frs. Open Tues.–Sun. 10–5:40.*

④ The **Parc Monceau,** which can be entered from avenue Velasquez, off boulevard Malesherbes, was laid out as a private park in 1778 and retains some of the fanciful elements then in vogue, including mock ruins and a phony pyramid. In 1797, Garnerin, the world's first-recorded parachutist, staged a landing in the park. The rotunda, known as the Chartres Pavilion, was originally a tollhouse and has well-worked iron gates.

Leave the Parc Monceau by these gates and follow rue Phalsbourg
and avenue de Villiers to the **Musée Jean-Jacques Henner.** Henner
(1829–1905), a nearly forgotten Alsatian artist, here receives a
sumptuous tribute. His obsessive fondness for milky-skinned, au-
burn-haired female nudes is displayed in hundreds of drawings and
paintings on the three floors of this gracious museum. *43 av. de
Villiers. Admission: 14 frs. Open Tues.–Sun. 10–noon and 2–5.*

Boulevard de Courcelles, which runs along the north side of the Parc
Monceau, leads west to rue Pierre-le-Grand (Peter the Great
Street). At the far end of that street, at 12 rue Daru, loom the unlikely gilt onion domes of the Russian Orthodox cathedral of
St-Alexandre Nevsky, erected in neo-Byzantine style in 1860. Inside,
the wall of icons that divides the church in two creates an atmosphere seldom found in Roman Catholic or Protestant churches.

From Orsay to Trocadéro

*Numbers in the margin correspond to points of interest on the Orsay
to Trocadéro map.*

The Left Bank has two faces: the cozy, ramshackle Latin Quarter
(*see* The Left Bank, *below*) and the spacious, stately 7th arrondissement. This tour covers the latter, then heads back across the Seine
for a look at the museums and attractions clustered around the place
du Trocadéro. The latest addition to the area is already the most
popular: the Musée d'Orsay. Crowds flock to this stylishly converted
train station to see the Impressionists, but also discover important
examples of other schools of 19th- and early 20th-century art.

The atmosphere of the 7th arrondissement is set by the National Assembly, down the river from Orsay, opposite place de la Concorde.
French deputies meet here to hammer out laws and insult each
other. They resume more civilized attitudes when they return
to the luxurious ministries that dot the nearby streets. The most famous is the Hôtel Matignon, official residence of the French prime
minister.

The majestic scale of many of the area's buildings is totally in character with the daddy of them all, the Invalides. Like the Champ de
Mars nearby, the esplanade in front of the Invalides was once used
as a parade ground for Napoléon's troops. In a coffin beneath the
Invalides dome, M. Bonaparte dreams on.

Musée d'Orsay

The **Musée d'Orsay** opened in December 1986. It is devoted to the
arts (mainly French) produced between 1848 and 1914, and its collections are intended to form a bridge between the classical collections of the Louvre and the modern collections of the Beaubourg.
The building began in 1900 as a train station for routes between Paris and the southwest of France. By 1939, the Gare d'Orsay had become too small for mainline travel, and intercity trains were
transferred to the Gare d'Austerlitz. Gare d'Orsay became a suburban terminus until, in the 1960s, it closed for good. After various
temporary uses (a theater and auction house among them), the
building was set for demolition. However, the destruction of the
19th-century Les Halles (market halls) across the Seine provoked a
furor among conservationists, and in the late 1970s, President
Giscard d'Estaing, with an eye firmly on establishing his place in the
annals of French culture, ordered Orsay to be transformed into a

Musée d'Orsay

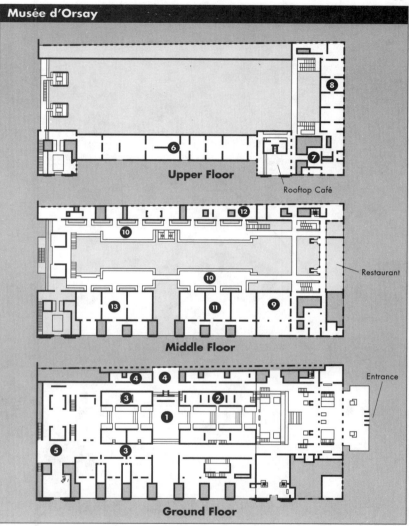

Upper Floor

Rooftop Café

Restaurant

Middle Floor

Entrance

Ground Floor

Sculpture 1850-1870, **1**

History Painting and the Portrait 1850-1880, **2**

Painting before 1870, **3**

Decorative Arts 1850-1880, **4**

Architecture 1850-1900, **5**

Impressionism and Post-Impressionism, **6**

Neo-Impressionism, **7**

Rousseau; the Pont-Aven School; the Nabis, **8**

Decorative Arts and Interiors of the Third Republic, **9**

Sculpture, **10**

Painting 1880-1900, **11**

Painting after 1900, **12**

Art Nouveau, **13**

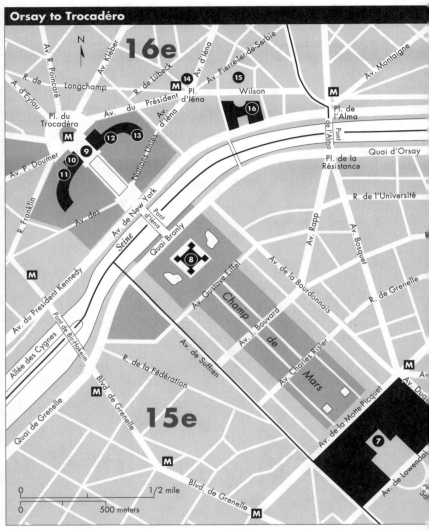

Orsay to Trocadéro

Ecole Militaire, **7**
Eiffel Tower, **8**
Hôtel des Invalides, **6**
Hôtel Matignon, **4**
Musée d'Art
Moderne de la Ville
de Paris, **16**
Musée de la Légion
d'Honneur, **2**

Musée de la
Marine, **11**
Musée de l'Homme, **10**
Musée des Monuments
Français, **12**
Musée d'Orsay, **1**
Musée du Cinéma, **13**
Musée Guimet, **14**
Musée Rodin, **5**

Palais Bourbon, **3**
Palais de Chaillot, **9**
Palais Galliera, **15**

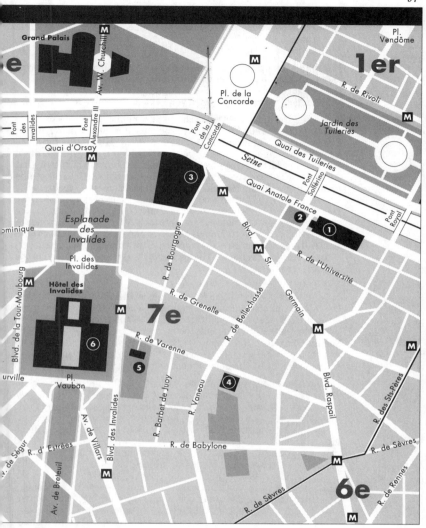

Grand Palais

Av. W. Churchill

Pl. Vendôme

1er

R. de Rivoli

Pl. de la
Concorde

Jardin des
Tuileries

Pont des
Invalides

Pont
Alexandre III

Quai d'Orsay

Pont
de la Concorde

Seine

Quai des Tuileries

Quai Anatole France

Pont Solférino

Pont Royal

3

Esplanade
des
Invalides

ominique

2

1

R. de Bourgogne

Blvd. St.

R. de l'Université

Pl. des
Invalides

Blvd. de la Tour-Maubourg

Hôtel des
Invalides

R. de Grenelle

R. de Bellechasse

Germain

7e

6

R. de Varenne

urville

Pl.
Vauban

5

R. Barbet de Jouy

R. Vaneau

4

Blvd. Raspail

R. des Sts-Pères

Av. de Ségur

R. d'Estrées

Av. de Breteuil

Av. de Villars

Blvd. des Invalides

R. de Babylone

R. de Sèvres

R. de Sèvres

6e

R. de Rennes

museum. The architects Pierre Colboc, Renaud Bardou, and Jean-Paul Philippon were commissioned to remodel the building, while Gae Aulenti, known for her renovation of the Palazzo Grassi in Venice, was hired to redesign the interior.

Exhibits take up three floors, but the visitor's immediate impression is of a single, vast, stationlike hall. The use of an aggressively modern interior design in a building almost a century old has provoked much controversy, which you'll want to resolve for yourself.

The chief artistic attraction is the Impressionists, whose works are displayed on the top floor, next to the museum café. Renoir, Sisley, Pissarro, and Monet are all well represented. Highlights for many visitors are Monet's *Poppy Field* and Renoir's *Le Moulin de la Galette*. The latter differs from many Impressionist paintings in that Renoir worked from numerous studies and completed it in his studio rather than painting it in the open air. Nonetheless, its focus on the activities of a group of ordinary Parisians amusing themselves in the sun on a Montmartre afternoon is typical of the spontaneity, the sense of the fleeting moment captured, that are the very essence of Impressionism. Where Monet, the only one of the group to adhere faithfully to the tenets of Impressionism throughout his career, strove to catch the effects of light, Renoir was more interested in the human figure.

The Post-Impressionists—Cézanne, van Gogh, Gauguin, and Toulouse-Lautrec—are all also represented on this floor. Some may find the intense, almost classical serenity of Cézanne the dominant presence here; witness his magnificent Mont Sainte-Victoire series, in which he paints and repaints the same subject, in the process dissolving form until the step to abstract painting seems almost an inevitability. Others will be drawn by the vivid simplicity and passion of van Gogh, or by the bold, almost pagan rhythms of Gauguin.

On the first floor, you'll find the work of Manet and the delicate nuances of Degas. Pride of place, at least in art historical terms, goes to Manet's *Déjeuner sur l'Herbe*, the painting that scandalized Paris in 1863 at the Salon des Refusés, an exhibit organized by those artists refused permission to show their work at the Academy's official annual exhibit. The painting shows a nude woman and two clothed men picnicking in a park. In the background, another naked girl bathes in a stream. Manet took the subject, poses and all, from a little-known Renaissance print in the Louvre. In that, of course, the clothed men wore contemporary 16th-century garb. In Manet's painting, the men also wear contemporary clothing, that of mid-19th-century France, complete with gray trousers and frock coats. What would otherwise have been thought a respectable "academic" painting thus became deeply shocking: two clothed men with two naked women! The loose, bold brushwork, a far cry from the polished styles of the Renaissance, added insult to artistic injury. Another reworking by Manet of a classical motif is his reclining nude, *Olympia*. Gazing boldly out from the canvas, she was more than respectable 19th-century Parisian proprieties could stand.

Those who prefer more correct academic paintings should look at Puvis de Chavannes's larger-than-life, classical canvases. The pale, limpid beauty of his figures is enjoying considerable attention after years of neglect. Those who are excited by more modern developments will make for the early 20th-century Fauves (meaning wild beasts, the name given them by an outraged critic in 1905)—particularly Matisse, Derain, and Vlaminck.

Sculpture at the Orsay means, first and foremost, Rodin (though there's more to enjoy at the Musée Rodin, *see below*). Two further highlights are the faithfully restored Belle Epoque restaurant and the model of the entire Opéra quarter, displayed beneath a glass floor.

The Musée d'Orsay, otherwise known as M.O., is one of Paris's star attractions. Crowds are smaller at lunchtime and on Thursday evenings. *1 rue de Bellechasse. Admission: 32 frs adults, 15 frs students and senior citizens and on Sun., under 18 free. Open Tues.– Sat. 10–6, Thurs. 10–9:30, and Sun. 9–6.*

Time Out There is no better place to take a break than the **Musée d'Orsay café,** handily but discreetly situated behind one of the giant station clocks close to the Impressionist galleries on the top floor. From the rooftop terrace, there is a panoramic view across the Seine toward Montmartre and the Sacré-Coeur.

② Across from the Musée d'Orsay stands the **Musée de la Légion d'Honneur.** French and foreign decorations are displayed in this stylish mansion by the Seine (officially known as the Hôtel de Salm). The original building, constructed in 1786, burned during the Commune in 1871 and was rebuilt in 1878. *2 rue de Bellechasse. Admission: 10 frs. Open Tues.–Sun. 2–5.*

Toward the Invalides

③ Continue along the left bank of the Seine to the 18th-century **Palais Bourbon** (directly across from place de la Concorde), home of the Assemblée Nationale (French Parliament). The colonnaded facade, commissioned by Napoléon, is a sparkling sight after a recent cleaning program (jeopardized at one stage by political squabbles as to whether cleaning should begin from the left or the right). There is a fine view from the steps across to place de la Concorde and the church of the Madeleine. *Not open to the public.*

The quiet, distinguished 18th-century streets behind the Palais Bourbon are filled with embassies and ministries. The most famous,
④ reached via rue de Bourgogne and rue de Varenne, is the **Hôtel Matignon,** residence of the French Prime Minister, and Left Bank counterpart to the President's Elysée Palace. "Matignon" was built in 1721 but has housed heads of government only since 1958. From 1888 to 1914, it was the embassy of the Austro-Hungarian Empire. *57 rue de Varenne. Neither house nor garden is open to the public.*

Take a peek a few doors down at **No. 51:** this is one of Paris's handful of private cul-de-sacs where concrete gives way to private mansions and grassy yards; it is closely guarded and admits residents only. At **No. 53** you can pay your respects to American novelist Edith Wharton, who lived and worked here from 1910 to 1920. She wrote of her abode, "My years of Paris life were spent entirely in the rue de Varenne—rich years, crowded and happy years."

Another glorious town house along rue de Varenne is the Hôtel
⑤ Biron, better known as the **Musée Rodin.** The splendid house, with its spacious vestibule, broad staircase, and light, airy rooms, retains much of its 18th-century atmosphere and makes a handsome setting for the sculpture of Auguste Rodin (1840–1917). You'll doubtless recognize the seated *Thinker (Le Penseur)*, with his elbow resting on his knee, and the passionate *Kiss.* There is also an outstanding white marble bust of Austrian composer *Gustav Mahler,* as well

as numerous examples of Rodin's obsession with hands and erotic subjects.

The second-floor rooms, which contain some fine paintings by Rodin's friend Eugène Carrière (1849–1906), afford views of the large garden behind the house. Don't go without visiting the garden: It is exceptional both for its rose bushes (over 2,000 of them, representing 100 varieties) and for its sculpture, including a powerful statue of the novelist Balzac and the despairing group of medieval city fathers known as the *Burghers of Calais*. *77 rue de Varenne. Admission: 26 frs, 17 frs Sun. Open Easter–Oct., Tues.–Sun. 10–6; Nov.–Easter, Tues.–Sun. 10–5.*

6 From the Rodin Museum, you can see the **Hôtel des Invalides,** along rue de Varenne. It was founded by Louis XIV in 1674 to house wounded (or "invalid") veterans. Although no more than a handful of old soldiers live at the Invalides today, the military link remains in the form of the **Musée de l'Armée**—one of the world's foremost military museums—with a vast, albeit somewhat musty, collection of arms, armor, uniforms, banners, and military pictures down through the ages.

The **Musée des Plans-Reliefs,** housed on the fifth floor of the right-hand wing, contains a fascinating collection of scale models of French towns made to illustrate the fortifications planned by Vauban in the 17th century. (Vauban was a superb military engineer who worked under Louis XIV.) The largest and most impressive is Strasbourg, which takes up an entire room. Not all of Vauban's models are here, however. As part of a cultural decentralization program, France's socialist government of the early 1980s decided to pack the models (which had languished for years in dusty neglect) off to Lille in northern France. Only half the models had been shifted when a conservative government returned to office in 1986 and called for their return. Ex-Prime Minister Pierre Mauroy, the socialist mayor of Lille, refused, however, and the impasse seems set to continue.

The museums are not the only reason for visiting the Invalides. The building itself is an outstanding monumental ensemble in late-17th-century Baroque, designed by Bruand and Mansart. The main, cobbled courtyard is a fitting scene for the parades and ceremonies still occasionally held here. The most impressive dome in Paris towers over the **Eglise du Dôme** (church of the Dome). Before stopping here, however, visit the 17th-century **Eglise St-Louis des Invalides,** the Invalides's original church, and the site of the first performance of Berlioz's *Requiem* in 1837.

The Dôme church was built onto the end of Eglise St-Louis but was blocked off from it in 1793—no great pity perhaps, as the two buildings are vastly different in style and scale. It was designed by Mansart and built between 1677 and 1735. The remains of Napoléon are here, in a series of no fewer than six coffins, one inside the next, within a bombastic tomb of red porphyry, ringed by low reliefs and a dozen statues symbolizing Napoléon's campaigns. Among others commemorated in the church are French World War I hero Marshal Foch; Napoléon's brother Joseph, erstwhile king of Spain; and fortification-builder Vauban, whose heart was brought to the Invalides at Napoléon's behest. *Hôtel des Invalides. Admission: 32 frs adults, 22 frs children and senior citizens. Open daily 10–6; 10–5 in winter.*

Time Out It's well worth the short trek down boulevard des Invalides to rue de Babylone, where, at No. 57 bis, you'll find Paris's only Asian **Pagoda,** now a movie theater and small tea room which offers an exotic environment for sipping hot tea and cooling your heels. *Open Mon.–Sat. 4–10, Sun. 2–8.*

Cross the pleasant lawns outside the Dôme church to place Vauban. Follow avenue de Tourville to the right, and turn left onto avenue de la Motte-Picquet.

The Eiffel Tower and the Trocadéro

A few minutes' walk will bring you face-to-face with the Eiffel Tower. Spare a thought for the **École Militaire** on your left; it is 18th-century architecture at its most harmonious. It is still in use as a military academy and therefore not open to the public.

The pleasant expanse of the **Champ de Mars** makes an ideal approach to the **Eiffel Tower,** whose colossal bulk (it's far bigger and sturdier than pictures suggest) becomes evident the nearer you get. It was built by Gustave Eiffel for the World Exhibition of 1889, the centennial of the French Revolution, and was still in good shape to celebrate its own 100th birthday. Recent restoration hasn't made the elevators any faster (lines are inevitable), but the nocturnal illumination is fantastic—every girder highlighted in glorious detail.

Such was Eiffel's engineering wizardry that even in the strongest winds his tower never sways more than 4½ inches. Today, it is Paris's best-known landmark and exudes a feeling of permanence. As you stand beneath its huge legs, you may have trouble believing that it nearly became 7,000 tons of scrap-iron when its concession expired in 1909. Only its potential use as a radio antenna saved the day; it now bristles with a forest of radio and television transmitters. If you're full of energy, stride up the stairs as far as the third deck. If you want to go to the top, you'll have to take the elevator. The view at 1,000 feet may not beat that from the Tour Maine-Montparnasse (*see* The Left Bank, *below*), but the setting makes it considerably more romantic. *Pont d'Iéna. Cost by elevator: 2nd floor, 18 frs; 3rd floor, 35 frs; 4th floor, 52 frs. Cost by foot: 10 frs (2nd and 3rd floors only). Open July–Aug., daily 9 AM–midnight; Sept.–June, daily 9:30 AM–11 PM.*

Just across the Pont d'Iena from the Eiffel Tower, on the heights of Trocadéro, is the muscular, sandy-colored **Palais de Chaillot**—a cultural center built in the 1930s to replace a Moorish-style building constructed for the World Exhibition of 1878. The gardens between the Palais de Chaillot and the Seine contain an aquarium and some dramatic fountains. The terrace between the two wings of the palace offers a wonderful view of the Eiffel Tower.

The Palais de Chaillot contains four large museums, two in each wing. In the left wing (as you approach from the Seine) are the Musée de l'Homme and the Musée de la Marine. The **Musée de l'Homme,** on the second and third floors, is an earnest anthropological museum with artifacts, costumes, and domestic tools from around the world, dating from prehistoric times to the recent past. *Admission: 25 frs adults, 15 frs children. Open Wed.–Mon. 9:45–5.*

The **Musée de la Marine,** on the first floor, is a maritime museum with a salty collection of ship models and seafaring paraphernalia, illustrating French naval history right up to the age of the nuclear submarine. *Admission: 28 frs adults, 14 frs senior citizens, students, and children. Open Wed.–Mon. 10–6.*

⑫ The other wing is dominated by the **Musée des Monuments Français,** an excellent introduction to French medieval architecture. This museum was founded in 1879 by architect-restorer Viollet-le-Duc (the man who more than anyone was responsible for the extensive renovation of Notre Dame). It pays tribute to French buildings, mainly of the Romanesque and Gothic periods (roughly 1000–1500), in the form of painstaking copies of statues, columns, archways, and frescoes. It is easy to imagine yourself strolling among ruins as you pass through the first-floor gallery. Substantial sections of a number of French churches and cathedrals are represented here, notably Chartres and Vézelay. Mural and ceiling paintings—copies of works in churches around the country—dominate the other three floors. The value of these paintings has become increasingly evident as many of the originals continue to deteriorate. On the ceiling of a circular room is a reproduction of the painted dome of Cahors cathedral, giving the visitor a more vivid sense of the skills of the original medieval painter than the cathedral itself. *Admission: 20 frs, 13 frs on Sun. Open Wed.–Mon. 9:45–5:15.*

⑬ The **Musée du Cinéma Henri Langlois,** located in the basement of this wing, traces the history of motion pictures since the 1880s. Henri Langlois devoted his life to collecting the memorabilia contained in this museum, which include scripts, photos, costumes, and Louis Lumière's first movie camera, dating from 1895. *Admission: 22 frs. Open Wed.–Mon. Guided tours only, at 10, 11, 2, 3, and 4.*

Time Out   For a tremendous view of the Eiffel Tower, splurge for lunch or a snack at **Les Monuments,** an elegant new restaurant in the Palais de Chaillot. To fill your belly rather than feast your eyes, head left from the Palais de Chaillot (down rue Franklin) to rue de Passy, a long, lively, narrow street full of shops and restaurants. **Pastavino,** at 30 rue de Passy, has excellent pasta and Italian wine in a room with gleaming modernistic decor. Around the corner, at 4 rue Nicolo, the intimate **Au Régal** has been serving up Russian specialties since 1934, abetted by a comradely welcome and ready supply of vodka.

The area around the Palais de Chaillot offers a feast for museum lovers. The **Musée Guimet** (down avenue du Président Wilson, at place
⑭ d'Iéna) has three floors of Indo-Chinese and Far Eastern art, and the largest collection of Cambodian art this side of Cambodia. The museum was founded by the Lyonnais industrialist Emile Guimet, who traveled around the world in the late 19th century amassing priceless objets d'art. Among the museum's bewildering variety of exhibits are stone buddhas, Chinese bronzes, ceramics, and painted screens. *6 pl. d'Iéna. Admission: 26 frs adults, 14 frs students and senior citizens. Open Wed.–Mon. 9:45–5:15.*

The museum recently opened a new gallery, the **Hotel Heidelbach–Guimet,** a minute's walk down avenue d'Iéna, which features Buddhist art from China and Japan. *19 av. d'Iena. Admission: 23 frs. Open Wed.–Mon. 9:45–6.*

⑮ Some 200 yards down avenue Pierre-Ier-de-Serbie is the **Palais Galliera,** home of the small and some would say overpriced Museum of Fashion and Costume. This stylish, late-19th-century town house hosts revolving exhibits of costume, design, and accessories, usually based on a single theme. *10 av. Pierre-Ier-de-Serbie. Admission: 26 frs adults, 17 frs students and senior citizens. Open Tues.–Sun. 10–5:40.*

⑯ The **Musée d'Art Moderne de la Ville de Paris** has both temporary exhibits and a permanent collection of modern art, continuing where the Musée d'Orsay leaves off. Among the earliest works are Fauvist paintings by Vlaminck and Derain, followed by Picasso's early experiments in Cubism. No other Paris museum exudes such a feeling of space and light. Its vast, unobtrusive, white-walled galleries provide an ideal background for the bold statements of 20th-century art. Loudest and largest are the canvases of Robert Delaunay. Other highlights include works by Braque, Rouault, Gleizes, Da Silva, Gromaire, and Modigliani. There is also a large room devoted to Art Deco furniture and screens, where Jean Dunand's gilt and lacquered panels consume oceans of wall space. There is a pleasant, if expensive, museum café, and an excellent bookshop specializing in 19th- and 20th-century art and architecture, with many books in English. *11 av. du Président Wilson. Admission: 15 frs, half-price on Sun. for permanent exhibitions only. Prices vary for special exhibitions. Open Tues.–Sun. 10–5:30, Wed. 10–8:30.*

The Left Bank

Numbers in the margin correspond to points of interest on the Left Bank map.

References to the Left Bank have never lost their power to evoke the most piquant of all images of Paris. Although the bohemian strain the area once nurtured has lost much of its vigor, people who choose it today as a place to live or work are, in effect, turning their backs on the formality and staidness of the Right Bank.

The Latin Quarter is the geographic and cerebral hub of the Left Bank, populated mainly by Sorbonne students and academics who fill the air of the cafés with their ideas—and their tobacco smoke. (The university began as a theological school in the Middle Ages and later became the headquarters of the University of Paris; in 1968, the student revolution here had an explosive effect on French politics, resulting in major reforms in the education system.) The name Latin Quarter comes from the university tradition of studying and speaking in Latin, a tradition that disappeared during the Revolution.

Most of the St-Germain cafés, where the likes of Sartre, Picasso, Hemingway, and de Beauvoir spent their days and nights, are patronized largely by tourists now, and anyone expecting to capture the feeling of this quarter when it was the epicenter of intellectual and artistic life in Paris will be disappointed. Yet the Left Bank is far from dead. It is a lively and colorful district, rich in history and character, with a wealth of bookshops, art stores, museums, and restaurants.

St-Michel to St-Germain

❶ **Place St-Michel,** named for the grandiose fountain at its hub depicting St-Michel striking down the dragon, is a good starting point for exploring the rich slice of Parisian life that the Left Bank offers. Leave your itineraries at home, and wander along the neighboring streets lined with restaurants, cafés, galleries, old bookshops, and all sorts of clothing stores, from tiny boutiques to haute couture showrooms.

If you follow quai des Grands Augustins and then quai de Conti west from St-Michel, you will be in full view of the Ile de la Cité and the Louvre, and you may catch a glimpse of the imposing dome of the Temple de l'Oratoire (built in 1621 and once one of the most impor-

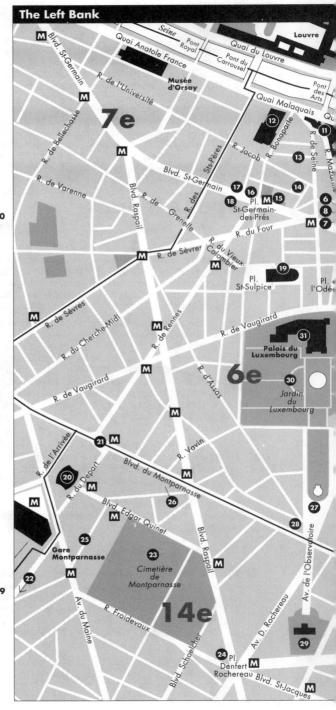

The Left Bank

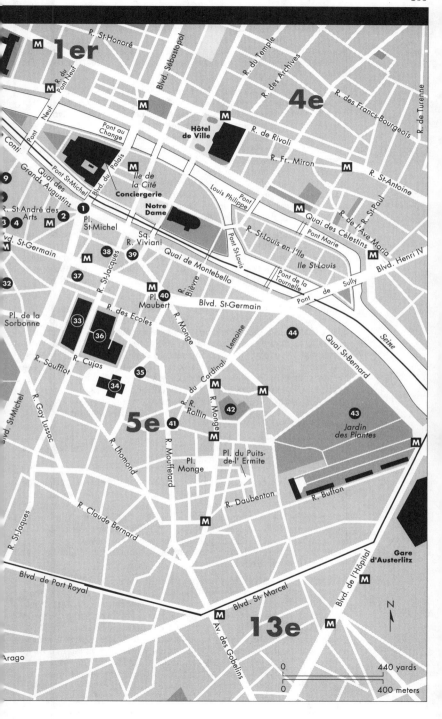

M 1er

R. St-Honoré

R. du Pont Neuf

Blvd. Sébastopol

R. du Temple

R. des Archives

4e

R. des Francs-Bourgeois

R. de Turenne

Conti

Pont Neuf

Pont St-Michel

Quai des Grands Augustins

R. St-André des Arts

Blvd. St-Germain

Pont au Change

Blvd. du Palais

Hôtel de Ville

R. de Rivoli

R. Fr. Miron

R. St-Antoine

Ile de la Cité

Conciergerie

Louis Philippe

Pont

Quai des Célestins

R. de l' Ave Maria

R. St-Paul

Pl. St-Michel

Notre Dame

Pont St-Louis

R. St-Louis en l'Ile

Pont Marie

Ile St-Louis

Blvd. Henri IV

Sq. R. Viviani

Quai de Montebello

Pont de la Tournelle

Pont de Sully

Seine

38

39

R. St-Jacques

R. Bièvre

37

Maubert

40 Pl. Maubert

Blvd. St-Germain

Quai St-Bernard

32

R. des Ecoles

R. Monge

R. du Cardinal-Lemoine

44

Pl. de la Sorbonne

33

36

R. Cujas

35

34

R. Soufflot

R. St-Michel

R. Gay Lussac

5e

R. R. Rollin

42

43 Jardin des Plantes

41

R. Lhomond

R. Mouffetard

Pl. du Puits-de-l' Ermite

Pl. Monge

R. Daubenton

R. Buffon

R. Claude Bernard

R. St-Jacques

Gare d'Austerlitz

Blvd. de Port Royal

Blvd. St-Marcel

Blvd. de l'Hôpital

N

Arago

Av. des Gabelins

13e

0 440 yards

0 400 meters

tant churches in France) across the Seine. The Hôtel des Monnaies (the mint), the Institut de France (home of the Académie Française), and the Ecole National des Beaux-Arts (Paris's fine-arts academy) together comprise a magnificent assembly of buildings on the river embankment that lies west of Paris's oldest bridge, the Pont Neuf.

For a route crowded more with humanity and less with car and bus traffic, pick up the pedestrian rue St-André des Arts at the southwest corner of place St-Michel. **Studio St-André des Arts,** at No. 30, is one of Paris's most popular experimental cinemas. Just before you reach the Carrefour de Buci crossroads at the end of the street, turn onto the **Cour du Commerce St-André.** Jean-Paul Marat printed his revolutionary newspaper, *L'Ami du Peuple,* at No. 8; and it was here that Dr. Guillotin conceived the idea for a new, "humane" method of execution that was used during the Revolution—it was rumored that he practiced it on sheep first—and that remained the means of executing convicted criminals in France until President Mitterrand abolished it in 1981.

Down a small passageway on the left stands one of the few remaining towers of the 12th-century fortress wall built by Philippe-Auguste. The passage leads you to the **Cour de Rohan,** a series of three cloistered courtyards that were part of the hôtel of the archbishops of Rouen, established in the 15th century; the name has been corrupted over the years to Rohan.

Rejoin the Cour du Commerce St-André and continue to the **Carrefour de Buci,** once a notorious Left Bank landmark. By the 18th century, it contained a gallows, an execution stake, and an iron collar for punishing troublemakers. In September 1792, the Revolutionary army used this daunting site to enroll its first volunteers, and many Royalists and priests lost their heads here during the bloody course of the Revolution. There's nothing sinister, however, about the Carrefour today. Brightly colored flowers spill onto the sidewalk at the **Grange à Buci** flower shop, on the corner of rue Grégoire-de-Tours. **Rue de Buci** has one of the best markets in Paris. *Open Tues.–Sun. till 1 PM.*

Time Out   If you happen to arrive when the market is closed, **La Vieille France** patisserie at 14 rue de Buci may help fill the gap.

Several interesting, smaller streets of some historical significance radiate from the Carrefour. **Rue de l'Ancienne-Comédie,** which cuts through to the busy place de l'Odéon, is so named because it was the first home of the now legendary French theater company, the Comédie Française. The street was named in 1770, the very year the Comédie left for the Tuileries palace. The company moved again later to the Odéon, before heading to its present home by the Palais-Royal (*see* The Historic Heart, *above*).

Across the street from the company's first home (No. 14) is the oldest café in Paris, **Le Procope.** Opened in 1686 by an Italian named Francesco Procopio (only three years before the Odéon itself opened), it has been a watering hole for many of Paris's most famous literary sons and daughters over the centuries; Diderot, Voltaire, Balzac, George Sand, Victor Hugo, and Oscar Wilde were some of its more famous and infamous regulars. Ben Franklin is said to have stopped in whenever business brought him to Paris. The fomenters of the French Revolution met at the Procope, too, so it is possible that old Ben may have crossed paths with the likes of Marat, Danton, Desmoulins, and Robespierre. Napoléon's hat, forgotten here, was encased in a glass dome. In 1988, Paris's second-largest restaurant group, Frères Blanc, bought the Procope (now really more of a restaurant), claiming to want to give it a "new lease on life and a new literary and cultural vocation."

Stretching north from the Carrefour de Buci toward the Seine is the **9 rue Dauphine,** the street that singer Juliet Greco put on the map when she opened the Tabou jazz club here at No. 33 in the '50s. It attracted a group of young intellectuals who were to become known as the Zazous, a St-Germain movement promoting the jazz culture, complete with all-night parties and free love. The cult author Boris Vian liked to play his trumpet through the night, an activity that did little to endear him to the club's neighbors. You may still find jazz played here, but the club is a shadow of its former self.

The next street that shoots out of the Carrefour (moving counter-**10** clockwise) is rue Mazarine. Here stands the **Hôtel des Monnaies,** the national mint. Louis XVI transferred the Royal Mint to this imposing mansion in the late 18th century. Although the mint was moved to Pessac, near Bordeaux, in 1973, weights and measures, medals, and limited-edition coins are still made here. In June 1988, an enlarged **Musée de la Monnaie** opened so that the vast collection of coins, documents, engravings, and paintings could be displayed. The workshops are on the second floor. On Tuesday and Friday at 2 PM you'll catch the coin and medal craftsmen at work; their ateliers overlook the Seine. *11 quai de Conti. Admission: 20 frs adults, 15 frs students and senior citizens. 15 frs Sun. Open Tues., Thurs.–Sun. 1–6, Wed. 1–9.*

11 Next door is the **Institut de France.** With its distinctive dome and commanding position over the quai at the foot of the Pont des Arts, it is not only one of France's most revered cultural institutions but also one of the Left Bank's most impressive waterside sights. The Tour de Nesle, which formed part of Philippe-Auguste's wall fortifications along the Seine, used to stand here, and, in its time, it had many royal occupants, including Henry V of England. The French novelist Alexandre Dumas (1824–1895) featured the stormy history of the Tour de Nesle—during which the lovers of a number of French queens were tossed from its windows—in a melodrama of the same name. In 1661, the wealthy Cardinal Mazarin left 2 million French pounds in his will for construction of a college here that would be dedicated to educating students from the provinces of Piedmont, Alsace, Artois, and Roussillon, all of which had been annexed to France during the years of his ministry. Mazarin's coat of arms is sculpted on the dome, and the public library in the east wing, which holds over 350,000 volumes, still bears his name. At the beginning of the 19th century, Napoléon stipulated that the Institut de France be transferred here from the Louvre. The **Académie Française,** the oldest of the five academies that comprise the Institut de France, was created by Cardinal Richelieu in 1635. Its first major task was to edit the French dictionary; today, among other functions, it is still charged with safeguarding the purity of the French language. Election to its ranks is the highest literary honor in the land, subject to approval by the French head of state, and there may only be 40 "immortal" members at any one time. The appointment of historian and authoress Marguerite Yourcenar to the Académie in 1986 broke the centuries-old tradition of the academy as a bastion of male-only linguistic and literary rule. The Institut also embraces the Académie des Beaux-Arts; the Académie des Sciences; the Académie des Inscriptions et Belles Lettres; and the Académie des Sciences Morales et Politiques. *Guided visits are reserved for cultural associations only.*

⑫ Just west along the waterfront, on quai Malaquais, stands the **Ecole Nationale des Beaux-Arts,** whose students can usually be seen painting and sketching on the nearby quais and bridges. The school—today the breeding ground for France's foremost painters, sculptors, and architects—was once the site of a convent, founded in 1608 by Marguerite de Valois, the first wife of Henri IV. During the Revolution, the convent was turned into a depot for works of art salvaged from the monuments that were under threat of destruction by impassioned mobs. Only the church and cloister remained, however, when the Beaux-Arts school was established in 1816. Allow yourself time to wander into the courtyard and galleries of the school to see the casts and copies of the statues that were once stored here, or stop in at one of the temporary exhibitions of professors' and students' works. *14 rue Bonaparte. Open daily 1–7.*

⑬ Tiny **rue Visconti,** running east–west off rue Bonaparte (to the left of the Beaux-Arts as you face the building), has a lot of history packed into its short length. In the 16th century, it was known as Paris's Little Geneva—named after Europe's foremost Protestant city—because of the Protestant ghetto that formed here. Racine, one of France's greatest playwrights and tragic poets, lived at No. 24 until his death in 1699. Balzac set up a printing shop at No. 17 in 1826, and the fiery Romantic artist Eugène Delacroix (1798–1863) worked here from 1836 to 1844.

Time Out The terrace at **La Palette** (43 rue de Seine) beckons as soon as you reach the rue de Seine, at the end of rue Visconti. This popular café has long been a favorite haunt of Beaux Arts students. One of them was allowed to paint an ungainly portrait of the *patron,* François, which presides with mock authority over the shaggy gathering of clients.

Swing right just after the next corner onto the pretty rue Jacob, where both Wagner and Stendhal once lived. Follow rue Jacob across rue des Saints-Pères, where it changes to rue de l'Université. You are now in the Carré Rive Gauche, the Left Bank's concentrated quarter-mile of art dealers and galleries. *Galleries are usually open 10–12:30 and 2–6, closed Mon.*

⑭ Return on rue Jacob until you are almost back to rue de Seine. Take the rue de Fürstemberg to the quiet place Fürstemberg, bedecked with white globe lamps and catalpa trees. Here is **Atelier Delacroix,** Delacroix's former studio, containing only a paltry collection of sketches and drawings by the artist; the garden at the rear of the studio is almost as interesting. Nonetheless, those who feel the need to pay homage to France's foremost Romantic painter will want to make the pilgrimage. *Place Fürstemberg. Admission: 12 frs adults, 8 frs ages 18–25 and over 60, 7 frs on Sun. Open Wed.–Mon. 9:45–5:15.*

⑮ Take rue de l'Abbaye to **St-Germain-des-Prés,** Paris's oldest church, which began as a shelter for a relic of the True Cross brought back from Spain in AD 542. Behind it, rue de l'Abbaye runs alongside the former Abbey palace, dating from AD 990 and once part of a powerful Benedictine abbey. The chancel was enlarged and the church then consecrated by Pope Alexander III in 1163. Interesting interior details include the colorful 19th-century frescoes in the nave by Hippolyte Flandrin, a pupil of the classical painter Ingres, depicting vivid scenes from the Old Testament. The church stages superb organ concerts and recitals; programs are displayed outside and in the weekly periodicals *Officiel des Spectacles* and *Pariscope. Open weekdays 8–7:30; weekends 8–9.*

Across the cobbled place St-Germain-des-Prés stands the celebrated **Les Deux Magots** café, named after the grotesque Chinese figures, or *magots*, inside. It still thrives on its post–World War II reputation as one of the Left Bank's prime meeting places for the intelligentsia. Though the Deux Magots remains crowded day and night, these days, you're more likely to rub shoulders with tourists than with philosophers. Yet those in search of the mysterious glamour of the Left Bank can do no better than to station themselves at one of the sidewalk tables—or at a window table on a wintry day—to watch the passing parade.

In the postwar years, Jean-Paul Sartre and Simone de Beauvoir would meet "the family" two doors down at the **Café de Flore** on boulevard St-Germain. "The family" was de Beauvoir's name for their close-knit group, which included fellow-graduates from the prestigious Ecole Normale Supérieure and writers from Gaston Gallimard's publishing house in the nearby rue Sébastien-Bottin. Today the Flore has become more of a gay hangout. Along with the Deux Magots and the pricey **Brasserie Lipp** across the street, where politicians and show-biz types come to wine and dine (after being "passed" by the doorman), it is a scenic spot that never lacks for action. In case you're in need of a sideshow, you'll also be able to see the street musicians—as likely to be playing Bolivian reed pipes or Scottish bagpipes as an old-style pump accordion—as well as acrobats and fire-eaters who perform in front of the church.

A large part of the area south of boulevard St-Germain, around rue de Grenelle and rue des Saints-Pères, has undergone enormous change but is still home to publishing houses, bookstores, and galleries.

For contrast, take rue du Vieux-Colombier through the Carrefour de La Croix Rouge to place St-Sulpice. This newly renovated square is ringed with cafés, and Yves St-Laurent's famous Rive Gauche store is at No. 6. Looming over the square is the enormous 17th-century church of **St-Sulpice.** The Marquis de Sade and Baudelaire were baptised here, and Victor Hugo tied the knot with Adele Foucher at the church's altar. The 18th-century facade was never finished, and its unequal towers add a playful touch to an otherwise sober design. The interior is baldly impersonal, however, despite the magnificent Delacroix frescoes—notably Jacob wrestling with the angel—in the first chapel on your right. If you now pick up the long rue de Rennes and follow it south, you'll soon arrive in the heart of Montparnasse.

Montparnasse

With the growth of Paris as a business and tourist capital, commercialization seems to have filled any area where departing residents and businesses have created a vacuum. Nowhere else is this more true than in and around the vaulting, concrete space and starkly functionalist buildings that have come to rule Montparnasse. Seeing it now, it is difficult to believe that in the years after World War I, Montparnasse replaced Montmartre as *the* place in which Parisian artists came to live.

The opening of the 59-story **Tour Maine-Montparnasse** in 1973 forever changed the face of this painters' and poets' haunt. (The name Montparnasse itself came from some 17th-century students, who christened the area after Mount Parnassus, the home of Apollo, leader of the Muses.) The tower was part of a vast redevelopment plan that aimed to make the area one of Paris's premier business and shopping districts. Fifty-two floors of the tower are taken up by offices, while a vast commercial complex, including a Galeries Lafayette department store, spreads over the first floor. Although it is uninspiring by day, it becomes a neon-lit beacon for the area at night. As Europe's tallest high rise, it affords stupendous views of Paris; on a clear day, you can see for 30 miles. (There's a snack bar and cafeteria on the 56th floor; if you go to the top-floor bar for drinks, the ride up is free.) It also claims to have the fastest elevator in Europe! *Admission: 40 frs adults, 30 frs students and senior citizens, 22 frs children 5–14. Open daily 9:30 AM–10:30 PM, weekdays 10 AM–9:30 PM in winter.*

㉑ Immediately north of the tower is **place du 18 Juin 1940,** part of what was once the old Montparnasse train station and a significant spot in Parisian World War II history. It is named for the date of the radio speech Charles de Gaulle made, from London, urging the French to continue resisting the Germans after the fall of the country to Nazi Germany in May 1940. In August 1944, the German military governor, Dietrich von Choltitz, surrendered to the Allies here, ignoring Hitler's orders to destroy the city as he withdrew; the French General Philippe Leclerc subsequently used it as his headquarters.

Behind the older train station, Gare Montparnasse, you'll see the huge new train terminal that serves Chartres, Versailles, and the west of France. Since 1990, the high-speed *TGV Atlantique* leaves here for Brittany (Rennes and Nantes) and the southwest (Bordeaux, via Tours, Poitiers, and Angoulême). South of this station is one of the oddest residential complexes to appear in this era of architectural experimentation. On the platform connecting the two stations is the newly completed **Jardin Atlantique,** a small park which contains benches for weary travelers sweating through a stopover, featuring an assortment of trees from all countries that—appropri-
㉒ ately—border on the Atlantic ocean. The nearby **Amphithéâtre,** built by Ricardo Boffil, is eye-catching but stark and lacking in human dimension.

㉓ The **Cimetière de Montparnasse** (Montparnasse cemetery) contains many of the quarter's most illustrious residents, buried only a stone's throw away from where they worked and played. It is not at all a picturesque cemetery (with the exception of the old windmill in the corner, which used to be a student tavern) but seeing the names of some of its inhabitants—Baudelaire, Maupassant, Saint-Saëns, and the industrialist André Citroën—may make the visit worthwhile. Nearby, at place Denfert-Rochereau, is the entrance to an
㉔ extensive complex of **catacombs** (*denfert* is a corruption of the word for hell, *enfer*). The catacombs are stocked with the bones of millions of skeletons that were moved here in 1785 from the area's charnel houses. *Admission: 27 frs adults, 15 frs students and senior citizens. Open Tues.–Fri. 2–4, weekends 9–11 and 2–4.*

Montparnasse's bohemian aura has dwindled to almost nothing, yet the area hops at night as *the* place in Paris to find movies of every description, many of them shown in their original language. Thea-
㉕ ters and theater-cafés abound, too, especially along seedy **rue de la Gaîté.** The Gaîté-Montparnasse, Le Théâtre Montparnasse, and Le Grand Edgar are among the most popular. Up boulevard du Montparnasse and across from the Vavin métro station are two of the better-known gathering places of Montparnasse's heyday, the **Dôme**
㉖ and **La Coupole** brasseries. La Coupole opened in 1927 as a bar/res-

taurant/dance hall and soon became a home away from home for some of the area's most famous residents, such as Apollinaire, Max Jacob, Cocteau, Satie, Stravinsky, and the ubiquitous Hemingway. It may not be quite the same mecca these days, but it still pulls in a classy crowd.

Across the boulevard, rue Vavin leads past two more celebrated Montparnasse cafés, the **Sélect** and the **Rotonde,** to the Jardin du Luxembourg. But stay on boulevard du Montparnasse for the inter-**㉗** section with boulevard St-Michel, where the verdant **avenue de l'Observatoire** begins its long sweep up to the Luxembourg gardens. Here you'll find perhaps the most famous bastion of the Left Bank **㉘** café culture, the **Closerie des Lilas.** Now a pricey bar/restaurant, the Closerie remains a staple on all literary tours of Paris not least because of the commemorative plaques fastened onto the bar, marking the places where renowned personages sat. Baudelaire, Verlaine, Hemingway, and Apollinaire are just a few of the names. Although the lilacs *(lilas)* have gone from the terrace, it is still a pretty place, opening onto the luxuriant green of the surrounding parkland, and as crowded in the summer as it ever was in the '30s.

㉙ The vista from the Closerie includes the **Paris Observatory** (to the right), built in 1667 by Louis XIV. Its four facades were built to align with the four cardinal points—north, south, east, and west—and its southern wall is the determining point for Paris's official latitude, 48° 50'11"N. French time was based on this Paris meridian until 1911, when the country decided to adopt the international Greenwich Meridian.

A tree-lined alley leads along the avenue de l'Observatoire to the gardens, but before the entrance, you'll pass Davioud's **Fontaine de l'Observatoire** (Observatory Fountain), built in 1873 and decked with four statues representing the four quarters of the globe. Look north from here and you'll have a captivating view of Montmartre and Sacré-Coeur, with the gardens in the foreground.

Palais du Luxembourg

㉚ From avenue de l'Observatoire walk up to the **Jardin du Luxembourg** (the Luxembourg Gardens), one of the city's few large parks. Its fountains, ponds, trim hedges, precisely planted rows of trees, and gravel walks are typical of the French fondness for formal gar-**㉛** dens. At the far end is the **Palais du Luxembourg,** gray and imposing, built, like the park, for Maria de' Medici, widow of Henri IV, at the beginning of the 17th century. Maria was born and raised in Florence's Pitti Palace, and, having languished in the Louvre after the death of her husband, she was eager to build herself a new palace, somewhere she could recapture something of the lively, carefree atmosphere of her childhood. In 1612, she bought the Paris mansion of the duke of Luxembourg, tore it down, and built her palace. It was not completed until 1627, and Maria was to live there for no more than five years. In 1632, Cardinal Richelieu had her expelled from France, and she saw out her declining years in Cologne, Germany, dying there almost penniless in 1642. The palace remained royal property until the Revolution, when the state took it over and used it as a prison. Danton, the painter David, and Thomas Paine were all detained here. Today, it is the site of the French Senate and is not open to the public.

㉜ The **Théâtre National de l'Odéon,** set at the north end of the Luxembourg Gardens, was established in 1792 to house the Comédiens Français troupe. The massive structure you see today replaced the original theater, which was destroyed by fire in 1807. Since World War II, it has specialized in 20th-century productions. It was the base for Jean-Louis Barrault's and Madeleine Renaud's theater company, the Théâtre de France, until they fell out of favor with the authorities for their alleged role in spurring on the student revolutionaries in May 1968. Today, the Théâtre de l'Odéon is the French home of the Theater of Europe and stages some excellent productions by major foreign companies.

The Sorbonne and the Latin Quarter

If you follow rue de Vaugirard (the longest street in Paris) one block east to boulevard St-Michel, you will soon be at the **place de la Sorbonne,** the hub of the Latin Quarter and nerve center of the student population that has always held such sway over Left Bank life. The square is dominated by the Eglise de la Sorbonne, whose outstanding exterior features are its cupola and 10 Corinthian columns. Inside is the white marble tomb of Cardinal Richelieu. (The church is open to the public only during exhibitions and cultural events.) The university buildings of La Sorbonne spread out around the church from rue Cujas down to the visitor's entrance on rue des Ecoles.

❸ The **Sorbonne** is the oldest university in Paris—indeed, one of the oldest in Europe—and has for centuries been one of France's principal institutions of higher learning. It is named after Robert de Sorbon, a medieval canon who founded a theological college here in 1253 for 16 students. By the 17th century, the church and university buildings were becoming dilapidated, so Cardinal Richelieu undertook to have them restored; the present-day Sorbonne campus is largely a result of that restoration. Despite changes in the neighborhood, the maze of amphitheaters, lecture rooms, and laboratories, and the surrounding courtyards and narrow streets, still have a hallowed air. For a glimpse of a more recent relic of Sorbonne history, look for Puvis de Chavannes's painting of the *Sacred Wood* in the main lecture hall, a major meeting point during the tumultuous student upheavals of 1968, and now a university landmark.

Behind the Sorbonne, bordering its eastern reach, is the rue St-Jacques. The street climbs toward the rue Soufflot, named to honor ❸ the man who built the vast, domed **Panthéon,** set atop place du Panthéon. One of Paris's most physically overwhelming sites—it was commissioned by Louis XV as a mark of gratitude for his recovery from a grave illness in 1744—the Panthéon is now a seldom-used church, with little of interest except for Puvis de Chavannes's monumental frescoes and the crypt, which holds the remains of Voltaire, Zola, Rousseau, and dozens of French statesmen, military heroes, and thinkers. In 1789—the year the church was completed—its windows were blocked by order of the Revolutionary Constituent Assembly, and they have remained that way ever since, adding to its sepulchral gloom. The dome, which weighs about 10,000 tons, is best appreciated from a distance. *Entrance on rue Clothilde. Admission: 26 frs, 17 frs ages 18–25, 6 frs children 7–17. Open daily 10–5:30.*

Diagonally across from the Panthéon on the corner of rue Clovis and ❸ rue Cujas stands the striking **St-Etienne-du-Mont.** This mainly 16th-century church's ornate facade combines Gothic, Baroque, and Renaissance elements. Inside, the fretted rood screen is the only one of its kind in Paris. Note the uneven-floored chapel behind the choir, which can be reached via a cloister containing some exquisite stained glass dating from the 17th century.

Up rue St-Jacques again and across from the Sorbonne are the **Lycée Louis-le-Grand** (Molière, Voltaire, and Robespierre studied here) and the elite **Collège de France,** whose grounds continue around the corner onto rue des Ecoles. In 1530, François I created this school as the College of Three Languages, which taught High Latin, Greek, and Hebrew, and any other subjects eschewed by academics at the Sorbonne. Diagonally across from the college, on the other side of rue des Ecoles, is the **square Paul-Painlevé;** behind it lies the entrance to the inimitable Hôtel et Musée de Cluny.

Built on the site of the city's enormous old Roman baths, the **Musée National du Moyen-Age** (formerly the **Musée de Cluny**) is housed in a 15th-century mansion that originally belonged to monks of Cluny Abbey in Burgundy. The remains of the baths that can still be seen are what survived a sacking by Barbarians in the 4th century. But the real reason people come to the Cluny is for its tapestry collection. The most famous series of all is the graceful *Lady and the Unicorn, or Dame à la Licorne,* woven in the 15th or 16th century, probably in the southern Netherlands. And if the tapestries themselves aren't enough at which to marvel, there is also an exhibition of decorative arts from the Middle Ages, a vaulted chapel, and a deep, cloistered courtyard with mullioned windows, set off by the *Boatmen's Pillar,* Paris's oldest sculpture, at its center. *Admission: 26 frs, 17 frs students and senior citizens and on Sun., under 18 free. Open Wed.–Mon. 9:45–5:45.*

Above boulevard St-Germain, rue St-Jacques reaches toward the Seine, bringing you past the elegant proportions of the church of **St-Séverin.** Rebuilt in the 16th century and noted for its width and its Flamboyant Gothic style, the church dominates a close-knit Left Bank neighborhood filled with quiet squares and pedestrian streets. In the 11th century, it was the parish church for the entire Left Bank. Louis XIV's cousin, a capricious woman known simply as the Grande Mademoiselle, adopted St-Séverin when she tired of the St-Sulpice church; she then spent vast sums getting Le Brun to modernize the chancel. Note the splendidly deviant spiraling column in the forest of pillars behind the altar. *Open weekdays 11–5:30, Sat. 11–10.*

Running riot around the relative quiet of St-Séverin are streets filled with restaurants of every description, serving everything from souvlaki-to-go to five-course haute cuisine. There is definitely something for every budget here. Rue de la Huchette is the most heavily trafficked of the restaurant streets and especially good for its selection of cheaper Greek food houses and Tunisian patisseries. In the evening, many restaurants put out full window displays of the foods to be offered on that night's menu in order to induce people away from the umbrella-covered terraces of neighboring cafés.

Time Out   If you end up in this area in the evening and are in the mood for entertainment with your supper, duck into **Le Cloître** (19 rue St-Jacques). It's an old, heavily wood-beamed bar with a one- and sometimes two-woman revue in the *cave,* or cellar, performing songs of old Paris from the '20s, '30s, and '40s. For a quieter diversion, stop at **Polly Maggoo** (11 rue St-Jacques).

Cross to the other side of rue St-Jacques. In Square René Viviani, which surrounds the church of **St-Julien-le-Pauvre,** stands an acacia tree that is supposed to be the oldest tree in Paris (although it has a rival claim from another acacia at the Jardin des Plantes). This tree-filled square also gives you one of the more spectacular views of Notre Dame. The tiny church here was built at the same time as Notre Dame (1165–1220), on a site where a whole succession of chapels once stood. The church belongs to a Greek Orthodox order today, but was originally named for St. Julian, bishop of Le Mans, who was nicknamed "Le Pauvre" after he gave all his money away.

Behind the church, to the east, are the tiny, elegant streets of the recently renovated **Maubert** district, bordered by quai de Montebello and boulevard St-Germain. Rue de Bièvre, once filled with tanneries, is now guarded at both ends to protect President Mitterrand's private residence.

Between St-Julien-le-Pauvre and place Maubert, two tiny streets—**rue des Anglais** and **rue des Irlandais**—mark the presence of foreign students who have come to study at Paris's academic and theological institutions over the centuries. Very basic board was provided by the small college for Irish students studying to become priests; although it has now been taken over by Polish students, it is still sometimes possible to get accommodation here (for men) if you are one for staying in humble, monklike quarters.

Public meetings and demonstrations have been held in place Maubert ever since the Middle Ages. Nowadays, most gatherings **40** are held inside or in front of the elegantly Art Deco **Palais de la Mutualité,** on the corner of the square, also a venue for jazz, pop, and rock concerts. On Tuesdays, Thursdays, and Saturdays, it is transformed into a colorful outdoor food market.

Head up rue Monge, turn right onto rue du Cardinal-Lemoine, and **41** you'll find yourself at the minute **place de la Contrescarpe.** It doesn't start to swing until after dusk, when its cafés and bars fill up. During the day, the square looks almost provincial, as Parisians flock to the daily market on rue Mouffetard. There are restaurants and cafés of every description on rue Mouffetard, and if you get here at lunchtime, you may want to buy yourself the makings for an alfresco lunch and take it to the unconventional picnic spot provided by the nearby **42** Gallo-Roman ruin of the **Arènes de Lutèce;** it begins on rue Monge, just past the end of rue Rollin. The ancient arena was discovered only in 1869 and has since been excavated and landscaped to reveal parts of the original Roman amphitheater. This site and the remains of the baths at the Cluny constitute the only extant evidence of the powerful Roman city of Lutetia that flourished here in the 3rd century. It is also one of the lesser-known delights of the Left Bank, so you are not likely to find it crowded.

43 The **Jardin des Plantes** is an enormous swath of greenery containing spacious botanical gardens and a number of natural history museums. It is stocked with plants dating back to the first collections here in the 17th century, and has been enhanced ever since by subsequent generations of devoted French botanists. It claims to shelter Paris's oldest tree, an *acacia robinia,* planted in 1636. There is also a small, old-fashioned zoo here; an alpine garden; an aquarium; a maze; and a number of hothouses. The **Musée Entomologique** is devoted to insects; the **Musée Paléontologique** exhibits fossils and prehistoric animals; the **Musée Minéralogique** houses an impressive collection of rocks and minerals. *Admission: 15–25 frs. Museums open Wed.–Mon. 9–11:45 and 1–4:45, weekends 2–4:45. Garden open daily 7:30–sunset.*

Time Out At the back of the gardens, in place du Puits-de-l'Hermite, you can drink a restorative cup of sweet mint tea in **La Mosquée,** a beautiful white mosque, complete with minaret. Once inside, you'll be convinced that you must be elsewhere than the Left Bank of Paris. The students from the nearby Jussieu and Censier universities pack themselves into the Moslem restaurant here, which serves copious quantities of couscous. The sunken garden and tiled patios are open to the public—the prayer rooms are not—and so are the *hammams,* or Turkish baths. *Baths open daily 11 AM–8 PM; Fri. and Sun. men only; Mon., Wed., Thurs., and Sat. women only. Admission: 15 frs, 65 frs for Turkish baths. Guided tours of mosque Sat.–Thurs. 10–noon and 2–5:30.*

In 1988, Paris's large Arab population gained another base: the huge
❹❹ **Institut du Monde Arabe,** which overlooks the Seine on quai St-Bernard, just beyond Université Jussieu. Jean Nouvel's harmonious mixture of Arabic and European styles in a striking glass and steel edifice was greeted with enthusiasm when the center first opened. Note on the building's south side the 240 shutter-like apertures that open and close to regulate light exposure. It contains a sound and image center, a vast library and documentation center, and an excellent art museum containing an array of Arab-Islamic art, textiles, and ceramics, with exhibits on Arabic mathematics, astronomy, and medicine. Glass elevators will take you to the ninth floor, where you can sip tea on the roof and enjoy (yet another) memorable view over the Seine and Notre Dame. *23 quai St-Bernard. Admission free. Open Tues.–Sun. 10–6.*

Montmartre

Numbers in the margin correspond to points of interest on the Montmartre map.

On a dramatic rise above the city is Montmartre, site of the Sacré-Coeur basilica and home to a once-thriving artistic community, a heritage recalled today chiefly by the gangs of third-rate painters clustered in the area's most famous square, the place du Tertre. Despite their presence, and the fact that the fabled nightlife of old Montmartre has fizzled down to some glitzy nightclubs and porn shows, Montmartre still exudes a sense of history, a timeless quality infused with that hard-to-define Gallic charm.

The crown atop this urban peak, the Sacré-Coeur is something of an architectural oddity. Its silhouette, viewed from afar at dusk or sunrise, looks more like a mosque than a cathedral. The Sacré-Coeur has been called everything from ugly to sublime; try to see it from as many perspectives as you can before drawing your own conclusion.

Seeing Montmartre means negotiating a lot of steep streets and flights of steps. If the prospect of trudging up and down them is daunting, you can tour parts of Montmartre by public transportation, aboard the Promotrain or the Montmartrobus. The Promotrain offers daily 40-minute guided tours of Montmartre between 10 AM and midnight. The cost is 25 francs for adults, 15 francs for children under 12, and departures are from outside the Moulin Rouge on place Blanche. The Montmartrobus is a regular city bus that runs around Montmartre for the price of a métro ticket. It departs from place Pigalle. If you're visiting only Sacré-Coeur, take the funicular that runs up the hill to the church near Anvers métro station.

Exploring Montmartre

❶ Begin your tour at **place Blanche,** site of the Moulin Rouge. Place Blanche—White Square—takes its name from the clouds of chalky dust churned up by the windmills that once dotted Montmartre (or *La Butte,* meaning "mound" or "hillock"). They were set up here not just because the hill was a good place to catch the wind—at over 300 feet, it's the highest point in the city—but because Montmartre was covered with wheat fields and quarries right up to the end of the 19th century. The carts carrying away the wheat and crushed stone trundled across place Blanche, turning the square white as they passed. Today, only two of the original 20 windmills are intact. A number have been converted to other uses, none more famous than **❷** the **Moulin Rouge,** or Red Windmill, built in 1885 and turned into a dance hall in 1900. It was a genuinely wild place in its early days, immortalized by Toulouse-Lautrec in his boldly simple posters and paintings. The place is still trading shamelessly on the notion of Paris as a city of sin: If you fancy a Vegas-style night out, with computerized light shows and troupes of bare-breasted girls sporting feather headdresses, this is the place to go *(see* The Arts and Nightlife, Chapter 7). The cancan, by the way—still a regular feature here—was considerably more raunchy when Lautrec was around.

For a taste of something more authentically French, walk past the **❸** Moulin Rouge, up **rue Lepic,** site of one of the most colorful and tempting food markets in Paris (closed Mon.).

Time Out Stop in at the tiny **Lux Bar** (12 rue Lepic) for coffee and a sandwich. The wall behind the bar is covered with a 1910 mosaic showing place Blanche at the beginning of the century.

❹ Turn left onto rue des Abbesses and walk along to **Cimetière de Montmartre** (Montmartre cemetery). It's by no means as romantic or as large as the better known Père Lachaise cemetery in the east of the city, but it contains the graves of many prominent French men and women, including the 18th-century painters Greuze and Fragonard; Degas; and Adolphe Sax, inventor of the saxophone. The Russian ballet dancer Nijinsky is also buried here.

Walk back along rue des Abbesses. Rue Tholozé, the second street on the left, was once a path over the hill, the oldest in Montmartre. **❺** It leads to the **Moulin de la Galette,** one of the two remaining windmills in Montmartre, which has been unromantically rebuilt. To **❻** reach it, you pass **Studio 28.** This seems to be no more than a generic little movie theater, but when opened in 1928, it was the first purposely built *art et essai,* or experimental theater, in the world. Over the years, the movies of directors like Jean Cocteau, François Truffaut, and Orson Welles have often been shown here before their official premieres.

❼ Return to rue des Abbesses, turn left, and walk to **place des Abbesses.** The little square is typical of the kind of picturesque and slightly countrified style that has made Montmartre famous. The entrance to the métro station, a curving, sensuous mass of delicate iron, is one of a handful of original Art Nouveau stations left in Paris. The austere, red brick **church of St-Jean l'Evangéliste** (1904) is worth a look, too. It was one of the first concrete buildings in France; the brick had to be added later to soothe offended locals. The **café St-Jean,** next to it, is a popular local meeting place, crowded on weekends.

Montmartre

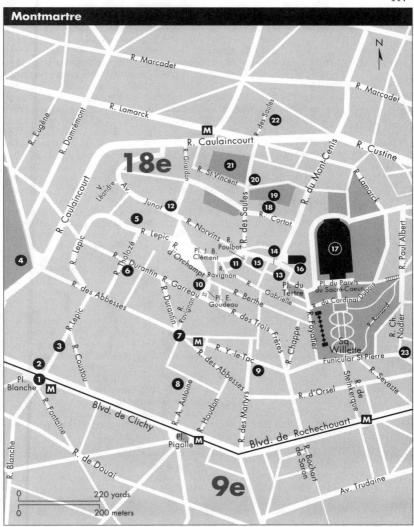

Basilique du Sacré-Coeur, **17**

Bateau-Lavoir, **10**

Chapelle du Martyre, **9**

Cimetière de Montmartre, **4**

Cité Internationale des Arts, **12**

Espace Dali, **15**

La Mère Catherine, **14**

Lapin Agile, **20**

Marché St-Pierre, **23**

Moulin de la Galette, **5**

Moulin de Paris, **11**

Moulin Rouge, **2**

Musée d'Art Juif, **22**

Musée du Vieux Montmartre, **18**

Place Blanche, **1**

Place des Abbesses, **7**

Place du Tertre, **13**

Rue Lepic, **3**

St-Pierre de Montmartre, **16**

St-Vincent Cemetery, **21**

Studio 28, **6**

Théâtre Libre, **8**

Vineyard, **19**

There are two competing attractions just off the square. Theater buffs should head down the tiny rue André-Antoine. At No. 37, you'll see what was originally the **Théâtre Libre,** or Free Theater, founded in 1887 by André Antoine and immensely influential in popularizing the work of iconoclastic young playwrights such as Ibsen and Strindberg. The other attraction is **rue Yvonne-le-Tac,** scene of a vital event in Montmartre's early history and linked to the disputed story of how this quarter got its name. Some say the name Montmartre comes from the Roman temple to Mercury that was once here, called the Mound of Mercury or *Mons Mercurii.* Others contend that it was an adaptation of *Mons Martyrum,* a name inspired by the burial here of Paris's first bishop, St-Denis. The popular version of his martyrdom is that he was beheaded by the Romans in AD 250, but arose to carry his severed head from rue Yvonne-le-Tac to a place 4 miles to the north, an area now known as St-Denis. He is commemorated by the 19th-century **Chapelle du Martyre** at No. 9, built over the spot where he is said to have been executed. It was in the crypt of the original chapel here that St. Ignatius of Loyola founded the Jesuit order in 1540, a decisive step in the efforts of the Catholic Church to reassert its authority in the face of the Protestant Reformation. A final twist on the name controversy is that Montmartre briefly came to be known as Mont-Marat during the French Revolution. Marat was a leading Revolutionary figure who was obliged to spend most of the day in the tub, the result of a disfiguring and severe skin condition. It was in his bath that Charlotte Corday, a fanatical opponent of the Revolutionary government, stabbed him to death.

From rue Yvonne-le-Tac, retrace your steps through place des Abbesses. Take rue Ravignan on the right, climbing to the summit via place Emile-Goudeau, an enchanting little cobbled square. Your goal is the **Bateau-Lavoir,** or Boat Wash House, at its northern edge. Montmartre poet Max Jacob coined the name for the old building on this site, which burned down in 1970. First of all, he said, it resembled a boat. Second, the warren of artists' studios within was always cluttered and paint-splattered, and looked to be in perpetual need of a good hosing down. The new building also contains art studios, but, if you didn't know its history, you'd probably walk right past it; it is the epitome of poured concrete drabness.

It was in the original Bateau-Lavoir that painters Picasso and Braque, early this century, made their first bold stabs at the concept of Cubism—a move that paved the way for abstract painting. The poet Apollinaire, who also kept a Bateau-Lavoir studio, helped Cubism gain acceptance with his book, *Les Peintures du Cubisme* (1913), which set the seal on the movement's historical significance.

Continue up the hill to place Jean-Baptiste Clément. The Italian painter and sculptor Modigliani (1884–1920) had a studio here at No. 7. Some have claimed he was the greatest Italian artist of the 20th century, the man who fused the genius of the Italian Renaissance with the modernity of Cézanne and Picasso. He claimed that he would drink himself to death—he eventually did—and chose the right part of town to do it in. This was one of the wildest areas of Montmartre. Its bistros and cabarets have mostly gone now, though, and only the **Moulin de Paris** still reflects a glimmer of the old atmosphere. Look for the octagonal tower at the north end of the square; it's all that's left of Montmartre's first water tower, built around 1840 to boost the area's feeble water supply.

Rue Norvins, formerly rue des Moulins, runs behind and parallel to the north end of the square. Turn left along it to reach stylish avenue Junot, site of the **Cité Internationale des Arts** (International Residence of the Arts), where the city authorities rent out studios to artists from all over the world. Retrace your steps back to rue Norvins and continue east past the bars and tourist shops, until you reach place du Tertre.

⑬ **Place du Tertre** *(tertre* means hillock) regains its village atmosphere only in the winter, when the somber buildings gather in the grays of the Parisian light and the plane tree branches sketch traceries against the sky. At any other time of year, you'll have to fight your way through the crowds to the southern end of the square and the breathtaking view over the city. The real drawback is the swarm of artists clamoring to dash off your portrait. If you're in the mood, however. . . . Most are licensed to be there, and, like taxi drivers, their prices are officially fixed. But there is no shortage of con men, sketch pads in hand, who will charge whatever they think they can get away with. If one produces a picture of you without having first asked, you're under no obligation to buy it, though that's not to say you won't have to argue your case. It's best just to walk away.

⑭ **La Mère Catherine,** the restaurant at the northern end of the square, has an honored place in French culinary history. It was a favorite with the Russian cossacks who occupied Paris in 1814 after Napoléon had been exiled to the island of Elba. Little did they know that when they banged on the tables and shouted *"bistro,"* the Russian word for "quick," they were inventing a new breed of French restaurant. For a restaurant catering almost entirely to the tourist trade, La Mère Catherine is surprisingly good, though prices are high for what's offered.

Time Out **Patachou,** opened in 1987, sounds the one classy note on place du Tertre (at No. 9). It offers exquisite, if expensive, cakes and teas.

⑮ Around the corner on rue Poulbot, the **Espace Dali** houses more than 300 works by Salvador Dali, who once kept a studio in the area. The museum's atmosphere is meant to approximate the surreal experience, with black walls, low lighting, and a new-agey musical score—punctuated by recordings of Dali's own voice. If you're interested in seeing some of Dali's less-familiar works, including a series of sculptures and bronzes, a visit will prove worthwhile. Those unmoved by this eccentric genius and showman may want to skip this stop in favor of strolling the place du Tertre. *11 rue Poulbot, tel. 42–64–40–10. Admission: 35 frs adults, 25 frs children. Open daily 10–6; until 8 in summer.*

It was in place du Tertre in March 1871 that one of the most destructively violent episodes in French history began, one that colored French political life for generations. Despite popular images of later-19th-century France—and Paris especially—as carefree and prosperous, for much of this period the country was desperately divided into two camps: an ever more vocal and militant underclass, motivated by resentment of what they considered an elitist government, and a reactionary and fearful bourgeoisie and ruling class. It was a conflict that went back at least as far as the French Revolution at the end of the 18th century, and one that twice flared into outbreaks of civil war and rebellion, in 1832 and 1848, as the country oscillated between republican and imperial forms of government. In 1870, France, under the leadership of an opportunistic but feeble Napoléon III (nephew of the great Napoléon), was drawn into a disastrous war with Bismarck's Prussia, which was rapidly growing into one of the most formidable military powers in Europe. (Soon after, Prussia was to dominate a newly united and aggressive Germany.) In September that year, Prussia invaded France, surrounded Paris, and laid siege to it. After four months of appalling suffering—during which time the Louvre became a munitions factory, the Gare de Lyon was converted into a cannon foundry, and the two elephants in the zoo, Castor and Pollux, were eaten by starving Parisians—the new government under French statesman Adolphe Thiers capitulated. Although mass starvation seemed imminent, fears that Thiers would restore an imperial rather than a republican government caused Parisians to refuse to surrender their arms to him. Thiers then ordered that the guns at Montmartre be captured by loyal government forces. Insurgents responded by shooting the two generals ordered to retake the guns. Almost immediately, barricades were thrown up across the city streets, and the fighting began in earnest. The antimonarchists formed the Commune, which for three heady months ruled Paris. In May, from his base at Versailles, Thiers ordered the city retaken. Estimates as to the numbers killed in the fighting vary greatly. Some say 4,000 Communards lost their lives; others claim 20,000. No one, however, doubts that upward of 10,000 Communards were executed by government troops after the collapse of the Commune.

In expiation for this bloodshed, the French government decided, in 1873 (after the downfall of Thiers), to build the basilica of the Sacré-Coeur. It was to be a sort of national guilt offering. Before visiting this landmark, walk to the church of **St-Pierre de Montmartre** at the east side of place du Tertre. It's one of the oldest churches in the city, built in the 12th century as the abbey church of a substantial Benedictine monastery. It's been remodeled on a number of occasions down through the years, and the 18th-century facade, built by Louis XIV, contrasts uncomfortably with the mostly medieval interior. Its setting is awkward, too: The bulk of the Sacré-Coeur looms directly behind it.

The **Basilique du Sacré-Coeur,** begun in 1873 and completed in 1910 (though not consecrated until 1919), symbolized the return of relative self-confidence to later-19th-century Paris after the turmoil of the Commune. Even so, the building was to some extent a reflection of political divisions within the country. It was largely financed by French Catholics fearful of an anticlerical backlash and determined to make a grand statement on behalf of the Church. Stylistically, the Sacré-Coeur borrows elements from Romanesque and Byzantine models, fusing them under its distinctive Oriental dome. Built on a grand scale, the effect is strangely disjointed and unsettling, rather as if the building had been designed by an architect of railway stations, with a pronounced taste for exoticism. (The architect, Abadie, died in 1884, long before the church was finished.) The gloomy, cavernous interior is worth visiting for its golden mosaics; climb to the top of the dome for the view over Paris.

More of Montmartre beckons north and west of the Sacré-Coeur. Take rue du Mont-Cenis down to rue Cortot, site of the **Musée du Vieux Montmartre.** Like the Bateau-Lavoir, the building that is now the museum sheltered an illustrious group of painters, writers, and assorted cabaret artists in its heyday toward the end of the 19th century. Foremost among them were Renoir—he painted the *Moulin de la Galette*, an archetypical Parisian scene of sun-drenched revels, while he lived here—and Maurice Utrillo, Montmartre painter par excellence. Utrillo was encouraged to paint by his mother, Suzanne Valadon, a regular model of Renoir's and a considerable painter in her own right. Utrillo's life was anything but happy, despite the considerable success his paintings enjoyed. He was an alcoholic continu-

ally in trouble with the police, and he spent most of his declining years in hospitals. Having taken the gray, crumbling streets of Montmartre as his subject matter, he discovered that he worked more effectively from postcards than from the streets themselves. For all that, almost all his best works were produced before 1916 (he died in 1955). They evoke the atmosphere of old Montmartre hauntingly. Look carefully at the pictures in the museum here and you can see the plaster and sand he mixed with his paints to help convey the decaying buildings of the area. Almost the best thing about the mu-
⑲ seum, however, is the view over the tiny **vineyard** on neighboring rue des Saules, the only vineyard in Paris, which still produces a symbolic 125 gallons of wine every year. It's hardly vintage stuff, but there are predictably bacchanalian celebrations during the October harvest. *Musée du Vieux Montmartre, 12 rue Cortot. Admission: 30 frs adults, 20 frs students and senior citizens. Open Tues.–Sun. 11–5:30.*

There's an equally famous Montmartre landmark on the corner of
⑳ rue St-Vincent, just down the road: the **Lapin Agile.** It's a bar-cabaret and originally one of the raunchiest haunts in Montmartre. Today, it manages against all odds to preserve at least something of its earlier flavor, unlike the Moulin Rouge. It got its curious name—it means the Nimble Rabbit—when the owner, André Gill, hung a sign outside (you can see it now in the Musée du Vieux Montmartre) of a laughing rabbit jumping out of a saucepan clutching a wine bottle. In those days, the place was still tamely called La Campagne (The Countryside). Once the sign went up, locals rebaptized the place Lapin à Gill, which, translated, means rabbit, Gill-style. When in 1886 it was sold to cabaret singer Jules Jouy, he called it the Lapin Agile, which has the same pronunciation in French as Lapin à Gill. In 1903, the premises were bought by the most celebrated cabaret entrepreneur of them all, Aristide Bruand, portrayed by Toulouse-Lautrec in a series of famous posters.

㉑ Behind the Lapin Agile is the **St-Vincent Cemetery;** the entrance is off little rue Lucien-Gaulard. It's a tiny graveyard, but serious students of Montmartre might want to visit to see Utrillo's burial place.

Continue north on rue des Saules, across busy rue Caulaincourt,
㉒ and you come to the **Musée d'Art Juif,** the Museum of Jewish Art. It contains devotional items, models of synagogues, and works by Pissarro and Marc Chagall. *42 rue des Saules. Admission: 20 frs adults, 15 frs students and children. Open Sun.–Thurs. 3–6.*

There are several routes you can take back over Montmartre's hill. Luxurious avenue Junot, from which you'll see the villa Léandre, one of Montmartre's most charming side streets, makes for a picturesque return from the area around the cemetery and the museum. Alternatively, you can turn east onto rue Lamarck, past several good restaurants, to circle around the quieter side of the Sacré-Coeur basilica. If you then take the little stairpath named after
㉓ Utrillo down to rue Paul Albert, you'll come upon the **Marché St-Pierre** (St. Pierre Market), the perfect place to rummage for old clothes and fabrics. Prices are low. *Open Tues.–Sun. 8–1.*

Take rue de Steinkerque, opposite the foot of the Sacré-Coeur gardens, then turn right onto boulevard de Rochechouart and continue down to **Place Pigalle** to complete your tour of the essential Montmartre. Despite the area's reputation as a tawdry red-light district, a number of trendy clubs have opened here. (*see* The Arts and Nightlife, Chapter 7.) If you choose to visit at night, however, be aware that dubious characters and lewd sex shows still prevail.

On the Fringe

The Bois de Boulogne

Class and style have been associated with "Le Bois," as it is known, ever since it was landscaped into an upper-class playground by Baron Haussmann in the 1850s at the request of Napoléon III. This sprawling, 2,200-acre wood, crisscrossed by broad, leafy roads, lies just west of Paris, surrounded by the wealthy residential districts of Neuilly, Auteuil, and Passy. Here you will discover rowers, joggers, strollers, riders, lovers, hookers, *pétanque*-players, and picnickers. Horse races at Longchamp and Auteuil are high up the social calendar and re-create something of a Belle Epoque atmosphere. The French Open tennis tournament at the beautiful Roland Garros Stadium in late May is another occasion when Parisian style and elegance are on full display. The manifold attractions of these woods include cafés, restaurants, lakes, gardens, and waterfalls. Rowboats are available at the two largest lakes, the Lac Inférieur and Lac Supérieur. A cheap and frequent ferry crosses to the idyllic island in the middle of the Lac Inférieur.

Buses traverse the Bois de Boulogne during the day (service 244 from Porte Maillot), but the métro goes only to the fringe: Alight at Porte Dauphine (east), Les Sablons (north), or Porte d'Auteuil (south). Porte Dauphine is one of the few stations still to possess an original Art Nouveau iron-and-glass entrance canopy, designed by métro architect Hector Guimard. It stands at the bottom of avenue Foch, connecting the Bois to the Champs-Elysées. It used to be known as the avenue de l'Impératrice in honor of the Empress Eugénie (wife of Napoléon III) and is Paris's grandest boulevard—for both its sheer size (330 yards wide) and its high-priced real estate.

One of the best ways of getting around the Bois is by bicycle. Bikes can be rented on Wednesdays and on weekends from Le Relais du Bois restaurant, Route de Suresnes (tel. 45–27–54–65). The cost is 25 francs an hour or 90 francs a day.

A word of warning: The Bois becomes a distinctly adult playground after dark, when walking, and even driving, are not advisable; the Bois's night population can be dauntingly aggressive.

Besides being a charming place to stroll or picnic, the Bois de Boulogne boasts several individual attractions worth a visit in their own right:

Parc de Bagatelle. This is a beautiful floral park with irises, roses, tulips, and water lilies among the showpieces; it is at its freshest and most colorful between April and June. The velvet green lawns and majestic 18th-century buildings (often host to art exhibitions) are fronted by a terrace with views toward the Seine—an attractive sight at any time of year. *Entrance: Route de Sèvres à Neuilly, or off Allée de Longchamp (Bus 244 or Métro: Pont de Neuilly). Admission: 10 frs adults, 5 frs children to park, 35 frs adults, 25 frs children to château buildings. Open 8:30 AM–8 PM.*

Jardin d'Acclimatation. This delightful children's amusement park on the northern edge of the Bois de Boulogne has plenty to enchant adults as well. There are boat trips along an "enchanted river," a zoo with a refreshing mix of exotic and familiar animals, a miniature railway, a high-towered folly, and various fairground stalls to keep young and old entertained. The zoo and amusement park can be

reached via the miniature railway—a surefire hit with children—
that runs from Porte Maillot (Wed. and weekends from 1:30; 4 frs).
Many of the attractions (though not the zoo, which is spread out
through the park) have separate entry fees, notably the child-ori-
ented **Musée en Herbe** (13 frs; 11 frs excluding garden; 20 frs with
workshop). There are plenty of open-air cafés for a refreshing
break. *Blvd. des Sablons (Métro: Les Sablons). Admission: 13 frs
adults, 6 frs children. Open Sun.–Fri. 10–6, Sat. 2–6.*

Musée des Arts et Traditions Populaires. This museum, situated
right alongside the Jardin d'Acclimatation in an ugly modern building, contains an impressive variety of artifacts related principally to
preindustrial rural life. Many exhibits have buttons to press and
knobs to twirl; however, there are no descriptions in English. The
museum is a favorite destination for school field trips, so avoid
weekday afternoons, except Wednesdays, when the children are not
in school. *6 av. du Mahatma-Gandhi (Métro: Les Sablons). Admission: 23 frs adults, 15 frs children and Sun. Open Wed.–Mon. 10–
5:15.*

Pré Catalan. This pleasant, well-tended area in the heart of the Bois
de Boulogne includes one of Paris's largest trees: a copper beech
over 200 years old. The "Shakespeare Garden" contains flowers,
herbs, and trees mentioned in Shakespearean plays. *Route de la
Grande Cascade (Bus 244 or Métro: Porte Dauphine). Guided tours
at 11, 1:30, 3, 5, and 5:30.*

The Bois de Vincennes

Situated to the southeast of Paris, sandwiched between the unexcit-
ing suburb of Charenton and the working-class district of Fontenay-
sous-Bois, the Bois de Vincennes is often considered a poor man's
Bois de Boulogne. Although the east of Paris has less to attract visitors than the west, the comparison is largely unfair. The Bois de
Vincennes is no more difficult to get to (bus 46; métro to Porte
Dorée) and has equally illustrious origins. It, too, was landscaped
under Napoléon III—a park having been created here by Louis XV
as early as 1731.

Also like the Bois de Boulogne, the Bois de Vincennes has several
lakes, notably Lac Daumesnil, with two islands, and Lac des
Minimes, with three. Rowboats can be hired at both. There is also a
zoo, a cinder-track racecourse (Hippodrome de Vincennes), a castle,
an extensive flower garden, and several cafés. The Foire du Trône, in
spring, is one big fun fair. Bikes can be rented from Château de Vincennes métro station (tel. 47–66–55–92). The cost is 25 francs an
hour or 100 francs a day.

Château de Vincennes. On the northern edge of the Bois is the historic Château de Vincennes, France's medieval Versailles, an imposing, high-walled castle surrounded by a dry moat and dominated by
a 170-foot keep through which guided tours are offered. The sprawling castle grounds also contain a replica (1379–1552) of the Sainte-
Chapelle on the Ile de la Cité, and two elegant, classical wings
designed by Louis Le Vau in the mid-17th century (now used for na-
val/military administration, and closed to the public). *Av. de Paris,
Vincennes (Métro: Château de Vincennes). Admission: 25 frs
adults, 14 frs students and senior citizens. Open daily 10–6; 10–4 in
winter. Guided tours of chapel every 45 minutes.*

Musée des Arts d'Afrique et d'Océanie. This museum, housed in a
building erected for the Colonial Exhibition of 1931, is devoted to

African and Oceanic Art and features headdresses, bronzes, jewelry, masks, statues, and pottery from former French colonies in Africa and the South Seas. There is also a tropical aquarium. *293 av. Daumesnil (Métro: Porte Dorée). Admission: 27 frs adults, 20 frs children and on Sun. Open Wed.–Mon. 10–5:30, weekends 10–6.*

Parc Floral. The 70-acre Vincennes flower garden includes a lake and water garden and is renowned for its seasonal displays of blooms. The "exotarium" contains tropical fish and reptiles. *Route de la Pyramide, Vincennes (Métro: Château de Vincennes). Admission: 5 frs, children under 6 free. Open daily 9:30–8, 9:30–5 in winter.*

Zoo. Some 600 mammals and 200 species of bird can be seen at Vincennes Zoo, the largest in France. One of the most striking features is an artificial rock 236 feet high, inhabited by wild mountain sheep. *53 av. de St-Maurice (Métro: Porte Dorée). Admission: 35 frs adults, 20 frs children. Open Apr.–Oct., daily 9–6; Nov.–Mar., daily 9–5:30.*

La Défense

You may be pleasantly surprised by the absence of high-rise buildings and concrete towers in central Paris; one of the reasons for this is that French planners, with their usual desire to rationalize, ordained that modern high-rise development be relegated to the outskirts of the capital. Over the last 20 years, La Défense, just to the west of Paris, across the Seine from Neuilly, has been transformed into a futuristic showcase for state-of-the-art engineering and architectural design.

A few people actually live here amid all this glass and concrete, but most come here to work. The soaring high rises of La Défense are mainly taken up by offices—often the French headquarters of multinational companies—with no expense spared in the pursuit of visual ingenuity. Outlines, shadows, reflections, plays of light, and swirling underpasses make up a stimulating, but slightly terrifying, cityscape. At its heart is the giant arch of La Défense, aligned with avenue de la Grande Armée, the Arc de Triomphe, the Champs-Elysées, and the Louvre. Tubular glass elevators whisk you to the top. *Métro or RER: La Défense. Admission: 35 frs, 25 frs under 18. Open Sun.–Fri. 9–6, Sat. 9–7.*

Père Lachaise Cemetery

This largest, most interesting, and most prestigious of Paris cemeteries dates back to the start of the 19th century. Situated on the eastern fringe of Paris, it is a veritable necropolis whose tombs compete in grandiosity, originality, and often, alas, dilapidation. Cobbled avenues, steep slopes, and lush vegetation contribute to a powerful atmosphere. The cemetery was the site of the Paris Commune's final battle on May 28, 1871, when the rebel troops were rounded up, lined against the **Mur des Fédérés** (Federalist's Wall; now in the southeast corner of the cemetery), and shot. Named after the Jesuit father—Louis XIV's confessor—who led the reconstruction of the Jesuit Rest House completed here in 1682, the cemetery houses the tombs of the French author Colette; the composer Chopin; the playwright Molière; the writers Honoré Balzac, Marcel Proust, Paul Eluard, and Oscar Wilde; the popular French actress Simone Signoret and her husband, singer-actor Yves Montand; and Edith Piaf. Perhaps the most noticeable shrine is to rock star Jim

Morrison: Lyrics scribbled on tombstones will lead you to the gravesite, where dozens of hippie faithfuls sit in silent homage to the songwriter. Get hold of a map at the entrance—and remember that Père Lachaise is an easy place to get lost in. *Rue des Rondeaux (Métro: Gambetta, Père Lachaise). Open daily 8–6, 8–dusk in winter.*

St-Denis

Although today St-Denis is a pretty seedy, downmarket northern suburb, its history—exemplified by its huge green-roof cathedral—is illustrious. The **Basilique de St-Denis** can be reached by métro from Paris and is worth visiting for several reasons. It was here, under dynamic prelate Abbé Suger, that Gothic architecture (typified by pointed arches and rib vaults) arguably made its first appearance. Suger's writings also show the medieval fascination with the bright, shiny colors that appear in stained glass. The kings of France soon chose St-Denis as their final resting place, and their richly sculpted tombs—along with what remains of Suger's church—can be seen in the choir area at the east end of the church. The vast 13th-century nave is a brilliant example of structural logic. Its elements—columns, capitals, and vaults—are a model of architectural harmony. The facade retains the rounded arches of the Romanesque style that preceded Gothic and is set off by a small rose window, reputedly the earliest in France. There was originally a left tower, with spire, as well as a right one; there is currently talk of reconstructing it. *Métro: St-Denis–Basilique. Admission to choir: 26 frs adults, 17 frs students and senior citizens. Open daily 10–7, 10–5 in winter, not open until noon on Sun. year-round.*

La Villette

The so-called **Cité des Sciences et de l'Industrie** is housed in the vast **Parc de la Villette,** created in the mid-1980s on the site of a former *abattoir* (slaughterhouse) in the unfashionable outskirts of northeast Paris. The sprawling complex includes a science and industry museum; planetarium; curved-screen cinema; an "inventorium," or children's play area; a concert hall (the Zénith—a major rock venue); and the huge iron-and-glass Grande Halle, used for concerts and exhibitions.

The **museum** tries to do for science and industry what the lookalike Pompidou Center does for modern art. It is a brave attempt to make technology seem fun and easy. The visual displays are bright and thought-provoking, while dozens of "try-it-yourself" contraptions make the visitor feel more participant than onlooker (though most displays are in French only). It's fascinating stuff and, perhaps, a forerunner of the museums of tomorrow—despite the huge, echoing main hall that is unpleasantly like a high-tech factory, and the lines (especially during school holidays), which can be absurdly long. *Métro: Porte de la Villette. Admission: 45 frs adults, 35 frs children (planetarium 15 frs extra). Open Tues.–Sun. 10–6.*

The **Géode** cinema, facing the museum building across the unruffled sheen of a broad moat, looks like a huge silver golf ball: It's actually made of polished steel. Thanks to its enormous, 180-degree-curved screen, it has swiftly become a cult movie venue. As its capacity is limited, we suggest you materialize in the morning or early afternoon to be sure of a same-day ticket. *Admission: 50 frs (joint ticket with museum 85 frs adults, 75 frs children). Screenings Tues.–Sun. 10–9.*

The futuristic outlines of the Géode and Science Museum shimmer in the canals that crisscross the Parc de la Villette, principally the barge-bearing Canal de l'Ourcq on its way from Paris to St-Denis. The whole area is ambitiously landscaped—there are sweeping lawns, a children's playground, canopied walkways, and weird, brightly painted pavilions—and is at last beginning to take shape, although a massive musical academy by the Porte de Pantin entrance will need several years of additional construction before completion.

The former slaughterhouse—the **Grande Halle**—is a magnificent structure that provides an intelligent link with the site's historic past: Its transformation into an exhibition-cum-concert center has been carried out as ingeniously as that of the former Gare (now Musée) d'Orsay. It is an intriguing sight at night, too, when strips of red neon along the roof and facade flicker on and off like a beating heart.

Off the Beaten Track

Académie de la Bière

Beer and *moules-frites* (mussels cooked in white wine and served with french fries) is more a Belgian than a French specialty, yet it's readily available in Paris, as if to underline the gastronomic as well as linguistic ties between the two neighbors. A good place to sample this satisfying combination is the friendly, unpretentious Académie de la Bière, near Montparnasse, the nearest Paris comes to the atmosphere of a British pub, with a cozy, wood-benched interior and pavement terrace for lazy summer evenings. There is a choice of 200 beers from numerous countries (several on draft), plus various snacks. *88 bis blvd. de Port-Royal, 5e, tel. 43–54–66–65. Open evenings 6 PM–2 AM; closed Sun. RER: Port-Royal.*

Bercy

This neighborhood, currently the focus of a massive renovation project scheduled for completion in 1996, is testament to the French genius for urban renewal. Tucked away on the Right Bank of the Seine, south of the Gare de Lyon in the 12th arrondissement, this colorful district was for decades filled with warehouses for the storing of wine from the provinces. Given the pace of transformation, there's little point checking the neighborhood map as you step out of Bercy métro station and come face-to-face with the mighty glass wall of the new **French Finance Ministry** which moved—grudgingly—to their new quayside offices from the Louvre in the late 1980s. To your left, the ingeniously sloping, green-walled **Palais Omnisports,** a stadium that hosts sports and music events and seats 17,000, looms like a moss-covered pyramid approached on all sides by gleaming white steps. These structures serve as cornerstones for the stretch of land that is to become the **Parc de Bercy,** which will have at its other pole a large **Food and Wine business complex** (including offices and a shopping center) and the new **American Center.** Designed by American architect Frank Gehry and open to the public in June of '94, the center contains a large art gallery, two theaters, studios, a bookstore, restaurant, and housing for visiting artists. Finally, to balance out the commercial with the residential, plans are underway to create new housing, schools, and public spaces in the neighborhood, eventually to be served by the new high-speed subway called the

Météor, which will run between Tolbiac in the 13th arrondissement to the Madeleine. *Métro: Bercy.*

Directly across the Seine in the 13th arrondissement is another one of the city's *grands travaux,* the **Bibliothèque de France** or the *Très Grand Bibliothèque* (Very Big Library) as some are facetiously calling it. Scheduled for completion sometime in late 1995, this project will subsume the majority of the collections in the old Bibliothèque Nationale, and with some 11 million volumes between its walls, will surpass the Library of Congress to become the largest library in the world. Architect Dominique Perrault's controversial design features four soaring 24-story towers that will house most of the books, while readers and visitors are relegated to underground reading rooms. *Métro: Quai de la Gare.*

Buttes-Chaumont

This is an immensely picturesque park in the downbeat 19th arrondissement of northeast Paris. It boasts a lake, waterfall, and clifftop folly or "belvedere." Until town planner Baron Haussmann got his hands on it in the 1860s, the area was a garbage dump and quarry—hence the steep slopes. *Rue Botzaris. Métro: Buttes-Chaumont, Botzaris.*

Canal St-Martin

Place de la République is the gateway to east Paris, a largely residential area often underestimated by tourists. One of its highlights is the Canal St-Martin, which starts just south of the Bastille but really comes into its own during the mile-long stretch north of République, across the 10th arrondissement. With its quiet banks, locks, and footbridges, the Canal St-Martin has an unexpected flavor of Amsterdam—and is much-loved by novelists and film directors. (Simenon's famous inspector Maigret solved many a mystery along its deceptively sleepy banks.) Major development has transformed the northern end of the canal, around the place de Stalingrad and its 18th-century rotunda, and there are boat trips along the once-industrial Bassin de la Villette to the nearby Parc de la Villette. *Métro: Jacques-Bonsergent, Colonel-Fabien, or Jaurès.*

Chinatown

Nestled between the high rises of rue de Tolbiac, avenue de Choisy, and boulevard Massena in the 13th arrondissement is the Chinatown of Paris. Neither as ornamental nor as self-contained as those of San Francisco or New York, Paris's Chinatown nevertheless offers a break for those weary of museum-going or monument-gazing. Explore the myriad of electronics and clothing stores, or stop for lunch at one of the dozens of restaurants that will draw you in with an exciting array of Chinese comestibles. Be sure to head down to No. 48 rue d'Ivry where the **Tang-Fréres** Chinese supermarket packs a serious crowd of shoppers on weekends. Under the platform at 37 rue du Disque is the **Temple d'Association des Residents d'Origine Chinoise,** a small Buddhist temple that looks like a cross between a school cafeteria and an exotic eastern enclave filled with Buddha figures, fruit, and incense.

Hôtel Drouot

Hidden away in a grid of narrow streets not far from the Opéra is Paris's central auction house, offering everything from stamps and toy soldiers to Renoirs and 18th-century commodes. Open six days a week, the Drouot's 16 salesrooms make for fascinating browsing and there's no obligation to bid. The mix of fur-coated ladies with money to burn, penniless art lovers desperate to unearth an unidentified masterpiece, and scruffy dealers trying to look anonymous makes up Drouot's unusually rich social fabric. *Entrance at the corner of rue Rossini and rue Drouot. Viewings Mon.–Sat. 11–noon and 2–6, with auctions starting at 2. Métro: Richelieu-Drouot.*

Les Catacombes

The catacombs consist of an extensive underground labyrinth built by the Romans, tunneling under much of the Left Bank and into the near suburbs. They were subsequently used to store bones from disused graveyards; then, during World War II, they became the headquarters of the French Resistance. You are well advised to take a flashlight with you. *1 pl. Denfert-Rochereau. Admission: 27 frs, 15 frs students and senior citizens. Open Tues.–Fri. 2–4, weekends 9–11 and 2–4. Guided tours on Wed. at 2:45; 20 frs extra. Métro and RER: Denfert-Rochereau.*

The Métro

Many visitors spend considerable time on the cheap and practical métro system without realizing it is a considerable attraction in its own right. For a start, it is not strictly a "subway" or "underground," inasmuch as it ventures out of its tunnels at several points to offer a delightful rooftop tour of the city. Part of **Line 2** (Dauphine–Nation) is above ground, yielding views of the Sacré-Coeur and the Canal St-Martin. Nearly all of **Line 6** (Nation–Etoile) is above ground and gives terrific views of the Invalides and Eiffel Tower. There is a charming glimpse of Notre Dame, Ile de la Cité, and Ile St-Louis as **Line 5** crosses the Seine between quai de la Rapée and Gare d'Austerlitz, continuing past the fine 17th-century Hôpital de la Salpêtrière.

A number of métro stations are attractions in themselves—the **Louvre** and **Varenne** stations are well-known for their museumlike feeling, **Cluny-Sorbonne** and **Pasteur** for their imaginative use of mosaics. The entrance canopies to **Porte Dauphine** and **Abbesses** stations are the best remaining examples of the florid, interlacing Art Nouveau ironwork created by Hector Guimard at the start of the century.

Nation Quarter

The towering, early 19th-century statue-topped columns on the majestic **place de la Nation** stand sentinel at the Gates of Paris, the eastern sector's equivalent of the Arc de Triomphe; the bustling but unpretentious Cours de Vincennes provides a down-to-earth echo of the Champs-Elysées. Place de la Nation (originally known as place du Trône, but Throne Square was far too monarchical a title to survive the Revolution) was the scene of over 1,300 executions at the guillotine in 1794. Most of these unfortunates were buried around the corner (via rue Fabre d'Eglantine) in the **Cimetière de Picpus,** a peaceful convent cemetery containing the grave of General Lafayette, identified by its U.S. flag. *35 rue Picpus. Open Tues.–Sun. 2–6, 2–4 in winter; closed Mon. Métro: Nation, Picpus.*

Sightseeing Checklists

Historic Buildings and Sites

American Center. Designed by American architect Frank Gehry, the new American Center is one of the central projects being carried out in the overhaul of the Bercy section of eastern Paris. A venue for American arts and culture, the building is worth a visit simply to view Gehry's kinetic and cubistic design. Métro: Bercy. (*See* Off the Beaten Track.)

Arc de Triomphe. Napoléon's triumphal arch forms part of the most imposing architectural vista in Europe, and dominates the circling traffic below it. Métro or RER: Etoile. (*See* From the Arc de Triomphe to the Opéra.)

Arènes de Lutèce. One of the two remaining vestiges of Gallo-Roman Paris (Museé National du Moyen-Age is the other; *see* Museums and Galleries, *below*). The arena, designed as a theater and circus, was almost totally destroyed by the barbarians in AD 280; you can still see part of the stage and tiered seating. Métro: Monge. (*See* The Left Bank.)

Bourse. The Paris Stock Exchange, a serene, colonnaded 19th-century building, is a far cry from Wall Street. Take your passport if you want to tour it. *Rue Vivienne (Métro: Bourse). Admission 10 frs; guided tours only (in French), weekdays, every half hour between 1:30 and 3.*

Bourse du Commerce. Paris's Commercial Exchange, an attractive, 18th-century circular building, now stands in contrast to the ultramodern Forum des Halles. Métro: Louvre, Les Halles; RER: Châtelet-Les Halles. (*See* The Historic Heart.)

Château de Vincennes. Known as the medieval Versailles, the château on the northern edge of the Bois de Vincennes is a majestic ensemble. Before you enter, walk around the outside for the best views of the fortified towers. Métro: Château de Vincennes. (*See* On the Fringe.)

Conciergerie. The fairy-tale towers of the Conciergerie disguise the fact that this was the grim prison that housed Marie Antoinette, Robespierre, and Danton during the French Revolution. The view of the building from quai de la Mégisserie across the Seine, especially at night, is memorable. Métro: Cité. (*See* The Historic Heart.)

Ecole Militaire. Still used as a military academy, the Ecole Militaire, overlooking the Champ de Mars and the Eiffel Tower, is not open to visitors, but you can admire its harmonious, 18th-century architecture from the Champ de Mars. Métro: Ecole Militaire. (*See* From Orsay to Trocadéro.)

Ecole Nationale des Beaux-Arts. The National Fine Arts College, founded at the beginning of the 17th century, occupies three large mansions on the Left Bank quayside. The school regularly stages temporary exhibits. Métro: St-Germain-des-Prés. (*See* The Left Bank.)

Eiffel Tower. The most famous landmark in Paris, built to celebrate the centennial of the French Revolution in 1889. Métro: Bir Hakeim; RER: Champ-de-Mars. (*See* From Orsay to Trocadéro.)

Hôtel de Lauzun. This is the only *hôtel particulier* on Ile St-Louis open to visitors. With its magnificent painted ceilings, tapestries, and gilded carvings, it provides a rich taste of aristocratic life in

17th-century Paris. Métro: Pont Marie. (*See* The Marais and Ile St-Louis.)

Hôtel de Sens. This is one of the few private mansions in Paris to have survived from the Middle Ages. Originally the home of the archbishops of Sens, it now houses a fine- and applied-arts library, the **Bibliothèque Forney,** and stages some excellent temporary exhibits. Métro: Pont Marie. (*See* The Marais and Ile St-Louis.)

Hôtel des Invalides. Built in the 17th century to house war veterans or "invalids," the Invalides now houses two museums, the **Musée de l'Armée** and the **Musée des Plans-Reliefs.** (*See* Museums and Galleries, *below.*) Métro: Latour-Maubourg, Varenne. (*See* From Orsay to Trocadéro.)

Hôtel de Sully. This superb 17th-century mansion houses the **Caisse Nationale des Monuments Historiques,** which organizes some excellent guided tours and conferences on historical monuments throughout the city. Métro: St-Paul. (*See* The Marais and Ile St-Louis.)

Hôtel de Ville. The Paris city hall has been splendidly cleaned and its vast square transformed into an elegant pedestrian area. Métro: Hôtel de Ville. (*See* The Marais and Ile St-Louis.)

Hôtel Matignon. The French prime minister's residence is obviously not open to visitors, but the courtyard of this elegant mansion, built in 1721, is worth a discreet peek. Métro: Varenne. (*See* From Orsay to Trocadéro.)

Institut de France. You will see the distinctive cupola of the French Institute standing out against the Left Bank skyline over the river from the Louvre. The Institute is home to the Académie Française and four other, lesser-known academies. Métro: Pont Neuf. (*See* The Left Bank.)

Memorial of the Unknown Jewish Martyr. Commemorating the 6 million Jews who were killed during the Holocaust, the memorial is housed in the Center for Contemporary Jewish Documentation, which also contains a library, archives, and a gallery with temporary exhibitions. *Métro: St-Paul.* (*See* The Marais and Ile St-Louis.)

Opéra. The Paris Opéra, with its monumental foyer and staircase, is a pastiche of architectural styles. Don't miss Marc Chagall's famous painted ceiling. Métro: Opéra; RER: Auber. (*See* From the Arc de Triomphe to the Opéra.)

Opéra de la Bastille. Argentinian architect Carlos Ott's gigantic new Paris opera, which has transformed place de la Bastille, opened on July 14, 1989, the bicentennial of the French Revolution. Métro: Bastille. (*See* The Marais and Ile St-Louis.)

Palais Bourbon. This 18th-century palace on the Left Bank, opposite place de la Concorde, is home to the French Parliament (Assemblée Nationale). Its colonnaded facade offers a superb view over the Seine. Métro: Assemblée Nationale. (*See* From Orsay to Trocadéro.)

Palais de l'Elysée. You can catch a glimpse of the French president's official residence, a sumptuous, early 18th-century mansion, from rue du Faubourg St-Honoré. Métro: Champs-Elysées–Clemenceau. (*See* From the Arc de Triomphe to the Opéra.)

Palais-Royal. Louis XIV lived in this palace, built by Cardinal Richelieu in the 1630s, before his move to Versailles. Today it houses the French Culture Ministry. Be sure to see the courtyard and the gardens. Métro: Palais-Royal. (*See* The Historic Heart.)

Panthéon. The Panthéon's huge dome, perched on the Montagne Ste-Geneviève, dominates the Sorbonne area. Built in the late 18th century, it houses the remains of many of the country's greatest men. Métro: Cardinal-Lemoine; RER: Luxembourg. (*See* The Left Bank.)

Place de la Bastille. This is the site of the infamous Bastille prison, destroyed on July 14, 1789. It's marked now by the July Column, commemorating the 1830 and 1848 uprisings. Métro: Bastille. (*See* The Marais and Ile St-Louis.)

Place de la Concorde. This huge square, built in the 1770s, was the gruesome scene of numerous deaths at the guillotine. The obelisk, in the center of the vast square, was salvaged from the ruins of the Egyptian Temple of Luxor; the viceroy of Egypt gave it to Charles X in 1829. Métro: Concorde. (*See* From the Arc de Triomphe to the Opéra.)

Place des Vosges. The oldest and most harmonious square in Paris, built by Henri IV at the beginning of the 17th century. Métro: St-Paul, Chemin-Vert. (*See* The Marais and Ile St-Louis.)

Place du Tertre. Once Montmartre's main village square, place du Tertre is best known for its artists and caricaturists. You will capture the former village atmosphere at its best in the morning; hordes of visitors and tourists transform it in the afternoon and evening. Métro: Abbesses. (*See* Montmartre.)

Place Vendôme. The most imposing square in the city was laid out by Mansart in the 17th century. Napoléon stands on the summit of the mighty central column. Métro: Opéra, Tuileries. (*See* From the Arc de Triomphe to the Opéra.)

Sorbonne. France's oldest university, founded in 1253 by Robert de Sorbon, was rebuilt and enlarged by Cardinal Richelieu in the 17th century and now forms a sprawling ensemble stretching from rue des Ecoles to rue Cujas in the heart of the Latin Quarter. Métro: Cluny-Sorbonne; RER: Luxembourg. (*See* The Left Bank.)

Théâtre National de l'Odéon (National Theater). The colonnaded Odéon theater looks out over the Luxembourg Gardens on one side and down to the busy place de l'Odéon on the other. This early 19th-century building is now the French base of the Theater of Europe. Métro: Odéon. (*See* The Left Bank.)

Museums and Galleries

Paris has a plethora of museums. Most are closed once a week, usually Monday or Tuesday. Admission prices vary. A few museums are free; most offer reductions for children, students, and senior citizens. The **Carte Musées et Monuments,** available at the main tourist office on the Champs-Elysées, is an extremely good deal, giving you access to more than 60 museums and monuments in Paris over a one-, three- or five-day period. Cost, respectively, is 60, 120, or 170 francs. Paris also boasts a wealth of art galleries, often housing temporary exhibits that aim to sell the works displayed but that the general public is welcome to visit. These galleries are too numerous for us to list; they are mainly situated in the Carré Rive Gauche on the Left Bank between St-Germain-des-Prés and the Musée d'Orsay or on the Right Bank off and along the Faubourg St-Honoré north of the Champs-Elysées. Among the most famous are **Galerie Schmit** (396 rue St-Honoré), **Galerie Malingue** (26 avenue Matignon), and **Galerie Gismondi** (20 rue Royale). **Hôtel Drouot** (9 rue Drouot), the Paris auction house east of Opéra, is a "living museum," with thousands of different objects on display each day.

Atelier de Gustave Moreau. Town house–cum–studio of Symbolist painter Gustave Moreau (1826–1898); those with a taste for the wilder shores of late-19th-century Romanticism will love it. Métro: Trinité. (*See* From the Arc de Triomphe to the Opéra.)

Atelier Delacroix. The small and carefully preserved studio of Romantic painter Eugène Delacroix is delightfully located on the quiet and leafy rue Fürstemberg. Métro: St-Germain-des-Prés. (*See* The Left Bank.)

Centre National de la Photographie. Rotating photography exhibits. *11 rue Berryer (Métro: George V). Admission: 30 frs adults, 15 frs students and children. Open Wed.–Mon. noon–7.*

Cité des Sciences et de l'Industrie de la Villette. Children adore this extensive and imaginatively laid out museum; it's very much a hands-on experience. Métro: Porte de la Villette. (*See* On the Fringe.)

Espace Dali. Dozens of Dali paintings and sculptures housed in a surrealistic atmosphere. Métro: Lamarck-Caulaincourt. (*See* Montmartre.)

Grand Palais. What was intended as no more than a temporary exhibit space back in the early years of the century has become a permanent part of the art scene in Paris; it houses major exhibits. Métro: Champs-Elysées–Clemenceau. (*See* From the Arc de Triomphe to the Opéra.)

Institut du Monde Arabe. A new addition to the Left Bank, opposite the east end of Ile St-Louis, it does for Arab culture what the Beaubourg does for modern art. Métro: Cardinal-Lemoine, Jussieu. (*See* The Left Bank.)

Maison de Balzac. This was the Paris home of France's great 19th-century novelist. It contains a wide range of exhibits charting his tempestuous life. *47 rue Raynouard (Métro: La Muette). Admission: 17 frs adults, 9 frs students and senior citizens. Open Tues.–Sun. 10–5:40.*

Maison de la Vigne et du Vin de France. The central headquarters of the French wine industry is a useful source of information about wine regions. Bottles and maps are on display. Métro: Franklin-Roosevelt. (*See* From the Arc de Triomphe to the Opéra.)

Maison de Victor Hugo. The elegant Paris home of prolific 19th-century French author Victor Hugo is filled with mementos of his varied life. Métro: St-Paul. (*See* The Marais and Ile St-Louis.)

Les Martyres de Paris. A one-of-a-kind museum of horror that showcases the history of torture and suffering in Paris. Complete with wax figures and amplified screams and moans. *Nouveau Forum des Halles, Porte du Louvre. (Métro: Châtelet/Les Halles.) Admission: 40 frs adults, 29 frs children. Open daily 10:30–6:30.*

Musée Bourdelle. Antoine Bourdelle (1861–1929) was a French artist whose sculpture reveals the influence of Auguste Rodin, with whom he worked. Bourdelle's bust of Rodin is here, along with other works displayed in Bourdelle's house, garden, and studio. There is a notable series of portraits of Beethoven. *16 rue Antoine-Bourdelle (Métro: Falguière). Admission: 25 frs adults, 18 frs children and students. Open Tues.–Sun. 10–5:30.*

Musée Bricard/Musée de la Serrure. The art of locks and lockmakers down the years. Métro: St-Paul. (*See* The Marais and Ile St-Louis.)

Musée Carnavalet. Maps, plans, furniture, and portraits reveal the history of Paris. Métro: St-Paul. (*See* The Marais and Ile St-Louis.)

Musée Cognacq-Jay. This lavish, 18th-century town house is home to one of the finest small collections of art and artifacts in the city. Métro: St-Paul. (*See* The Marais and Ile St-Louis.)

Musée Dapper. Pre-colonial African art is beautifully displayed in a tranquil four-story hôtel particulier. *50 av. Victor Hugo (Métro: Victor Hugo). Admission: 15 fr adults, 7 fr children; free Wed. Open daily 11–7.*

Musée d'Art Juif. Paris's small Jewish museum contains devotional items, synagogue models, and a few works by Pissarro and Chagall. Métro: Lamarck-Caulaincourt. (*See* Montmartre.)

Musée d'Art Moderne de la Ville de Paris. A collection of 20th-century pictures and sculpture. Métro: Iéna. (*See* From Orsay to Trocadéro.)

Musée National du Moyen-Age (formerly the **Musée de Cluny**). The atmospheric medieval former headquarters of the abbots of Cluny is now one of the most fascinating museums in the city, filled with Roman and medieval works of art. Métro: Cluny–Sorbonne. *(See* The Left Bank.)

Musée de la Chasse et de la Nature. A collection of paintings, guns, and traps. Métro: Rambuteau. *(See* The Marais and Ile St-Louis.)

Musée de la Curiosité. Housed in a 16-century cellar in the Marais section of Paris, this new museum contains antique magic paraphernalia, including some of Houdini's old toys. Magic show every hour. *11 rue St-Paul (Métro: St-Paul). Admission: 45 frs adults, 30 frs children. Open Wed., Sat., and Sun., 2–7.*

Musée de la Femme et Collection d'Automates. A curious mixture of feminine artifacts and automata. The clockwork collection bursts into life every afternoon at 3 (guided tours only). *12 rue du Centre, Neuilly (Métro: Pont de Neuilly). Admission: 12 frs adults, 6 frs children and senior citizens. Open Wed.–Mon. 2:30–5.*

Musée de la Holographie. The Museum of Holography has a suitably modern setting in the Forum des Halles. *15 Grand Balcon, Forum des Halles (Métro/RER: Les Halles). Admission: 32 frs adults, 26 frs students and senior citizens. Open Mon.–Sat. 10–7, Sun. 1–7.*

Musée de la Légion d'Honneur. The headquarters of the most prestigious civilian awards in France. Métro: Solférino; RER: Musée d'Orsay. *(See* From Orsay to Trocadéro.)

Musée de la Marine. Those with salt in their veins will not want to miss this extensive maritime museum in the Palais de Chaillot. Métro: Trocadéro. *(See* From Orsay to Trocadéro.)

Musée de la Musique Mécanique. A pleasantly rustic museum, stuck down a dead end near the Pompidou Center, featuring mechanical musical instruments (hourly tours with working demonstrations). *Impasse Berthaud (Métro: Rambuteau). Admission: 30 frs adults, 20 frs children under 12. Open weekends 2–7.*

Musée de la Poste. This museum of postal history, spread over five floors, includes displays of international and French stamps (since 1849), postmen's uniforms and postboxes, sorting and stamp-printing machines, and the balloon used to send mail out of Paris during the Prussian siege of 1870. *34 blvd. de Vaugirard (Métro: Falguière). Admission: 25 frs adults, 12.50 frs students and senior citizens, children under 6 free. Open Mon.–Sat. 10–6.*

Musée de la Vie Romantique. Now a museum devoted to a collection of documents, artwork, and household possessions which formerly belonged to mid–19th-century novelist George Sand, this house was for years the site of Friday evening *salons* hosted by painter Ary Schiffer and including the likes of Ingres, Delacroix, Turgenev, Chopin, and Sand. Literary buffs will appreciate the myriad of objects collected from Sand's house at Nohant, including portraits, furniture, and her cigarette box. *16 rue Chaptal (Métro: St-George, Place Blanche). Admission: 35 frs adults, 25 frs under 18. Open Tues.–Sun. 10–5:40.*

Musée de l'Armée. The glorious and sometimes not-so-glorious history of the French army is traced in this imposing museum in Les Invalides. Métro: Latour-Maubourg, Varenne. (*See* From Orsay to Trocadéro.)

Musée de l'Art Africain et des Arts Océaniques. Artifacts from Africa and the South Seas are intriguingly displayed in this sizable museum. Métro: Porte-Dorée. (*See* On the Fringe.)

Musée de l'Art Naïf Max Fourny. Varied exhibitions of the "Naïf" painters (including Maria Kloss, M. Rolly, and J. Guerra), whose innovative use of bright colors and imaginative themes can be traced to the French Dadaists. *2 rue Ronsard (Métro: Anvers). Admission: 22 frs adults, 16 frs students and senior citizens. Open Tues.– Sat. 10–10, Sun. and Mon. 10–6.*

Musée de l'Histoire de France. It contains everything from Marie Antoinette's last letter to the Edict of Nantes to the sumptuous apartments of 18th-century French aristocrats. The museum includes the **Archives Nationales,** with thousands of documents charting French history back to the 10th century. (*See* The Marais and Ile St-Louis.)

Musée de l'Homme. This is the city's principal anthropological museum, housed in the Palais de Chaillot. Métro: Trocadéro. (*See* From Orsay to Trocadéro.)

Musée de l'Opéra. The Opéra museum contains paintings and operatic mementos of the lavish Paris opera house. Métro: Opéra. (*See* From the Arc de Triomphe to the Opéra.)

Musée de l'Orangerie. Twentieth-century French paintings are housed in this elegant neoclassical pavilion at the west end of the Tuileries Gardens. Métro: Concorde. (*See* From the Arc de Triomphe to the Opéra.)

Musée de l'Ordre de la Libération. The Order of Liberation was created by General de Gaulle after the fall of France in 1940 to honor those who made outstanding contributions to the Allied victory in World War II. (Churchill and Eisenhower figure among the rare foreign recipients.) Some 200 display cabinets evoke various episodes of the war: De Gaulle's Free France organization, the Resistance, the Deportation, and the 1944 Liberation. *51 bis blvd. de Latour-Maubourg (Métro: Latour-Maubourg). Admission: 10 frs. Open Mon.–Sat. 2–5.*

Musée des Arts Décoratifs. French decorative arts down the centuries are covered in this quiet museum in the Louvre complex. Métro: Palais-Royal. (*See* The Historic Heart.)

Musée des Arts et Traditions Populaires. Preindustrial objects from all the regions of France. Métro: Les Sablons. (*See* On the Fringe.)

Musée des Monuments Français. If you have any interest in French medieval architecture, make a point of seeing this excellent museum; it's one of the most imaginative and instructive in the city. Métro: Trocadéro. (*See* From Orsay to Trocadéro.)

Musée des Plans-Reliefs. Plans and models of French-fortified towns and cities in the 17th century make for a museum that is substantially more interesting than many visitors realize. It's located in the Hôtel des Invalides. Métro: Latour-Maubourg, Varenne. (*See* From Orsay to Trocadéro.)

Musée d'Orsay. One of the Big Three museums in Paris, rivaling the Louvre and the Beaubourg (Pompidou Center) for the extent of its collection. It covers art in France from 1848 to 1914. For many, the Impressionists are the major draw. Métro: Solférino; RER: Musée d'Orsay. (*See* From Orsay to Trocadéro.)

Musée du Cinéma. This is one of a number of museums near Trocadéro at the Palais de Chaillot; it charts the history of movies in colorful and vibrant detail. Métro: Trocadéro. (*See* From Orsay to Trocadéro.)

Musée du Jeu de Paume. The former home of the Impressionists reopened in 1991 with a redesigned, shiny white interior featuring temporary exhibits of brash contemporary art. Métro: Concord. (*See* From the Arc de Triomphe to the Opéra.)

Musée du Louvre. This is the world's biggest museum, legendary home of the *Mona Lisa*. Recent renovations—from the 1989 inauguration of I. M. Pei's controversial pyramids to the recent reopening of the Richelieu wing, Coeur Carrée, and the creation of an under-

So, you're getting away from it all.

Just make sure you can get back.

AT&T Access Numbers
Dial the number of the country you're in to reach AT&T.

*AUSTRIA††	022-903-011	*GREECE	00-800-1311	NORWAY	800-190-11
*BELGIUM	078-11-0010	*HUNGARY	00◇-800-01111	POLAND†◆2	0◇010-480-0111
BULGARIA	00-1800-0010	*ICELAND	999-001	PORTUGAL†	05017-1-288
CANADA	1-800-575-2222	IRELAND	1-800-550-000	ROMANIA	01-800-4288
CROATIA†◆	99-38-0011	ISRAEL	177-100-2727	*RUSSIA† (MOSCOW)	155-5042
*CYPRUS	080-90010	*ITALY	172-1011	SLOVAKIA	00-420-00101
CZECH REPUBLIC	00-420-00101	KENYA†	0800-10	S. AFRICA	0-800-99-0123
*DENMARK	8001-0010	*LIECHTENSTEIN	155-00-11	SPAIN•	900-99-00-11
*EGYPT† (CAIRO)	510-0200	LITHUANIA◆	8◇196	*SWEDEN	020-795-611
*FINLAND	9800-100-10	LUXEMBOURG	0-800-0111	*SWITZERLAND	155-00-11
FRANCE	19◇-0011	F.Y.R. MACEDONIA	99-800-4288	*TURKEY	00-800-12277
*GAMBIA	00111	*MALTA	0800-890-110	UKRAINE†	8◇100-11
GERMANY	0130-0010	*NETHERLANDS	06-022-9111	UK	0500-89-0011

Countries in bold face permit country-to-country calling in addition to calls to the U.S. **World Connect**℠ prices consist of **USADirect**® rates plus an additional charge based on the country you are calling. Collect calling available to the U.S. only. *Public phones require deposit of coin or phone card. ◇Await second dial tone. †May not be available from every phone. ††Public phones require local coin payment through the call duration. ◆Not available from public phones. • Calling available to most European countries. ¹Dial "02" first, outside Cairo. ²Dial 010-480-0111 from major Warsaw hotels. ©1994 AT&T.

Here's a travel tip that will make it easy to call back to the States. Dial the access number for the country you're visiting and connect right to AT&T. It's the quick way to get English-speaking AT&T operators and can minimize hotel telephone surcharges.

If all the countries you're visiting aren't listed above, call **1 800 241-5555** for a free wallet card with all AT&T access numbers. Easy international calling from AT&T. **TrueWorld Connections.**

AT&T

American Express offers Travelers Cheques built for two.

Cheques *for Two*ˢᴹ from American Express are the Travelers Cheques that allow either of you to use them because both of you have signed them. And only one of you needs to be present to purchase them.

Cheques *for Two* are accepted anywhere regular American Express Travelers Cheques are, which is just about everywhere. So stop by your bank, AAA* or any American Express Travel Service Office and ask for Cheques *for Two*.

ground shopping center-cum-parking lot—make the museum a must see. Métro: Palais-Royal. *(See* The Historic Heart.)

Musee du Parfum. Fragonard, the legendary French perfume manufacturer, has created a museum which demonstrates the traditional process of perfume distillation using miniature machinery. Fragonard products are sold at factory prices. Métro: Opéra. *(See* From the Arc de Triomphe to the Opéra).

Musée du Rock. A multimedia rock 'n' roll hall of fame, with wax figures depicting everyone from Buddy Holly to Madonna. *Nouveau Forum des Halles. Porte du Louvre (Métro: Châtelet-Les-Halles). Admission: 43 frs adults, 32 frs students and children. Open daily 10:30–6:30.*

Musée du Sport. A sports museum housed at the French national stadium in southwest Paris, featuring posters, trophies, equipment, and other sporting paraphernalia. *Parc des Princes, 24 rue du Commandant-Guilbaud (Métro: Porte de St-Cloud). Admission: 20 frs adults, 10 frs children and senior citizens. Open Sun.–Tues., Thurs., and Fri. 9:30–12:30 and 2–5.*

Musée du Vieux Montmartre. The history of rowdy and picturesque Montmartre is traced in this likable little museum. Métro: Lamarck-Caulaincourt. *(See* Montmartre.)

Musée du Vin (Wine Museum). This museum is pretty, petite, and a gourmet's treat. Devoted to the vine and traditional wine-making artifacts, it is housed in the cellars of a former 13th-century abbey. The premises double as a medieval wine bar: A selection of wines is served by the glass, along with excellent cheese and meat platters. *Caveau des Échansons, rue des Eaux (Métro: Passy). Admission and wine-tasting: 26 frs. Open daily noon–6.*

Musée Grévin. This waxworks museum, founded in 1882, ranks with London's Madame Tussaud's. Dozens of wax renderings of historical and contemporary celebrities are on display. *10 blvd. Montmartre (Métro: Rue Montmartre). Admission: 48 frs adults, 34 frs children under 14. Open daily 1–7, during school holidays 10–7.*

Musée Guimet. Indo-Chinese and Far Eastern art are housed in this elegant museum. Métro: Iéna. *(See* From Orsay to Trocadéro.)

Musée Jacquemart-André. A sumptuous, 19th-century town house is the setting for this little-known museum that contains a rich collection of Renaissance and 18th-century art. Métro: St-Phillipe-du-Roule. *(See* From the Arc de Triomphe to the Opéra.)

Musée Marmottan. Paris's "other" Impressionist museum (after the Musée d'Orsay) is beautifully situated in a 19th-century mansion on the edge of the Bois de Boulogne. The Marmottan boasts a collection of more than 100 works by Claude Monet (including *Impression-Sunrise*, from which the term "Impressionist" derives). There are also fine Impressionist works by other artists like Pissarro, Renoir, and Sisley. The first and second floors boast some magnificent medieval illuminated manuscripts and the original furnishings of a sumptuous early 19th-century Empire mansion. Marmottan is one of the most underestimated museums in Paris. *2 rue Louis-Boilly (Métro: La Muette). Admission: 35 frs adults, 15 frs children and senior citizens. Open Tues.–Sun. 10–5:30.*

Musée National d'Art Moderne. The largest collection of modern art in the world is housed in the brash and vibrant **Beaubourg.** Métro: Rambuteau. *(See* The Marais and Ile St-Louis.)

Musée National de la Céramique, in St-Cloud park, displays hundreds of Sèvres porcelain creations, together with the manufacturing premises. *Pl. de la Manufacture, Sèvres (Métro: Pont de Sevres). Admission: 23 frs, 15 frs on Sun. Open Wed.–Mon. 10–5:15.*

Musée National des Techniques. The former church and priory of St-

Martin des Champs were confiscated during the Revolution and used first as an educational institution, then as an arms factory before becoming, in 1799, the Conservatoire des Arts et Métiers. Today, the 11th- to 13th-century church, with its fine belfry and skillfully restored east end, forms part of the Musée National des Techniques, an industrial museum with a varied collection of models (locomotives, vehicles, and agricultural machinery), astronomical instruments, looms, and glass, together with displays on printing, photography, and the history of television. The splendid 13th-century refectory, a large hall supported by central columns, is now used as a library. *270 rue St-Martin (Métro: Arts et Métiers). Admission: 20 frs, 10 frs on Sun. Open Tues.–Sun. 10–5:15.*

Musée Notre Dame. A small museum charting the turbulent history of the most venerable building in Paris. Métro: Cité. *(See* The Historic Heart.)

Musée Picasso. The elegant Hôtel Salé provides the setting for the largest collection of Picassos in existence. Métro: St-Sébastien. *(See* The Marais and Ile St-Louis.)

Musée Rodin. This is probably the best single-artist museum in Paris. An elegant town house is filled with sculptures, plans, and drawings by the prolific 19th-century sculptor. Métro: Varenne. *(See* From Orsay to Trocadéro.)

Musée Zadkine. Russian-born sculptor Ossip Zadkine (1890–1967) trained in London before setting up in Paris in 1909. The works on exhibit here, in Zadkine's former house and studio, reveal the influences of Rodin, African art, and Cubism. *100 bis rue d'Assas (Métro: Vavin). Admission: 17 frs adults, 9 frs students and senior citizens, Sun. free. Open Tues.–Sun. 10–5:40.*

Nouveau Musée Grévin (Les Halles). This branch of the Musée Grévin *(see above)* is situated in the Forum des Halles and boasts waxwork scenes from Belle Epoque Paris. *Grand Balcon, Forum des Halles (Métro/RER: Les Halles). Admission: 42 frs adults, 32 frs children under 14. Open Mon.–Sat. 10:30–7:30, Sun. 1–7.*

Palais de la Découverte. Substantial science museum, complete with planetarium, adjoining the Grand Palais. Métro: Champs-Elysées–Clemenceau. *(See* From the Arc de Triomphe to the Opéra.)

Petit Palais. This is the smaller twin of the Grand Palais *(see above)*, housing a collection of 19th-century French paintings and furniture. Métro: Champs-Elysées–Clemenceau. *(See* From the Arc de Triomphe to the Opéra.)

Churches

Paris boasts numerous historic churches. Those of outstanding interest are detailed in the Exploring sections above and are also listed here, along with some others that are well worth a visit if you are in the neighborhood. Most are open 9–noon and 2–5, but there are no set hours. Some stage daily services at lunchtime. Quiet and appropriate dress are expected.

Paris is rich in churches of two architectural styles: late Gothic (the Flamboyant style of the 14th and 15th centuries, with its intricate stone tracery) and 17th-century Baroque (columns, rounded arches, and smaller windows inspired by classical antiquity and the Italian Renaissance). Another feature is the phenomenal number of wall paintings, to be found mainly in side chapels and dating, for the most part, from the first half of the 19th century.

American Cathedral of the Holy Trinity. A neo-Gothic structure built between 1885 and 1888. Métro: Alma-Marceau. *(See* From the Arc de Triomphe to the Opéra.)

American Church in Paris. Another neo-Gothic church, this one built rather later (1927–1931), on the Left Bank. *65 quai d'Orsay (Métro: Alma-Marceau), tel. 47–05–07–99.*

Basilique de St-Denis. Built between 1136 and 1286, this is in some ways the most important Gothic church in the Paris region, the first in which the guiding principles of Gothic architecture were fully developed. Today, it's in a seedy northern suburb. Métro: St-Denis–Basilique. *(See* On the Fringe.)

Basilique du Sacré-Coeur. A major and highly visible landmark, Sacré-Coeur contains golden mosaics and provides sweeping views of Paris. Métro: Anvers. *(See* Montmartre.)

Cathédrale Notre Dame. If you visit only one church in Paris, it should be Notre Dame, the most historic and dominant church in the city. Métro: Cité. *(See* The Historic Heart.)

Eglise de la Madeleine. The stern neoclassical exterior of the Madeleine belies the richly harmonious, if dimly lit, interior. Métro: Madeleine. *(See* From the Arc de Triomphe to the Opéra.)

Eglise du Dôme. Under the dome of this magnificently commanding Baroque church, part of Les Invalides, Napoléon rests in imperial splendor. Métro: St-François-Xavier. *(See* From Orsay to Trocadéro.)

Eglise St-Louis des Invalides. The Baroque church at Les Invalides. Métro: Latour-Maubourg. *(See* From Orsay to Trocadéro.)

Mosquée de Paris. Not far from the Jardin des Plantes, you can plunge into a Moslem atmosphere beneath the arcades and minaret of an authentic mosque (built 1922–1925) decorated in the style of Moorish Spain. *Pl. du Puits de l'Ermite (Métro: Monge). Open Sat.–Thurs. 9–noon and 2–5.* (*See* The Left Bank.)

Notre-Dame de l'Assomption. This 1670 church, with its huge dome and solemn interior, was the scene of Lafayette's funeral in 1834. It is now used as the chapel of the Polish community. *Rue Cambon (Métro: Concorde).*

Notre-Dame des Blancs Manteaux. The Blancs Manteaux were white-robed 13th-century mendicant monks, whose monastery once stood on this spot. For the last 100 years, this late 17th-century church has boasted an imposing 18th-century facade that belonged to a now-destroyed church on the Ile de la Cité. Unfortunately, the narrow streets of the Marais leave little room to step back and admire it. The inside boasts some fine woodwork and a Flemish-style Rococo pulpit whose marquetry panels are inlaid with pewter and ivory. *Rue des Blancs-Manteaux (Métro: Rambuteau).*

Notre-Dame de Bonne Nouvelle. This wide, soberly neoclassical church is tucked away off the Grands Boulevards near Strasbourg-St-Denis. The church is unusual in that it faces north-south instead of east-west. The previous church on the spot (the second) was ransacked during the Revolution, and the current one, built 1823–1829 after the restoration of the French monarchy, was ransacked by Communard hooligans in May 1871. The highlight of the interior is the semicircular apse behind the altar, featuring some fine 17th-century paintings beneath a three-dimensional, 19th-century grisaille composition by Abel de Pujol. A wide variety of pictures, statues, and works of religious art can be found in the side chapels and in the church museum (ask at the sacristy to the left of the altar). *Rue de la Lune (Métro: Bonne-Nouvelle).*

Notre-Dame de Lorette. This little-known church below Montmartre was built from 1823 to 1836 in the neoclassical style popular at the time. Of principal interest is the vast array of religious wall paintings; they are of varying quality but have been successfully restored. *Rue de Châteaudun (Métro: Notre-Dame-de-Lorette).*

Notre-Dame des Victoires. You'll want to visit this 17th-century church, built from 1666 to 1740, to see the 30,000 ex voto tablets that adorn its walls. *Place des Petits-Pères (Métro: Sentier, Bourse)*.

St-Alexandre Nevsky. The onion domes of the Russian Orthodox cathedral of Paris are among the city's most distinctive landmarks. Métro: Courcelles. *(See* From the Arc de Triomphe to the Opéra.)

Sainte-Chapelle. Built by Louis IX (1226–1270) to house what he believed to be the Crown of Thorns from Christ's crucifixion and fragments of the True Cross, the Ste-Chapelle is one of the supreme architectural achievements of the Middle Ages. Metro: Cité. *(See* The Historic Heart.)

Ste-Clotilde. This neo-Gothic church (1846–1858) is chiefly of note for its imposing twin towers, visible from across the Seine. French classical composer César Franck was the organist here from 1858 to 1890. *Rue Las-Cases (Métro: Solférino)*.

Ste-Croix-St-Jean. This much-restored church, erected in 1624, is now used as the Armenian Cathedral of Paris. Its chancel contains some splendid 18th-century gilded paneling. The exterior underwent extensive cleaning and restoration in 1988. *Rue du Perche (Métro: Rambuteau)*.

St-Denis du St-Sacrement. This severely neoclassical edifice (close to the Picasso Museum in the Marais) dates from the 1830s. It is a formidable example of architectural discipline, oozing restraint and monumental dignity (or banality, according to taste). The grisaille frieze and gilt fresco above the semicircular apse have clout if not subtlety; the Delacroix *Deposition* (1844), in the front right-hand chapel as you enter, has both. *Rue de Turenne (Métro: St-Sébastien)*.

Ste-Elisabeth. This studied essay (1628–1646) in Baroque has a pleasantly unpretentious feel to it; there's no soaring bombast here. There are brightly restored wall paintings and a wide, semicircular apse around the choir, with stupendous carved 17th-century wood paneling featuring biblical scenes (transferred from an abbey at Arras in northern France). *Rue du Temple (Métro: Temple)*.

St-Etienne du Mont. This church (1492–1632) in the shadow of the Panthéon has two major claims to fame: its mishmash facade and its curly, carved rood screen (1525–1535), separating nave and chancel, the only one of its kind in Paris. Métro: Cardinal Lemoine. *(See* The Left Bank.)

St-Eustache. The "Cathedral of the Right Bank" was built between 1532 and 1637 and offers a considerable contrast to the brash modernity of the neighboring Forum des Halles. Métro or RER: Les Halles. *(See* The Historic Heart.)

St-Germain-des-Prés. Graceful St-Germain-des-Prés, in the heart of the Left Bank, is the oldest church in the city; its classical facade disguises its late-Romanesque interior. Métro: St-Germain-des-Prés. *(See* The Left Bank.)

St-Germain l'Auxerrois. Built from the 13th to the 16th centuries, this rich, late-Gothic church opposite the east end of the Louvre was once the royal church in Paris. Métro: Louvre. *(See* The Historic Heart.)

St-Gervais-St-Protais. Built from 1494 to 1657, this church stands on the site of what was the oldest church in the city. Métro: Hôtel de Ville. *(See* The Marais and Ile St-Louis.)

St-Jean l'Evangéliste. Church of St-Jean is an innovative 1904 essay in concrete, which has since been clad in reassuring red brick. Métro: Abbesses. *(See* Montmartre.)

St-Louis-en-l'Ile. Built from 1664 to 1726, this is the only church on the Ile St-Louis. *(Métro: Pont-Marie.)*

St-Louis de la Salpêtrière. This is the church of the Salpêtrière Hospital next to the Gare d'Austerlitz, an unmistakable sight with its lantern-topped octagonal dome. The church, built 1670–1677 according to the designs of Libéral Bruant, is shaped like a Greek cross. *Blvd. de l'Hôpital (Métro: Gare d'Austerlitz).*

St-Médard. The nave and facade, with its large late-Gothic window, date from the late 15th century. The 17th-century choir is in the contrasting classical style. A picturesque churchyard lines rue Censier. *Square St-Médard (Métro: Censier-Daubenton).*

St-Nicolas des Champs. Here's another Parisian example of Gothic colliding with Renaissance: The round-arched, fluted Doric capitals in the chancel date from 1560 to 1587, a full century later than the pointed-arched nave (1420–1480). There is a majestic mid-17th-century organ and a fine *Assumption of the Virgin* (1629) above the high altar by Simon Vouet. The south door (1576) in rue au Maire is gloriously carved and surrounded by a small but unexpectedly well-tended lawn complete with rosebushes. *Rue St-Martin (Métro: Arts et Métiers).*

St-Nicolas du Chardonnet. The first church on the site was apparently built in a field of thistles *(chardons* in French), and over recent years, St-Nicolas has been a thorn in the side of the Catholic Church by refusing to abandon Latin mass. Stubborn priests are not, however, the most visible attraction of this pleasant Baroque edifice (1656–1709) on the bustling Left Bank. There is a Corot study for the *Baptism of Christ* in the first chapel on the right and a *Crucifixion* by Brueghel the Younger in the sacristy. *Rue St-Victor (Métro: Maubert-Mutualité).*

Ste-Odile. The colossal, dark-brick tower of this modern church (built 1938–1946) surges into the northern Paris skyline like a stumpy rocket, reminiscent of something out of Soviet Russia. The inside, however, smacks more of Scandinavian architecture, with its harmony, simple lines, and decorative restraint. *Av. Stéphane-Mallarmé (Métro: Porte de Champerret).*

St-Pierre de Montmartre. Much-restored little church dating from the 12th century and now overshadowed by Sacré-Coeur. Métro: Anvers. (*See* Montmartre.)

St-Roch. A dynamically Baroque church, built between 1635 and 1740, in the swanky heart of the Right Bank. Métro: Tuileries. (*See* The Historic Heart.)

St-Sulpice. Built from 1646 to 1780, this is the "Cathedral of the Left Bank." Métro: St-Sulpice. (*See* The Left Bank.)

St-Vincent de Paul. With its pair of square towers, this early 19th-century church (1824–1844) stands out in the midst of the undistinguished streets surrounding the Gare du Nord. The facade is lent drama by a pedimented portico and the majestic flight of steps leading up from a cheerful square. Inside, the outstanding feature is the glittering gold fresco high up the nave walls by Hippolyte Flandrin, depicting an endless procession of religious figures. *Place Franz-Liszt (Métro: Poissonnière).*

Temple de l'Oratoire. Built from 1616 to 1630 by Le Mercier as mother church for the Carmelite Congregation of the Oratory, although the Jesuit-style facade dates from the 18th century and the main portal from 1845. During the Revolution, the church became an arms depot, a storehouse, and then, from 1811, a Protestant church. *Rue de l'Oratoire (Métro: Louvre).*

Temple Ste-Marie. This building, constructed 1632–1634 by François Mansart as the chapel of the Convent of the Visitation, is now a Protestant church. The dome above the distinctive nave rotunda is one of the earliest in Paris and is said to have influenced Christopher Wren when planning St. Paul's Cathedral in London. *Rue St-Antoine (Métro: Bastille).*

Parks and Gardens

Bois de Boulogne. These 2,200 acres of woodland and lakes on Paris's western outskirts are crisscrossed by broad, leafy roads and include a children's amusement park. Métros: Porte Dauphine (east), Les Sablons (north), and Porte d'Auteuil (south). *(See* On the Fringe.)

Bois de Vincennes. Another vast area of woodland, on the southeast outskirts of Paris, with a sprawling castle, a zoo, and a floral park. Métro: Château de Vincennes (north), Porte Dorée (south). *(See* On the Fringe.)

Buttes-Chaumont. In the 1860s Haussmann transformed this former steep-sloped quarry into an immensely picturesque park with lake, waterfalls, and oft-painted belvedere—and a charming restaurant. Métro: Buttes-Chaumont, Botzaris. (*See* Off the Beaten Track.)

Champ de Mars. This long, formal garden, landscaped at the start of the century, lies between the Eiffel Tower and Ecole Militaire. It was previously used as a parade ground and site of the World Exhibitions of 1867, 1889 (date of the construction of the Eiffel Tower), and 1900. Métro: Bir-Hakeim; RER: Champ-de-Mars. *(See* From Orsay to Trocadéro.)

Jardin Atlantique. This little tree-lined park on the platform covering the tracks at the Gare Montparnasse is a great spot to relax during layovers. Métro: Montparnasse–Bienvenue. (*See* the Left Bank.)

Jardin des Halles. This urban park near the church of St-Eustache is geared mainly for children—there's an old-fashioned carousel—but it's also a pleasant place to stroll. Watch out for rhino-shaped bushes. (*Métro and RER: Les Halles.*)

Jardin des Plantes. Paris's botanical gardens house a zoo, an alpine garden, greenhouses, an aquarium, a maze, various museums, and a *robinia* tree planted in 1636. Métro: Monge, Jussieu. *(See* The Left Bank.)

Jardin des Tuileries. Le Nôtre's masterpiece, with its understated elegance, fountains, and statues, runs from the Louvre to place de la Concorde. It's ideal for a stroll or a drink in an open-air café. Métro: Tuileries. *(See* From the Arc de Triomphe to the Opéra.)

Jardin du Luxembourg. These formal gardens are in the heart of Paris, with fountains, statues, and tree-lined alleys. They are built around the Palais du Luxembourg, home to the French Senate. Métro: Odéon, Cluny-Sorbonne; RER: Luxembourg. *(See* The Left Bank.)

Jardin du Palais-Royal. A delightful, little-known oasis bordered by arcades. Come here to see Daniel Buren's controversial black-and-white striped columns in the courtyard. Métro: Palais-Royal. *(See* The Historic Heart.)

Jardins Albert-Kahn. On the Paris side of the Seine, across from Parc de St-Cloud (*see below*), these gardens add a surprising note of oriental greenery to the undistinguished suburb of Boulogne. (*Métro: Boulogne–Pont de St-Cloud.*) *Admission: 10 frs adults, 5 frs children.*

Moorish Gardens (Mosquée de Paris). The patio and arcades under the minaret of the Paris mosque make the setting a mecca for garden and mint-tea lovers. *Pl. du Puits de l'Ermite (Métro: Monge). Tours Sat.–Thurs. 2–5; closed Fri.*

Parc Andre-Citroën. In the 15th arrondissement, this innovative park, built on the site of the former car factory, features open, grassy space, elegant greenhouses filled with exotic plants and flowers, Japanese rock gardens, and rambling wildflowers. To the delight of children there is also a computer-programmed "dancing fountain." (*Métro: Javel or Balard.*)

Parc de Bagatelle. A beautiful floral park famous for its rose gardens on the west side of Bois de Boulogne. Métro: Pont de Neuilly. *(See On the Fringe.)*

Parc de Bercy. Still being built at press time, this park is at the heart of a *tour de force* of urban renewal in the 12th arrondissement, which includes the Omnisports de Bercy and the Ministry of Finance, as well as the new Frank Gehry American Center, a Food and Wine business complex, and new housing and business space in the neighborhood. Métro: Bercy. *(See Off the Beaten Track.)*

Parc Monceau. An 18th-century park in the chic 17th arrondissement, with lake, rotunda, and mock ruins. Métro: Monceau. *(See From the Arc de Triomphe to the Opéra.)*

Parc Montsouris. Very pretty, English-style gardens in the south of the city, with cascades, a lake, and a meteorological observatory disguised as a Tunisian Palace. *(Métro: Glacière; RER: Cité Universitaire.)*

Parc de St-Cloud. This tumbling, wooded park on a hill to the southwest of Paris offers some superb views of the city. *(Métro: Boulogne–Pont de St-Cloud.)*

Parc de la Villette. A vast new park now surrounds the glimmering science-and-industry museum complex, with a children's play area, the Inventorium. It's a pleasant place for a stroll near the Canal de l'Ourcq, in the once-unfashionable 19th arrondissement in the northeast of Paris. Métro: Porte de Pantin, Porte de la Villette. *(See On the Fringe.)*

Serres d'Auteuil. A bewildering variety of plants and flowers are grown in these greenhouses for use in Paris's municipal parks and in displays at official occasions. Tropical and exotic plants sweat it out in the mighty hothouses, while the surrounding gardens' leafy paths and well-tended lawns offer cooler places to admire floral virtuosity. *3 av. de la Porte d'Auteuil (Métro: Porte d'Auteuil). Admission: 5 frs. Open daily 10–5:30.*

Cemeteries

This is not such a macabre listing as it sounds. The cemeteries of Paris are remarkable for their statues, elaborate monuments, tombs of the famous, and melancholy disrepair. They are usually open from 7:30 to 6 in summer and from 8 to 5:30 in winter.

Cimetière de Montmartre. Situated on the west side of the Montmartre hill, this cemetery, built in 1795, houses the tombs of the writer Stendhal, the composer Berlioz, the painter Degas, and the famous French film director François Truffaut. Métro: Place de Clichy. *(See Montmartre.)*

Cimetière de Montparnasse. High walls encircle the Montparnasse cemetery, a haven of peace in one of Paris's busiest shopping and business areas. You can visit the tombs of Jean-Paul Sartre, Baudelaire, Bartholdi—who designed the Statue of Liberty—and André Citroën. Métro: Raspail, Edgar Quinet. *(See The Left Bank.)*

Cimitière de Picpus. This convent cemetery marks the spot where thousands were guillotined in 1794. The grave of General Lafayette is also here. Métro: Nation, Picpus. *(See Off the Beaten Track.)*

Cimetière du Père Lachaise. This cemetery—the largest in Paris— is also the most attractive. Métro: Gambetta, Père Lachaise. *(See On the Fringe.)*

What to See and Do with Children

Aquariums A spell of fish-gazing is a soothing, mesmerizing experience for young and old alike. There are two principal aquariums in Paris, plus the exciting marine center dreamt up by the famous ocean explorer Jacques Cousteau.

Aquarium Tropical, *293 av. Daumesnil, 12e. Admission: 25 frs, 15 frs on Sun. Open Wed.–Mon. 10–noon and 1:30–5:30. Métro: Porte Dorée.*
Centre de la Mer et des Eaux, *195 rue St-Jacques, 5e. Admission: 25 frs adults, 15 frs children. Open Tues.–Fri. 10–12:30 and 1:15–5:30, weekends 10–5:30. RER: Luxembourg.*

Boating Rowboats can be rented at the **Lac Inférieur** in the Bois de Boulogne and at **Lac des Minimes** and **Lac Daumesnil** in the Bois de Vincennes.

Boat Trips An hour on the Seine on a Bateau Mouche or Vedette is good fun and a great way to get to know the capital. The cost is 30–40 francs for adults, 15–20 francs for children under 10. Departures every half-hour from:

Eiffel Tower, *7e. Métro: Bir-Hakeim.*
Pont de l'Alma, *8e. Métro: Alma-Marceau.*
Square du Vert Galant, *1er. Métro: Pont-Neuf.*

Circus There's no need to know French to enjoy a circus. Tickets range from 40 to 180 francs. There are evening and weekend matinee performances. Check for details with:

Cirque de Paris, *corner of av. Hoche and Commune de Paris, Nanterre, tel. 47–24–11–70. RER: Nanterre Ville.*
Cirque d'Hiver, *110 rue Amelot, 11e, tel. 47–00–12–25. Métro: Filles-du-Calvaire.*
Cirque Grüss, *21 av. de la Porte de Chatillon, 14e, tel. 45–41–48–63. Metro: Porte d'Orléans.*
Cirque Moreno, *Square Réjane, 20e, tel. 43–56–00–61. Métro: Nation, Porte de Vincennes.*
Cité des Sciences et de l'Industrie de la Villette. This futuristic museum housed in the Parc de la Villette includes a science and industry museum, planetarium, curved screen "Geode" cinema, and a children's play area. *Metro: Porte de la Villette. (See* On the Fringe.*)*

Eiffel Tower Climb, and then ride the elevator to the top level of the Eiffel Tower for a breathtaking view of Paris and beyond.

Fairs Twice a year—usually during August and Christmas—the rue de Rivoli side of the **Tuileries Gardens** is transformed into a *foire* or fairgrounds, complete with rides, shooting galleries and a huge ferris wheel that affords a spectacular view of the heart of Paris *(Métro: Tuileries).*

The **Foire du Trône,** every spring in the Bois de Vincennes *(Métro: Porte Dorée),* is a big event that goes until the wee hours. Consult the weekly *Pariscope* for details.

Ice Cream An ice cream is an ice cream, but the city's best (with a choice of some 30 flavors) is sold at **Berthillon's** on the Ile St-Louis. *31 rue St-Louis-en-l'Ile, 4e; closed Mon. and Tues. Métro: Pont-Marie.*

Ice Skating Every winter from December to March, weather permitting, a small skating rink is erected on the Rivoli side of the Tuileries Gardens. *Admission: 35 frs (including rental). Open 10–10.*

Another rink is near the Buttes-Chamont park to the northeast. *30 rue Edouard-Pailleron, 19e, tel. 42–08–72–26. Admission: 25 frs adults, 20 frs children under 16 (skate hire 15 frs). Open weekdays 3–9, Sat. 10–5 and 8:30–midnight, Sun. 10–6. Métro: Bolivar.* A short RER ride away, Euro Disney's Hotel New York has an outdoor skating rink complete with skating Disney characters (ticket to the park not necessary). *Euro Disneyland, Marne-la-Vallée, tel. 60–45–73–00. Admission: 50 frs adults, 30 frs children (including skate rental). Open daily Nov.–Mar. 2:30–10. RER A: Marne-la-Vallée.*

Jardin d'Acclimatation This charming children's play-park in the Bois de Boulogne boasts a miniature train, boat rides, a zoo, and a game area, plus fairground stalls and cafés. *Admission: 13 frs adults, 6 frs children. Open daily 10–6. Métro: Les Sablons.*

Parc Floral de Paris This is the east Paris equivalent of the Jardin d'Acclimatation, situated in the Bois de Vincennes near the château. It features a miniature train, a game area, and miniature golf. *Route de la Pyramide, Vincennes. Admission: 5 frs, children under 6 free. Open daily 9:30–8 (to 5 in winter). Métro: Château de Vincennes.*

Movies There is no shortage of English movies in Paris, some (often cartoons) geared for children. Consult *Pariscope* or *L'Officiel des Spectacles* for details.

Museums **Musée de la Curiosité.** This new museum contains antique magic paraphernalia including some objects from Houdini's bag of tricks, and features an hourly magic show. *11 rue St-Paul. Admission: 45 frs adults, 30 frs children. Open Wed., Sat., and Sun. 2–7. Métro: St-Paul.*

Musée de la Femme et Collection d'Automates. The collection of automata and clockwork dolls bursts into life each afternoon; it's well worth making the short trip to Neuilly, especially since the Jardin d'Acclimatation and Bois de Boulogne (*see above*) are close at hand. *12 rue du Centre, Neuilly. Admission: 12 frs adults, 6 frs children. Open Wed.–Mon. 2:30–5; guided tours at 3. Métro: Pont de Neuilly.*

Musée de l'Homme. Paris's anthropological museum contains models and artifacts from prehistoric to recent times, with entertaining temporary exhibitions ideal for children. *Palais de Chaillot. Admission: 25 frs adults, 15 frs children. Open Wed.–Mon. 9:45–5. Métro: Trocadéro.*

Musée Grévin. A visit to a waxwork museum is a good way to spend a rainy afternoon. The long-established boulevard Montmartre museum concentrates on imitations of the famous, the newer one in Les Halles on recapturing the Belle Epoque. *10 blvd. Montmartre, 9e. Admission: 48 frs adults, 34 frs children under 14. Open 1–7, 10–6 during school holidays. Métro: Rue Montmartre.* **Nouveau Musée Grévin.** *Forum des Halles, 1er. Admission: 38 frs adults, 28 frs children under 14. Métro: Les Halles. Open Mon.–Sat. 10:30–7:30, Sun. 1–7.*

Parks Paris is not renowned as an open-space city. Its major parks (Bois de Boulogne and Bois de Vincennes) are on the outskirts, but there is room to stroll and play at:

Arènes de Lutèce, *5e. Métro: Monge.*
Champs de Mars, *7e. Métro: Ecole Militaire.*
Jardin des Halles, *1er. Métro: Les Halles.*

Jardin des Plantes, *5e. Métro: Jussieu.*
Jardin des Tuileries, *1er. Métro: Tuileries.*
Jardin du Luxembourg, *6e. RER: Luxembourg.*
Jardin du Ranelagh, *16e. Métro: La Muette.*
Parc André-Citroën, *15e. Métro: Javel.*
Parc de la Villette, *19e. Métro: Porte de la Villette.*
Parc de Montsouris, *14e. RER: Cité Universitaire.*
Parc des Buttes-Chaumont, *19e. Métro: Buttes-Chaumont.*
Parc Monceau, *8e. Métro: Monceau.*

Puppet Shows On most Wednesday, Saturday, and Sunday afternoons, the Guignol, the French equivalent of Punch and Judy, can be seen going through their ritualistic battles in several of Paris's parks, including the Champs de Mars *(15e, Métro: Ecole Militaire);* the Jardin du Luxembourg *(6e, Métro: Vavin);* and the Parc Montsouris *(14e, Métro: Porte d'Orléans).*

Or try one of Paris's several puppet theaters. Though shows are usually not in English, they're enjoyable for kids nonetheless.

Guignol du Parc de Choisy, *149, av. de Choisy, 13e, tel. 43–66–72– 39. Admission: 10 frs. Shows Tues., Sat., and Sun. at 3:30. Métro: Place d'Italie, Tolbiac.*
Marionnettes de Vaugirard, *Square Georges Brassens, rue Brancion, 15e, tel. 48–42–51–80. Admission: 14 frs. Shows Wed. at 3, 4, and 5, Sat. and Sun. at 3:30 and 4:30. Métro: Porte de Vanves.*
Marionnettes des Champs-Elysées. *Rond Point des Champs-Elysées, 8e, corner of avs. Matignon and Gabriel, tel. 42–57–43–34. Admission: 12.50 frs. Shows Tues., Sat., and Sun. at 3, 4, and 5. Métro: Champs-Elysées–Clemenceau.*

Roller Skating Paris's unofficial outdoor roller-skating venue is the concourse between the two wings of the Palais de Chaillot at Trocadéro. Or try: **La Main Jaune,** *rue du Caporal-Peugeot, 17e, tel. 47–63–26–47. (Métro: Porte de Champerret.) Admission: 40 frs (skate hire 10 frs). Open Wed. and weekends 2:30–7.*

Swimming Though every arrondissement has its own public pool or *piscine*, the best place to take kids is **Aquaboulevard de Paris,** an aquatic park and athletic super-center which features an enormous indoor wave pool with waterslides and a simulated outdoor beach during the summer. The center also has facilities for tennis and bowling (as well as a health club for adults). *4–6 rue Louis Armand, 15e, tel. 40–60–10– 00. Admission: weekdays, 68 frs adults, 19 frs children, weekends, 75 frs adults, 55 frs children. Open daily 8 AM to midnight. Métro: Balard or Porte de Versailles.*

Zoos Monkeys, deer, birds, and farm animals star at the **Jardin d'Acclimatation** *(see above)*, while the **Ménagerie** in the Jardin des Plantes also boasts elephants, lions, and tigers. *57 rue Cuvier, 5e. Admission: 25 frs adults, 13 frs children. Open daily 9–6 (9–5 in winter). Métro: Jussieu, Monge.*

Paris's biggest zoo is the **Parc Zoologique de Paris** in the **Bois de Vincennes,** which in addition to wild beasts includes a museum, films, and exhibitions. *53 av. de St-Maurice, 12e. Admission: 35 frs adults, 20 frs children. Open daily 9–6 (9–5 in winter). Métro: Porte Dorée.*

4 Shopping

*By Corinne
LaBalme*

*Corinne
LaBalme is a
Paris-based
freelance
writer and a
contributing
editor for
United
Airlines'*
Hemispheres.

Window-shopping is one of Paris's great spectator sports. Tastefully displayed wares—luscious cream-filled éclairs, lacy lingerie, rare artwork, gleaming copper pots—entice the eye and awaken the imagination. And shopping is one of the city's greatest pastimes, a chance to mix with Parisians and feel the heartbeat of the country. Who can understand the magic of French cuisine until they've explored a French open-air produce market on a weekend morning? Or resist the thrill of seeing a Chanel evening gown displayed in its own glossy Paris boutique—where the doorknobs are shaped like Chanel crystal perfume bottle stoppers?

Happily, the shopping opportunities in Paris are endless and geared to every taste. You can price emerald earrings at Cartier, spend an afternoon browsing through bookstalls along the Seine, buy silk-lined gloves at Dior, tour the high-gloss department stores, or haggle over prices in the sprawling flea markets on the outskirts of town. For many, perfume and designer clothing are perhaps the most coveted Parisian souvenirs. However, even on haute couture's home turf, bargains are surprisingly elusive. Foreign visitors, subject to the slings and arrows of international exchange rates, are advised to know prices in their own country before arrival. A Pierre Cardin tie or a Lalique bottle of *L'Air du Temps* may possibly be cheaper at the mall back home . . . although it won't be as much fun to buy.

Bargain hunters should watch for the word *soldes* (sale). Sales are generally held in July and January. The relatively meager French mark-downs (10%–15%) used to disappoint international visitors—but no more! One recession side-effect is markdowns of 30%–50%. Outside of sales, there are other good deals to be had, particularly in some of the discount shops, often located on the edge of town. Some of these are listed below.

You'll be spending most of your time in Paris sightseeing rather than shopping. Keep in mind that Paris's museums have some gloriously chic gift shops. Some of the best are in the Louvre (books, posters, reproduction statues, and jewelry), the Opéra Garnier (scarves, cards, cassettes, accessories), and the Musée des Arts Décoratifs (unusual craft items and reproductions of historic china, toys, linens, and glassware from the museum collections). Museum-quality art and antiques are also in ready supply here, and reputable dealers handle the necessary paperwork and shipping.

Paris is highly cosmopolitan, with numerous outlets for Burberry raincoats, Benetton sweaters, and Levi's jeans. We've concentrated our listings on characteristically French products.

Credit Cards Even stores that accept currency other than francs will generally give you a lower rate of exchange than banks or exchange offices. You're better off using credit cards, which are more widely used in France than in the United States. Even the corner newstand or flea market salesperson is likely to honor plastic. VISA is the most common and preferred card, followed closely by MasterCard/EuroCard. American Express, Diners Club, and Access are accepted in the larger international stores.

Duty-Free Shopping Visitors from outside the European Union, aged 15 and over, whose stay in France and/or the EU is less than six months can benefit from VAT (Value Added Tax) reimbursements, known in France as TVA or *détaxe*. To qualify, non-EU residents must spend at least 2,000F in a single store. Refunds vary from 13% to 18.6% and are mailed to you by check or credited to the purchaser's charge card. The major department stores have simplified the process with special détaxe desks where the *bordereaux* (export sales invoices) are prepared. Most high-profile shops with international clients have détaxe forms, but stores are not required to do this paperwork. If the discount is extremely important to you, ask if it is available before making your purchase. Invoices and bordereaux forms must be presented to French customs upon leaving the country. The items purchased should also be available for inspection.

Mailing Purchases Home Smaller shops are reluctant to mail purchases overseas, in case the goods get lost. Mailing goods oneself is possible—all French post offices sell self-sealing mailing boxes—but postage is costly. Remember that if you are claiming a Value Added Tax deduction (*see above*), you should have the goods with you when you leave the country.

Shopping Areas

Avenue Montaigne The names atop the showcase windows lining this elegant boulevard are the honor roll of haute couture: Chanel, Dior, Nina Ricci, Christian Lacroix, Emanuel Ungaro, Céline, Valentino, Per Spook, Escada, Thierry Mugler, Hanae Mori. Here you'll also find Louis Vuitton, accessorists S. T. Dupont and Isabel Canovas, and the lively new boutique run by former Chanel super-model Inès de la Fressange. Yves St-Laurent's salon is nearby, at 5 avenue Marceau.

Left Bank Browsing through the antiques shops, bookstores, and art galleries of St-Germain-des-Prés, Paris's intellectual core, is window-shopping at its most varied. High fashion arrived here in the '70s, when **YSL** opened **Rive Gauche** boutiques for men and women on the place Saint-Sulpice. The area around rue de Grenelle and rue Saint-Pères is known for intimate designer boutiques (Sonia Rykiel, Claude Montana) and shoe shops (Maud Frizon, Charles Jourdan, Stéphane Kélian, and Carel).

Le Marais The elegant mansions and tiny kosher food stores that characterized the low-lying area between the Beaubourg and place des Vosges were overtaken by New Wave fashion and trendy gift shops in the 1980s. Avant-garde designers Azzedine Alaia, Lolita Lempicka, Issey Miyake, and Romeo Gigli have boutiques within a few blocks of the stately Picasso and Carnavalet museums. Shopping for off-beat decorative household items is also excellent here.

Les Halles Most of the narrow pedestrian streets on the former site of Paris's wholesale food market are lined with fast-food joints, sex shops, jeans outlets, and garish souvenir stands, but the rue du Jour (home of the Agnès b. boutiques) is an attractive exception. Street artists claim the plaza in front of the Pompidou Center, and prostitutes rule the nearby rue St-Denis. In the middle of the action, the **Forum des Halles**—a multilevel underground shopping mall—caters to a noisy teenage clientele.

Opéra to Madeleine Three major department stores—Au Printemps, Galeries Lafayette, and the British Marks and Spencer (*see* Department Stores, *below*)—are clustered behind Paris's ornate 19th-century opera house. The place de la Madeleine is home to two luxurious food stores, Fauchon and Hédiard, plus a 75-shop mall, Les Trois Quartiers. Lalique and Baccarat Crystal also have opulent showrooms near the Madeleine Church.

Montparnasse The bohemian mecca for artists and writers in the '20s and '30s, Montparnasse is better known for bars and restaurants than shops. A recently built commercial center near the train station boasts a Galeries Lafayette outlet but is too charmless to attract many tour-

Right Bank Shopping

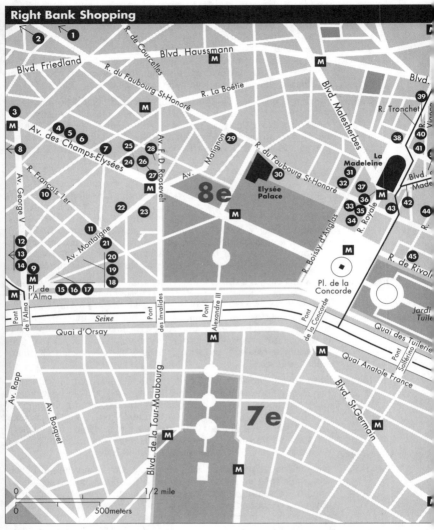

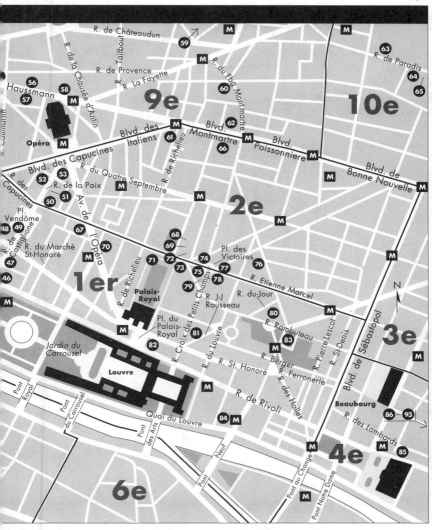

Agatha, **5, 16**
Au Bon Marché, **15**
Cacharel Stock, **26**
Carré Rive Gauche, **1**
Chipie Stock, **25**
Dominique
Morlotti, **14**
Dorothée bis Stock, **24**
FNAC, **17**
Galeries Lafayette, **19**
Guerlain, **6**
Jadis et
Gourmande, **22**
Kenzo, **8**
La Bagagerie, **10**
Le Monde en
Marche, **3**
Marie Papier, **21**
Poilâne, **11**
Shakespeare and
Company, **2**
Sonia Rykiel, **7**
Sonia Rykiel
Enfant, **9**
Souleido, **4**
SR Store, **23**
Tati, **18**
Tea and Tattered
Pages, **20**
Village Voice, **12**
YSL Rive Gauche, **13**

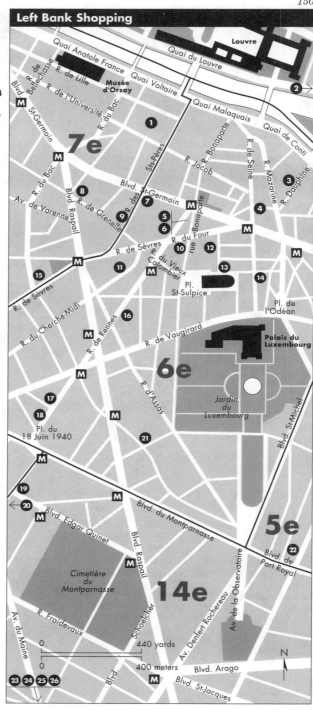

Left Bank Shopping

ists. The rue d'Alésia on the southern fringe of Montparnasse is known for discount clothing shops.

Place des Victoires Françoise Chassagnac, the canny retailer who "discovered" Azzedine Alaia and Angelo Tarlazzi, put this graceful, circular plaza near the Palais-Royal on the fashion map when she opened her Victoire boutique in 1967. Kenzo, Thierry Mugler, and Cacharel soon followed. Avant-garde boutiques like Chantal Thomass, Jean-Charles de Castelbajac, and En Attendant les Barbares have since fanned into the sidestreets, while Jean-Paul Gaultier has his shop in the nearby Galerie Vivienne arcade.

Place Vendôme and Rue de la Paix The magnificent 17th-century place Vendôme, and the rue de la Paix leading north from Vendôme, have attracted the world's most elegant jewelers: Cartier, Boucheron, Buccellati, Van Cleef and Arpels, Répossi, Mellerio, Mauboussin, and Mikimoto. This super-posh pedestrian square was repaved with silver-gray granite in 1992, and shines brighter than ever.

Rue du Faubourg St-Honoré The presence of the Elysée Palace and the official residences of the American and British ambassadors mean this chic shopping and residential street is well patrolled by the police. The Paris branch of Sotheby's and renowned antiques galleries such as Didier Aaron and Odermatt-Cazeau add artistic flavor. Boutiques include Hermès, Lanvin, Karl Lagerfeld, Reveillon Furs, Louis Feraud, and Christian Lacroix.

Trocadéro–Victor Hugo This aristocratic and conservative neighborhood in the 16th arrondissement attracts predictably classic retailers, most of whom are centered around the place Victor Hugo. Bargain hunters know that the secondhand shops in this wealthy area offer exceptionally fine goods. **Réciproque** (123 rue de la Pompe) is one of the biggest and best, with three storefronts of nearly new designer fashions and gifts for both men and women.

Champs-Elysées Cafés and movie theaters keep the once-chic Champs-Elysées active 24 hours a day, but the invasion of exchange banks, car showrooms, and fast-food chains has lowered the tone. Four glitzy 20th-century arcade malls (**Galerie du Lido, Le Rond-Point, Le Claridge,** and **Elysées 26**) capture most of the retail action.

Bastille The faddiest (and most ephemeral) teenager boutiques are clustered between art galleries, bars, and furniture outlets in this rapidly gentrifying neighborhood. Jean-Paul Gaultier established his **Junior** boutique on the rue Faubourg St-Antoine in 1994.

Department Stores

Paris's top department stores offer both convenience and chic. Some are open until 10 PM one weekday evening, and all six major stores listed below have multilingual guides, international welcome desks, détaxe offices, and restaurants.

Opéra area **Au Printemps** (64 blvd. Haussmann, 9e, tel. 42–82–50–00) is a glittery three-store complex that includes "La Maison," for housewares and furniture; "La Mode," for ladies and children; and "Brummel," a six-floor emporium devoted to menswear. Flo Prestige, the celebrated Parisian brasserie chain, caters the in-house restaurants. *Open Mon.–Sat. 9:30–7.*

Galeries Lafayette (40 blvd. Haussmann, 9e, tel. 42–82–34–56) is equally elegant, and it spices up its Parisian aura with periodic exhibits featuring crafts from exotic countries. Be sure and look up while in the main store: The glorious Belle Epoque stained-glass dome is a Parisian landmark. Stylish private-label fashions (Briefing and Jodphur) offer good value, and the elegant floor-wide gourmet shop includes several sophisticated snack/wine bars. *Open Mon.–Sat. 9:30–6:45. Another branch is at Centre Commercial Montparnasse, 15e, tel. 45–38–52–87.*

Marks & Spencer (35 blvd. Haussmann, 9e, tel. 47–42–42–91) is a British store chiefly noted for its moderately priced sportswear and its excellent English grocery and take-out food service. *Open Mon.–Sat. 9:30–7, Tues. 10–7.*

Louvre–Pont Neuf area   **La Samaritaine** (19 rue de la Monnaie, 1er, tel. 40–41–20–20), a sprawling four-store complex, is rapidly shedding its fusty, grandmotherly image. Especially good for kitchen supplies, housewares, and furniture, it's famous for its rooftop snackbar that offers a marvelous view of Notre Dame. *Open Mon.-Sat. 9:30–7, Thurs. 9:30–10.*

Hôtel de Ville/Marais area   **Bazar de l'Hôtel de Ville** (52–64 rue de Rivoli, 4e, tel. 42–74–90–00), affectionately called BHV, houses an enormous basement hardware store that sells everything from doorknobs to cement mixers! The fashion offerings are minimal, but BHV is noteworthy for quality household goods, home decor materials, and office supplies. *Open Mon.–Sat. 9:30–7, Wed. 9:30–10.*

Left Bank   **Au Bon Marché** (22 rue de Sèvres, 7e, tel. 44–39–80–00), founded in 1852, is chiefly known for linens, table settings, and high-quality furniture. La Grande Epicerie, a grocery store and deli here, is a gourmet's delight, and the sleek restaurant was designed by jet-set decorator Andrée Putman. The basement is a treasure trove for books, records, and arty gifts. *Open Mon.–Fri. 9:30–6:30, Sat. 9:30–7.*

Budget   Most Parisians dash into their neighborhood **Monoprix** or **Prisunic** stores—with branches throughout the city—at least once a week. These handy shops stock inexpensive cosmetics, toothpaste, groceries, toys, typing paper, bathmats—a little of everything. Clothing often represents good value: Noted designers like Elisabeth de Senneville occasionally create special low-price lines for these stores.

Tati stores are known for bargain-basement prices, although goods are not always top quality. One of the largest is at 140 rue de Rennes, 6e.

Specialty Shops

Antiques   Antiques shops and art gallery enclaves are scattered throughout the city. For a full day's browsing, try:

Louvre des Antiquaires (2 pl. du Palais-Royal, 1er), is an elegant multifloor complex where 250 of Paris's leading dealers showcase their rarest objects.
Carré Rive Gauche is a compact Left Bank district, bordered by the quai Voltaire and the rue de l'Université, whose narrow sidestreets shelter dozens of fine arts and antiques galleries.

Bags and Luggage   **La Bagagerie** (41 rue du Four, 6e, tel. 45–48–85–88; also 11 rue Fbg. St-Honoré, 8e, tel. 47–42–79–13, and 12 rue Tronchet, 8e, tel. 42–65–03–40) features brightly colored bags and belts with youthful style and moderate prices.
Hermès (24 rue Fbg. St-Honoré, 8e, tel. 40–17–47–17) was established as a saddlery in 1837 but since went on to scarves and more:

Its most famous leather creation is the eternally chic Kelly bag, created for Grace Kelly. Prices are astronomical.

Louis Vuitton (78 av. Marceau, 8e, tel. 47–20–47–00; also 54 av. Montaigne, 8e, tel. 45–62–90–43) sells the world's best-known, monogram-patterned luxury luggage and accessories.

Le Monde du Bagage (4 rue des Petits Champs, 2e, tel. 42–86–90–45) features crushable-but-chic, leather-trimmed canvas carry-alls and knapsacks.

English-Language Books

An eternal Parisian pastime is strolling by the open-air bookstalls along the Seine.

W.H. Smith (248 rue de Rivoli, 1er, tel. 44–77–88–89) carries an excellent range of travel and language books, cookbooks, and fiction for adults and children.

Brentano's (37 av. de l'Opéra, 2e, tel. 42–61–52–50) is another well-stocked general bookstore.

Village Voice (6 rue Princesse, 6e, tel. 46–33–36–47), known for its selection of contemporary authors, hosts regular literary readings.

Shakespeare and Company (37 rue de la Bûcherie, 5e, no phone) is a sentimental Left Bank favorite, specializing in expatriate literature.

Tea and Tattered Pages (24 rue Mayet, 6e, tel. 40–65–94–35) sells cheap, secondhand English tomes.

Clothing (Women's) Classic Chic

Chanel (42 av. Montaigne, 8e, tel. 47–23–74–12, and 29 rue Cambon, 1er) has experienced a radical transformation under Karl Lagerfeld, who has added leather 'n' chains to classic suits and accessories.

Christian Dior (30 av. Montaigne, 8e, tel. 40–73–54–44) is a pearl gray palace selling ladies' and menswear, perfumes, jewelry, lingerie, furs, leather goods, porcelain, and gifts.

Givenchy Boutique (8 av. Georges V, 8e, tel. 47–20–81–31) presents slightly more affordable versions of the designer's elegant ready-to-wear.

Nina Ricci (39 av. Montaigne, 8e, tel. 47–23–78–88) clothes are supremely ladylike, and the lingerie is luxuriantly romantic.

Trendsetters

Christian Lacroix (26 av. Montaigne, 8e, tel. 47–20–68–95, and 73 rue du Fbg. St-Honoré, 8e) turns haute couture into a Provençal carnival with daring cuts and candy-coated colors.

Jean-Paul Gaultier (6 rue Vivienne, 2e, tel. 42–86–05–05), Madonna's clothier, specializes in outrageously attention-getting garments for men and women.

Lolita Lempicka (13 bis rue Pavée, 4e, tel. 42–74–50–48) serves up sharp suits and whimsical silk dresses. **Lolita bis,** a lower-priced junior line, is sold in a shop across the street.

Romeo Gigli (46 rue de Sévigné, 4e, tel. 48–04–57–05) offers the oversized Renaissance-style clothing for men and women that has bestowed cult status upon this Milan-based designer.

Thierry Mugler (10 pl. des Victoires, 2e, tel. 42–60–06–37, and 49 av. Montaigne, 8e, tel. 47–23–37–62), with kinky lace-up dresses and sexy cat-suits, keeps fans coming back for more—menswear is next door at No. 8.

Victoire (12 pl. des Victoires, 2e, tel. 42–61–09–02) is a discreet boutique that taps into new trends.

Chic and Casual

Agnes b. (3 and 6 rue du Jour, 1er, tel. 45–08–49–89) has knitwear separates that are wardrobe basics for young Parisians.

Inès de la Fressange (14 av. Montaigne, 8e, tel. 47–23–08–94), the former Chanel super-model creates casual looks based on evergreen V-neck sweaters and slim, velvet jeans.

Sonia Rykiel (175 blvd. St-Germain, 6e, tel. 49–54–60–60 and 79 rue Fbg. St-Honoré, 8e, tel. 42–65–20–81) singlehandedly made cotton velour into a recognized fashion statement.

Suzette Idier (9 rue de Birague, 4e, tel. 42–77–72–52) runs an intimate, pocket-sized boutique chockful of sexy cocktail gowns, colorful daywear, and all the latest Paris accessories.

Clothing (Men's) **Brummel** (Au Printemps department store, 64 blvd. Haussmann, 9e, tel. 42–82–50–00) is Paris's menswear fashion leader: six floors of suits, sportswear, underwear, coats, ties, and accessories in all price ranges.

Charvet (28 pl. Vendôme, 1er, tel. 42–60–30–70) is the Parisian equivalent of a London tailor or New York's Brooks Brothers: a conservative, aristocratic institution famed for made-to-measure shirts and exquisite ties and accessories.

Dominique Morlotti (25 rue St-Sulpice, 6e, tel. 43–54–89–89) offers an easy-going approach to menswear. Moderately priced designer separates have that debonair Parisian flair.

Kenzo (3 pl. des Victoires, 2e, tel. 40–39–72–03, and 17 blvd. Raspail, 7e, tel. 45–49–33–75) brings exhuberant color and fantasy to his menswear collections. Move on if you're looking for a classic three-piece suit.

Lanvin (2 rue Cambon, 1er, tel. 42–60–38–83, and 15 rue Fbg. St-Honoré, 8e) offers elegant tailoring plus fine sportswear. The branch for women is at 15 rue Fbg. St-Honoré.

Clothing (Children) Top Paris designers now offer mini-couture: **Baby Dior** (28 av. Montaigne, 8e, tel. 40–73–55–14) features velvet suits and ballgowns for little princes and princesses; **Sonia Rykiel Enfant** (4 rue de Grenelle, 6e, tel. 49–54–61–10) has sturdy but sophisticated fashions in washable velour and waxed cotton for infants and toddlers; and **Kenzo Bébé** (3 pl. des Victoires, 1er, tel. 40–39–72–87) has colorful kilts and jackets.

Natalys (32 rue St-Antoine, 4e, tel. 48–87–77–42, and 92 av. des Champs-Elysées, 8e, tel. 43–59–17–65) is a major French chain selling clothing, toys, furniture, and accessories for newborns and grade-school children.

Clothing (Resale) **Réciproque** (95, 101, and 123 rue de la Pompe, 16e, tel. 47–04–30–28 [women's] and 47–27–93–52 [menswear]) is Paris's most exclusive swap shop. Anyone hoping to sell designer cast-offs here must make an appointment weeks in advance (no appointment is necessary to buy). There's not much in the way of service or space, but savings are significant: 4,200 frs for a brocade Nina Ricci dinner suit, 300 frs for Camille Unglick shoes. Closed Mondays and from the end of July through August.

Catherine Baril (14–16–25 rue de la Tour, 16e, tel. 45–20–95–21), smaller than Réciproque and even more exclusive, has one-of-a-kind haute couture in addition to designer ready-to-wear.

Clothing (Discount) *Rue d'Alésia* This street in the 14th arrondissement is lined with stock shops selling last season's items at a discount. Be forewarned: Dressing rooms are not always provided.

SR Store (64 rue d'Alésia, 14e, tel. 43–95–06–13) slices 50% off last year's prices for Sonia Rykiel fashions for men, women, and children, and still manages to hold 20–30% sales in January and July.

Cacharel Stock (114 rue d'Alésia, 14e, tel. 45–42–53–04) offers impressive savings for men's, women's, and children's clothing (plus even bigger markdown sales racks on the second floor).

Chipie Stock (82 rue d'Alésia, 14e, tel. 45–42–07–52) has jeans and sweaters for the whole family.

Dorothée bis Stock (74 rue d'Alésia, 14e, tel. 45–42–17–11) practices multiple markdowns on selected gowns and sportswear.

Central Paris **Mendès** (65 rue Montmartre, 2e, tel. 42–36–83–32), the manufacturer of Yves St-Laurent's Rive Gauche and Variations lines for women, sells last season's clothes at half price.

Fabrics **Rodin** (36 av. Champs-Elysées, 8e, tel. 43–59–58–82) and **Bouchara** (54 blvd. Haussmann, 9e, tel. 42–80–66–95) sell top-quality apparel and upholstery fabrics.

Discount **Marché Saint Pierre** (2 rue Charles Nodier, 18e, tel. 46–06–92–25), a raucous, four-floor warehouse in Montmartre, supplied designers like Kenzo in his salad days. It offers cheap end-of-bolt specials, upholstery, and wall fabrics.

Food **Poilâne** (8 rue du Cherche-Midi, 6e, tel. 45–48–42–59) produces the
Bread most famous bread in the world. The chewy sourdough loaves are sold in hundreds of Paris restaurants and shops and are airmailed to United States and Tokyo restaurants every day.

Candy and **A la Mère de Famille** (35 rue du Fbg. Montmartre, 9e, tel. 47–70–83–
Chocolate 69) is an enchanting shop specializing in old-fashioned bonbons, sugar candy, and more.
Jadis et Gourmande (49 bis av. Franklin Roosevelt, 8e, tel. 42–25–06–04; 27 rue Boissy d'Anglas, 8e, tel. 42–65–23–23; and 88 blvd. de Port-Royal, 5e, tel. 43–26–17–75) personalizes chocolate bars with names and initials.
La Maison du Chocolat (52 rue François 1er, 8e, tel. 47–23–38–25) is heaven for cocoa purists. Take home chocolates, ice cream, and other treats, or meet a friend in the tearoom for sinfully rich hot chocolate and chocolate-mousse *frappés* (cold drinks). Take-out only at 8 blvd. de la Madeleine, 9e, tel. 47–42–86–52 and 225 rue Fbg. St-Honoré, 8e, tel. 42–27–39–44.

Gourmet Shops **Fauchon** (26–28–30 pl. de la Madeleine, 8e, tel. 47–42–60–11) and **Hédiard** (21 pl. de la Madeleine, 8e, tel. 42–66–44–36) sell prestigious house brands of paté, mustard, honey, jellies, and private label champagne, plus sumptuous produce from around the world. The **Galeries Lafayette Gourmet shop** (40 blvd. Haussmann, 9e, tel. 42–82–34–56) is equally chic, with its gold shopping carts and bistro-style snackbars for caviar and smoked salmon, but less intimidating. The Grande Epicerie, on the ground floor of **Au Bon Marché** (22 rue de Sèvres, 7e, tel. 44–39–80–00), has an excellent array of fine French foodstuffs.

Jewelry Most of the big names are based near the place Vendôme. Designer costume and semiprecious jewelry is sold in most of the av. Montaigne and rue du Faubourg St-Honoré boutiques.

Cartier (7 and 23 pl. Vendôme, 1er, tel. 42–61–55–55) has two less formal "Les Must" boutiques, which carry lighters, pens, watches, key-chains, and other gift items.

Costume **Agatha** (97 rue de Rennes, 6e, tel. 45–48–81–30; 45 rue Bonaparte, 6e, tel. 46–33–20–00; and 12–14 av. Champs-Elysées, 8e, tel. 43–59–68–68) has trendy but moderately priced seasonal collections.
Isabel Canovas (16 av. Montaigne, 8e, tel. 47–20–10–80) offers faux bijoux, that, while not cheap, are prized by fashion mavens for their wittiness and glamour.

Linens **Porthault** (18 av. Montaigne, 8e, tel. 47–20–75–25) makes hand-embroidered table linens, luxurious old world-style sheets, and the most sumptuous layettes in town.

Lingerie **Chantal Thomass** (1 rue Vivienne, 1er, tel. 40–15–02–36) sets the right mood for her trademark black-lace hosiery, satin corsets, and feather-trimmed negligees in this plush, pink velvet boutique that resembles a Victorian bordello.
Natari (7 pl. Vendôme, 1er, tel. 42–96–22–94) seduces all, with selections for every pocketbook. Movie-star lingerie and peignoir sets come in pure silk or washable synthetic versions.

Music/Records **FNAC** (Forum des Halles, 1er, tel. 40–41–40–00; 26 av. Ternes, 17e, tel. 44–09–18–00; and 136 rue de Rennes, 6e, tel. 49–54–30–00) is a high-profile French chain selling music; photo, TV, and audio equipment; and books.
Virgin Megastore (52–60 av. des Champs-Elysées, 8e, tel. 40–74–06–48) has acres of CDs and tapes—everything from classic to rap—plus a book division.

Perfumes **Annick Goutal** (14 rue de Castiglione, 1er, tel. 42–60–52–82) sells this exclusive signature perfume line.
Guerlain (68 av. des Champs-Elysées, 8e, tel. 47–89–71–84, and 47 rue Bonaparte, 6e, tel. 43–26–71–19) boutiques are the only authorized Paris outlets for legendary perfumes like Shalimar, Jicky, Vol de Nuit, Mitsouko, and Chamade.

Discount **Michel Swiss** (16 rue de la Paix, 2nd Floor, 2e, tel. 42–61–61–11, and 24 av. de l'Opéra, 1er, tel. 47–03–49–11) offers large savings on perfumes and fashion accessories. Service is not helpful; know what you want before flagging a salesperson.

Scarves **Hermès** (24 rue Fbg. St-Honoré, 8e, tel. 40–17–47–17) clocks a scarf sale every 20 seconds before the Christmas holidays! The all-silk *carrés*—truly fashion icons—are legendary for their brilliant colors and intricate designs, which change yearly.
Souleiado (78 rue de Seine, 6e, tel. 43–54–62–25, and 83 av. Paul Doumer, 16e, tel. 42–24–99–34) uses traditional Provençal patterns for cotton scarves, quilted bags, and linens.

Shoes **Laurent Mercadel** (31 rue Tronchet, 8e, tel. 42–66–01–28, and 3 pl. des Victoires, 1er, tel. 45–08–84–44) offers classic styles updated with unusual accents.
Stéphane Kélian (23 blvd. de la Madeleine, 1er, tel. 42–96–01–84, and 6 pl. des Victoires, 2e, tel. 42–61–55–60) creates chic, high-style, comfortable shoes for men and women.

Stationery **Marie Papier** (26 rue Vavin, 6e, tel. 43–26–46–44) sells an extraordinary variety of colored writing paper and notebooks.

Tablewares **Au Bain Marie** (8 rue Boissy d'Anglas, 8e, tel. 42–66–59–74) is an
China and enchanted kingdom for amateur and professional cooks. Come here
Crystal for crockery, porcelain, and a world-class collection of cookbooks.
Lalique (11 rue Royale, 8e, tel. 42–66–52–40) crystal vases and statuettes are prized for their sinuous, romantic forms and delicate design.
Geneviève Lethu (28 rue St-Antoine, 4e, tel. 42–74–21–25) is a homey, casual shop selling tea services, potpourri mixtures, and table linens for your real or imagined country house.

Discount The **rue de Paradis** in the 10th arrondissement is lined with china and crystal showrooms. Shoppers with style numbers, pocket calculators, and comparison prices from home often profit from serious savings on fine Limoges porcelain.
La Tisanière (21 rue de Paradis, 10e, tel. 47–70–22–80) sells china "seconds."
Arts-Céramiques (15 rue de Paradis, 10e, tel. 48–24–83–70) has special promotional sales in its back room.

NOTE: Although there aren't any bargains at the **Baccarat Crystal showroom** (30 bis rue de Paradis, 10e, tel. 47–70–64–30), this elegant, red-carpeted spot with a fascinating in-house museum is well worth a visit.

Silver **Christofle** (24 rue de la Paix, 2e, tel. 42–65–62–43, and 9 rue Royale, 8e, tel. 49–33–43–00), founded in 1830, presents the finest French silver services in sumptuous velvet display cases.
Jean-Pierre de Castro (17 rue des Francs-Bourgeois, 4e, tel. 42–72–04–00) is a dusty secondhand shop selling old-fashioned silver settings by the kilo-weight. The inexpensive bracelets made of Victorian silver spoons and forks make marvelous gifts.

Toys **Au Nain Bleu** (406–410 rue Fbg. St-Honoré, 8e, tel. 42–60–39–01) is a high-price wonderland, with elaborate dollhouses, miniature sports cars, and enchanting hand-carved rocking horses.
Le Monde en Marche (34 rue Dauphine, 6e, tel. 43–26–66–53) specializes in unusual, old-fashioned wooden toys.

Drugstores

The **Pharmacie Les Champs-Elysées** (84 av. des Champs-Elysées, 8e, tel. 45–62–02–41) is open 24 hours a day, 365 days a year.
Pharmacie Les Petits Champs (21 rue des Petits Champs, 1er, tel. 42–96–97–20; open daily 8–8).
Drugstore Saint-Germain (149 blvd. St-Germain, 6e, tel. 42–22–80–00; open daily 9 AM–2 AM).
Pharmacie Européene de la Place Clichy (6 pl. Clichy, 9e, tel. 48–74–65–18; open daily 8 AM–1 AM).

Shopping Arcades

The various shopping arcades, or *passages*, scattered around Paris offer a pleasant shopping alternative, especially those dating back to the 19th century, most of which have been splendidly restored. Their arching glass roofs, mosaic or marble flooring, and brass lamps are now set off to full advantage.

Most arcades are conveniently located in the central 1st and 2nd arrondissements on the Right Bank. Our favorite is **Galerie Vivienne** (4 rue des Petits-Champs, 2e) between the Stock Exchange (Bourse) and the Palais-Royal. It has a range of interesting shops and an excellent tearoom and is home to **Cave Legrand,** a quality wine shop. **Galerie Véro-Dodat** (19 rue Jean-Jacques Rousseau, 1er) has painted ceilings and slender copper pillars. You'll find an arcade called **Passage des Pavillons** at 6 rue de Beaujolais, 1er, near the Palais-Royal gardens; and **Passage des Princes** at 97 rue de Richelieu, 2e. **Passage des Panoramas** (11 blvd. Montmartre, 2e) is the oldest of them all, opened in 1800. Across the Grands Boulevards is **Passage Jouffroy** (12 blvd. Montmartre, 9e), with shops selling toys, perfumes, original cosmetics, and dried flowers: Try **Pain d'Epices** (No. 29) and **Au Bonheur des Dames** (No. 39).

Markets

Food Markets Paris's open-air food markets are among the city's most colorful attractions. Every *quartier* (district) has one, although many are open only a few days each week. Sunday morning, till 1 PM, is usually a good time to go; Monday is the day these markets are likely to be closed. The local markets usually concentrate on food, but they always have a few brightly colored flower stalls. The variety of cheeses is always astounding.

Many of the better-known markets are in areas you'd visit for sightseeing; our favorites are on **rue de Buci**, 6e (open daily); **rue Mouffetard,** 5e; and **rue Lepic** in Montmartre (the latter two best on weekends). The **Marché d'Aligre** (open Sat., Sun., and Mon. mornings) is a bit farther out, beyond the Bastille on rue d'Aligre in the 12th arrondissement, but you won't see many tourists in this less-affluent area of town, and Parisians from all over the city know it and love it. The prices come tumbling down as the morning draws to a close.

Flower and Bird Markets Paris's main flower market is located right in the heart of the city on Ile de la Cité, between Notre Dame and the Palais de Justice. It's open every day except Sunday, when a bird market takes its place, and Monday, when it's closed. Birds and a host of other animals are also sold in the shops and stalls on the quai de la Mégisserie on the Right Bank of the Seine. Other colorful flower markets are held beside the Madeleine church, 8er, on place des Ternes, 17e, down the road from the Arc de Triomphe. Both are open daily except Monday.

The Stamp Market Philatelists should head for Paris's unique stamp market on avenue Marigny and avenue Gabriel, overlooking the gardens at the bottom of the Champs-Elysées. *Open Thurs., Sat., Sun., and public holidays.*

Flea Markets The **Marché aux Puces** on Paris's northern boundary (Métro: Porte de Clignancourt) still attracts the crowds, but its once unbeatable prices are now a feature of the past. This century-old labyrinth of alleyways packed with antiques dealers' booths and junk stalls now spreads for over a square mile. Early birds often pick up the most worthwhile loot. But be warned—if there's one place in Paris where you need to know how to barter, this is it! For lunch, stop for mussels and fries in one of the rough-and-ready cafés. *Open Sat., Sun., and Mon.*

There are other, less-impressive flea markets on the southern and eastern slopes of the city—at **porte de Montreuil** and **porte de Vanves**—but they have a depressing amount of real junk and are best avoided, except by obsessive bargain hunters.

5 Dining

By Robert Noah

Updated by William Echikson and Baty Landis.

Whether your dream meal is savoring truffle-studded foie gras from Limoges china, or breaking the crust of a steaming cassoulet in a thick crockery bowl, you can find it in Paris. Despite rumblings about lowered standards and increasingly bland fare, Paris remains one of the world's great food capitals. For most visitors, the prospect of eating here is exciting; for many, it's the main reason for a trip.

It's not unusual to hear of mediocre food, haughty service, and outrageous prices in Paris restaurants. It's certainly possible to have a bad meal here. Yet the city's restaurants exist principally for the demanding Parisians themselves, for whom every meal is—if not a way of life—certainly an event worthy of their undivided attention. Most restaurants that cannot attain the high standard of their French patrons will not last long. If you want to dine well, therefore, look for restaurants where the French go, and avoid places that cater to tourists. Keep in mind, however, that world-famous restaurants are bound to be frequented by foreigners as well as Parisians, and that a Midwestern accent at the next table is not always a bad sign.

In making the selections for this guide, we have tried to include restaurants with a variety of styles and price levels, from formal dining rooms serving haute cuisine to cheery wine bars offering open-faced sandwiches and not much more. More than half are in the 1st–8th arrondissements, within easy reach of hotels and sights; many others are in the 14th and 16th arrondissements, also popular visitor areas. In addition, we have included a number of restaurants with excellent food, atmosphere, and service that are off the beaten tourist path. In this we follow the lead of the French, for whom a good meal is worth a trip. Because space is at a premium, our selection is limited to places with primarily French rather than ethnic dishes.

Restaurant Types

What's the difference between a bistro and a brasserie? Can you order food at a café? Do you go to a restaurant for just a snack? The following definitions should help.

A **restaurant** traditionally serves a three-course (first, main, and dessert) meal at both lunch and dinner. Although this category includes the most formal, three-star establishments, it also applies to humble neighborhood spots. Don't expect to grab a quick snack. In general, restaurants are what you choose when you want a complete meal and when you have the time to linger over it. Wine is typically drunk with restaurant meals. Hours are fairly consistent; *see* Mealtimes, *below.*

Many say **bistros** served the world's first fast food. After the fall of Napoléon, the Russian soldiers who occupied Paris were known to bang on zinc-topped café bars, crying "bistrot"—"hurry" in Russian. In the past, bistros were simple places with minimum decor and service. Although many nowadays are quite upscale, with beautiful interiors and chic clientele, most remain cozy establishments serving straightforward, frequently gutsy cooking, with plenty of variety meats and long-simmered dishes such as *pot-au-feu* and veal *blanquette.*

Brasseries—ideal places for quick, one-dish meals—originated when Alsatians fleeing German occupiers after the Franco-Prussian War came to Paris and opened restaurants serving specialties from home. Pork-based dishes, *choucroute* (sauerkraut and sausages), and beer (brasserie also means brewery) were—and still are—mainstays here. The typical brasserie is convivial and keeps late hours. Some are open 24 hours a day—a good thing to know, since many restaurants stop serving at 10:30 PM.

Like bistros and brasseries, **cafés** come in confusing variety. Usually informal neighborhood hangouts, cafés may also be veritable show-places attracting chic, well-heeled crowds. At most cafés, regulars congregate at the bar, where coffee and drinks are cheaper than at tables. At lunch, tables are set and a limited menu is served. Sand-wiches, usually with *jambon* (ham) or *fromage* (cheese, often Gru-yere or Camembert), or *mixte* (ham and cheese) are served throughout the day. Cafés are for lingering, for people-watching, and for daydreaming.

Wine bars, or *bistrots à vins,* are a newer phenomenon. These infor-mal places serve very limited menus, often no more than open-faced sandwiches (*tartines*) and selections of cheeses and cold cuts (*char-cuterie*). Owners concentrate on their wine lists, which often in-clude less well known, regional selections, many of them available by the glass. Like today's bistros and brasseries, some wine bars are very fancy indeed, with costly wine lists and full menus. Most re-main friendly and unassuming, good places for sampling wines you might otherwise never try.

If you're not very hungry or want to eat at an odd hour, consider one of Paris's many **charcuteries.** Today's charcuterie is virtually a res-taurant (though without waiter service), and the pâtés and meat products that once filled the shelves have moved over to make room for prepared salads, quiches, breads, and desserts. Choose what ap-peals to you most and take it to one of the city's green spaces for your own *déjeuner sur l'herbe.* Or you can put together your picnic by vis-iting a number of shops, including **boulangeries** (bakeries), **pâtisse-ries** (pastry shops), and **fromageries** (cheese shops).

Mealtimes Generally, Paris restaurants are open from noon to about 2, and from 7:30 or 8 to 10 or 10:30. Brasseries have longer hours and often serve all day and late into the evening; some are open 24 hours. The iconoclastic wine bars do as they want, frequently serving hot food only through lunch and cold assortments of *charcuterie* and cheese until a late afternoon or early evening close.

We have included days closed in all our listings, as well as yearly va-cations when known. Assume a restaurant is open seven days a week, year-round, unless otherwise indicated. Surprisingly, many prestigous restaurants close on Saturday as well as Sunday. July and August are the most common months for annual closings, but Paris in August is no longer the wasteland it used to be, and many restaurants now close for a few weeks in winter instead. The past couple of years have been hard for many Paris restaurants, and man-agement may hesitate to announce vacation dates too far in advance or suddenly decide not to close after all. We suggest you call ahead to confirm that the establishment of your choice will be open when you plan to visit.

Because most restaurants are open for only a few set hours for lunch and dinner, and because meals are much longer affairs here than they are in the United States, we strongly advise you to make reser-vations. Most wine bars do not take reservations; reservations are also unnecessary for brasserie and café meals at odd hours. In the reviews below, we have indicated where reservations are advised or required (and when booking weeks or months in advance is neces-sary), and where reservations are not accepted. If you want nonsmoking, make this clear when you reserve. Though the law re-quires all restaurants to provide a nonsmoking area, this is some-times limited to a very few tables.

Menus All establishments must post their menus outside, so study them carefully before deciding to enter. Most restaurants offer two basic types of menu: à la carte and fixed price (*prix fixe*, or *un menu*). The prix-fixe menu will usually offer the best value, though choices are limited. Most menus begin with a first-course section, often subdivided into cold and hot starters, followed by fish and poultry, then meat; it's rare today that anyone orders something from all three. However, outside of brasseries, wine bars, and other simple places, it's inappropriate to order just one dish, as you'll understand when you see the waiter's expression. In recent years, the *menu dégustation* has become popular; consisting of numerous small courses, it allows for a wide sampling of the chef's offerings. In general, consider the season when ordering. Daily specials are usually based on what's freshest in the market that day.

Following are a number of menu items that appear frequently on French menus and throughout the reviews that follow. *See also* our Menu Guide at the end of the book for additional guidance.

bavarois—usually, a dessert of whipped cream, custard, and gelatin; it can also be savory, made with vegetables or fish.
blanquette—a stew—often veal—with a white-sauce base.
bouef à la Bourguignonne—a beef stew cooked in red wine, with onions, mushrooms, and bacon.
boeuf à la ficelle—pieces of beef tied with string and simmered in stock.
bouef à la mode—a refined beef stew.
boudin blanc—sausage made with white meat.
boudin noir—sausage made with pig's blood.
brandade—creamy cod purée, sometimes incorporating potato purée and garlic.
charcuterie—a selection of cold, pork-based products such as sausages, pâtés, and terrines.
choucroute—hearty dish of sauerkraut, usually accompanied by sausage, pork, and sometimes duck; also called *choucroute garnie*.
clafoutis—a hearty, flan-like tart with a base of seasonal fruit.
confit—meat (often duck), cooked in fat and preserved.
coq au vin—a classic preparation of chicken cooked in red wine and garnished with pearl onions, mushrooms, and bacon.
daube—beef stew.
fondant—traditionally, a shiny glaze used to decorate cakes and other desserts. Today, the word has a number of meanings, including flourless cake.
fricassée—any of several kinds of stews and braised dishes.
langoustine—a type of crustacean, similar to crawfish but smaller.
mille-feuille—a classic dessert composed of alternate layers of puff pastry and pastry cream (Napoléon in English).
navarin—a kind of stew, frequently made with lamb.
pastilla—originally a flaky pastry used in Moroccan cuisine. Today's French chefs use it to encase a variety of foods.
profiterole—a small cream puff with a savory or sweet filling (often ice cream).
quenelle—a dumpling, usually of fish or poultry.
ragoût—a kind of stew.
rillettes—potted, minced meat, often pork or goose.
sabayon—traditionally, an egg-and-wine-based dessert; also a savory preparation based on an egg-and-wine mixture.

Wine The wine that suits your meal is the wine you like. The traditional rule of white with fish and red with meat no longer applies. If the restaurant has a *sommelier*, let him help you. Most sommeliers are knowledgeable about their lists, and will suggest what is appropriate after you've made your tastes and budget known. In addition to the wine list, informal restaurants will have a *vin de la maison* (house wine) that is less expensive. Simpler spots will have wines *en carafe* or *en pichet*. Except for wine bars and brasseries, most restaurants do not sell wine by the glass. If you'd like something before the meal, consider ordering your wine for the meal ahead of time, or sample a typical French *apéritif*.

Dress Code Perhaps surprisingly, casual dress is acceptable at all but the fanciest restaurants. Use your judgment, of course, and remember that casual to the French does not mean without style. When in doubt, leave the sloppier blue jeans behind. In the reviews below, we have indicated where a jacket and tie are advised or required, and where casual attire is appropriate.

Prices Although prices are high, a trend toward cheaper, more informal eateries continues. We have made an effort to include a number of lower-priced establishments below. All prices include tax and tip (*service compris* or *prix nets*). No additional tip is expected, though pocket change left on the table in simple places, or an additional 5% of the bill in better restaurants, is appreciated.

The following credit card abbreviations are used: AE, American Express; DC, Diners Club; MC, MasterCard; and V, Visa.

Highly recommended restaurants are indicated by a ★.

Category	Cost*
$$$$	over 550 frs
$$$	300 frs–550 frs
$$	175 frs–300 frs
$	under 175 frs

* *per person, including tax and service but not drinks*

1st Arrondissement (Louvre)
See Right Bank Dining map

$$$$ **Le Grand Véfour.** This sumptuously decorated restaurant is perhaps the prettiest in Paris, and its 18th-century origins make it one of the oldest. Chef Guy Martin impresses with his unique blend of sophisticated yet rustic dishes, including cabbage ravioli with truffle cream. Luminaries from Napoléon to Colette to Jean Cocteau have frequented this intimate address under the arcades of the Palais-Royal; you can request to be seated at their preferred table. *17 rue Beaujolais, Métro: Palais-Royal, tel. 42–96–56–27. Reservations 1 week in advance advised. Jacket and tie required. AE, DC, MC, V. Closed Sat., Sun., and Aug.*

$$$ **Le Carré des Feuillants.** Star chef Alain Dutournier pays homage to the cuisine of his native Southwest France. Many of the restaurant's ingredients are delivered from there, including poultry, beef, and game in season. The decor, with its mix of homey and elegant, includes gorgeous Venetian glass, handsome *faux-bois* painted walls, and fanciful *trompe-l'oeil* ceilings. The Carré has one of the finest wine lists in Paris, and a special wine-and-food menu lets you sample a variety. The visible kitchen adds to the conviviality of this friendly restaurant. *14 rue Castiglione, Métro: Tuileries, tel. 42–86–82–82.*

Right Bank Dining

A. Beauvilliers, **51**
A La Cloche
des Halles, **42**
A La Courtille, **59**
Amphyclès, **14**
Apicius, **15**
Astier, **63**
Au Couchon d'Or, **57**
Au Petit Colombier, **11**
Au Pied de Cochon , **40**
Au Pressoir, **76**

Au Trou Gascon, **78**
Augusta, **17**
Aux Négotiants, **52**
Aux Petites Pères, **45**
Baracane, **66**
Batifol, **39**
Bistrot de l'Etoile
Lauriston, **9**
Bistrot des Deux
Théâtres, **50**
Brasserie Flo, **55**

Café Drouant, **44**
Casa Olympe, **49**
Chartier, **48**
Chez Bruno, **54**
Chez Fernand, **60**
Chez Georges, **43**
Chez Géraud, **1**
Chez Jenny, **65**
Chez Pauline, **32**
Chez Philippe/
Pyrénées-
Cévennes, **61**

Coconnas, **67**
Drouant, **44**
Gaya, **31**
Guy Savoy, **19**
Jacques Mélac, **64**
Jamin/Robuchon, **7**
Julien, **56**
La Butte Chaillot, **6**
La Ferme
St. Hubert, **29**
La Fermette
Marbeuf, **23**

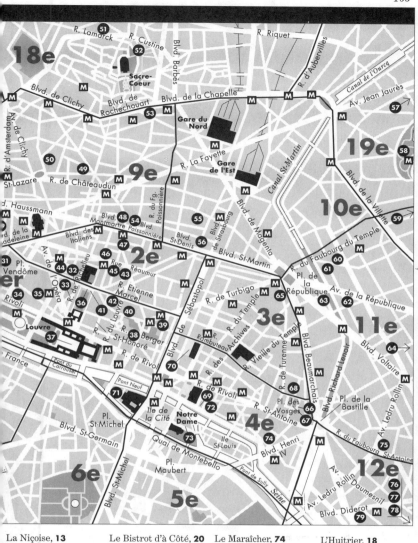

Left Bank Dining

Louvre

1er

3e

4e

Quai Anatole France

R. de l'Université

Blvd. St-Germain

Seine

R. de Bellechasse

de Grenelle

R. de Varenne

Blvd. Raspail

R. des Sts-Pères

R. Jacob

R. Mazarine

Ile de la Cité

Notre Dame

Ile St-Louis

Pl. St-Michel

R. St. Jacques

Quai de Montebello

R. du Four

Blvd. St-Germain

R. de Sèvres

R. de Rennes

R. du Cherche-Midi

R. de Vaugirard

R. d'Assas

Pl. St-Sulpice

Pl. de l'Odéon

6e

Jardin du Luxembourg

l'Observatoire

Pl. Maubert

R. des Ecoles

Ile St-Louis

5e

Pl. du Panthéon

R. Gay Lussac

R. Mouffetard

Pl. Monge

R. Monge

Jardin des Plantes

R. Claude Bernard

Pl. du 18 Juin 1940

Blvd. du Montparnasse

Cimetière de Montparnasse

Blvd. Raspail

Av. du Maine

Av. de

Av. du G¹. Leclerc

Av. R. Coty

Blvd. St-Jacques

Blvd. Arago

Blvd. de Port Royale

Blvd. St-Marcel

Av. des Gobelins

Blvd. de l'Hôpital

13e

Pl. d'Italia

Blvd. Vincent Auriol

Blvd. Auguste Blanqui

4e

10 11 12 17 18 19 20 21 14 15 16 22 23 24 25 26 27 28 29

0   1/2 mile

0   500 meters

Reservations advised. Dress: casual but elegant. AE, DC, MC, V. Closed Sat. lunch, Sun., and Aug.

Pierre. M. and Mme. Dez are always on hand to greet you in their long, two-dining-room address, a classic Parisian restaurant next to the Comédie Française. The many habitués return for the house specialties and want no contemporary gastronomic foolishness. Try the foie gras, pike *quenelles, beef à la ficelle,* and *tarte Tatin.* Dinner starts at 7 PM to accommodate Comédie Française theatergoers. *10 rue de Richelieu, Métro: Palais-Royal, tel. 42–96–09–17. Reservations advised. Dress: casual but elegant. AE, DC, MC, V. Closed Sat., Sun., and Aug.*

$$–$$$ **Chez Pauline.** This classic restaurant near the Palais Royal has be-
★ come a neighborhood institution. The setting, with wood-paneled walls, is warm and welcoming. The cooking is bourgeois, old-fashioned, and delicious. Chef André Gelin has been here for decades and his touch is sure and swift. Try the oysters in cream sauce. The wine list is filled with classic Burgundies; the lunch menu provides good value. *5 rue Villedo, Métro: Pyramides or Palais-Royal, tel. 42–96–20–70. Reservations advised. Dress: casual but elegant. AE, MC, V. Closed Sat. dinner, Sun., and 2 weeks in Aug.*

$$ **Au Pied de Cochon.** This landmark brasserie in the former Les Halles district has been popular since its founding in 1946; today, tourists make up the bulk of the clientele. Recent renovation has given it an Italian look incongruous to its classic French menu of shellfish, onion soup, steaks and, of course, the eponymous pig's feet. It's open 24 hours a day, and the terrace is a good spot for people-watching in fine weather. *6 rue Coquillière, Métro: Les Halles, tel. 42–36–11–75. Reservations advised. Dress: casual. AE, DC, MC, V.*

Gaya. Come here for seafood in all its guises, from marinated anchovies to fish soup, to grilled sole—much of it with a Mediterranean accent. The colorful Portuguese azulejos on the ground floor are delightful; upstairs is less attractive. *17 rue Duphot, Métro: Madeleine, tel. 42–60–43–03. Reservations advised. Dress: casual. AE, MC, V. Closed Sun.*

Le Grand Louvre. The austere metal-and-wood decor is in keeping with this restaurant's location under the pyramid of the Louvre. Cuisine from the southwest of France predominates and includes foie gras with raisins, pigeon terrine with walnuts, and prune ice cream with Armagnac. After dinner, the hushed, illuminated pyramid will seem to belong to you alone. *Louvre, Métro: Palais-Royal, tel. 40–20–53–41. Reservations 48 hours in advance essential. Dress: casual. AE, DC, MC, V. Closed Tues.*

$–$$ **La Tour du Montlhéry.** When the centuries-old Les Halles marketplace became an aseptic shopping mall, many neighborhood bistros closed or went upscale. With sagging wood-beamed ceilings, red-checked tablecloths, and exposed brick walls lined with creative portraits, the Montlhéry has managed to hang on to the old market feel. If you don't mind passing under hanging samples of your future meal (sausages, etc.) on your way into the dining room, jovial waiters will serve you simple grilled food. Try the *Côte de Boeuf* and wash it down with a good Beaujolais. *5 rue des Prouvaires, Métro: Les Halles, tel. 42–36–21–82. Reservations advised. Dress: casual. MC, V. Closed Sat., Sun., and July 14–Aug. 15.*

Willi's Wine Bar. This English-owned wine bar, a renowned haunt for Anglophiles as well as a chic French crowd, is a Paris phenomenon. The simple, frequently original menu changes to reflect the market's offerings and might include chicken liver terrine, sea trout with lemon butter, or guinea hen with herb vinaigrette; crème brûlée is the favorite dessert. The wine list includes more than 250 listings with an emphasis on Rhônes. The quality of the service can vary. *13 rue des Petits-Champs, Métro: Bourse, tel. 42–61–05–09. Reservations advised. Dress: casual. MC, V. Closed Sun.*

$ **A La Cloche des Halles.** Get here by 12:30 PM if you want to lunch at this small and popular wine bar in the Les Halles neighborhood. Forgive the tacky decor and enjoy quiches, omelets, and the assortments of high-quality cheeses and charcuterie. Wines, served by the glass or bottle, include some good Beaujolais. The simple menu is served until closing at 10 PM. *28 rue Coquillière, Métro: Les Halles, tel. 42–36–93–89. Reservations advised for lunch. Dress: casual. No credit cards. Closed Sun.*

Batifol. Casual tourists and business people come together comfortably in the bright, spacious original of what is now a popular Parisian chain. "Batifol" technically refers to a musical bistro, and this modern interpretation carries on the tradition with brass instruments and music-themed prints hanging side by side on the walls. This is a good place for solo diners, who can have a full meal or snack at the counter, in the company of the friendly bartenders. The food is nothing spectacular, but it's a good value and a trusty standby. *14 rue Montédour, Métro: Etienne Marcel, tel. 42–36–85–50. Dress: casual. AE, DC, MC, V.*

Le Rubis. This humble, neighborhood wine bar enjoys tremendous popularity with everyone from executives to laborers. One or two hearty plats du jour, such as *petit salé* (salted, slow-cooked pork ribs) with lentils and boudin noir plus omelettes, cheeses, and charcuterie assortments, make up the menu here. There's an eclectic selection of adequate wines by the glass or bottle. *10 rue du Marché St. Honoré, Métro: Tuileries, tel. 42–61–03–34. No reservations. Dress: casual. No credit cards. Closed Sat. eve., Sun., and mid-Aug.*

La Taverne Henri IV. This informal wine bar near the Pont Neuf, on the tip of the Ile de la Cîté, is an excellent choice for a quick lunch or snack. No full meals are served, but a selection of open-faced sandwiches on Poilâne bread (from the celebrated bakery), cheese and charcuterie plates, and varied wines by the glass or bottle make for a satisfying meal. *13 pl. du Pont Neuf, Métro: Pont Neuf, tel. 43–54–27–90. Reservations advised for lunch. Dress: casual. No credit cards. Closed Sat. dinner, Sun., and Aug.*

2nd Arrondissement (Stock Exchange)
See Right Bank Dining map

$$$$ **Drouant.** A costly renovation recently restored the luster to this Paris landmark, founded in 1880. Amid stylish Art Deco decor, diners enjoy the creations of celebrated chef Louis Grondard, whose menu might include charlotte of langoutines with eggplant, and salted veal kidney. *18 rue Gaillon, Métro: Opéra, tel. 42–65–15–16. Reservations advised. Jacket and tie required. AE, DC, MC, V.*

$$–$$$ **Pile ou Face.** This restaurant serves the most interesting and creative food around the Stock Exchange. Housed in a narrow building on two floors, it offers an intimate setting for discussing big business. The cooking is inventive, the service attentive. Try the rabbit paté and the scrambled eggs with mushrooms, then move on to the

sweetbreads and the exquisite roast chicken. *52 bis rue de Notre Dame des Victoires, Métro: Bourse, tel. 42–33–64–33. Reservations advised. Dress: casual. MC, V. Closed Sat., Sun., and Aug.*

$$ Aux Petits Pères. This old-fashioned restaurant serves fresh, cream-filled cooking in a sedate, country-style room with rustic wood-paneled walls. Try the chicken in cream and mushrooms, or the stuffed pheasant with cauliflower. The appetizers and desserts are simple, so concentrate on the main course. *6 rue Notre Dame des Victoires, Métro: Bourse, tel. 42–60–91–73. Reservations advised. Dress: casual. AE, MC, V. Closed Sat., Sun., and 1 week in Feb. and Aug.*

Café Drouant. The Café across the hall from Drouant (*see above*) shares its illustrious history and 1930s decor, but the limited menu highlighting grilled foods is one-half the price (à la carte at noon, prix-fixe at dinner). The Café serves until midnight, and its proximity to the Opéra makes it a good choice for after the ballet. *Pl. de Gaillon, Métro: Opéra, tel. 42–65–15–16. Reservations advised. Dress: casual. AE, DC, MC, V.*

Chez Georges. At this classic bistro, the atmosphere beats the food, but the food isn't bad. The wood-paneled entry leads you to an elegant yet unpretentious dining experience. One long, white-clothed stretch of table lines the mirrored walls, and attentive waiters sweep efficiently along the entire length. Enjoy the herring, the sole, the kidneys, and *frites* (French fries). *1 rue du Mail, tel. 42–60–07–11. Métro: Sentier. Reservations advised. Dress: casual. AE, DC, MC, V. Closed Sun. and Aug.*

Le Vaudeville. Like the other six Parisian brasseries of Jean-Paul Bucher, the Vaudeville has history and a good-looking clientele (many of them from the stock exchange across the street), and represents an excellent value, thanks to its assortment of fixed-price menus. Shellfish, house smoked salmon, and desserts are particularly fine. You can enjoy the handsome 1930s decor and joyful din until 2 AM daily. *29 rue Vivienne, Métro: Bourse, tel. 40–20–04–62. Reservations advised. Dress: casual. AE, DC, MC, V. Closed Christmas eve.*

3rd Arrondissement (Le Marais/Beaubourg)
See Right Bank Dining map

$ Chez Jenny. Order the filling choucroute Jenny and a carafe of Alsa-
★ tian wine, then sit back and watch the bustle at this large Alsatian brasserie decorated with museum-quality marquetry and woodwork. Waitresses in regional costume wend their way through many salons on two levels, serving forth hearty fare. Though the clientele is not the chic crowd of some other brasseries, everyone's having just as much fun. *39 blvd. du Temple, Métro: République, tel. 42–74–75–75. Reservations advised. Dress: casual. AE, DC, MC, V.*

4th Arrondissement (Le Marais/Ile St-Louis)
See Right Bank Dining map

$$$$ L'Ambroisie. This tiny, romantic restaurant on the patrician place
★ des Vosges is one of the best in Paris. Chef-owner Bernard Pacaud's refined, oft-imitated cuisine featuring such dishes as mousse of red bell peppers and braised oxtail is served in a jewel-like Italianate setting of flowers, tapestries, and subdued lighting. *9 pl. des Vosges, Métro: St-Paul, tel. 42–78–51–45. MC, V. Reservations one month in advance essential. Dress: casual but elegant. Closed Sun., Mon., Aug., and mid-Feb.*

\$\$\$ Miravile. This latest Miravile—the third for successful young owners Gilles and Muriel Epié—has vaguely California decor and a Provençal-inspired menu. Mr. Epié's celery *remoulade* with foie gras, and chocolate mille-feuille exemplify his full-flavored style. The restaurant is popular with staff members from the adjacent Hôtel de Ville (city hall). *72 quai de l'Hôtel de Ville, Métro: Pont-Marie, tel. 42–74–72–22. Reservations advised. Dress: casual. MC, V. Closed Sat. lunch, Sun.*

\$\$ Coconnas. On a soft summer evening, there may well be no prettier place in Paris than a terrace table at this restaurant on the place des Vosges. When the weather forces you inside, the red-brick interior is welcoming, with its large oil paintings depicting the place des Vosges in its heyday. The owner, Claude Terrail, also owns the Tour d'Argent; as at that celebrated restaurant, the emphasis here is more on the setting than the food. Certainly, you won't eat badly: Chicken stewed with vegetables and souffléd madeleines are just a couple of the many tempting specialties. *2 pl. des Vosges, Métro: Chémin Vert or St-Paul, tel. 42–78–58–16. Reservations advised. Dress: casual. AE, DC, MC, V. Closed Mon. and Dec. 20–Jan. 20; also closed Tues. in winter (Oct.–Feb.).*

Le Vieux Bistrot. Forgive the corny name and touristy location next to Notre Dame. This really *is* generations old, and its menu is full of bistro classics such as beef fillet with marrow, giant éclairs, and *tarte tatin*, the French version of apple pie, flambé. Decor is nondescript, but the frequently fancy crowd doesn't seem to notice. *14 rue du Cloître-Notre-Dame, Métro: Hôtel de Ville, tel. 43–54–18–95. Reservations advised. Dress: casual. MC, V.*

\$ ★ Baracane. This is one of the best values in the Marais district. The owner oversees the menu, full of the robust specialties of his native Southwest France, including rabbit confit, veal tongue, and pear poached in wine and cassis. There's a reasonable dinner menu and cheaper menu at lunch. *38 rue des Tournelles, Métro: Bastille, tel. 42–71–43–33. Reservations advised. Dress: casual. MC, V. Closed Sat. lunch, Sun.*

Le Grizzli. It's said this turn-of-the-century bistro was one of the last to have dancing bears as entertainment—thus the name. Today's owner gets many of his ingredients—especially the wonderful ham and cheeses—from his native Auvergne. Several dishes are cooked on hot slate, including salmon and lamb. There's an interesting selection of wines from Southwest France. Prices here are at the low end of our Moderate range. *7 rue St. Martin, Métro: Châtelet, tel. 48–87–77–56. Reservations advised. Dress: casual. MC, V. Closed Sun.*

Le Maraîcher. With its exposed stone walls and wood beams, this intimate little restaurant on a quiet street in the Marais is very *vieux Paris*. The young owner worked at the renowned Lucas-Carton, which may account for the table settings and service, which are surprisingly refined considering the reasonable prices. Freshness and seasonality are hallmarks of such dishes as roasted lamb filet with eggplant and coquilles St-Jacques with potato pulp in a balsamic vinaigrette. For dessert, try the caramelized apple mille-feuille with cream, or the bittersweet chocolate mousse. *5 rue Beautreillis, Métro: Sully-Morland, tel. 42–71–42–49. Reservations advised. Dress: casual. MC, V. Closed Sat. lunch, Sun., late July–early Aug.*

Trumilou. Popular with students, artist types, and others on a budget, the Trumilou serves unremarkable bistro cuisine such as leg of lamb and apple tart. But the homely non-decor is somehow homey, and the staff is friendly despite the crowd. The location facing the Seine and the Ile St-Louis is especially pleasant in nice weather, when you can sit on a narrow terrace under the trees. *84 quai de l'Hôtel de Ville, Métro: Pont-Marie, tel. 42–77–63–98. Reservations accepted. Dress: casual. MC, V. Closed Mon.*

5th Arrondissement (Latin Quarter)
See Left Bank Dining map

$$$$
★ **La Tour d'Argent.** Dining at this temple to haute cuisine is a theatrical and unique event—from apéritifs in the ground-floor bar to dinner in the top-floor dining room, with its breath-taking view of Notre Dame. Come for the setting; the food does not reach the same heights. In recent years elegant owner Claude Terrail has hired a series of young chefs, and today's menu is a mix of Tour classics and contemporary creations. Venerable favorites such as *caneton* Tour d'Argent (pressed duck), quenelles André Terrail, and filets de sole Cardinal have been lightened, and new dishes added, including scallop salad with truffles and double-thick lamb chops with carrots. The wine list is one of the greatest in the world. Visit the cellars before or after a meal. The lunch menu is suprisingly affordable. *15 quai de la Tournelle, Métro: Cardinal Lemoine, tel. 43–54–23–31. Reservations required at least 1 week in advance. Jacket and tie required at dinner, advised at lunch. AE, DC, MC, V. Closed Mon.*

$$–$$$
★ **La Timonerie.** Only a few steps along the quai from La Tour d'Argent, this small, elegant restaurant avoids all theatrics and sticks to fine cooking. Philippe de Givenchy works with a small staff and his proposals are consistently interesting and well-executed. In his hands, simple products such as rosemary and lemon mackerel are turned into high-class eating experiences. *35 quai de la Tournelle, Métro: Maubert Mutalité, tel. 43–25–44–42. Reservations advised. Jacket and tie advised. MC, V. Closed Sun. and Mon.*

$$
★ **Campagne et Provence.** The talented young owners of the Miravile (*see* 4th Arrondissement, *above*) also run this small establishment on the quai across from Notre Dame. Fresh, colorful, Provençal-inspired cuisine includes vegetables stuffed with cod brandade, and ratatouille. The list of reasonably priced regional wines helps keep prices down. *25 quai de la Tournelle, Métro: Maubert-Mutualité, tel. 43–54–05–17. Reservations advised. Dress: casual. MC, V. Closed Mon. lunch, Sat. lunch, Sun.*

Moissonnier. Mr. and Mme. Moissonnier are always present to greet their faithful habitués. The Lyonnais cuisine includes *saladiers Lyonnais* (assorted cold salads), pike quenelles, eggs in a *meurette* (red wine) sauce, and, to drink, a variety of Beaujolais. With its homey decor, this is the perfect place to experience a typical French Sunday lunch. Ask to be seated in the ground-floor dining room. *28 rue des Fossés-St-Bernard, Métro: Cardinal Lemoine, tel. 43–29–87–65. Reservations advised. Dress: casual. MC, V. Closed Sun. eve., Mon., Aug.*

$
Chez René. This reliable address at the eastern end of the blvd. St-Germain has satisfied three generations of Parisians, who count on finding Burgundian dishes such as boeuf à la Bourguignonne and coq au vin, and the wines of the Maconnais and Beaujolais. The dining rooms are cozy. *14 blvd. St-Germain, Métro: Cardinal Lemoine, tel. 43–54–30–23. Reservations advised. Dress: casual. MC, V. Closed Sat., Sun., Aug., and Dec. 23–Jan. 3.*

6th Arrondissement (Luxembourg)
See Left Bank Dining map

$$ **Lipp.** At this classic Left Bank brasserie, politicians, entertainers, rubber-necking tourists, and everyone else vie for tables, especially in the ground-floor dining room. Being sent up to the second floor is the best sign that you count for nothing in Paris. All the socializing distracts you from the food, which is classic brasserie-style stuff: herring in cream, choucroute, and mille-feuille. The pretty decor is straight from the 1920s, and the ceramics are landmarked. *151 blvd. St-Germain, Métro: St-Germain-des-Prés, tel. 45–48–53–91. No reservations; expect lines. Dress: jacket and tie required. AE, DC, MC, V. Closed mid-July–mid-Aug.*

Le Petit Zinc. It's hard to believe the extravagant *fin-de-siècle*-style decor is new. The kitchen does a creditable job with shellfish, veal liver, and duck confit. Careful ordering will lessen the cost of your meal. Le Muniche, next door, has the same owners and lively atmosphere. *11 rue St-Benoît, Métro: St-Germain-des-Prés, tel. 42–61–20–60. Reservations strongly advised. Dress: casual. AE, DC, MC, V.*

La Rôtisserie d'En Face. A long rotisserie is part of the attractive country-elegant decor at this bistro created by renowned chef Jacques Cagna. Overcrowding sometimes results in lowered cooking standards, but this is one of the most popular of the "chef-bistros" sprouting up across the city. The cuisine includes roast chicken with mashed potatoes and grilled salmon with spinach. The menu is fixed-price only, and it's cheaper at lunch. Dinner is two set seatings only. *2 rue Christine, Métro: Odéon, tel. 43–26–40–98. Reservations advised. MC, V. Closed Sat. dinner.*

$ **Claude Sainlouis.** For 35 years now, Claude Piau has depended on the same formula: inexpensive steak, fries, and salad. There's not much variety, but all of Paris—professionals, tourists, lovers—crowd boisterously into the dark, red dining room for lunch and dinner. *27 rue du Dragon, Métro: St-Germain des Prés, tel. 45–48–29–68. Dress: casual. No credit cards. Closed Sat. dinner, Sun., Aug., and 15 days at Easter and Christmas.*

7th Arrondissement (Invalides)
See Left Bank Dining map

$$$$ **L'Arpège.** This small, striking restaurant one block from the Rodin
★ Museum is currently one of the most talked-about of Paris's restaurants. It features the cuisine of young chef-owner Alain Passard, whose menu is both original (lobster/turnip starter in a sweet-sour vinaigrette, stuffed sweet tomato) and classic (beef Burgundy, pressed duck). The problem here is inconsistency: one sublime meal followed by a mediocre experience. With its curving, hand-crafted wood panels and wrought-iron window frames, the decor is unusually minimalist. Service, although young and energetic, sometimes falls behind. The fixed-price lunch is a steal. *84 rue de Varenne, Métro: Varenne, tel. 45–51–47–33. Reservations advised. Dress: casual but elegant. AE, DC, MC, V. Closed Sat., Sun. lunch, Aug.*

Duquesnoy. This pretty, pastel dining room is one of the most enjoyable restaurants in Paris. Mr. Duquesnoy's cuisine is original without pretense or excess, with seasonal dishes such as truffle and potato ravioli, cabbage, and baby *babas au rhum*. An excellent wine list, professional service (overseen by the charming Mme. Duquesnoy), and a discreet atmosphere complete the picture. *6 av.*

Bosquet, Métro: Ecole Militaire, tel. 47–05–96–78. Reservations advised. Dress: casual but elegant. AE, MC, V. Closed Sat. lunch, Sun., Aug.

Jules Verne. Distinctive all-black decor, stylish service, and the new, top-ranked chef Alain Reix—not to mention a location at 400 feet, on the second level of the Eiffel Tower—have made the Jules Verne one of the hardest dinner reservations to get in Paris. Soufflé of giant crab and lobster tournedos in a veal and butter sauce are examples of Chef Reix's colorful, flavorful cuisine. The restaurant is open daily, and a lunch table is easier to snag. *Eiffel Tower, Métro: Bir-Hakeim, tel. 45–55–61–44. Reservations 2 months in advance for dinner at window table. Jacket and tie required. AE, DC, MC, V.*

$$$–$$$$ **Le Divellec.** This is perhaps Paris's best and most expensive fish restaurant. Located on the place des Invalides, it counts President Mitterand among its celebrated customers. Most dishes are very light. The specialty of the house is created using one of only three lobster presses in the world; the lobster is boiled, pressed, lightly creamed, and daintily garnished. The restaurant's decor pays homage to the sea with blue, wave-inspired paneling and nautical decor. *107 rue de l'Université, Métro: Invalides, tel. 45–51–91–96. Reservations 2 weeks in advance advised. Dress: elegant. AE, DC, MC, V. Closed Sun.*

$–$$ **L'Oeillade.** Come here for great value. The decor of blond-wood paneling and interesting, 20th-century paintings is without pretention, and there's a low-key clientele to match. Sample the avocado beignets and move on to the coquilles St-Jacques with endive fondu. Watch out for the wines—they will intoxicate your bill. *10 rue de St-Simon, Métro: Rue du Bac, tel. 42–22–01–60. Reservations advised. Dress: casual. MC, V. Closed Sat. lunch, Sun.*

$ **Aux Fins Gourmets.** What would the far western end of the blvd. St-Germain be without this comforting bistro? Solid country dishes prevail: *pipérade* (mixture of eggs, peppers, onions, tomatoes, and garlic), duck confit, and cassoulet. Pastries come from the excellent shop Peltier. In warm weather, dinner or lunch on the sidewalk terrace, under the shady plane trees, is a delight. *213 blvd. St-Germain, Métro: Bac, tel. 42–22–06–57. Reservations advised. Dress: casual. No credit cards. Closed Sun., Mon. lunch, Aug.*

Chez l'Ami Jean. Neighborhood families comprise a large portion of the clientele, and it's easy to see why they find this homey Basque restaurant so welcoming. The haphazard decor includes banners, baskets, and photos of the staff and regulars. Enjoy the *pipérade*— scrambled eggs and tomatoes. Try the duck or goose confits, and end your meal with the nutty *gâteau basque. 27 rue Malar, Métro: La Tour Maubourg, tel. 47–05–86–89. Reservations advised. Dress: casual. MC, V. Closed Sun. and Aug.*

Thoumieux. Virtually everything at this third-generation restaurant is made on the premises, including foie gras, rillettes, duck confit, cassoulet, and the homey desserts. The red velour banquettes, mellow yellow walls, and bustling waiters in long, white aprons are delightfully Parisian. *79 rue St. Dominique, Métro: Invalides, tel. 47–05–49–75. Reservations advised. Dress: casual. MC, V.*

8th Arrondissement (Champs-Elysées)
See Right Bank Dining map

$$$$ **Ledoyen.** Chef Ghislaine Arabien is the most talked about up-and-
★ coming chef in Paris. She sets gastronomic fashion by concentrating
on northern French cuisine, and creates specialties featuring beer
sauces, including *coquilles St-Jacques à la bière*. The elegant restaurant, with its gilded ceilings and walls, plush armchairs, and a
candelabra on each table, is set in an equally posh location off the
Champs-Elysées near place de la Concorde. *1 av. du Tuit, on the
Carré des Champs-Elysées, Métro: Place de la Concorde or
Champs-Elysées–Clemenceau, tel. 47–42–23–23. Reservations essential. Dress: elegant. AE, DC, MC, V. Closed weekends.*

Les Ambassadeurs. This dining room in the opulent Crillon is un-
doubtedly the finest hotel restaurant in Paris. Respected chef
Christian Constant is a master at giving even the humblest ingredients sophistication, as exemplified by his *petit salé* of cod, his rabbit
with marjoram, and his pork with spider crab. Some find the all-
marble dining room, with its crystal chandeliers, mirrors, and
heavy blue draperies, to be stiff and inhospitable. But no one can
fault the view onto the place de la Concorde, the distinguished service, or the memorable wine list. Lunch is more affordable, though
still expensive; there's also a good brunch. *10 pl. de la Concorde,
Métro: Concorde, tel. 44–71–16–16. Reservations essential. Jacket
and tie required at dinner. AE, DC, MC, V.*

Lucas-Carton. Chef Alain Senderens continues to create a provocative blend of nouvelle and classic cuisine, including foie gras
wrapped in cabbage, a very spicy duck Apicius, and pastilla of rabbit. The beautiful dining rooms glow with Belle Epoque splendor,
and the crowd is international and one of the dressiest in Paris. *9 pl.
de la Madeleine, Métro: Madeleine, tel. 42–65–22–90. Reservations
at least 3 weeks in advance essential. Jacket and tie required at dinner. MC, V. Closed Sat. lunch, Sun., Christmas week, and Aug.*

★ **Taillevent.** Many say it's the best restaurant in Paris. Within the
wood-paneled main dining rooms of this mid-19th-century mansion
you will find exceptional service that is never over-bearing, a stellar
wine list, and the tempered classic cuisine of young chef Philippe Le-
gendre. Among his signature dishes are lobster boudin and lamb
with cabbage. Pastry chef Gilles Bajolle is one of the finest in Paris.
Try his *nougatine glacée aux poires* (thin layers of nougatine and
pear sherbet) or tarte Tatin with quince. Book three to four weeks
ahead. *15 rue Lamennais, Métro: Charles de Gaulle/Etoile, tel. 45–
63–39–94. Reservations essential. Jacket and tie required. AE,
MC, V. Closed weekends, Aug.*

$$$ **Le Carré des Champs-Elysées.** This luxury brasserie sits below the
landmark restaurant Ledoyen (*see above*). For about $50 a dinner,
wine included, you can sample chef Ghislaine Arabian's cooking, in-
cluding her specials served at Ledoyen. The handsome, curved din-
ing room is a pleasure year-round, and the terrace is a special treat
in warm weather. *Carré des Champs-Elysées, Métro: Champs-
Elysées–Clemenceau, tel. 47–42–23–23. Reservations advised.
Dress: casual but elegant. AE, DC, MC, V. Closed Sun.*

$$–$$$ **Le Bistrot du Sommelier.** The 30-page wine list is the chief attraction
at this restaurant owned by Philippe Faure-Brac, elected the
world's Best Sommelier in 1992. The jolly Faure-Brac welcomes you
into his warm establishment and particularly recommends the res-
taurant's selections from the Rhône Valley. Decor includes harvest-

themed tapestries and frescoes, and dishes include ravioli with
fresh herbs and cheese or with truffles and fattened pullet in yellow
wine. The dinner menu for about $60 offers six dishes with six
wines. *97 blvd. Haussmann, Métro: St-Augustin, tel. 42–65–24–85.
Reservations essential. Dress: casual. AE, DC, MC, V. Closed
Sat., Sun., and Aug.*

$$ La Fermette Marbeuf. It's a favorite haunt of French TV and movie
★ stars, who like the spectacular Belle Epoque mosaics, tiles, and
stained glass (discovered by accident when the restaurant was being
redecorated), and appreciate the solid, updated classic cuisine. Try
gâteau of chicken livers and sweetbreads, lamb navarin with vegeta-
bles, and bitter chocolate fondant. Prices here are exceptional, con-
sidering the quality of the food, the surroundings, and the
neighborhood. La Fermette becomes animated late, around 9. *5 rue
Marbeuf, Métro: Franklin D. Roosevelt, tel. 47–20–63–53. Reser-
vations advised. Dress: casual but elegant. AE, DC, MC, V.*

Savy. This 60-year-old restaurant still wears an honest, homey face,
despite its rarified avenue Montaigne location. Expect 1950s decor
and substantial cuisine, with specialties of central France such as
stuffed cabbage, roast lamb shoulder, and apple tart. *23 rue Ba-
yard, Métro: Franklin D. Roosevelt, tel. 47–23–46–98. MC, V. Res-
ervations advised. Dress: casual. Closed weekends and Aug.*

Sébillon. The original Sébillon has nurtured chic residents of the
fashionable suburb of Neuilly for generations, and this elegant, pol-
ished new branch off the Champs-Elysées should do as well. The
menu is similar, with lobster salad, lots of shellfish, and—its great
specialty—roast leg of lamb sliced at table and served in unlimited
quantity. Service is notably friendly. *66 rue Pierre Charron, Métro:
Franklin D. Roosevelt, tel. 43–59–28–15. Reservations advised.
Dress: casual chic. AE, DC, MC, V.*

$ La Ferme St. Hubert. Reserve ahead for lunch, as this unpretentious
spot serving primarily cheese dishes is mobbed then. The owner has
a cheese shop next door—one of the best in the city—and from its
shelves come the main ingredients for fondue, raclette, and the best
croque St-Hubert (toasted cheese sandwich) in Paris. The house
wines are decent, and the location is convenient to the fancy food
shop, Fauchon, on the place de la Madeleine. *21 rue Vignon, Métro:
Madeleine, tel. 47–42–79–20. Reservations essential at lunch, ad-
vised at dinner. Dress: casual. AE, MC, V. Closed Sun.*

9th Arrondissement (Opéra)
See Right Bank Dining map

$$$ La Table d'Anvers. One of the best restaurants near Montmartre, it
★ serves an interesting menu, with Italian and Provençal touches in
dishes like gnocchi of langoustines and *girolles* (wild mushrooms),
saddle of rabbit with polenta, and *croustillant* of asparagus with
scampi. La Table's wide range of chocolate desserts is among the
best in Paris; serious sweet-tooths can indulge in an all-dessert
menu, which includes a single token fish dish. *2 pl. d'Anvers, Métro:
Anvers, tel. 48–78–35–21. Reservations advised. Dress: casual but
elegant. AE, MC, V. Closed Sat. lunch, Sun., mid-Aug.*

$$ Casa Olympe. Beginning in the 1970s, a few feminist pioneers began
★ to break into the exclusive world of haute cuisine. Among them,
Dominique Nahmias, alias Olympe, displays a rare creativity. The
modern, no-frills dining room of her new restaurant below Mont-
martre is the setting for her limited but strong menu spotlighting

masterful renditions of French dishes like steak tartare. Everyone from professionals to Montmartre hipsters is starting to pour into this sedate eating place, already one of the hottest spots in town. *48 rue St-Georges, Métro: St-Georges, tel. 42–85–26–01. Reservations advised. Dress: casual. MC, V. Closed Sat., Sun., and Aug.*

$ Bistrot des Deux Théâtres. Quality is high and prices are low in this well-run restaurant in the Pigalle/Clichy area. The prix-fixe menu includes apéritif, first and main courses, a cheese or dessert course, half a bottle of wine, and coffee. The food is far from banal; try salad of foie gras and the apple tart flambéed with Calvados. *18 rue Blanche, Métro: Trinité, tel. 45–26–41–43. Reservations advised. Dress: casual. MC, V.*

Chartier. This cavernous turn-of-the-century restaurant enjoys a huge following among the budget-minded, including students, solitary bachelors, and tourists. You may find yourself sharing a table with strangers as you study the long, old-fashioned menu of such favorites as hard-boiled eggs with mayonnaise, pâté, and roast veal with spinach. *7 rue du Faubourg-Montmartre, Métro: Rue Montmartre, tel. 47–70–86–29. No reservations. Dress: casual. No credit cards.*

Chez Bruno. In a theater neighborhood with few good, inexpensive restaurants, this jazzy bistro stands out. The dim, casual interior, photos and posters, and soft music all bow to Jazz. A solid 60-franc menu gets you three courses; 130 francs does the same but serves a homemade foie gras with the house special of fondu Bourguignonne. There's also an interesting, inexpensive afternoon tea service. *5 rue Bergère, Métro: Rue Montmartre, tel. 45–23–24–42. Reservations advised. Dress: casual. AE, MC, V. Closed Sat. lunch, Sun.*

10th Arrondissement (République)
See Right Bank Dining map

$$ Brasserie Flo. This, the first of brasserie king Jean-Paul Bucher's seven Paris addresses, is hard to find down its passageway near the Gare de l'Est, but worth the effort. The rich wood- and stained-glass interior is typically Alsatian, the service enthusiastic, and the brasserie standards such as shellfish, steak tartare, and choucroute tasty. Order one of the carafes of Alsatian wine. It's open until 1:30 AM, with a special night-owl menu from 11 PM. *7 cour des Petites Ecuries, Métro: Château d'Eau, tel. 47–70–13–59. Reservations advised. Dress: casual but elegant. AE, DC, MC, V.*

Julien. Another Bucher brasserie (*see above*), this one is a kind of poor man's Maxim's, with dazzling Belle Epoque decor. The menu offers brasserie fare, with smoked salmon, foie gras, cassoulet, and good sherbets. The crowd is ebullient and lots of fun. There's service until 1:30 AM, with a special night-owl menu from 11 PM. *16 rue du Faubourg St. Denis, Métro: Strasbourg-St-Denis, tel. 47–70–12–06. Reservations advised. Dress: casual but elegant. AE, DC, MC, V.*

11th Arrondissement (Bastille)
See Right Bank Dining map

$$ Chez Fernand. The chef-owner of this neighborhood spot near the place de la République is more concerned with his Normandy-inspired cuisine than with his restaurant's inconsequential decor. Mackerel rillettes, skate with Camembert, and duck are examples of his varied style. Also try the selection of Camemberts. The owner's smaller Fernandises, next door, is even less expensive. *17 rue Fontaine-au-Roi, Métro: République, tel. 43–57–46–25. Reservations advised. Dress: casual. MC, V. Closed Sun., Mon., Aug.*

★ **Chez Philippe/Pyrénées-Cévennes.** Old-timers still refer to this comfortable bistro by its original name—Pyrénées-Cévennes—while others know it as Chez Philippe. The eclectic menu combines the cooking of Burgundy, central France—even Spain—in such dishes as snails in garlic butter, cassoulet, and paella. An attentive staff bustles amid cozy surroundings, with beamed ceiling and polished copper. *106 rue de la Folie-Méricourt, Métro: République, tel. 43–57–33–78. Reservations advised. Dress casual. MC, V. Closed weekends, Aug.*

$ **Astier.** You'll find remarkable value at this pleasant restaurant, where the prix-fixe menu (there's no à la carte) includes first and main courses, cheese (excellent), and dessert. Among high-quality seasonal dishes, try mussel soup with saffron, fricassée of beef cheeks, and plum clafoutis. Service can be rushed, but the enthusiastic crowd does not seem to mind. Study the excellent wine list, which has some surprising buys. *44 rue Jean-Pierre Timbaud, Métro: Parmentier, tel. 43–57–16–35. Reservations advised. Dress: casual. AE, MC, V. Closed weekends, Aug.*

★ **Jacques Mélac.** There's robust cuisine to match the noisy camaraderie at this popular wine bar–restaurant, owned by mustachioed Jacques Mélac. Charcuterie, a salad of preserved duck gizzards, braised beef, and cheeses from central France make good choices here. Mr. Mélac has his own miniature vineyard out the front door and hosts a jolly party at harvest time. *42 rue Léon Frot, Métro: Charonne, tel. 43–70–59–27. Dress: casual. MC, V. Closed Mon. dinner, weekends Aug.*

Le Passage. The friendly Passage is located in the rather obscure Passage de la Bonne Graine, not far from the place de la Bastille. Though it bills itself as a wine bar, it has a full menu, including five styles of *andouillettes* (chitterling sausage). The wine list is excellent. *18 Passage de la Bonne Graine (enter by 108 av. Ledru-Rollin), Métro: Ledru-Rollin, tel. 47–00–73–30. Reservations advised. Dress: casual. AE, MC, V. Closed Sat. lunch, Sun.*

Le Villaret. The owner of this newcomer once ran the excellent Astier (*see above*), and his experience shows. Menu choices are often interesting, always well prepared. Try salmon tart, hot foie gras salad, duck confit, and seasonal fruit clafoutis. Decor, with exposed stone and half-timbering, combines traditional and modern styles. The restaurant does not serve lunch, but makes up for that by serving dinner until 1 AM. *13 rue Ternaux, Métro: Parmentier, tel. 43–57–89–76. Reservations advised. Dress: casual. MC, V. Closed lunch, Sun., Aug.*

12th Arrondissement (Gare de Lyon)
See Right Bank Dining map

$$$ **Au Pressoir.** This excellent restaurant in the eastern part of Paris deserves more attention than it receives. Chef-owner Henri Séguin's menu is original, with exciting choices such as fricassée of lobster with morels, pigeon with eggplant blinis, and chocolate soup with brioche. The wine list is tops, and service is friendly and professional. *257 av. Daumesnil, Métro: Michel Bizot, tel. 43–44–38–21. Reservations advised. Dress: casual. MC, V. Closed weekends, mid-Feb., Aug.*

Au Trou Gascon. The success of this Belle Epoque establishment off the place Daumesnil enabled owner Alain Dutournier to open the now-renowned Carré des Feuillants in the 1st arrondissement (*see above*). He's still the owner here, too, and continues to serve his personal version of the cuisine of Gascony, a region of outstanding ham, foie gras, lamb, and poultry. His white chocolate mousse is now a classic. *40 rue Taine, Métro: Daumesnil, tel. 43–44–34–26. Reservations advised. Dress: casual. AE, DC, MC, V. Closed weekends, Christmas week, Aug.*

★ **L'Oulette.** Chef-owner Marcel Baudis once ran his restaurant from a smaller location in the 4th arrondissement, but success encouraged him to open this larger, fancier spot, with lean, modern decor. Although something indefinable was lost in the move, the cuisine of Baudis's native Southwest France is as good as ever. Recommended dishes include oxtail with foie gras, fresh cod with celeriac and walnuts, and *pain d'épices* (spice cake). The restaurant, in the rebuilt Bercy district, is a bit hard to find. *15 pl. Lachambeaudie, Métro: Dugommier, tel. 40–02–02–12. Reservations advised. Dress: casual. AE, MC, V. Closed Sat. lunch, Sun.*

Le Train Bleu. This historic brasserie in the Gare de Lyon was recently restored, and its gorgeous 19th-century frescos are more impressive than ever. Chef Michel Comby heads the kitchen, and turns out standard brasserie fare, such as herring in cream and hot sausage. Prices are high, but if you come to the station to catch a train, consider stopping here, even if just for a drink. *Gare de Lyon, Métro: Gare de Lyon, tel. 43–43–09–06. Reservations advised. Dress: casual. AE, DC, MC, V.*

13th Arrondissement (Les Gobelins)
See Left Bank Dining map

$$$ Au Petit Marguéry. Both staff and diners seem to be having a good time in this warm, convivial bistro run by three brothers. The menu goes beyond the usual bistro classics to include such dishes as cold lobster, cod fillet with spices, and excellent lamb of the Pyrénées. Prices are at the low end of this category. *9 blvd. de Port Royal, Métro: Les Gobelins, tel. 43–31–58–59. Reservations advised. Dress: casual. AE, DC, MC, V. Closed Sun., Mon., Christmas week, Aug.*

14th Arrondissement (Montparnasse)
See Left Bank Dining map

$$$ La Cagouille. This is one of the best fish restaurants in Paris. Bearlike Gérard Allemandou moved his intimate and very successful *bistro à poissons* to this vast, modern space on the somewhat sterile place Brancusi several years ago. But his style remains the same: Few sauces or adornments mask the fresh, clean flavors of fish, from elegant sole and turbot to more pedestrian sardines and mackeral. Besides its excellent wine list, La Cagouille has the finest collection of Cognacs in the city. There's a large terrace for warm-weather dining. *10–12 pl. Brancusi, Métro: Gaîté, tel. 43–22–09–01. Reservations advised. Dress: casual but elegant. AE, MC, V.*

$$ Contre-Allée. This large, simply decorated restaurant is popular with a Left Bank crowd of students and professor-types. The interesting menu includes original choices, such as squid salad with mussels, and roast cod with parmesan. Homemade fresh pasta accompanies many dishes. A sidewalk terrace enlivens shady

Denfert-Rochereau. The restaurant serves until 11:30 PM. *83 av. Denfert-Rochereau, Métro: Denfert-Rochereau, tel. 43–54–99–86. Reservations advised. Dress: casual. AE, DC, MC, V. Closed Sat. lunch.*

La Coupole. This world-renowned, cavernous address in Montparnasse practically defines the term brasserie. Many find it too large, too noisy, and too expensive. But everyone from Left Bank intellectuals (Jean-Paul Sartre and Simone de Beauvoir were regulars) to bourgeois grandmothers come here. Owner Jean-Paul Bucher (of the Flo group of brasseries) had the sense to leave well enough alone when he restored it, simply polishing and cleaning the famous murals. Expect the usual brasserie menu, including perhaps the largest shellfish presentation in Paris, choucroute, and a big choice of desserts. The buffet breakfast from 7:30 to 10:30 daily is an excellent value. *102 blvd. du Montparnasse, Métro: Vavin, tel. 43–20–14–20. Reservations advised. Dress: casual. AE, DC, MC, V.*

★ **Le Pavillon Montsouris.** This bucolic building on the edge of Parc Montsouris was recently restored, and the pretty pastel interior and large terrace facing the park make for a charming spot on a sunny day. A multichoice, prix-fixe menu is a real bargain, and dishes prepared by the bright, young chef are fresh and interesting, and rarely repeated. Service can slow down during peak times; give yourself you have time for a leisurely meal. *20 rue Gazan, Métro: RER Cité-Universitaire, tel. 45–88–38–52. Reservations advised. Dress: casual. AE, DC, MC, V.*

$ **La Régalade.** This is one of the most talked about new restaurants in
★ Paris. The address, right next to the highway, is nothing to write home about, but Yves Camdeborde's cooking is stunning. Although a veteran of the Crillon, he has kept his prices remarkably low—$30 for a three-course feast. Tables are booked as much as a month in advance, but service does continue until midnight and often you can sneak in later in the evening. *49 av. Jean-Moulin, Métro: Alesia, tel. 45–45–68–58. Reserve 1 month in advance. Dress: casual. MC, V. Closed Sat. lunch, Sun., Mon., Aug.*

Le Bistrot du Dôme. This cheery yellow fish bistro in Montparnasse belongs to the fancy and expensive Dôme, and benefits from that elegant brasserie's excellent sources of fish. The many seafood dishes are always very fresh and simply presented; try the poached stingray in a vinaigrette sauce. Decor includes colorful tiles and pretty Italian glass light fixtures. Jovial service and a limited but affordable wine list add to the enjoyment. *1 rue Delambre, Métro: Vavin, tel. 43–35–32–00. Reservations advised. Dress: casual. AE, MC, V.*

15th Arrondissement (Front de Seine)
See Left Bank Dining map

$$$ **Pierre Vedel.** Burly Pierre Vedel's very Parisian bistro attracts entertainers and other fashionable patrons, which may account for some surly service if you are not well-known. Mr. Vedel's menu changes according to what looks good in the market, but generally includes Mediterranean-inspired dishes such as brandade, poached eggs with tomato sauce, *osso bucco* (braised veal shanks) with lemon, and peach soup with mint. *19 rue Duranton, Métro: Boucicaut, tel. 45–58–43–17. Reservations advised. Dress: casual chic. MC, V. Closed weekends.*

★ **Morot-Gaudry.** Located on top of a building near the Ecole Militaire, this popular address offers the luxury of well-spaced tables and an unusual outlook over Paris. Chef-owner Jean-Pierre Morot-Gaudry prepares a personalized cuisine that's a combination of classic and modern. Seasonal dishes might include scallops with Jerusalem artichokes, veal blanquette, and chocolate mille-feuille with wild raspberries. The menu marries a different wine with each dish; the prix-fixe lunch menu is less expensive. *6 rue de la Cavalerie, Métro: Motte-Picquet, tel. 45-67-06-85. Reservations advised. Dress: casual. AE, MC, V. Closed weekends.*

$$ **Le Barrail.** A favorite with staff from nearby *Le Monde*, this good neighborhood spot offers hospitable service in an unassuming setting. Impeccable ingredients go into such dishes as foie gras aux pommes and the increasingly hard-to-find potatoes *Dauphine* (potatoes mashed with pâté à choux and deep-fried). Ordering the prix-fixe menu here will lessen the cost of your meal. *17 rue Falguière, Métro: Pasteur, tel. 43-22-42-61. Reservations advised. Dress: casual. AE, MC, V. Closed weekends, early Aug.*

Le Clos Morillons. The chef here has made many trips to the Far East, and his cuisine incorporates such oriental flavorings as sesame and ginger. But the menu is unmistakably French, with its delicious terrine of potato with foie gras, roast guinea fowl, and the all-chocolate dessert (several kinds of chocolate desserts on one plate). Added pluses are the professional service in the quiet dining room, an interesting wine list emphasizing Loire wines, and less-expensive fixed-price menus at lunch and dinner. *50 rue Morillons, Métro: Convention, tel. 48-28-04-37. Reservations advised. Dress: casual. MC, V. Closed Sat. lunch, Sun., middle 2 weeks of Aug.*

$ **L'Armoise.** At this quiet neighborhood restaurant near the Front de Seine development, chef-owner Georges Outhier prepares one of the best veal livers in Paris, along with such treats as a delicious duck breast with honey and pot-au-feu de la mer. Madame Outhier is an attentive hostess in the salmon-pink dining rooms. *67 rue des Entrepreneurs, Métro: Charles Michel, tel. 45-79-03-31. Reservations advised. Dress: casual. MC, V. Closed Sat. lunch, Sun. mid-Feb., Aug.*

16th Arrondissement (Trocadéro/Bois de Boulogne)
See Right Bank Dining map

$$$$ **Jamin/Robuchon.** Surely it's the hardest reservation to obtain in
★ France. Chef-owner Joël Robuchon, though under 50, has already attained cult status, and his influence on cooks around the globe is great. Under his inspired vision, everything from John Dory with ginger and cream of cauliflower with caviar to saddle of lamb in a salt crust and even pig's head become visual and gustatory revelations. Antoine Hernandez, chef-sommelier, is a gentle guide through the impressive wine list, and service in general is attentive and professional. The big news here is that Robuchon has moved out of his old cramped quarters into a brighter, more airy space in a sparkling new *hôtel particulier*. *59 av. Raymond Poincaré, Métro: Victor Hugo, tel. 47-27-12-27. Reservations essential. Jacket required, jacket and tie advised. MC, V. Closed weekends, July.*

Le Pré Catalan. Dining beneath the chestnut trees on the terrace of this fanciful palace restaurant in the Bois de Boulogne is a Belle Epoque fantasy. Chef Roland Durand has brought new life to the cuisine of this venerable establishment, with elegant dishes such as risotto with langoustines, sweetbreads with morels and asparagus tips, and chocolate and pistachio cake. The lunch menu is more reasonably priced. *Bois de Boulogne, rte. de Surèsnes, Métro: Porte*

Dauphine, tel. 45–24–55–58. Reservations essential. Jacket and tie advised. AE, DC, MC, V. Closed Sun. eve., Mon., mid-Feb.

★ **Le Vivarois.** Chef-owner Claude Peyrot is one of the most inspired and creative of contemporary French chefs, though his cooking can be uneven. He is a master with fish and puff pastry, his *bavarois* of red bell pepper (a creamy, molded concoction) is oft-imitated, and his original dishes shine: scallops with sesame and ginger, *rissolette* of lamb's feet with artichokes and basil, and chocolate soufflé with chicory ice cream. Service is not always up to par. *192 av. Victor Hugo, Métro: Rue de la Pompe, tel. 45–04–04–31. Reservations advised. Dress: casual. AE, DC, MC, V. Closed weekends, Aug.*

★ **Port Alma.** The charming welcome of Mme. Canal and the nautical-blue and pastel decor of this very pretty restaurant will have you feeling festive from the start. Mr. Canal, the chef, is from Southwest France near Spain, and his cuisine is bursting with full, sunny flavors. Try turbot with thyme, sea bass in a salt crust with fennel gratin, or *bouillabaisse* (ordered ahead). Look forward to attentive, polite service, too. *10 av. de New York, Métro: Alma-Marceau, tel. 47–23–75–11. Reservations advised. Dress: casual. AE, DC, MC, V. Closed Sun., Aug.*

$$–$$$ **Le Relais du Parc.** Facing an interior garden in a luxury hotel in
★ Paris's posh 16th arrondissement is the long-awaited second restaurant of Joël Robuchon of Jamin fame (*see above*). The menu is a mix of original, sparkling creations such as *croustillant* of salmon and lacy fried potatoes, and substantial, traditional fare such as skate with cabbage and succulent beef tail with carrots. The warm *tarte fine* of apples is fabulous. Prices are lower and service less formal than at Jamin, but this is still a most elegant restaurant. Though larger and easier to book than the original, standards sometimes slip due to an overworked staff. *55 av. Raymond Poincaré, Métro: Trocadéro, tel. 44–05–66–10. Reservations essential. Dress: casual. AE, DC, MC, V.*

$$ **La Butte Chaillot.** This, the latest of star-chef Guy Savoy's fashionable bistros, is the largest and most impressive: A dramatic iron staircase connects two levels, decorated in turquoise and earth colors. Dining here is part theater, as the *à la mode* clientele will attest, but it's not all show: The very good food includes tasty raviolis of Royans (tiny cheese pillows), roast chicken with mashed potatoes, and stuffed veal breast with rosemary. A wide sidewalk terrace fronts tree-shaded avenue Kléber. *112 av. Kléber, Métro: Trocadéro, tel. 47–27–88–88. Reservations advised. Dress: casual chic. AE, MC, V.*

Bistrot de l'Etoile Lauriston. Another bistro from Guy Savoy (*see above*), this attractive, subdued establishment features full-flavored dishes such as stuffed, gratinéed zucchini, raviolis with *pistou* and lamb sautéed with rosemary. An upscale crowd includes many Americans. *19 rue Lauriston, Métro: Kléber, tel. 40–67–11–16. Reservations advised. Dress: casual. AE, MC, V. Closed Sat. lunch, Sun.*

Chez Géraud. Cherubic, jolly Géraud Rongier runs this fairly new bistro in the chic Passy district. Dishes such as salad of preserved duck gizzards, roast pigeon with Port sauce, and bitter chocolate cake exemplify the robust cuisine here. Rongier's knowledge of wine is vast, and his eclectic wine list has everything from great chateaux to little-known regional bottles. Notice the pretty tile mural at the back of the dining room. *31 rue Vital, Métro: Passy, tel. 45–20–33–*

00. Reservations advised. Dress: casual. AE, MC, V. Closed weekends, Aug.

$ **L'Auberge du Bonheur.** Food is not the reason to come to this informal spot behind the Grande Cascade restaurant in the Bois de Boulogne. Instead, come in warm weather to dine on the huge gravel terrace, surrounded by chestnut and plane trees, wisteria, and bamboo. Order simply: Salads and grilled meats are best. *Allée de Longchamp, Métro: Porte Maillot, tel. 42–24–10–17. Reservations advised. Dress: casual. AE, MC, V. Closed Feb., Sat. in winter.*

17th Arrondissement (Monceau/Clichy)
See Right Bank Dining map

$$$$ **Amphyclès.** Young chef-owner Philippe Groult had already made a
★ name for himself before opening this much-anticipated restaurant a few years ago. Since then Groult, trained under Joël Robuchon (*see above*), has not disappointed, and his exciting menu includes cauliflower soup with caviar, herb salad, and duck with coriander and orange. Service is excellent, and Amphyclès is one of the few grand Parisian restaurants that still proffers desserts from a pastry trolley. *78 av. des Ternes, Métro: Ternes, tel. 40–68–01–01. Reservations one week in advance. Dress: casual. AE, DC, MC, V. Closed Sat. lunch, Sun.*

Apicius. Chef-owner Jean-Pierre Vigato excels at mixing the humble with the rarified, as he does here in dishes from duck *tourte* (pie) and pig's foot to roasted sweetbreads and Bresse chicken cooked in salt. A good-looking crowd occupies the airy, flower-filled dining rooms. *122 av. de Villiers, Métro: Pereire, tel. 43–80–19–66. Reservations advised. Dress: casual but elegant. AE, DC, MC, V. Closed weekends and Aug.*

Guy Savoy. Guy Savoy is one of a handful of top chefs in Paris today, and his four bistros have not managed to distract him too much from his handsome luxury restaurant near the Arc de Triomphe. Savoy's oysters in aspic, sea bass with spices, and poached and grilled pigeon reveal the magnitude of his talent. His *mille-feuille* is a contemporary classic. *18 rue Troyon, Métro: Charles de Gaulle–Etoile, tel. 43–80–40–61. Reservations advised. Dress: casual. AE, MC, V. Closed Sat. lunch, Sun.*

$$$ **Augusta.** In this fine fish restaurant in a prosperous corner of the 17th arrondissement, the menu combines fish classics with chef Lionel Maître's original creations. Sample mussels with garlic butter, bouillabaisse with potatoes, or langoustines with vanilla. At least one meat dish is always offered. The comfortable dining room invites lingering. *98 rue de Toqueville, Métro: Malesherbes, tel. 47–63–39–97. Reservations advised. Dress: casual but elegant. MC, V. Closed Sat. lunch, and Sun., Oct.–Apr., weekends May–Sept.*

$$–$$$ **Au Petit Colombier.** It's a perennial favorite among Parisians, who come to eat comforting *cuisine bourgeoise* in the warm dining rooms, accented with wood and bright copper. Menu standards include milk-fed lamb chop *en cocotte* and *coq au vin*. Service is friendly and unpretentious. It's open for Sunday dinner. *42 rue des Acacias, Métro: Charles de Gaulle–Etoile, tel. 43–80–28–54. Reservations advised. Dress: casual. AE, MC, V. Closed Sat., Sun. lunch.*

Le Graindorge. Chef-owner Bernard Broux, formerly at the immensely popular Trou Gascon (*see* 12th Arrondissement, *above*), recently opened his own establishment. Here he prepares an original mix of the cuisines of Southwest France and of his native Flanders. Try his succulent eel terrine in a delicious herb aspic (seasonal), pork cheeks with juniper, and caramelized brioche *galette* (pancake). Mme. Broux oversees the pleasant dining rooms, and can help you choose one of the fine beers offered here. *15 rue de l'Arc-de-Triomphe, Métro: Charles De Gaulle–Etoile, tel. 47–54–00–28. Reservations advised. Dress: casual but neat. AE, MC, V. Closed Sat. lunch, Sun.*

$$ La Niçoise. Posters of Nice adorn the simple upstairs dining room, and Mediterranean flavors emerge from the kitchen at this enjoyable Niçoise oasis. Try ricotta ravioli with basil, or *petits farcis Niçois* (stuffed vegetables). Moderately priced Provençal wines help keep prices down. *4 rue Pierre Demours, Métro: Ternes, tel. 45–74–42–41. Reservations advised. Dress: casual. AE, MC, V. Closed Sat. lunch, Sun.*

La Rôtisserie d'Armaillé. Admire the handsome oak paneling, cranberry and green upholstery, and the very Parisian crowd at star-chef Jacques Cagna's third restaurant. The prix-fixe menu has many tempting choices, among them *pastilla* of guinea hen and a terrific chocolate cake. Wines are a little pricey. *6 rue d'Armaillé, Métro: Argentine, tel. 42–27–19–20. Reservations advised. Dress: casual. AE, MC, V. Closed Sat. lunch, Sun.*

La Table de Pierre. The Louis XVI–style setting is somewhat surprising in this, one of the best Basque restaurants in Paris. Such dishes as peppers stuffed with cod brandade, *émincé* (thin slices) of squid, duck confit, and *gâteau Basque* are full of the colors and flavors of the *Pays Basque*. Owner Pierre Darrieumerlou is an agreeable host. *116 blvd. Péreire, Métro: Péreire, tel. 43–80–88–68. Reservations advised. Dress: casual. AE, MC, V. Closed Sat. lunch, Sun.*

Le Bistrot d'à Côté. Chef Michel Rostang was one of the first to start the trend toward the chef-bistro, and his place remains one of the best, offering simple, sumptuous cooking. Specials include a succulent veal in a red wine sauce, and a chocolate and pear crêpe. Still more impressive is that they've managed to pack so many knick-knacks—books, vases, old-fashioned radios—and marble-topped tables into such a tiny joint. Most patrons know to expect the cramped quarters, so the bistro tends to draw a laid-back, friendly crowd. *10 rue Gustav-Flaubert, Métro: Courcelles, tel. 42–67–05–81. Reservations advised. Dress: casual. MC, V. Closed Sat. lunch, Sun., Aug. 1–15.*

L'Huitrier. Come here if you share the Parisians' craving for oysters. Owner Alain Bunel will describe the different kinds available, and you can follow these with any of several fish specials offered daily. The excellent cheeses are from the outstanding shop of Roger Alléosse. Blond wood and cream colors prevail. *16 rue Saussier-Leroy, Métro: Ternes, tel. 40–54–83–44. Reservations advised. Dress: casual. AE, MC, V.*

18th Arrondissement (Montmartre)
See Right Bank Dining map

$$$$ A. Beauvilliers. Pickwickian owner Edouard Carlier is a born party-giver, and his flower-filled restaurant is one of the most festive in Paris. The three dining rooms are filled with his personal collection of paintings and valuable *bibelots*, and a tiny, vine-covered terrace makes for delightful summer dining. Chefs here come and go, but

Mr. Carlier maintains quality, serving both original creations and reinterpreted classics. Recommended are the red mullet *en escabèche* (in a peppery marinade) and foie gras, lobster, and sweetbread *tourte*. The mouth-puckering lemon tart is not to be missed. One drawback: Service can be distant if you are not known. *52 rue Lamarck, Métro: Lamarck-Caulaincourt, tel. 42–54–54–42. Reservations essential. Jacket and tie advised. AE, MC, V. Closed Mon. lunch, Sun.*

$ **Aux Négotiants.** This wine bar in Montmartre has zero decor, but gives a warm welcome to its mix of neighborhood regulars and well-heeled clientele. One or two hot plates are offered daily; otherwise, enjoy the terrines, cheeses, and other simple choices, served with affordable wines by the glass or bottle. *27 rue Lambert, Métro: Château Rouge, tel. 46–06–15–11. Reservations advised. Dress: casual. No credit cards. Closed weekends, Mon. and Fri. dinner.*

19th Arrondissement (La Villette)
See Right Bank Dining map

$$$ **Au Cochon d'Or.** This old-fashioned restaurant on the outskirts of northeast Paris serves meat and plenty of it—fitting for its location near a former Paris slaughterhouse. Everything bespeaks sturdy tradition here, from the overblown decor to the rich, filling cuisine—pepper steak, souffléed potatoes, and crêpes flambéed in Calvados. The faithful serving staff and the crowd of regulars heighten the mood of old-time Paris. The restaurant is convenient to the Parc de la Villette and the Cité des Sciences et de l'Industrie. *192 av. Jean Jaurès, Métro: Porte de Pantin, tel. 42–45–46–46. Reservations advised. Dress: casual. AE, DC, MC, V.*

Le Pavillon Puebla. This turn-of-the-century building in the spectacular Parc des Buttes-Chaumont is a bit hard to find, but feels wonderfully removed from the bustle of the city. Chef Vergès prepares an original, flavorful cuisine, including oyster ravioli with curry, lamb tournedos with truffle juice, and *gâteau* of crêpes and apples. Mme. Vergès oversees the elegant dining rooms and large terrace. *Parc Buttes-Chaumont (entrance rue Botzaris), Métro: Buttes-Chaumont, tel. 42–08–92–62. Reservations advised. Dress: casual but elegant. MC, V. Closed Sun., Mon., mid-Aug.*

20th Arrondissement (Père Lachaise)
See Right Bank Dining map

$ **A La Courtille.** This large wine bar–restaurant with a trendy following has a spectacular view of Paris over the new Parc de Belleville. (Notice the black and white photos of the quaint old Belleville neighborhood before the wrecking ball.) The kitchen prepares modernized versions of bistro classics and fresh, light creations such as marinated salmon with dill, roast cod with zucchini, and veal liver. An excellent wine list offers many choices by the glass. There's a large terrace, and service until 11 PM. *1 rue des Envierges, Métro: Pyrénées, tel. 46–36–51–59. Reservations advised. Dress: casual chic. DC, MC, V.*

6 Lodging

Updated by Corinne LaBalme

Winding staircases, geranium pots in the windows, a concierge who seems to have stepped from a 19th-century novel—all of these still exist in abundance in Paris hotels. So do palatial rooms with marble baths, Belle Epoque lobbies, and a polished staff at your beck and call. In Paris, unlike some international cities, there are wonderful hotels for every taste and budget. The Paris Tourist Office's annual lodging guide lists well over 1,000 member hotels in the city's 20 arrondissements. The true count, though, is closer to 2,000—some 80,000 rooms in all.

Our criteria when selecting the hotels reviewed below, were quality, location, and—where possible—character. Few chain hotels are listed, since they usually lack the charm and authenticity found in typical Parisian lodgings. Similarly, we do not list many hotels in outlying arrondissements (the 10th to the 15th, the 18th to the 20th) because these are far from the sites most visitors want to see. Generally, there are more Right Bank hotels offering luxury—or at any rate formality—than there are on the Left Bank, where hotels tend to be smaller but often loaded with character. The Right Bank's 1st, 2nd, and 8th arrondissements are still the most sought-after for lodging, and prices here reflect this. Less-expensive alternatives on the Right Bank are the fashionable Marais quarter (3rd and 4th arrondissements), where hotels have mushroomed in recent years, and the 11th and 12th, near the Opéra Bastille.

Once upon a time, obvious high and low seasons existed in Paris. Nowadays, the city is as likely to be overrun in November or February as in summer. The French in general and the Parisians in particular take their vacations in July and August, so most of the trade fairs and conventions that fill hotels the rest of the year come to a halt at this time, freeing up rooms for tourists. The French Tourist Office publishes a calendar showing peak periods.

Despite the huge choice of hotels here, you should always reserve well in advance, especially if you're determined to stay in a specific hotel. You can do this by telephoning ahead, then writing or faxing for confirmation. If you are asked to send a deposit, make sure you discuss refund policies before mailing your check or money order. Always ask for some form of written confirmation of your reservation, detailing the duration of your stay, the price, location and type of your room (single or double, twin beds or double), and bathroom (*see below*).

As part of a general upgrade of the city's hotels in recent years, dozens of well-worn, inexpensive Paris lodgings have disappeared, replaced by good-value establishments in the lower-to-middle price ranges. Despite widespread improvement, however, many Paris hotels still have idiosyncrasies—some charming, others less so. Rooms are not always perfectly square, floors not always perfectly flat. The standard French double bed is slightly smaller than its American counterpart. In many smaller hotels, you'll find a long bolster (*traversin*) instead of pillows (*oreillers*). (If you prefer pillows, request them when you are shown the room.) Air-conditioning is uncommon in all but the most luxurious hotels. (Paris's hot-weather season doesn't last long.)

The most enduring example of quirkiness is French plumbing, which sometimes looks like avant-garde sculpture. Shared toilets or bathrooms down the hall, though increasingly rare, are still found in many modest establishments. Never assume that what is billed as a bathroom (*salle de bain*) will necessarily contain a tub. Some rooms have toilets (what the French call *wc* or *cabinet de toilet*), some have *bidets* only—but no tub or shower. Others have a shower but no toilet, and still others have only washstands. Our reviews indicate the number of rooms with full bath facilities including tub (*baignoire*) or shower (*douche*), and number of rooms with shared baths. Make sure you know what you are getting when you book.

Almost all Paris hotels charge extra for breakfast, with prices ranging from 30 francs to over 100 francs per person in luxury establishments. Hotels generally assume you will be having breakfast there, and will add the breakfast charge to your bill automatically. If you don't want to have breakfast at the hotel, say so when you check in. For anything more than the standard Continental breakfast of *cafe au lait* (coffee with hot milk) and *baguette* (bread) or croissants, the price will be higher. Some hotels have especially pleasant breakfast areas, and we have noted this where applicable. Luxury hotels often have restaurants, but finding a restaurant is rarely a problem in Paris.

You'll notice that the French government grades hotels from four-star deluxe to one star, and that the stars appear on a shield on the hotel's facade. Theoretically, the ratings depend on amenities and price. They can be misleading, however, since many hotels prefer to be understarred for tax reasons. Many two- and three-star establishments offer excellent price-to-quality ratios. We list hotels by price, but often a hotel in a certain price category will have a few rooms that are less expensive; it's worthwhile to ask. Rates must be posted in all rooms, and all extra charges clearly shown. A nominal **séjour** tax (per person, per night) was introduced in 1994 to pay for increased promotion of tourism in Paris.

Unless otherwise stated, the hotels reviewed below have elevators, and rooms have TVs and telephones. Additional facilities, such as restaurants and health clubs, are listed at the end of each review.

The following credit card abbreviations are used: AE, American Express; DC, Diners Club; MC, MasterCard; and V, Visa.

Highly recommended lodgings are indicated by a star ★.

Category	Cost*
$$$$	over 1,200 frs
$$$	750 frs–1,200 frs
$$	450 frs–750 frs
$	under 450 frs

* *All prices are for a standard double room, including tax and service.*

1st Arrondissement (Louvre)
See Right Bank Lodging map

$$$$ **Inter-Continental.** An aura of elegant luxury reigns throughout this
★ exquisite late-19th-century hotel, one of the largest of the city's top hotels. It was designed by the architect of the Paris Opéra, Charles Garnier. Three of its gilt and stuccoed public rooms are official historic monuments. Spacious guest rooms overlook quiet inner courtyards. In summer, breakfast on the patio is a delicious experience. Service is impeccable. *3 rue de Castiglione, 75001, Métro: Concorde, tel. 44–77–11–11, fax 44–77–14–60. 378 rooms with bath, 72 suites*

with bath. English spoken. Facilities: 2 restaurants, bar, patio. AE, DC, MC, V.

★ **Meurice.** The Meurice, one of the finest hotels in the city, is now owned by the Italian CIGA chain. The sumptuous Versailles-style first-floor salons have all been renovated, and the bedrooms are adorned with Persian carpets. Most bathrooms are done in pink marble. The hotel's fabled restaurant opens on to the garden. You'll have to book well in advance if you want one of the few rooms or suites overlooking the Tuileries Gardens, but you won't be disappointed by the opulence and plushness of the others. *228 rue de Rivoli, 75001, Métro: Tuileries, tel. 44–58–10–10, fax 44–58–10–15. 148 rooms with bath, 40 suites with bath. English spoken. Facilities: restaurant. AE, DC, MC, V.*

★ **Ritz.** Surrounded by the city's finest jewelers, the Ritz is the crowning gem on the newly sparkling place Vendôme. Festooned with gilt and ormolu, dripping with crystal chandeliers and tapestries, and swathed in heavy silk, this dazzling hotel, which opened in 1896, is the epitome of fin-de-siècle Paris. It's surprisingly intimate, too. The hotel has no lobby for the express purpose of discouraging paparazzi and sightseers who could annoy the privileged clientele. Legendary suites are named after ritzy former residents like Marcel Proust and Coco Chanel. The Hemingway Bar (which the writer claimed to have "liberated" in 1945) closed in the early 1990s but will hopefully re-open soon. The handsome Vendôme Bar and the Espadon restaurant remain elite meeting spots, and the lower-level health club has a magnificent indoor swimming pool surrounded by bucolic frescoes and towering columns. There's warm-weather seating in the charming adjacent garden. *15 pl. Vendôme, 75001, Métro: Madeleine, tel. 42–60–38–30, fax 42–86–00–91. 142 rooms and 45 suites, all with bath. English spoken. Facilities: 2 restaurants, bar, indoor pool, health club, shopping gallery, cooking school, beauty salon. AE, DC, MC, V.*

$$$ **Normandy.** The Belle Epoque decor, warm welcome, and central location near the Palais-Royal and theaters make this hotel a fine choice. The comfortable rooms are individually decorated. Some are much smaller than others, and a handful of the least expensive have shower only. A wonderful wood-paneled bar with roaring fireplace is frequented by hotel guests and well-heeled theatergoers. *7 rue de l'Echelle, 75001, Métro: Pyramides, tel. 42–60–30–21, fax 42–60–45–81. 116 rooms with bath, 6 with shower, 7 suites with bath. English spoken. Facilities: restaurant (closed weekends), bar. AE, DC, MC, V.*

★ **Régina.** Set in the handsome place des Pyramides, this Art Nouveau gem stuffed with fine antiques is pleasantly old-fashioned. Request a room overlooking the Louvre and the Tuileries Gardens. *2 rue des Pyramides, 75001, Métro: Tuileries, tel. 42–60–31–10, fax 40–15–95–16. 120 rooms and 10 suites, all with bath. English spoken. Facilities: restaurant (closed August), bar, conference rooms. AE, DC, MC, V.*

$$ **Britannique.** A friendly, family-owned hotel in a restored 19th-century building, the Britannique has a handsome winding staircase and nicely decorated, soundproofed rooms. Ask for a room on one of the top three floors. *20 av. Victoria, 75001, Métro: Châtelet, tel. 42–33–74–59, fax 42–33–82–65. 25 rooms with bath, 15 with shower. English spoken. AE, DC, MC, V.*

Londres Stockholm. An appealing combination of character and comfort singles out this small hotel. The lobby has exposed oak beams, statues in niches, and rustic-looking stone walls. The freshly repainted, rough-cast white walls in the rooms are offset by deep

Right Bank Lodging

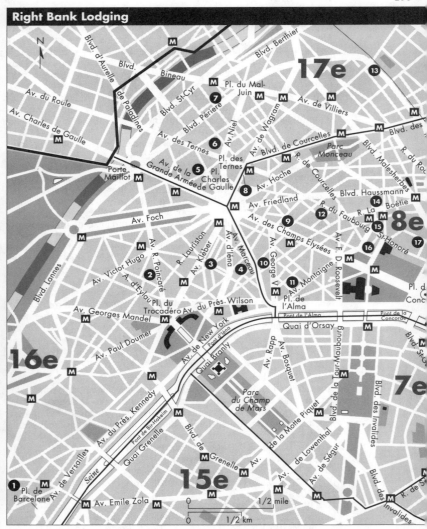

Alison, **17**	Ceramic, **8**	Hôtel du Marais, **45**	Le Laumière, **37**
Argenson, **14**	Choiseul-Opéra, **30**	Hôtel du Pré, **33**	Lille, **26**
Axial Beaubourg, **41**	Crillon, **18**	Hôtel du 7ᵉ Art, **50**	Londres Stockholm, **23**
Bradford, **12**	Duex-Iles, **49**	Inter-Continental, **20**	Lutèce, **48**
Bretonnerie, **43**	Etoile-Pereire, **7**	Jules-César, **53**	Méridional, **40**
Britannique, **27**	Gaillon-Opéra, **28**	Keppler, **4**	Meurice, **21**
Caron de Beaumarchais, **44**	Garden-Hotel, **39**	Kléber, **3**	Modern Hôtel-Lyon, **55**
Castex, **51**	George V, **10**	Kléber, **3**	Normandy, **25**
	Grand Hotel Inter-Continental, **31**	Lancaster, **9**	
		Le Bristol, **15**	

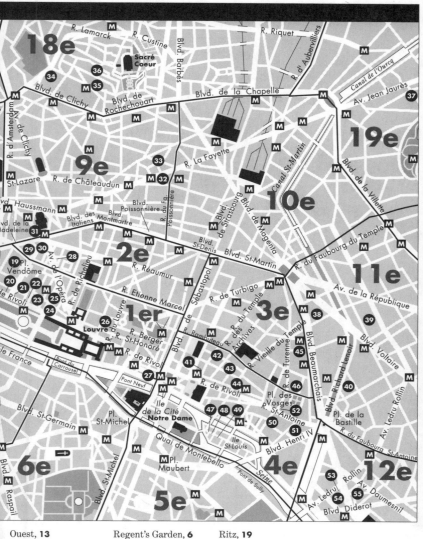

Left Bank Lodging

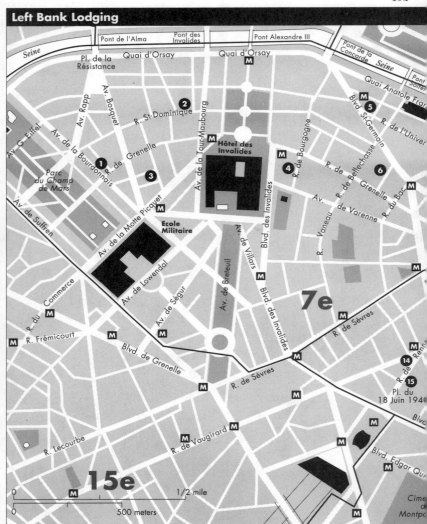

Acacias
St-Germain, **15**

Aramis-
St-Germain, **14**

Champ de Mars, **3**

Collège de France, **28**

Duc de Saint-Simon, **6**

Elysa Luxembourg, **25**

Esméralda, **29**

Fleurie, **8**

Grandes Ecoles, **23**

Hôtel d'Angleterre, **9**

Istria, **18**

Jardin des Plantes, **22**

Kensington, **1**

L'Abbaye
St-Germain, **13**

Lenox–
Montparnasse, **16**

L'Hôtel, **10**

Marronniers, **11**

Midi, **19**

Oriental, **27**

Panthéon, **24**

Parc Montsouris, **20**

Pavillon, **2**

Relais Christine, **12**

Résidence les
Gobelins, **21**

Royal, **17**

Solférino, **5**

Sorbonne, **26**

Université, **7**

Varenne, **4**

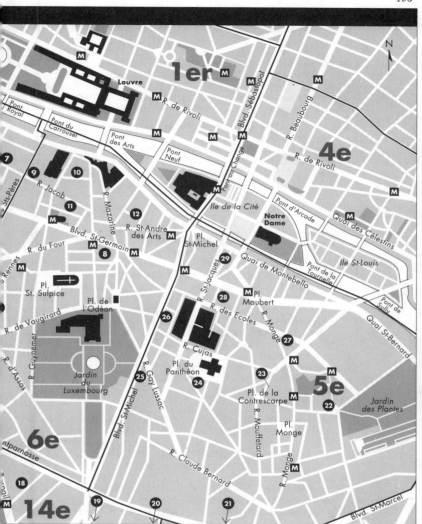

red carpeting. There's no restaurant or bar, but limited room service is available. *13 rue St-Roch, 75001, Métro: Pyramides, tel. 42–60–15–62, fax 42–60–16–00. 29 rooms with bath, 2 with shower. English spoken. AE, MC, V.*

★ **Tamise.** Just off the rue de Rivoli and Tuileries Gardens, this small hotel was once a private town house. Modestly luxurious, it boasts many English antiques in its charming rooms. *4 rue d'Alger, 75001, Métro: Tuileries, tel: 42–60–51–54, fax 42–86–89–97. 15 rooms with bath, 4 with shower. English spoken. MC, V.*

$ **Lille.** You won't find a less expensive base for exploring the Louvre than this hotel, located a short distance from the Cour Carrée. The facade got a face-lift a few years ago, but the somewhat shabby interior and minimal plumbing down long corridors was not upgraded. Hence the rock-bottom prices. Still, the Lille is a slice of Old Paris. There's no elevator, and not all rooms have TVs or phones. *8 rue du Pélican, 75001, Métro: Palais-Royal, tel. 42–33–33–42. 6 rooms with shower, 7 with shared bath. Some English spoken. No credit cards.*

2nd Arrondissement (Stock Exchange)
See Right Bank Lodging map

$$$$ **Westminster.** This former private mansion was built in the mid-19th century on what was then the most elegant street between the Opéra and place Vendôme. Tastefully renovated several years ago, the hotel has preserved its gracious turn-of-the-century atmosphere, with marble fireplaces, chandeliers, and parquet floors. Air-conditioning has been added, and the large bathrooms are clad with gray marble. The pleasant piano bar is a popular rendezvous. The hotel's restaurant serves excellent classic French cuisine. *13 rue de la Paix, 75002, Métro: Opéra, tel. 42–61–57–46, fax 42–60–30–66. 102 rooms and 20 suites, all with bath. English spoken. Facilities: parking lot (on pl. Vendôme), restaurant, tearoom, bar. AE, DC, MC, V.*

$$ **Gaillon-Opéra.** The oak beams, stone walls, and marble tiles of the ★ Gaillon-Opéra single it out as one of the most charming hotels in the Opéra neighborhood. The plants throughout and a flower-filled patio also delight. *9 rue Gaillon, 75002, Métro: Opéra, tel. 47–42–47–74, fax 47–42–01–23. 26 rooms and 1 suite, all with bath. English spoken. AE, DC, MC, V.*

Choiseul-Opéra. The historic, classical facade of the Choiseul-Opéra, located between the Opéra and place Vendôme, belies the strictly functional interior. The entrance hall, salon, and breakfast room were remodeled in 1992, and many rooms were freshened up. Service is relaxed but efficient, and the staff are happy to try out their English on guests. *1 rue Daunou, 75002, Métro: Opéra, tel. 42–61–70–41, fax 42–86–91–96. 28 rooms with bath, 14 with shower, 2 suites with bath. English spoken. AE, DC, MC, V.*

3rd Arrondissement (Le Marais/Beaubourg)
See Right Bank Lodging map

$$$$ **Pavillon de la Reine.** The best hotel in the Marais, it's set around two ★ flower-filled courtyards behind the historic Queen's Pavilion on the 17th-century place des Vosges. Although this cozy mansion looks old, it was actually reconstructed from scratch in 1986 following original plans and using period timbers, rough-hewn paving stones, Louis XIII fireplaces, and antiques. Ask for a duplex with French windows overlooking the first courtyard (there are no rooms over-

looking the place des Vosges). Breakfast is served in a vaulted cellar. *28 pl. des Vosges, 75003, Métro: Chemin Vert, tel. 42–77–96–40, fax 42–77–63–06. 31 rooms with bath, 24 suites with bath. English spoken. Facilities: parking. AE, DC, MC, V.*

$ Hôtel du Marais. On the edge of the Marais, this small hotel in a restored old building is near the Bastille Opéra and the Picasso Museum. For extremely reasonable rates you get amenities generally reserved for more expensive hotels, such as minibars and color TVs in rooms. Some rooms have exposed beams; all are functional, soundproofed, and clean. *2 bis rue Commines, 75003, Métro: Filles-du-Calvaire, tel. 48–87–78–27, fax 48–87–09–01. 12 rooms with bath, 27 with shower. Some English spoken. AE, MC, V.*

4th Arrondissement (Le Marais/Ile St-Louis)
See Right Bank Lodging map

$$$ Deux-Iles. This converted 17th-century mansion on the Ile St-Louis
★ has long won plaudits for charm and comfort. Flowers and plants are scattered around the stunning hall. The fabric-hung rooms, though small, have exposed beams and are fresh and airy. Ask for a room overlooking the little garden courtyard. The lounge is dominated by a fine chimneypiece and doubles as a bar. If the hotel is full, go to the Lutèce (*see below*) down the road; it belongs to the same owners. *59 rue St-Louis-en-l'Ile, 75004, Métro: Pont-Marie, tel. 43–26–13–35, fax 43–29–60–25. 8 rooms with bath, 9 with shower. English spoken. No credit cards.*

Lutèce. You'll find the same friendly reception, fabric-hung rooms, and clean, whitewashed stone walls here as at the neighboring Deux-Iles (*see above*). Try for rooms on the top floor; they offer terrific views over rooftops to the dome of the Panthéon. *65 rue St-Louis-en-l'Ile, 75004, Métro: Pont-Marie, tel. 43–26–23–52, fax 43–29–60–25. 13 rooms with bath, 10 with shower. English spoken. No credit cards.*

St-Louis. The St-Louis is another of the Ile St-Louis's converted 17th-century town houses. Antique furniture and oil paintings decorate the public areas. The bedrooms are elegantly simple, with exposed beams and stone walls. Blue-gray or light brown tiles adorn bathrooms. Breakfast is served in the atmospheric cellar. *75 rue St-Louis-en-l'Ile, 75004, Métro: Pont-Marie, tel. 46–34–04–80, fax 46–34–02–13. 15 rooms with bath, 6 with shower. English spoken. No credit cards.*

$$ Axial Beaubourg. Opened in 1990, this three-star hotel in a 17th-century building is one of the better deals in the Marais. There are beamed ceilings in the lobby and in the six first-floor rooms; decor is functional. The clientele is a mix of Europeans and Americans. The Beaubourg and Picasso Museums are a five-minute walk away. *11 rue du Temple, 75004, Métro: Hôtel de Ville, tel. 42–72–72–22, fax 42–72–03–53. 34 rooms with bath, 5 with shower. English spoken. AE, V.*

Bretonnerie. This small three-star hotel is located on a tiny street in the Marais, a few minutes' walk from the Beaubourg. The snug rooms are decorated in Louis XIII style, but vary considerably in size from spacious to cramped. Some boast antiques, beamed ceilings, and marble-clad bathrooms. There's a breakfast room in the vaulted cellar. *22 rue Ste-Croix-de-la-Bretonnerie, 75004, Métro: Hôtel de Ville, tel. 48–87–77–63, fax 42–77–26–78. 30 rooms with bath, 2 suites with bath. English spoken. MC, V. Closed Aug.*

★ Caron de Beaumarchais. The design theme of this elegant three-star hotel in the heart of the Marais is the work of Caron de Beaumarchais, the 18-century author who wrote the *Marriage of Figaro* in 1778. First-edition copies of his books adorn the public spaces, and 18th-century prints and reproduction wallpapers decorate the bedrooms, which have soundproof windows that keep out the noise from busy rue de Rivoli. Top-floor rooms have private balconies with a view of the Panthéon. All rooms are air-conditioned and have minibar, private safe, fax connection, and cable TV with CNN. *12 rue Vieille-du-Temple, 75004, Métro: St-Paul, tel. 42–72–34–12, fax 42–72–34–63. 17 rooms with bath, 2 with shower. English spoken. AE, DC, MC, V.*

Hôtel du 7e Art. The decor of this small Marais two-star hotel is 1940s–60s Hollywood movies, complete with posters and photographs (the name means "Seventh Art," what the French call filmmaking). Rooms have brown carpets and beige walls; they're small and sparsely furnished, but clean and quiet. The clientele tends to be young, and Americans are made to feel welcome. Breakfast and snacks are served in handsome ground-floor or cellar rooms with stone walls, and there's also a pleasant bar. No elevator. *20 rue St-Paul, 75004, Métro: St-Paul, tel. 42–77–04–03, fax 42–77–69–10. 6 rooms with bath, 15 with shower, 2 suites with bath. English spoken. Facilities: bar. AE, DC, MC, V.*

★ **Vieux Marais.** As its name implies, this charming, two-star hotel lies in the heart of the Marais. The rooms and bathrooms are simply decorated in light, refreshing colors and are impeccably clean. Try to get a room overlooking the courtyard. Breakfast is served in a pretty lounge. The staff is exceptionally courteous. *8 rue du Plâtre, 75004, Métro: Hôtel de Ville, tel. 42–78–47–22, fax 42–78–34–32. 22 rooms with bath, 8 with shower. English spoken. MC, V.*

$ ★ **Castex.** This family-run, two-star hotel in a 19th-century building is a real find. It was remodeled from top to bottom in 1989, and rooms are squeaky clean. The decor is strictly functional, but the extremely friendly owners and rock-bottom prices mean the Castex is often fully booked months ahead. There's a large American clientele. The eight least expensive rooms, two per floor, share toilets on the immaculate, well-lit landings. There's no elevator, and TV is in the lobby only. *5 rue Castex, 75004, Métro: Bastille, tel. 42–72–31–52, fax 42–72–57–91. 4 rooms with bath, 23 with shower. English spoken. MC, V.*

★ **Place des Vosges.** A loyal American clientele swears by this small hotel on a charming street just off the exquisite square of the same name. Oak-beamed ceilings and rough-hewn stone in public areas and some of the guest rooms add to the atmosphere. Ask for the top-floor room, the hotel's largest, with a view of Marais rooftops. There's a welcoming little breakfast room. *12 rue de Birague, 75004, Métro: Bastille, tel. 42–72–60–46, fax 42–72–02–64. 11 rooms with bath, 5 with shower. English spoken. AE, DC, V.*

5th Arrondissement (Latin Quarter)
See Left Bank Lodging map

$$$ ★ **Panthéon.** In a handsome 18th-century building facing the Panthéon, this excellent three-star hotel has prices that range from moderate to expensive. Some of the charming rooms have exposed beams, balconies, and stunning views; a vaulted breakfast room and impressive lobby are additional attractions. The desk staff is very helpful. *19 pl. du Panthéon, 75005, Métro: Luxembourg, tel. 43–54–32–95, fax 43–26–64–65. 33 rooms with bath, 1 with shower. English spoken. AE, DC, V.*

$$ Collège de France. The Collège de France offers peace and quiet in the heart of the Latin Quarter. Rooms are simply decorated in pale greens and light browns. The prettiest three, which are more expensive and sleep four, have oak beams and are on the sixth floor under the eaves. *7 rue Thénard, 75005, Métro: Maubert-Mutualité, tel. 43–26–78–36, fax 46–34–58–29. 23 rooms with bath, 6 with shower. Some English spoken. AE, MC, V.*

★ **Elysa Luxembourg.** The Elysa is what the French call an *hôtel de charme.* Though the building is not large, most rooms are surprisingly spacious, and all are exquisitely maintained and refurbished yearly. Cream-colored furniture is set against pale blue or pink fabrics. You'll find a minibar in every room and a breakfast lounge serving Continental or buffet breakfasts. The Elysa is one of the rare hotels in the city with a sauna. *6 rue Gay Lussac, 75005, Métro: Luxembourg, tel. 43–25–31–74, fax 46–34–56–27. 25 rooms with bath, 5 with shower. English spoken. Facilities: sauna. AE, DC, MC, V.*

★ **Grandes Ecoles.** Recently upgraded from no stars to two, this delightful hotel in three small old buildings is set far off the street in a beautiful garden. There are parquet floors, antiques, and a (nonworking) piano in the breakfast area. Most rooms have beige carpets and flowery wallpaper. It's hard to find a quieter, more charming hotel for the price. There's a faithful American clientele, including some backpackers. The rooms with bathroom facilities on the well-lit landings are inexpensive. *75 rue du Cardinal Lemoine, 75005, Métro: Cardinal Lemoine, tel. 43–26–79–23, fax 43–25–28–15. 29 rooms with bath, 10 with shower, 9 with shared bath. English spoken. AE, MC, V.*

★ **Jardin des Plantes.** Across the street from the lovely Jardin des Plantes botanical gardens on the edge of the Latin Quarter, this pleasant two-star hotel offers botanical-theme decor and very reasonable prices. There's a fifth-floor terrace where you can breakfast or sunbathe in summer, and a sauna and ironing room in the cellar. *5 rue Linné, 75005, Métro: Jussieu, tel. 47–07–06–20, fax 47–07–62–74. 29 rooms with bath, 4 with shower. English spoken. Facilities: sauna, bar-tearoom, terrace. AE, DC, MC, V.*

Sorbonne. This pretty, early 18th-century hotel, located right by the Sorbonne, was transformed in 1988 when its handsome stone facade was cleaned. Fresh flowers adorn each room, and great clusters of geraniums hang from the windows. Try for a room overlooking the little garden. Top floor rooms are tiny even by Paris standards. *6 rue Victor-Cousin, 75005, Métro: Luxembourg, tel. 43–54–58–08, fax 40–51–05–18. 11 rooms with bath, 26 with shower. English spoken. MC, V.*

$ Esméralda. One either loves it or hates it. The Esméralda, which boasts a fine (though noisy) location in a fusty 17th-century building across from Notre Dame, is famed for its cozy, eccentric charm. Some closet-size rooms are nearly overpowered by gaudy imitation antiques. Request a room with a view of the cathedral. Animal lovers will enjoy the friendly dogs and cats that snooze in the lobby. The price of the best rooms creep upward; singles with showers on the landings are very cheap. *4 rue St-Julien-le-Pauvre, 75005, Métro: St-Michel, tel. 43–54–19–20, fax 40–51–00–68. 15 rooms with bath, 4 with shower on the landing. Some English spoken. No credit cards.*

Oriental. This no-frills one-star in an old building has clean rooms, and is located near the Arènes de Lutèce. Not all rooms have complete bathrooms; facilities can be found on the landings. Some of the largest have TV. *2 rue d'Arras, 75005, Métro: Jussieu, tel. 43–54–*

38–12, fax 40–51–86–78. 2 rooms with bath, 20 with shower, 3 with shared bath. Some English spoken. AE, MC, V.

6th Arrondissement (Luxembourg)
See Left Bank Lodging map

$$$$ **L'Hôtel.** Rock idols and movie stars adore this expensive and eccentric Left Bank hotel filled with flowers and antiques. Oscar Wilde died here in room 16 ("I am dying beyond my means," he wrote). One small double is decorated entirely in leopardskin; another handsome suite features the mirrored, Art Deco boudoir furniture that belonged to vaudeville star Mistinguett. Many rooms are extremely small. The hotel has a fine restaurant, Le Belier, whose decor includes a fountain and a live tree. The bar, open until 1 AM, is popular with a well-heeled international crowd. *13 rue des Beaux-Arts, 75006, Métro: St-Germain-des-Prés, tel. 43–25–27–22, fax 43–25–64–81. 16 rooms with bath, 8 with shower, 3 suites with bath. English spoken. Facilities: restaurant, bar. AE, DC, MC, V.*

★ **Relais Christine.** The Relais Christine is one of the most appealing of the Left Bank hotels, impeccably luxurious yet oozing charm. The hotel is located on a quiet street between the Seine and the boulevard St-Germain and occupies some precious 16th-century cloisters. The best rooms look out over the central lawn. All are spacious and comfortable, particularly the duplexes on the upper floors. Air-conditioning and double-glazed windows add to their appeal. There's no restaurant, and only guests may use the bar. *3 rue Christine, 75006, Métro: St-Michel, tel. 43–26–71–80, fax 43–26–89–38. 34 rooms and 17 suites, all with bath. English spoken. Facilities: parking, bar. AE, DC, MC, V.*

$$$ **Hôtel d'Angleterre.** Some claim the Hôtel d'Angleterre is the ultimate Left Bank hotel—a little small and shabby, but elegant and perfectly (albeit snobbishly) managed. The 18th-century building was originally the British ambassador's residence; later, Hemingway made it his Paris home. Room sizes and rates vary greatly, though all rooms are individually decorated. Some are imposingly formal, others are homey and plain. Ask for one overlooking the courtyard. *44 rue Jacob, 75006, Métro: St-Germain-des-Prés, tel. 42–60–34–72, fax 42–60–16–93. 26 rooms and 3 suites, all with bath. English spoken. Facilities: bar, patio. AE, DC, MC, V.*

★ **L'Abbaye St-Germain.** This delightful hotel, entirely renovated in 1993, is a former 18th-century convent near St-Sulpice in the heart of the Left Bank. The first-floor rooms open onto flower-filled gardens. Some rooms on the top floor have oak beams and alcoves. The entrance hall is sturdily authentic, with stone vaults. All bathrooms are decorated with colored marble. The bar is for guests only. *10 rue Cassette, 75006, Métro: St-Sulpice, tel. 45–44–38–11, fax 45–48–07–86. 42 rooms and 4 suites, all with bath. English spoken. Facilities: bar. AE, MC, V.*

★ **Fleurie.** Entirely air-conditioned, this spiffy family-run hotel established in 1988 offers good location (a quiet side street near the place de l'Odéon), prettily furnished pastel rooms, and many luxury amenities: built-in hairdryers, minibars, private safe deposit boxes, marble-clad bathrooms, heated towel racks, and color TV with CNN. *32-34 rue Grégoire-de-Tours, 75006. Métro: Odéon, tel. 43–29–59–81, fax 43–29–68–44. 29 rooms with bath. English spoken. Facilities: bar/salon. AE, DC, MC, V.*

$$ **Acacias St-Germain.** This three-star hotel in a 19th-century building near Montparnasse was completely remodeled in 1992. It offers spotlessly clean rooms decorated in summery fabrics and colors, and a small, flower-filled patio. Check into the remarkable low-season and weekend discounts. *151 bis rue de Rennes, 75006, Métro: St-Placide, tel. 45–48–97–38, fax 45–44–63–57. 24 rooms with bath, 17 with shower. English spoken. Facilities: 24-hour room service, babysitting, tour guides, conference room, parking. AE, DC, MC, V.*

Aramis-St-Germain. Despite its location on busy rue de Rennes, the Aramis-St-Germain, opened in 1985, has proved a hit. All windows are double-glazed (keeping out street noise), and rooms are individually decorated. Several have Jacuzzis. There's no restaurant. Harvey's Piano Bar on the first floor is popular. *124 rue de Rennes, 75006, Métro: St-Placide, tel. 45–48–03–75, fax 45–44–99–29. 36 rooms with bath, 6 with shower. English spoken. Facilities: bar. AE, DC, MC, V.*

★ **Marronniers.** Accessed through an appealing courtyard off the chic rue Jacob, the Marronniers is a sentimental favorite for many budget-conscious tourists. The management began a room-by-room renovation in January 1994, to clean up the cobwebs that had started to obscure its charm. (Good news: Prices are to stay roughly the same.) The salon/breakfast room, in a glassed-in veranda, is an oasis of calm and greenery. *21 rue Jacob, 75006, Métro: St-Germain-des-Prés, tel. 43–25–30–60, fax 40–46–83–56. 17 rooms with bath, 20 with shower. English spoken. Facilities: bar. No credit cards.*

7th Arrondissement (Invalides)
See Left Bank Lodging map

$$$$ **Duc de Saint-Simon.** Set back from a peaceful little street leading to
★ boulevard St-Germain, the Saint-Simon is a favorite with American visitors. Parts of the building date back to the 17th century, others date from the 18th. Try for one of the rooms with a terrace; they look over the courtyard and neighboring gardens. There's a pleasant bar and a cellar lounge for breakfast. The regular doubles are significantly less expensive than the suites. *14 rue St-Simon, 75007, Métro: Bac, tel. 45–48–35–66, fax 45–48–68–25. 29 rooms and 5 suites, all with bath. English spoken. Facilities: bar. No credit cards.*

$$$ **Université.** This appealingly converted 17th-century town house is
★ located between boulevard St-Germain and the Seine. Rooms have their original fireplaces and are decorated with English and French antiques. Ask for one of the two rooms with a terrace on the fifth floor. Though there's no restaurant, you can rent the vaulted cellar for parties. Rooms with shower are moderately priced. *22 rue de l'Université, 75007, Métro: Bac, tel. 42–61–09–39, fax 42–60–40–84. 20 rooms with bath, 7 with shower. English spoken. AE, MC, V.*

$$ **Pavillon.** The entrance to the family-run Pavillon lies behind a garden at the end of an alley off rue St-Dominique, guaranteeing peace and quiet. Although some rooms in this former 19th-century convent are tiny, all have been redecorated and feature Laura Ashley wallpaper and old prints. Breakfast is served in the little courtyard in summer. There's no elevator, but the hotel is only two stories high. *54 rue St-Dominique, 75007, Métro: Invalides, tel. 45–51–42–87, fax 45–51–32–79. 3 rooms with bath, 15 with shower. English spoken. AE, MC, V.*

Solférino. Located across the street from the Musée d'Orsay, the Solférino is a charming little hotel with a variety of rooms, many of them inexpensive (those with shower only and shared bath). Decor is light and summery, and the breakfast room/lounge has a skylight. *91* *rue de Lille, 75007, Métro: Musée d'Orsay, tel. 47–05–85–54, fax 45–55–51–16. 22 rooms with bath, 5 with shower, 5 with shower and shared wc. English spoken. MC, V. Closed Christmas–New Year's.*

Varenne. The Varenne stands in a flower-filled courtyard set back from the street; windows of rooms facing the road are double-glazed to reduce noise. Decor is contemporary—and at times basic—with oak furniture and colorful curtains and wallpaper. *44 rue de Bourgogne, 75007, Métro: Varenne, tel. 45–51–45–55, fax 45–51–86–63. 17 rooms with bath, 7 with shower. English spoken. AE, MC, V.*

$ **Champ de Mars.** This simple, clean two-star hotel has one-star prices. Don't expect luxury or atmosphere, just a very good deal, in a nice neighborhood near the Eiffel Tower and Invalides. *7 rue du Champ de Mars, 75007, Métro: Ecole Militaire, tel. 45–51–52–30. 19 rooms with bath, 6 with shower. Some English spoken. MC, V. Closed two weeks in mid-Aug.*

Kensington. Perhaps the main reason for wanting to stay in this small two-star hotel is the superb view of the Eiffel Tower from the two top floors. Rooms are tiny and uninspiring with white Formica, but they are freshly decorated and always impeccably clean; all have double-glazed windows. There's no restaurant, but limited room service is available. *79 av. de la Bourdonnais, 75007, Métro: Ecole-Militaire, tel. 47–05–74–00, fax 47–05–25–81. 12 rooms with bath, 14 with shower. English spoken. AE, DC, MC, V.*

8th Arrondissement (Champs-Elysées)
See Right Bank Lodging map

$$$$ ★ **Crillon.** The Crillon is the crème de la crème of Paris's "palace" hotels, set as it is in two 18th-century town houses on the place de la Concorde, site of the French Revolution's infamous guillotine. Marie-Antoinette, who met her end there, took singing lessons at the Hôtel de Crillon, where one of the original *grands appartements*, now sumptuous salons protected by the French National Historic Landmark Commission, has been named for the Queen. Guests must pay dearly for a balcony overlooking the great square, with seemingly all of Paris at their feet; only the suites have them. Lesser mortals still get magnificent digs, individually decorated with Rococo and Directoire antiques, crystal and gilt wall sconces, and gold fittings. Most double rooms have separate sitting rooms, and the bathrooms, stocked with wonderful Annick Goutal toiletries, are clad in marble. The sheer quantity of the marble downstairs—in the lobby, the adjacent lounge, and especially the grand, top-rated Les Ambassadeurs restaurant—is staggering. The staff anticipates your every need. *10 pl. de la Concorde, 75008, Métro: Concorde, tel. 44–71–15–00, fax 44–71–15–02. 120 rooms and 43 suites, all with bath. English spoken. Facilities: 2 restaurants, 2 bars, shop. AE, DC, MC, V.*

George V. Some say the George V lacks the "this-could-only-be-Paris" atmosphere of other superdeluxe Parisian hotels. Its style is more international. Most rooms are impeccably decorated and imposing, though the penthouse suites are the only ones to enjoy a commanding view over the city. There are two restaurants; the better is Les Princes, where, in summer, you can eat on the leafy patio. *31 av. George V, 75008, Métro: George V, tel. 47–23–54–00, fax 47–20–40–00. 298 rooms and 53 suites, all with bath. English spoken. Facilities: 2 restaurants, bar, tea salon, hairdresser. AE, DC, MC, V.*

★ **Lancaster.** The phrase "small is beautiful" sums up the appeal of the

Lancaster, located just off the Champs-Elysées. This charming, old-fashioned hotel—behind a now-gleaming facade—offers all the same services as its bigger and better-known sisters, but with the atmosphere of a luxurious private home. All rooms are individually decorated with Louis XV and Louis XVI furniture. Bathrooms vary, but most are clad with marble. A fountain, statues, and flowers fill the pretty garden. *7 rue de Berri, 75008, Métro: George V, tel. 40-76-40-76, fax 40-76-40-00. 58 rooms and 8 suites, all with bath. English spoken. Facilities: restaurant, 2 private dining rooms. AE, DC, MC, V.*

★ **Le Bristol.** Luxury and discretion are the Bristol's trump cards. The understated facade on rue du Faubourg St-Honoré might mislead the unknowing, but the Bristol ranks among Paris's top four hotels. Some of the air-conditioned and spaciously elegant rooms have authentic Louis XV and Louis XVI furniture. Moreover, the management has filled public areas with Old Master paintings, sculptures, sumptuous carpets, and tapestries. The marble bathrooms are simply magnificent. Nonguests can take tea in the vast garden or dine in the tented summer restaurant or wood-paneled winter restaurant; later, you can listen to the pianist in the bar, open till 1 AM. There's an enclosed pool on the roof, complete with solarium and sauna for guests only. The service throughout is impeccable. *112 rue du Fbg. St-Honoré, 75008, Métro: St-Philippe du Roule, tel. 42-66-91-45, fax 42-66-68-68. 155 rooms and 45 suites, all with bath. English spoken. Facilities: restaurant, bar, pool, sauna, fitness machines, solarium, parking. AE, DC, MC, V.*

Plaza-Athénée. With its distinctive turn-of-the-century facade, accented with wrought iron and red awnings, the Plaza is set among the haute-couture houses on avenue Montaigne and is just a short stroll away from the Champs-Elysées. The rooms and suites, overlooking either the courtyard or the tree-lined avenue, are decorated in Louis XV, Louis XVI, or Regency styles. Forty-five cooks create the haute cuisine served at Le Régence, an elegant, candlelit restaurant. The art deco Relais restaurant is an upscale grill room. The bar is a long-standing rendezvous and is always busy. *25 av. Montaigne, 75008, Métro: F.D. Roosevelt, tel. 47-23-78-33, fax 47-20-20-70. 215 rooms and 42 suites, all with bath. English spoken. Facilities: 2 restaurants, bar, hairdresser, theater ticket agency, tearoom. AE, DC, MC, V. Relais restaurant closed in Aug.*

Résidence Maxim's de Paris. Fashion king Pierre Cardin has transformed this hotel at the foot of the Champs-Elysées into a sumptuous museum of a hotel. Every suite—there are only four regular double rooms—is decorated in an entirely different style, unified only by opulent luxury. There are 17th-century rooms, Chinese rooms, Art Nouveau rooms, English country manor rooms, and more. *42 av. Gabriel, 75008, Métro: Champs-Elysées-Clemenceau, tel. 45-61-96-33, fax 42-89-06-07. 35 suites, 4 double rooms, all with bath. English spoken. Facilities: 2 restaurants, bar. AE, DC, MC, V.*

$$$ **Bradford.** The turn-of-the-century, family-run Bradford has an appealing, old-fashioned feel. An old wooden elevator carries you from the flower-filled lobby to the spacious, comfortable rooms, some equipped with Louis XVI-style furniture, brass beds, and fireplaces. Some rooms with shower are less expensive off-season. *10 rue St-Philippe-du-Roule, 75008, Métro: St-Philippe-du-Roule, tel. 45-63-20-20, fax 45-63-20-07. 36 rooms with bath, 12 with shower, 2 suites with bath. English spoken. Facilities: bar. AE, DC, MC, V.*

$$ **Alison.** Conveniently located near the place de la Madeleine on a pleasant side street, the Alison is a small, friendly hotel in a 19th-century building. The rooms are decorated in simple, modern style. *21 rue de Surène, 75008, Métro: Madeleine, tel. 42–65–54–00, fax 42–65–08–17. 24 rooms with bath, 11 with shower. English spoken. Facilities: bar. AE, DC, MC, V.*

Ceramic. These are the lowest rates you'll pay this close to the Arc de Triomphe—just a few hundred yards away. The hotel has a handsome Belle Epoque tiled facade and a crystal chandelier in the reception area. The rooms haven't been remodeled in some time but are still comfortable. Those facing the street (among them 412, 422, 442) boast bay windows and intricate plaster moldings. Those facing the courtyard are quieter but less appealing. *34 av. de Wagram, 75008, Métro: Etoile, tel. 42–27–20–30, fax 46–22–95–83. 27 rooms with bath, 26 with shower. English spoken. MC, V.*

$ **★** **Argenson.** This friendly, family-run hotel provides what may well be the best value in the swanky 8th arrondissement. Some of the city's greatest sights are just a 10-minute walk away. Old furniture, molded ceilings, and skillful flower arrangements add to the charm. Ongoing room-by-room renovation means new bathrooms in many. The best rooms have full bath, but they are pricier; reserve well in advance for one of these. The smallest rooms have shared baths. *15 rue d'Argenson, 75008, Métro: Miromesnil, tel. 42–65–16–87, fax 47–42–02–06. 5 rooms with bath, 19 with shower, 3 with shared bath. Some English spoken. MC, V.*

9th Arrondissement (Opéra)
See Right Bank Lodging map

$$$$ **Grand Hotel Inter-Continental.** Paris's biggest luxury hotel has endless hallways and a facade that seems as long as the Louvre. And after a thorough restoration completed mid-1991, this 1862 gem sparkles like new. The grand salon's Art Deco dome and the painted ceilings of the Opéra and Café de la Paix restaurants are registered landmarks. Rooms are spacious and light, decorated in Art Nouveau style with pastel colors. The famed Café de la Paix is one of the city's great people-watching spots. *2 rue Scribe, 75009, Métro: Opéra, tel. 40–07–32–32, fax 42–66–12–51. 470 rooms, 23 suites, all with bath. English spoken. Facilities: 3 restaurants, 2 bars, health club, shops, parking. AE, DC, MC, V.*

$$ **Hôtel du Pré.** Located near the pretty square Montholon, slightly off the beaten track, this three-star hotel was thoroughly remodeled in the 1980s. Its reasonable prices, charming and sunny public areas, comfortable rooms done in summery colors, and large bathrooms make it a very good deal. The owners also run the equally good Relais du Pré and Résidence du Pré on the same street (at numbers 16 and 15). *10 rue Pierre-Sémard, 75009, Métro: Poissonière, tel. 42–81–37–11, fax 40–23–98–28. 22 rooms with bath, 19 with shower. English spoken. Facilities: bar. AE, DC, MC, V.*

$ **Riboutté-Lafayette.** This small, cozy two-star hotel in a 19th-century building near the busy rue La Fayette is family-run and filled with charming bric-a-brac and old furniture. The clean, sunny rooms are decorated in pastel colors, and those on the top floor have sloping ceilings. *5 rue Riboutté, 75009, Métro: Cadet, tel. 47–70–62–36, fax 48–00–91–50. 15 rooms with bath, 9 with shower. English spoken. AE, DC, MC, V.*

11th Arrondissement (Bastille)
See Right Bank Lodging map

$$ **Méridional.** This three-star hotel in a 19th-century building is a five-minute walk from either the Bastille or the Marais. It's located on a handsome but busy tree-lined boulevard. Though the lobby is a bit garish, the comfortable, quiet rooms are simply decorated in earthtones or floral prints. The hotel was entirely remodeled in 1991. *36 blvd. Richard Lenoir, 75011, Métro: Bréguet-Sabin, tel. 48–05–75–00, fax 43–57–42–85. 26 rooms with bath, 10 with shower. English spoken. AE, DC, MC, V.*

$ **Garden-Hotel.** Set on a pretty garden square in a quiet residential neighborhood just 10 minutes from Père-Lachaise cemetery, this family-run, two-star hotel is spotlessly clean. Rooms in front have lovely views; all units have double-glazed windows and are soberly decorated with brown carpets and beige walls. Note that bathtubs are half-size in rooms with baths. *1 rue du Général-Blaise, 75011, Métro: Saint-Ambroise or Voltaire, tel. 47–00–57–93, fax 47–00–45–29. 3 rooms with bath, 39 with shower. No English spoken. MC, V.*

★ **Résidence Alhambra.** This hotel is on the edge of the historical Marais quarter and is conveniently close to five Métro lines. The Alhambra's gleaming white exterior, backyard garden, and flower-filled window boxes provide a bright spot in an otherwise drab neighborhood. The smallish guest rooms are painted in fresh pastel shades or cool ivory. The lobby is filled with plants and leather armchairs. Most rooms have color TV. The reception area and breakfast room were remodeled in 1992. *11 bis–13 rue de Malte, 75011, Métro: République, tel. 47–00–35–52, fax 43–57–98–75. 10 rooms with bath, 48 with shower. English spoken. MC, V.*

12th Arrondissement (Gare de Lyon)
See Right Bank Lodging map

$$ **Paris-Lyon Palace.** Although neighboring a seedy sex shop, this 3-star hotel conveniently located near the Gare de Lyon has an attentive uniformed doorman and an extremely impressive plant-filled lobby. Bedrooms are modern and strictly functional. There's no restaurant, but the bar is open from lunch till 1 AM. *11 rue de Lyon, 75012, Métro: Gare de Lyon, tel. 43–07–29–49, fax 46–28–91–55. 64 rooms with bath, 64 with shower. English spoken. Facilities: bar. AE, DC, MC, V.*

$ **Jules-César.** The address may be unfashionable, but the Bastille, Jardin des Plantes, and Ile St-Louis are a short walk away, and the Gare de Lyon is just around the corner. The hotel, built in 1914, has been restored: The lobby is rather glitzy, but the guest rooms are more subdued. Rooms facing the street are larger than those in the back and have a somewhat better view. *52 av. Ledru-Rollin, 75012, Métro: Gare de Lyon, tel. 43–43–15–88, fax 43–43–53–60. 4 rooms with bath, 44 with shower. English spoken. MC, V.*
Modern Hôtel-Lyon. This three-star, family-run hotel, conveniently located between the Bastille and the Gare de Lyon, changed ownership in 1992. As a result, rooms have been remodeled and redecorated in light colors, and many bathrooms are being upgraded. The new owners are as friendly and helpful as their predecessors. *3 rue Parrot, 75012, Métro: Gare de Lyon, tel. 43–43–41–52, fax 43–43–81–16. 36 rooms with bath, 12 with shower. English spoken. Facilities: bar. AE, MC, V.*

13th Arrondissement (Les Gobelins)
(See Left Bank Lodging map)

$ **Résidence les Gobelins.** Located five minutes from the Latin Quarter, this simple, small two-star hotel on a quiet street offers pleasant rooms in warm, coordinated colors. The breakfast room faces a small flower-filled garden. *9 rue des Gobelins, 75013, Métro: Gobelins, tel. 47-07-26-90, fax 43-31-44-05. 18 rooms with bath, 14 with shower. English spoken. AE, MC, V.*

14th Arrondissement (Montparnasse)
See Left Bank Lodging map

$$ **Istria.** This small, charming two-star hotel was once a Montparnasse artists' hangout. Totally rebuilt in 1988 around a flower-filled courtyard on a quiet street, it is now a family-run establishment with simple, clean, and comfortable rooms decorated in soft, summery colors. *29 rue Campagne-Première, 75014, Métro: Raspail, tel. 43-20-91-82, fax 43-22-48-45. 4 rooms with bath, 22 with shower. English spoken. AE, MC, V.*

Lenox-Montparnasse. You'll want to stay in this new hotel mainly to take advantage of its location in the heart of Montparnasse; it's just around the corner from the famous Dôme and Coupole brasseries, and close to the Luxembourg Gardens. Room decor varies considerably. The best rooms have original fireplaces, old mirrors, and exposed beams; others are decorated in functional modern styles. All have TV with CNN and gleaming white-tile bathrooms with built-in hairdryers. There's no restaurant, but snacks are served in the bar from 5 PM to 2 AM, and room service is available. *15 rue Delambre, 75014, Métro: Edgar-Quinet, tel. 43-35-34-50, fax 43-20-46-64. 36 rooms with bath, 10 with shower, 6 suites with bath. English spoken. Facilities: bar, laundry. AE, DC, MC, V.*

★ **Royal.** This small hotel, set in a late-19th-century building on attractive boulevard Raspail, has won much praise, especially from American guests. The mood throughout is stylish yet simple, with salmon-pink rooms and a wood-paneled, marble-floored lobby filled with plants. You can sit in the small conservatory, where drinks are served; there's no bar or restaurant. *212 blvd. Raspail, 75014, Métro: Raspail, tel. 43-20-69-20, fax 42-79-95-23. 33 rooms with bath, 15 with shower. English spoken. AE, DC, MC, V.*

$ **Midi.** This hotel is close to both Montparnasse and the Latin Quarter, and there are Métro and RER stations nearby. Don't be put off by the nondescript facade and reception area; most of the rooms are adequately furnished, and those facing the street are both large and quiet. *4 av. Réné-Coty, 75014, Métro: Denfert-Rochereau, tel. 43-27-23-25, fax 43-21-24-58. 20 rooms with bath, 21 with shower, 9 with shared bath. Some English spoken. V.*

Parc Montsouris. This modest two-star hotel in an early 1900s building is on a charming and quiet residential street next to the lovely Parc Montsouris. Remodeled in 1991, its smallish rooms are decorated with pastel colors and modern furniture. Some rooms with shower are very inexpensive. Suites sleep four. *4 rue du Parc-Montsouris, 75014, Métro: Porte d'Orléans or RER Cité-Universitaire, tel. 45-89-09-72, fax 45-80-92-72. 18 rooms with bath, 17 with shower, 7 suites with bath. English spoken. AE, MC, V.*

16th Arrondissement (Trocadéro/Bois de Boulogne)
See Right Bank Lodging map

$$$$ **Parc Victor Hugo.** The newest (1992) luxury hotel on the Right Bank
★ was decorated by Nina Campbell with cozy chintz. Perfumed by floral potpourri, with sleek lighting and up-to-date amenities (CNN,
air-conditioning, VCRs), the Victor Hugo is a gracious tribute to
English country-house charm. A gourmet plus: Joël Robuchon's celebrated restaurant is right next door. *55-57 av. Raymond-Poincaré,
75116, Métro: Victor Hugo, tel. 44–05–66–66, fax 44–05–66–00. 104
rooms with bath, 11 suites with bath. English spoken. Facilities:
restaurant, bar, room service, valet parking, non-smoking floor.
AE, DC, MC, V.*

$$$ **Kléber.** Located just a short walk from Etoile and Trocadéro, the lit-
tle Kléber benefits greatly from the calm and greenery of nearby
place des Etats-Unis. Decor is strictly modern throughout, but
the thick blue carpets, set against beige walls, create a warm
atmosphere. The hotel is impeccably clean. Though there's no res-
taurant, there's a comfortable first-floor lounge and bar. Rooms
on the 2nd and 5th floors have balconies. Those with shower are
moderate. *7 rue de Belloy, 75016, Métro: Etoile, tel. 47–23–80–
22, fax 49–52–07–20. 11 rooms and 1 suite with bath, 10 rooms
with shower. English spoken. Facilities: bar, parking. AE, DC,
MC, V.*

$$ **Keppler.** Ideally located on the edge of the 8th and 16th arrondissements near the Champs-Elysées, this small two-star hotel in a 19th-
century building boasts many three-star features (room service,
small bar) at extremely reasonable prices. The spacious and airy
rooms are simply decorated with modern furnishings. Some rooms
with shower are less expensive. *12 rue Keppler, 75116, Métro: Kléber, tel. 47–20–65–05, fax 47–23–02–29. 31 rooms with bath, 18 with
shower. English spoken. Facilities: bar. AE, MC, V.*
Queen's Hotel. One of only a handful of hotels located in the desirable residential district around rue la Fontaine, Queen's is within
walking distance of the Seine and the Bois de Boulogne. The hotel is
small and functional, but standards of comfort and service are high.
Flowers on the facade add an appealing touch. Most rooms with
shower are inexpensive. *4 rue Bastien-Lepage, 75016, Métro:
Michelange-Auteuil, tel. 42–88–89–85, fax 40–50–67–52. 7 rooms
with bath, 15 with shower. English spoken. MC, V.*

17th Arrondissement (Monceau/Clichy)
See Right Bank Lodging map

$$$ **Regent's Garden.** The large number of repeat visitors is a safe indica-
★ tion that this is a special place. Located near the Arc de Triomphe,
the hotel was built in the mid-19th century by Napoleon III for his
doctor. Inside, it is every bit as you would imagine, with marble fire-
places, mirrors, gilt furniture, and stucco work. But the real attrac-
tion is the garden—a room overlooking it is something to be
treasured. The levels of service match the spectacular architecture
and decor. *6 rue Pierre-Demours, 75017, Métro: Etoile, tel. 45–74–
07–30, fax 40–55–01–42. 39 rooms with bath, 1 with shower. English
spoken. AE, DC, MC, V.*

$$ **Etoile-Pereire.** Pianist Ferrucio Pardi, owner and manager here, has
★ created a unique small hotel, set behind a quiet, leafy courtyard in a
chic residential district. Renovated in 1986, rooms and duplexes are
decorated in soothing pastels—pinks, grays, and apricots—with

Laura Ashley curtains and chair covers, and prints on the walls. There's no house restaurant, but room service can be arranged, and a copious breakfast is available—with 40 different jams and jellies. The bar is always busy in the evening. For a lively, personally run hotel, few places beat this likable spot. *146 blvd. Péreire, 75017, Métro: Péreire, tel. 42–67–60–00, fax 42–67–02–90. 18 rooms with bath, 3 with shower; 4 duplexes and 1 suite, all with bath. English spoken. Facilities: bar. AE, DC, MC, V.*

$ **Ouest.** Although this unpretentious hotel overlooks the railroad near Pont-Cardinet station, you can be sure of a quiet night's sleep, since all the rooms are soundproofed. Some are lighter and more spacious than others, so be sure to make your preference known. The area may not have much to interest tourists, but Montmartre, Parc Monceau, and the *grands magasins* (top department stores) are all within easy reach. *165 rue de Rome, 75017, Métro: Rome, tel. 42–27–50–29, fax 42–27–27–40. 18 rooms with bath, 30 with shower. English spoken. Facilities: parking, bar. MC, V.*

Palma. This prim and proper two-star hotel located between the Arc de Triomphe and Porte Maillot is run by the friendly and efficient Couderc family. Small and charming, it is one of the best modest hotel deals in the city. Ask for a top-floor room with a view. All rooms have cable TV with CNN. Breakfast is included in the price. *46 rue Brunel, 75017, Métro: Argentine, tel. 45–74–74–51, fax 45–74–40–90. 15 rooms with bath, 22 with shower. English spoken. MC, V.*

18th Arrondissement (Montmartre)
See Right Bank Lodging map

$$ **Timhotel Montmartre.** The reason for listing what is only one of eight Timhotels in Paris is simply the location of the Montmartre member of the chain—right in the leafy little square where Picasso lived at the turn of the century. A total renovation completed in spring 1994 means that this basic-but-functional hotel is priced higher than other chain members. *11 rue Ravignan, 75018, Métro: Abbesses, tel. 42–55–74–79, fax 42–55–71–01. 6 rooms with bath, 57 with shower. English spoken. AE, DC, MC, V.*

$ **Regyn's Montmartre.** Despite small rooms (all recently renovated), this owner-run hotel on Montmartre's place des Abbesses is rapidly gaining an enviable reputation for simple, comfortable accommodations. A predominantly young clientele and a correspondingly relaxed atmosphere have made this an attractive choice for some. Try for one of the rooms on the upper floors, with great views over the city. *18 pl. des Abbesses, 75018, Métro: Abbesses, tel. 42–54–45–21, fax 42–23–76–69. 14 rooms with bath, 8 with shower. English spoken. MC, V.*

Utrillo. Newly renovated, the Utrillo is on a quiet side street at the foot of Montmartre. The decor is appealing, with prints in every room and a marble-topped breakfast table. Because the color white is emphasized throughout, the hotel seems light, clean, and more spacious than it actually is. *7 rue Aristide-Bruant, 75018, Métro: Blanche, tel. 42–58–13–44, fax 42–23–93–88. 5 rooms with bath, 25 with shower. English spoken. Facilities: sauna. AE, DC, MC, V.*

19th Arrondissement (La Villette)
See Right Bank Lodging map

$ **Le Laumière.** Though it's located some distance from downtown, the low rates of this family-run, two-star hotel, close to the rambling Buttes-Chaumont park, are hard to resist. Most rooms are functional only, but some of the larger ones overlook the garden. The staff is exceptionally helpful. Shared baths (both showers and wc) are on well-lit landings. *4 rue Petit, 75019, Métro: Laumière, tel. 42–06–10–77, fax 42–06–72–50. 18 rooms with bath, 28 with shower, 8 with shared bath. English spoken. MC, V.*

Apartment Rentals

If you want to do your own cooking or need a base large enough for a family, consider a furnished rental. Among companies that rent apartments in Paris are **French Experience** (370 Lexington Ave., New York, NY 10017, tel. 212/986–1115, fax 212/986–3808) and **Chez Vous** (220 Redwood Hwy., Suite 129, Mill Valley, CA 94941, tel. 415/331–2535, fax 415/331–5296).

7 The Arts and Nightlife

The Arts

Updated by Alexandra Siegel

Parisians consider their city a bastion of art and culture, and indeed it is. But surprisingly, much of the theater, opera, music, and ballet here is not on a par with what you'll find in London, New York, or Milan. Mime and contemporary dance performances are often better bets, and they pose no language problems.

The music season usually runs from September to June. Theaters stay open during the summer, but many productions are at summer festivals elsewhere in France. The weekly magazines *Pariscope*, *L'Officiel des Spectacles*, and *7 à Paris* are published every Wednesday and give detailed entertainment listings. The Paris Tourist Office has set up a **24-hour hotline** (tel. 49–52–53–56) in English with information about weekly events. The best place to buy tickets is at the venue itself. Otherwise, try your hotel or a travel agency such as **Paris-Vision** (214 rue de Rivoli). Tickets for some events can be bought at the **FNAC** stores—especially Alpha-FNAC (1–5 rue Pierre Lescot, 1e, Forum des Halles, third level down). **Virgin Megastore** (52 av. des Champs-Elysées) sells theater and concert tickets. Half-price tickets for many same-day theater performances are available at the **Kiosque Théâtre** across from 15 place de la Madeleine; expect a line (open Tues.–Sat. 12:30–8, Sun. 12:30–6). There's another branch at Châtelet RER station (closed Sun.).

Theater A number of theaters line the Grands Boulevards between Opéra and République, but there is no Paris equivalent to Broadway or the West End. Shows are mostly in French. **Le Mogador** (25 rue de Mogador, 9e, tel. 42–85–45–30) is one of Paris's most sumptuous theaters. Classical drama is performed at the distinguished **Comédie Française** (Palais-Royal, 1er, tel. 40–15–00–15). You can reserve seats in person about two weeks in advance, or turn up an hour beforehand and wait in line for returned tickets.

The intimate **Gymnase** (38 blvd. de Bonne-Nouvelle, 10e, tel. 42–46–79–79) and the homely **Renaissance** (20 blvd. St-Martin, 10e, tel. 42–08–18–50), once home to Belle Epoque star Sarah Bernhardt, rub shoulders along the Grands Boulevards. The rue de la Gaîté near Montparnasse, lined with some of the raunchier Paris theaters since the 19th century, is still home to the stylish, old-fashioned **Gaîté-Montparnasse** (26 rue de la Gaîté, 14e, tel. 43–22–16–18).

The avant-garde is well represented by a number of small, offbeat theaters in the Marais and Bastille neighborhoods, or go a little farther north to Peter Brooks's **Bouffes du Nord** (37 bis blvd. de la Chapelle, 10e, tel. 46–07–34–50), offering wonderful experimental productions.

Ionesco admirers should visit the tiny Left Bank **Théâtre de la Huchette** (23 rue de la Huchette, 5e, tel. 43–26–38–99), where the playwright's short modern plays make a deliberate mess of the French language. In the Latin Quarter, the popular and inexpensive **Nouveau Théâtre Mouffetard** (73 rue Mouffetard, 5e, tel. 43–31–11–99) is great fun.

Many Paris theaters are worthy of a visit based solely on architectural merit and ambience, such as the elegantly restored **Théâtre des Champs-Elysées** (15 av. Montaigne, 8e, tel. 49–52–50–00), a plush Art Deco temple that hosts concerts and ballet as well as plays.

A particularly Parisian form of theater is *Café-Théâtre*—a mixture of satirical sketches and variety show riddled with slapstick humor and viewed in a café setting. It's fun if you have a good grasp of

French. We suggest either the **Café de la Gare** (41 rue du Temple, 4e, tel. 42–78–52–51) or Montmartre's pricier **Chez Michou** (80 rue des Martyrs, 18e, tel. 46–06–16–04).

Concerts Before the new Opéra de la Bastille opened, the **Salle Pleyel** (252 rue du Fbg. St-Honoré, 8e, tel. 45–63–07–96), near the Arc de Triomphe, was Paris's principal home of classical music. The Paris Symphony Orchestra and other leading international orchestras still play here regularly. Paris isn't as richly endowed as New York or London when it comes to orchestral music, but the city compensates with a never-ending stream of inexpensive lunchtime and evening concerts in churches. The candlelit concerts held in the **Sainte-Chapelle** are outstanding—make reservations well in advance. **Notre Dame** is another church where you can combine sightseeing with good listening. Others that offer concerts are **St-Eustache**, near Les Halles; **St-Germain-des-Prés**, on the Left Bank; **St-Louis-en-l'Ile**; **St-Roch**, north of the Louvre; and the lovely **St-Louis des Invalides.**

Both the **Musée du Louvre** (34 quai du Louvre, 1er, tel. 40–20–51–51) and the **Musée d'Orsay** (1 rue de Bellechasse, 7e, tel. 45–49–48–14) hold concerts, often at lunchtime.

Rock Concerts Unlike French jazz, French rock is not generally considered to be on par with its American and British cousins. Even so, Paris is a great place to catch some of your favorite groups, because concert halls tend to be smaller and tickets less expensive. Most places charge from 80 to 100 francs for entrance and get going around 11 PM. Leading English and American groups usually play at the large **Bercy** or **Zenith** halls in eastern Paris; check posters and papers for details. To hear live rock in a more intimate setting, try **Le Bataclan** (50 blvd. Voltaire, 11e), **Elysées Montmartre** (72 blvd. Rochechouart, 18e), **La Cigale** (124 blvd. Rochechouart, 18e), or the elegant **Casino de Paris** (16 rue Clichy, 9e). The legendary **Olympia** (28 blvd. des Capucines, 9e, tel. 47–42–25–49), once favored by Jacques Brel and Edith Piaf, still hosts leading French singers.

Opera The **Opéra** itself, or **Opéra Garnier** (pl. de l'Opéra, 9e, tel. 47–42–53–71) has alas conceded its role as Paris's main opera house to the **Opéra Bastille** (pl. de la Bastille, tel. 44–73–13–00). The old Opéra now devotes itself to classical dance; French ballet superstar Patrick Dupont is the reigning artistic director. The Opéra Bastille, meanwhile, has had its share of start-up and management problems, and many feel it is not living up to its promise of grand opera at affordable prices. In the lofty old hall of the **Opéra Comique** (5 rue Favart, 2e, tel. 42–90–12–20), you'll hear often excellent comic operas and lightweight musical entertainments. The **Théâtre Musical de Paris,** better known as the Théâtre du Châtelet (2 pl. du Châtelet, 1er, tel. 40–28–28–28) offers opera and ballet for a wider audience, at more reasonable prices.

Dance The highlights of the Paris dance year usually take place at the **Opéra Garnier,** which, in addition to being the sumptuous home of the well-reputed Paris Ballet, also bills dozens of major foreign troupes ranging from classical to modern. Other major venues include the **Théâtre de la Ville** at Châtelet (tel. 42–74–22–77), the **Palais des Congrès** at Porte Maillot (tel. 40–68–22–22), and the **Palais des Sports** at the Porte de Versailles (tel. 48–28–40–48). As a rule, more avant-garde or up-and-coming choreographers can be found in the smaller dance spaces around the Bastille and the Marais. Check the weekly *Pariscope* for listings.

Movies Parisians are far more addicted to the cinema as an art form than are Londoners or New Yorkers. There are hundreds of movie theaters in the city, and a number of them, especially in principal tourist areas such as the Champs-Elysées and the boulevard des Italiens near the Opéra, run English films. Check the *Officiel du Spectacle* or *Pariscope* for a movie of your choice. Look for the initials "v.o.," which mean *version originale;* i.e., not subtitled or dubbed. Cinema admission runs from 40 francs to 55 francs; there are reduced rates on Wednesdays and, in some cinemas, for morning shows. Most theaters will post two show times: the first is the *séance*, or period of commercials and previews. The film usually starts 10–25 minutes later.

Real movie buffs should visit the **Pompidou Center,** with lots of classics and obscure films. The **Musée du Cinéma** at the Palais de Chaillot houses a fabulous collection of posters, costumes, set designs, and props from all over the world. The **Cinémathèque Française** at Trocadéro has a reference library and photograph collection as well as an outstanding collection of films. The **Vidéothèque de Paris,** in the Forum des Halles, is a public archive of films and videos on the city of Paris.

The Champs-Elysées bristles with cinemas, among them the **Pathé Marignan-Concorde** (No. 27), **Gaumont Ambassade** (No. 50), **Gaumont Champs-Elysées** (No. 66), **Publicis** (No. 129), and the **George V** (No. 146). Big-screen fanatics should try the **Gaumont Grand Ecran** (30 pl. d'Italie, 13e), the **Max Linder Panorama** (24 blvd. Poissonière, 9e), the **Kinopanorama** (60 av. de la Motte-Piquet, 15e), or the **Grand Rex** (1 blvd. Poissonière, 2e), which sometimes doubles as a rock venue.

On the Left Bank, the Action chain of cinemas, including the **Action Ecoles** (23 rue des Ecoles, 5e), **Action Rive Gauche** (5 rue des Ecoles, 5e), and **Action Christine** (4 rue Christine, 6e), show offbeat films and reruns; so do the **Studio Galande** (42 rue Galande, 5e), the **Saint-André-des-Arts** (30 rue Saint-André-des-Arts, 6e), and the **Lucernaire Forum** (53 rue Nôtre-Dame-des-Champs, 6e). The Chinese-style **Pagoda** (57 rue de Babylone, 7e) is a national monument, and well worth a visit.

Nightlife

The French are definitely nightbirds, though these days that means smart, elegant *bars de nuit* rather than frenetic discos. The **Champs-Elysées,** that ubiquitous cabaret land, is making a comeback, though the clientele remains predominantly foreign. The tawdry **Pigalle** and down-at-the-heels **Bastille** areas are trendy these days, and the **Left Bank** boasts a bit of everything. During the week, people are usually home after closing hours at 2 AM, but weekends mean late-night partying.

Cabaret Paris's nightclubs are household names, shunned by wordly Parisians and beloved of foreign tourists, who flock to the shows. Prices can range from 350 francs (simple admission plus one drink) to more than 1,000 francs (dinner plus show). For 600 francs, you can get a good seat plus half a bottle of champagne.

The **Crazy Horse** (12 av. George V, 8e, tel. 47–23–32–32) is one of the best known clubs for pretty girls and dance routines, lots of humor, and lots less clothes. The **Moulin Rouge** (pl. Blanche, 18e, tel. 46–06–00–19), that old favorite in Montmartre, mingles the cancan and crocodiles in an extravagant spectacle. The **Lido** (116 bis av. des

Champs-Elysées, 8e, tel. 40–76–56–10) stars the famous Bluebell Girls and tries to win you over through sheer exuberance. The legendary **Folies Bergère,** depicted in Edouard Manet's 1881 painting, (32 rue Richer, 9e, tel. 42–46–77–11), reopened at the end of 1993 after closing briefly due to financial trouble. The new and improved cabaret includes ornate costumes, masterful lighting, and a show that returns to its music hall origins.

Other leading haunts include the **Milliardaire** (68 rue Pierre-Charron, 8e, tel. 42–25–25–17), with lots of leather and lace; the lively, crowded, and trendy **Paradis Latin** (28 rue du Cardinal-Lemoine, 5e, tel. 43–29–07–07); the **Nouvelle Eve** (25 rue Fontaine, 9e, tel. 48–78–37–96), which has a postwar music-hall flavor, with songs, dance, and magicians; and the **Eléphant Bleu** (49 rue de Ponthieu, 8e, tel. 43–59–58–64), a cabaret-cum-restaurant with an exotic (usually oriental) touch to most of its shows.

Bars and Nightclubs The more upscale Paris nightclubs tend to be both expensive (1,000 francs for a bottle of gin or whiskey) and private—in other words, you'll usually need to know someone who's a member in order to get through the door. It helps to be famous—or look like a model—to get into **Les Bains** (7 rue du Bourg-l'Abbé, 3e) and **Niel's** (2 av. Ternes, 17e). **Keur Samba** (73 rue La Boétie, 8e) has a jungle setting. The Pigalle area in Montmartre is becoming the place to be nowadays, despite its reputation as a seedy red-light district. Among hot places here are: **Moloko** (26 rue Fontaine, 9e), a smoky late-night bar with a small dance floor; **Le Dépanneur** (next door, at 27 rue Fontaine), which caters to more of a gin-drinking yuppie crowd; **Lili la Tigresse** (98 rue Blanche, 9e), a sexy bar with a trendy crowd; and—not to be missed—the brasserie **Pigalle** (22 blvd. de Clichy, 18e), whose '50s frescoes and ceramics have been classified as a national treasure.

The nightlife is still hopping in and around the Bastille, and includes the **China Club** (50 rue de Charenton, 12e), a trendy bar with an Orient Express theme; **Le Casbah** (18 rue de la Forge Royale, 11e), a bar and dance club with a touch of Casablanca; **Cafe de la Plage** (59 rue de Charonne, 11e), an arty-jazzy bar; **Le Wah-Wah** (11 rue Daval, 11e), a jewel of a bar with strange, religious imagery on the walls; and **Le Pistou Pelican** (15 rue de Bagnolet, 20e), a favorite among Beaux-Arts students with a laid-back ambience and occasional live music.

Literary types will head for **Harry's Bar** (5 rue Daunou, 2e), a cozy, wood-paneled hangout for Americans that's haunted by the ghosts of Ernest Hemingway and F. Scott Fitzgerald. Also highly popular among the nostalgic set are the many hotel bars in the city, including at the **Ritz** (15 pl. Vendôme, 1er), the **Lutètia** (45 blvd. Raspail, 6e), the **Bristol** (112 rue du Fbg. St-Honoré, 8e), the **Normandy** (7 rue de l'Echelle, 1er), and the **Bélier** at **l'Hôtel** (13 rue des Beaux Arts, 6e).

Other popular spots are **Le Rosebud** (11 bis rue Delambre, 14e) a cult spot for the Jeunesse Dorée (young and fashionable) of the Left Bank; **Le Comptoir** (4 rue Vauvilliers, 1er), a popular locale which draws a hip Les Halles crowd and featuring a drink aptly called a "Sexy"; **La Perla** (26 rue François Miron, 4e) an intimate Tex-Mex-style café/bar; and **le Forum** (4 blvd. Malesherbes, 8e), an archetypical French cocktail bar with one of the best selection of drinks in Paris.

Other fun places for an evening out include: **Caveau des Oubliettes.** Listen to Edith Piaf songs in a medieval cellar that was once the dungeons of a prison. It's complete with minstrels, troubadours, and serving wenches—and tourists love it. *11 rue St-Julien-le-Pauvre, 5e. Admission: 130 frs. Open 9 PM–2 AM. Closed Sun.*

Au Lapin Agile. It considers itself the "doyen of cabarets," and Picasso once paid for a meal with one of his paintings. The setting in Montmartre is touristy but picturesque. *22 rue des Saules, 18e. Admission: 120 frs. Open 9 PM–2 AM. Closed Mon.*

La Rôtisserie de l'Abbaye. French, English, and American songs are accompanied by the guitar in a medieval setting. You can dine here, too. *22 rue Jacob, 6e. Admission: 200–350 frs. Open evenings only.*

Madame Arthur. A wacky, burlesque transvestite-and-drag show that's not for the faint-hearted. *75 bis rue des Martyrs, 19e. Admission: 280 frs, including show. Open evenings only.*

L'Ane Rouge. A mixed Parisian and foreign crowd frequent this typical French cabaret. The emphasis is on laughs, and entertainment includes singers, magicians, comedians, and ventriloquists. *3 rue Laugier, 17e. Admission starts at 200 frs including show. Open 8 PM–midnight.*

Jazz Clubs The French take jazz seriously, and Paris is one of the great jazz cities of the world, with plenty of variety, including some fine, distinctive local coloring. (You're in Europe now, so why insist on American performers?) For nightly schedules, consult the specialty magazines *Jazz Hot* or *Jazz Magazine.* Remember that nothing gets going till 10 or 11 PM, and that entry prices can vary widely from about 35 francs to over 100 francs.

Start on the Left Bank at the **Caveau de la Huchette** (5 rue de la Huchette, 5e), a smoke-filled shrine to the Dixieland beat. **Le Petit Journal** (71 blvd. St-Michel, 5e), opposite the Luxembourg gardens, serves up good food and traditional jazz. **Le Bilboquet** (13 rue Saint-Benoît, 6e) plays mainstream jazz in a faded Belle Epoque decor. Nearby, the **Montana** (28 rue Saint-Benoît, 6e) is a well-known spot for jazz lovers. **La Villa** (29 rue Jacob, 6e), a newcomer on the jazz scene, has been attracting serious musicians.

Elsewhere in the city, **Au Duc des Lombards** (42 rue des Lombards, 1er) is an ill-lit, romantic venue. **Le Petit Opportun** (15 rue des Lavandières-Ste-Opportun, 1er) is a converted bistro that sometimes features top-flight American soloists with French backup. The **Slow Club** (130 rue de Rivoli, 1er) plays swing and Dixieland jazz. **New Morning** (7 rue des Petites Ecuries, 10e) is a premier spot for visiting musicians and French bands. The **Lionel Hampton jazz club** at the Meridien Hotel near Porte Maillot (81 blvd. Gouvion-St-Cyr, 17e) also boasts top jazz artists. The **Passage du Nord-Ouest** (13 rue du Faubourg-Montmartre, 9e) attracts a younger crowd.

Discos Discos aren't as hot as they once were here; you'll find more Parisians seeking moody little cocktail bars these days. Still, stalwarts continue to seek the beat. A Paris disco's life is often short and sweet, so don't be surprised if some of those listed here have closed their doors or changed their names. The **Balajo** (9 rue de Lappe, 11e), is an old Java ballroom which specializes in salsa and techno. On the same street, the **Chapelle des Lombards** (19 rue de Lappe, 11e) goes for an Afro-Cuban beat. Those with a penchant for Latin rhythms should try the **Trottoirs de Buenos-Aires** (37 rue des Lombards, 1er) for some mambo, samba, and salsa. **Le Tango** (13 rue Au-Maire, 4e) attracts a sensuous dance crowd. **La Java** (105 rue du Faubourg du Temple, 11e), where Edith Piaf made her name, still seems hung up on the '60s, while **Club Zed** (2 rue des Anglais, 6e) is a prime rock'n'roll venue for all ages. The famed **Le Palace** (8 rue du

Faubourg-Montmartre, 9e) saw its heyday come and go in the '80s, but is still fun for a night out. Music ranges from techno to pop to African beat.

Pubs The number of Paris bars that woo English-speaking clients with a pub atmosphere and dark beer are becoming increasingly popular with Parisians too. The **Académie de la Bière** (88 bis blvd. de Port-Royal, 5e) serves more than 100 foreign brews to accompany good french fries and *moules marinière* (mussels cooked in white wine). The **Bar Belge** (75 av. de Saint-Ouen, 17e) is an authentically noisy Flemish drinking spot, while the **Mayflower** (49 rue Descartes, 5e) is a classy, Left Bank spot, British-style. The **Micro-Brasserie** (106 rue de Richelieu, 2e), just off the Grands Boulevards, brews its own beer. Quaff Guinness in an Irish mode at **Kitty O'Shea** (10 rue des Capucines, 2e) or at the animated **Finnegan's Wake** (42 rue des Boulangers, 5e) in the Latin Quarter. The somewhat snooty **Bedford Arms** (17 rue Princesse, 6e) is open until dawn for draft beer and darts, while the **London Tavern** (3 rue du Sabot, 6e) offers piano and jazz. In the Bastille area, pubs are popping up at a rapid rate. The doyen is the seedy but colorful **Café de la Plage** (59 rue de Charonne, 11e).

Gay and Gay and lesbian bars and clubs are mostly concentrated in the
Lesbian Marais and include some of the most happening addresses in the city. However, trendy clubs fall in and out of favor at lightning speed and one-night discos and tea dances are always popping up, so check the local papers to see what's hot.

The very trendy **Banana Café** (13 rue de la Ferronnerie, 1er) attracts an energetic and scantily-clad mixed crowd; dancing on the tables is the norm. **Queen** (102 av. des Champs-Elysées, 8e) is currently one of the most talked about nightclubs in Paris: Gays, lesbians, and heterosexuals are all lining up to get in. **Amnesia Café's** (42 rue Vielle du Temple, 4e) under-lit bar and art deco ceiling paintings attract a young, yuppie gay and lesbian crowd. **Les Planches** (36 rue Doudeauville, 18e) offers two roomy lounges and a summer terrace for evening get-togethers. You might also try the friendly, artsy atmosphere—and reasonable prices—of **Le Central** (33 rue Vieille du Temple, 4e).

For men, **Le Quetzal** (10 rue de la Verrerie, 4e) features a chrome-and-blue-light atmosphere and gets very crowded and smoky on weekends; **The Trap** (10 rue Jacob, 6e) contains a ground floor video bar with a staircase leading to a darker, more social area; **Subway** (35 rue St-Croix-de-la-Bretonnerie, 4e) looks like a roadside dive and caters to an older, jean-sporting crowd; and **Club 18** (8 rue de Beaujolais, 1er), the oldest gay disco in Paris, took on a modern look in 1993 but is as popular and casual as ever, particularly on theme nights.

For women, **La Champmesle** (4 rue Chabanais, 2e) is the hub of lesbian nightlife with a back room reserved for women only; **Le Privilege** (3 cité Bergere, 9e) is expensive, but cheery and relaxed; **El Scandalo** (21 rue Keller, 11e) gets started late but is always lively; and **Le Memorie's** (2 pl. de Porte Maillot, 16e), though situated in a staid neighborhood, is Paris's most renowned lesbian dance club.

Casinos The nearest public casino, **Casino d'Enghien** (tel. 34–12–90–00), is by the lake at Enghien-les-Bains, 10 miles to the north of Paris.

All-night Chances are that some of your nocturnal forays will have you looking
Restaurants for sustenance at an unlikely hour. If so, you might find it handy to know that the following restaurants stay open round the clock:

Alsace (39 av. des Champs-Elysées, 8e, tel. 43–59–44–24), a stylish brasserie-restaurant, serves seafood and sauerkraut to famished night owls along the Champs-Elysées.

Au Pied de Cochon (6 rue Coquillière, 1er, tel. 42–36–11–75), near St-Eustache church in Les Halles, once catered to the all-night workers at the adjacent Paris food market. Today, its Second Empire decor has been restored, and traditional dishes like pig's trotters and chitterling sausage still grace the menu.

Au Chien Qui Fume (33 rue du Pont Neuf, 1er, tel. 42–36–07–42), open until 2 AM, has a chocolate mousse worth waiting up for.

Le Congrès (80 av. de la Grande-Armée, 17e, tel. 45–74–17–24), a lesser-known haunt beyond the Arc de Triomphe, is worth checking out if you're in search of a late-night T-bone steak.

Le Grand Café (4 blvd. des Capucines, 9e, tel. 47–42–75–77), whose exuberant turn-of-the-century dining room matches the mood of the neighboring Opéra, provides excellent oysters, fish, and meat dishes at rather hefty prices.

For more suggestions, *see* Dining, Chapter 5.

8 Excursions

Chantilly and Senlis

Updated by
Elva
Harding

Romantic Chantilly, with its faux Renaissance château, eye-popping art collection, splendid Rococo stables, classy racecourse, and vast (nearly 16,000-acre) forest, lies just 30 minutes north of Paris, yet it attracts far fewer sightseeing hordes than Versailles or Fontainebleau. It is a perfect setting for a day away from the capital. A trip here can easily be combined with a visit to Senlis, 6 miles to the east, whose maze of crooked streets is dominated by the soaring spire of its Gothic cathedral.

Getting There

By Car   Highway A1 runs just past Senlis; Chantilly is 6 miles west along the pretty D924.

By Train   Chantilly is 30 minutes from the Gare du Nord; a shuttle bus links Chantilly to Senlis.

Tourist Information

Office du Tourisme, 23 av. Maréchal-Joffre, 60500 Chantilly, tel. 16/ 44–57–08–58; 1 pl. du Parvis Notre-Dame, 60300 Senlis, tel. 16/44– 53–06–40.

Exploring

While the lavish exterior of the **Château de Chantilly** may be overdone—the style is 19th-century Renaissance pastiche—the building itself houses the Musée Condé, an outstanding collection of medieval manuscripts and European paintings, including masterpieces by Raphael, Watteau, and Ingres. *Admission: 35 frs adults, 27 frs students, 10 frs children under 12. Open Wed.–Mon. 10–6, 10:30–12:45 and 2–5 Nov.–Feb. Orchestra performance every afternoon during the summer and Christmas holidays. Admission 80 frs.*

Les Grandes Ecuries (the stables), near the château and adjoining the racecourse, are majestic 18th-century buildings housing the **Musée du Cheval** (Museum of the Horse). The spacious stables were built to accommodate 240 horses and more than 400 hounds for stag and boar hunts. *Admission: 45 frs adults, 35 frs children under 12. Open Wed.–Mon. 10:30–6:30 in summer; 2–4:30 Wed.–Fri., 10:30– 5:30 weekends Nov.–Mar.*

The **Cathédrale Notre Dame** in Senlis (place du Parvis) dates from the second half of the 12th century. The superb spire—arguably the most elegant in France—was added around 1240. This is one of France's oldest (and narrowest) cathedrals.

The **Musée de la Vénerie** (Hunting Museum), across from the cathedral, within the grounds of the ruined royal castle, claims to be Europe's only full-fledged hunting museum, with related artifacts, prints, and paintings (including excellent works by 18th-century animal portraitist Jean-Baptiste Oudry). *Château Royal. Admission: 13 frs adults, 7 frs students, (grounds only, 6 frs). Open Wed. 2–6, Thurs.–Mon. 10:30–noon and 2–6. Closed Tues. and mid-Dec.– mid-Jan.*

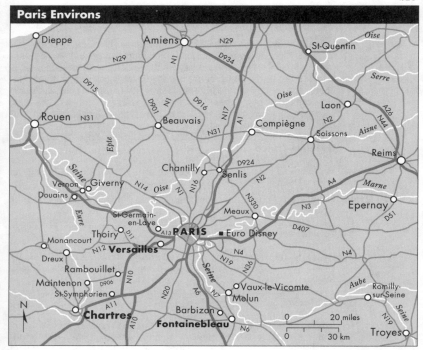

Paris Environs

Dining

Chantilly **Relais Condé.** Although this is probably the classiest restaurant in Chantilly—pleasantly situated across from the racecourse—there's a reasonable fixed-price menu (180 francs) that makes it a suitable lunch spot. The new chef has enlivened the menu with such dishes as lobster terrine and duck breast with honey and spices. *42 av. du Maréchal-Joffre, Chantilly, tel. 16/44-57-05-75. Reservations essential. Dress: informal. AE, V. Closed Tues. $$*

Senlis **Les Gourmandins.** This is a cozy, two-floor restaurant in old Senlis, serving some interesting dishes and offering a fine wine list. The 120-franc fixed-price menu is a good bet for a weekday lunch. *3 pl. de la Halle, Senlis, tel. 16/44-60-94-01. Reservations advised. Dress: informal. V. Closed Mon. eve., Tues., and last 3 weeks in Aug. $$*

Chartres

Although Chartres is chiefly visited for its magnificent Gothic cathedral with world-famous stained-glass windows, the whole town—one of the prettiest in France, with old houses and picturesque streets—is worth leisurely exploration.

Worship on the site of the cathedral goes back to before the Gallo-Roman period; the crypt contains a well that was the focus of Druid ceremonies. The original cult of the fertility goddess merged into that of the Virgin Mary with the arrival of Christianity. In the late 9th century, King Charles the Bold presented Chartres with what was believed to be the tunic of the Virgin. This precious relic attracted hordes of pilgrims, and Chartres swiftly became—and has remained—a prime destination for the faithful. Pilgrims trek to Chartres from Paris on foot to this day.

The noble, soaring spires of Chartres compose one of the most famous sights in Europe. Try to catch a glimpse of them surging out of the vast golden grainfields of the Beauce as you approach from the northeast.

Getting There

By Car   The A11/A10 expressways link Paris to Chartres (55 mi). To get to Rambouillet from Paris, take A13 toward Versailles, then A12 N10 (33 mi). D906 continues to Maintenon (15 mi), then to Chartres (12 mi).

By Train   There are hourly trains from Paris (Gare Montparnasse) to Chartres (travel time is 50–70 minutes, depending on service), many of which stop at Rambouillet and Maintenon.

Guided Tours

Paris Vision (214 rue de Rivoli, tel. 42–60–31–25) and **Cityrama** (4 pl. des Pyramides, tel. 44–55–61–00) can arrange guided visits to a number of sites in the Paris region. Both feature half-day trips to Chartres on Tuesday, Thursday, and Saturday afternoons (250 frs); and combined excursions to Chartres and Versailles (435 frs) on Tuesday and Saturday. Additional trips are scheduled in summer; call for information.

Tourist Information

Office du Tourisme, pl. de la Cathédrale, 28000 Chartres, tel. 16/37–21–50–00.

Exploring

Today's **Chartres cathedral** is the sixth church to occupy the same spot. It dates mainly from the 12th and 13th centuries, having been erected after the previous, 11th-century building burned down in 1194. A well-chronicled outburst of religious fervor followed the discovery that the Virgin's relic had miraculously survived unsinged. Reconstruction went ahead at a breathtaking pace. Just 25 years were needed for Chartres cathedral to rise again, and it has remained substantially unchanged ever since.

The lower half of the facade is all that survives from the 11th-century Romanesque church. (The Romanesque style is evident in the use of round, rather than pointed, arches.) The main door—the **Portail Royal**—is richly sculpted with scenes from the life of Christ. The flanking towers are also Romanesque, though the upper part of the taller of the two **spires** (380 feet as against 350 feet) dates from the start of the 16th century, and its fanciful flamboyance contrasts with the stalwart solemnity of its Romanesque counterpart. The **rose window** above the main portal dates from the 13th century. The three windows below it contain some of the finest examples of 12th-century stained glass in France.

The interior is somber, and your eyes will need time to get used to the darkness. Their reward will be a view of the gemlike richness of the stained glass, with the famous deep "Chartres blue" predominating. The oldest window, and perhaps the most stunning, is *Notre*

Portail Royal, **1**
New Tower, **2**
Old Tower, **3**
Vendôme
Chapel, **4**
Portail Sud, **5**
Notre Dame de
la Belle
Verrière, **6**
Crypt
entrance, **7**
St-Piat Chapel, **8**
Sacristy, **9**
Portail Nord, **10**
Staircase, **11**
Clocktower, **12**

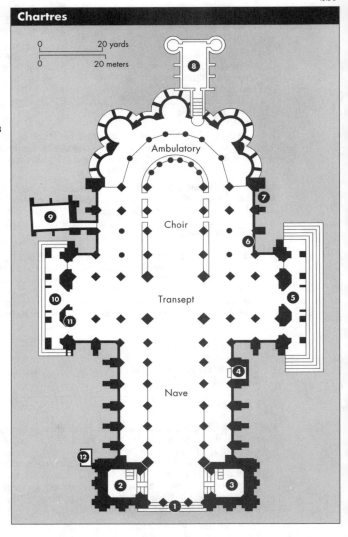

Chartres

0 20 yards

0 20 meters

Ambulatory

Choir

Transept

Nave

Dame de la Belle Verrière (literally, Our Lady of the Beautiful Window), in the south choir. It is well worth taking a pair of binoculars to pick out the details. If you wish to know more about stained-glass techniques and the motifs used, visit the small exhibit in the gallery opposite the north porch. The vast black-and-white medieval pattern on the floor of the nave is the only one of its kind to have survived from the Middle Ages. The faithful were expected to travel along its entire length (some 300 yards) on their knees.

Guided tours of the crypt start from the Maison de la Crypte opposite the south porch. The Romanesque and Gothic chapels running around the crypt have recently been stripped of the 19th-century paintings that used to disfigure them. You will also be shown a 4th-century Gallo-Roman wall and some 12th-century wall paintings.

Admission: 10 frs adults, 7 frs children and students. Guided tours of crypt: Easter–Oct. daily 11, 2:15, 3:30, 4:30, 5:15; Nov.–Easter daily 11, 4. English guide 30 frs.

Just behind the cathedral stands the **Musée des Beaux-Arts,** a handsome 18th-century building that used to serve as the bishop's palace. Its varied collection includes Renaissance enamels, a portrait of Erasmus by Holbein, tapestries, armor, and some fine, mainly French paintings of the 17th, 18th, and 19th centuries. There is also a room devoted to the forceful 20th-century works of Maurice de Vlaminck, who lived in the region. *29 cloître Notre Dame. Admission: 15 frs (20 frs for special exhibitions). Open Apr.–Oct. Wed.–Mon. 10–6, Nov.–Mar. 10–noon and 2–5, closed Tues.*

The museum gardens overlook the old streets that tumble down to the river Eure. Take rue Chantault down to the river, cross over, and head right, along rue de la Tannerie (which becomes rue de la Foulerie) as far as rue du Pont St-Hilaire. From here, there is a picturesque view of the roofs of old Chartres nestling beneath the cathedral. Then cross the bridge and head up to the Gothic **Eglise St-Pierre,** whose own magnificent windows date back to the early 14th century. There is yet more stained glass (17th century) to admire at the **Eglise St-Aignan** nearby, just off rue St-Pierre.

Wander among the steep, narrow streets, with the spires of the cathedral as your guide. Near the station is the striking monument to Jean Moulin, martyred World War II Resistance hero and onetime prefect of Chartres.

The River Eure snakes northeast from Chartres to the town of **Maintenon,** whose Renaissance **château** once belonged to Louis XIV's mistress and morganatic spouse, Madame de Maintenon. Her private apartments are open to visitors. The square, 12th-century keep is the sole vestige of a fortress that once occupied this site. The formal gardens stretch behind the château to the ivy-covered arches of the ruined **aqueduct**—one of the Sun King's most outrageous projects. His aim: to provide the ornamental ponds in the gardens of Versailles (30 miles away) with water from the Eure. In 1684, some 30,000 men were signed up to construct a three-tier, 3-mile aqueduct as part of this project. Many died of fever before the enterprise was called off in 1689. *Admission: 28 frs adults, 20 frs children. Open Apr.–Oct. Wed.–Mon. 2–6, Nov.–Mar. weekends 2–5:30. Closed Jan.*

Rambouillet, surrounded by a huge forest, was once the residence of kings and dukes; today it is the occasional home of the French president. When he's not entertaining visiting dignitaries here, the **château** and its extensive **grounds** (lake, islands, and flower beds) are open to the public. Most of the buildings date from the early 18th century, but the brawny **Tour François I,** named for the king who breathed his last here in 1547, was part of the 14th-century fortified castle that first stood on this site. *Admission: 26 frs adults, 17 frs children and senior citizens. Open Wed.–Mon. 10–11:30 and 2–5:30 (4:30 in winter).*

Dining

Chartres **La Vieille Maison.** Situated close to Chartres cathedral, in the same narrow street as Le Buisson Ardent (*see below*), La Vieille Maison is an intimate spot centered around a flower-decked patio. The menu changes regularly but invariably includes regional specialties such as truffles and asparagus with chicken. Prices, though justified, can be steep; the 155-franc lunch menu is a good bet. *5 rue au Lait, tel. 16/37–34–10–67. Reservations advised. Jacket and tie required. AE, MC, V. Closed Mon., Sun. evening. $$$*

Le Buisson Ardent. This wood-beamed restaurant offers attentive service, fixed-price menus, imaginative food, and a view of Chartres cathedral. Try the chicken ravioli with leeks or the rolled beef with spinach. *10 rue au Lait, tel. 16/37–34–04–66. Reservations advised. Dress: informal. AE, DC, MC, V. Closed Sun. evening. $–$$*

St-Symphorien **Château d'Esclimont.** This is a magnificent restored Renaissance château, 4 miles west of the Ablis exit on expressway A11 and about 15 miles from both Rambouillet and Chartres. Set in luxuriant grounds, with lawns and lake, this member of the Relais et Châteaux chain is a regular target for high-profile Parisian businessmen. The cuisine is sophisticated and reliably rich. Quail, hare fricassée (in season), and lobster top the menu. *St-Symphorien-le-Château, tel. 16/37–31–15–15. Reservations essential. Jacket and tie required. MC, V. $$$*

Euro Disney

In April 1992, American pop culture secured a mammoth outpost just 32 kilometers (20 miles) east of Paris. Euro Disney Resort, set on 1,500 acres in Marne-la-Vallée, boasts thousands of hotel rooms, a convention center, sports facilities, an entertainment and shopping complex and, of course, the main attraction: Euro Disneyland. Although great fanfare greeted the opening of Euro Disney, the resort has had its share of troubles: image problems, reports of technical glitches, feuds with neighbors objecting to noisy fireworks, and—worst of all—low attendance levels. Europe's economic woes are partially to blame: The devaluation of currency in Great Britain, Italy, and Spain in late 1992 made a trip to Euro Disney a costly venture for many Europeans. But even Parisians have not welcomed their new neighbor with open arms, visiting the park in far smaller numbers than had been forecast. It remains to be seen whether an improved economy among EU countries can bring in the hoped-for crowds.

In the meantime, there's plenty to see here. The theme park is made up of five "lands": Main Street U.S.A., Frontierland, Adventureland, Fantasyland, and Discoveryland. The central theme of each land is relentlessly echoed in every detail, from attractions, to restaurant menus, to souvenirs.

Top attractions at **Frontierland** are the chilling Phantom Manor, haunted by holographic spooks, and the thrilling runaway mine train of Big Thunder Mountain, a roller coaster that plunges wildly through floods and avalanches in a setting meant to evoke Monument Valley. Whiffs of Arabia, Africa, and the West Indies give **Adventureland** its exotic cachet; the spicy meals and snacks served here rank among the best food in the theme park. Don't miss Adventureland's Pirates of the Caribbean, an exciting *mise en scène* populated by eerily human, computer-driven figures, or Disney's newest attraction, **Indiana Jones and the Temple of Doom,** a breathtaking ride that relives some of our luckless hero's most exciting moments. **Fantasyland** charms the youngest park-goers with familiar cartoon characters and attractions featuring the stars of such Disney film classics as Snow White, Pinocchio, Dumbo, and Peter Pan. The focal point of Euro Disney—and its emblem—is Sleeping Beauty's Castle, a 140-foot, bubble-gum pink structure topped with 16 blue- and gold-tipped turrets. Officially known as Le Château de la Belle au Bois Dormant, its design was allegedly inspired by illustrations from a medieval Book of Hours. The castle's dungeon conceals a scaly green, two-ton dragon who rumbles and grumbles in his sleep, and occasionally rouses to roar—an impressive feat of engineering that terrifies every tot in the crowd! Cross the drawbridge from the castle to Central Plaza and walk left to **Discoveryland,** a futuristic setting for high-tech Disney entertainment. Robots on roller skates welcome visitors bound for Star Tours, a pitching, plunging, sense-confounding ride through intergalactic space. In Le Visionarium, blast off on a journey through time and space, presented in wraparound CircleVision by 9-Eye, a staggeringly realistic robot.

Euro Disney Resort includes six hotels with more than 5,000 rooms. Predictably, each has a theme, from the pseudo-Victorian splendor of the luxury-class Disneyland Hotel to the make-believe wilderness of Camp Davy Crockett, the resort's cheapest accommodation (also the farthest from Euro Disneyland). For entertainment outside the hotels and theme park, check out Festival Disney, a vast pleasure dome designed by architect Frank Gehry. Featured are American-style restaurants (a crab shack, a diner, a deli, a steak house), a disco, and a dinner theater where Buffalo Bill stages his Wild West Show twice nightly. An 18-hole golf course is open to the public (for information, tel. 64–74–30–00). *Admission to Euro Disneyland (prices vary according to season): 175–250 frs adults, 125–175 frs children under 12; 2-day passport 335–475 frs adults, 240–335 frs children; 3-day passport 440–630 frs adults, 315–440 frs children. Open mid-June–mid-Sept., daily 9–10; mid-Sept.–mid-June, daily 10–6, 10–9 during Dec. and spring school holidays.*

Getting There

By Bus Shuttle buses link Euro Disney to Roissy (56 km/35 mi) and Orly (50 km/31 mi) airports. Fare is 65 frs one way.

By Car The Strasbourg-bound A4 expressway leads from Paris to Euro Disney, at Marne-la-Vallée, a journey of 32 kilometers (20 miles) that in normal traffic will take about 30 minutes. The 4-kilometer (2½-mile) route from the expressway to the entrance of the theme park is clearly marked. Disney hotel guests should proceed to their hotel's "resident" parking lot; day visitors must head for the Parking Visiteurs, which costs 40 francs per car and is 600 yards from the theme-park entrance.

By Train Euro Disney's new suburban train station (Marne-la-Vallée-Chessy) is just 100 yards from the entrance to both the theme park and Festival Disney. Trains run every 10 to 20 minutes from central Paris RER-A stations at Charles de Gaulle-Etoile, Auber, Châtelet-Les Halles, Gare de Lyon, and Nation. The trip takes about 40 minutes and costs 70 francs round-trip (including the métro to the RER). A TGV station is expected to open right next to the RER station in June 1994, with trains running frequently from Gare Montparnasse.

Tourist Information

Contact **Walt Disney World Central Reservations** (Box 10,100, Lake Buena Vista, FL 32830-0100, tel. 407/934–7639) or **Euro Disney S.C.A.** (Central Reservations Office, BP 104 77777, Marne-la-Vallée, Cedex 4 France, tel. 49–41–49–10, fax 49–30–71–00).

Dining

Euro Disneyland is peppered with places to eat, ranging from snack bars and fast-food joints to full-service restaurants—all with a distinguishing theme. In addition, all Disney hotels and Festival Disney have restaurants that are open to the public. But since these are outside the theme park, it is not recommended that you waste time traveling to them for lunch. Euro Disneyland has recently relaxed its no alcohol policy and now serves wine and beer in select areas of the theme park, as well as at the hotels and restaurants. Eateries serve nonstop as long as the park is open. *AE, DC, MC, V at sit-down restaurants; no credit cards at others. Reservations recommended for sit-down restaurants.*

Fontainebleau

Fontainebleau, with its historic château, is a favorite place for excursions, especially since a lush forest (containing the painters' village of Barbizon) and the superb château of Vaux-le-Vicomte are close by.

Like Chambord in the Loire Valley or Compiègne to the north of Paris, Fontainebleau earned royal esteem as a hunting base. As at Versailles, a hunting lodge once stood on the site of the current château, along with a chapel built in 1169 and consecrated by exiled (later murdered and canonized) English priest Thomas à Becket. The palace you see today was begun under the flamboyant Renaissance king, François I, the French contemporary of England's Henry VIII. The king hired Italian artists Il Rosso (a pupil of Michelangelo) and Primaticcio to embellish his château. In fact they did much more: By introducing the pagan allegories and elegant lines of Mannerism to France, they revolutionized French decorative art. Their extraordinary frescoes and stuccowork can be admired in the Galerie François I and the glorious Salle de Bal, which was completed under Henri II, François's successor.

Although Sun King Louis XIV's architectural fancy was concentrated on Versailles, he commissioned Mansart to design new pavilions and had André Le Nôtre replant the gardens at Fontainebleau, where he and his court returned faithfully each autumn for the hunting season. However, it was Napoléon who made a Versailles, as it were, out of Fontainebleau, by spending lavishly to restore it to its former glory. He held Pope Pius VII prisoner here in 1812, signed the second Church-State concordat here in 1813, and, in the cobbled Cour des Adieux, bade farewell to his Old Guard in 1814 as he began his brief exile on the Mediterranean island of Elba.

Another courtyard—the Cour de la Fontaine–was commissioned by Napoléon in 1812 and adjoins the Etang (or pond) des Carpes. Ancient carp are alleged to swim here, although Allied soldiers drained the pond in 1915 and ate all the fish, and, in the event they missed some, Hitler's hordes did likewise in 1940.

Getting There

By Car   Take A6 then N7 to Fontainebleau from the Porte d'Orléans or Porte d'Italie (45 miles from Paris). N7 or N37 run close to Barbizon, 5 miles northwest of Fontainebleau. Vaux-le-Vicomte, near Melun, is 13 miles north of Fontainebleau. Take N6 north to Melun, then N36 (northeast), turning right 2 miles out of Melun along D215.

By Train Fontainebleau is about 50 minutes from the Gare de Lyon; take a bus to complete the trip from the station to the château. Barbizon and Vaux-le-Vicomte are not accessible by train.

Guided Tours

Paris Vision and **Cityrama** offer half-day trips to Fontainebleau and Barbizon (*see* Guided Tours in Chartres, *above*, for addresses). *Cost: 295 frs. Departures 1:30 Wed., Fri., and Sun.*

Tourist Information

Office du Tourisme, 31 pl. Napoléon-Bonaparte, Fontainebleau, tel. 16/64–22–25–68.

Exploring

The **château of Fontainebleau** dates from the 16th century, although additions were made by various royal incumbents over the next 300 years. The famous **horseshoe staircase** that dominates the Cour du Cheval Blanc (which later came to be called the Cour des Adieux, or Courtyard of Farewell) was built by Androuet du Cerceau for Louis XIII (1610–1643). The **Porte Dauphine** is the most beautiful of the various gateways that connect the complex of buildings; its name commemorates the fact that the Dauphin—the heir to the throne, later Louis XIII—was christened under its archway in 1606.

Napoléon's apartments occupied the first floor. You can see a lock of his hair, his Légion d'Honneur medal, his imperial uniform, the hat he wore on his return from Elba in 1815, and one bed in which he definitely did sleep (almost every town in France boasts a bed in which the emperor supposedly spent a night). There is also a throne room—Napoléon spurned the one at Versailles, a palace he disliked, and established his imperial seat in the former King's Bedchamber, a room with a suitably majestic decor—and the **Queen's Boudoir,** known as the room of the six Maries (occupants included ill-fated Marie Antoinette and Napoléon's second wife, Marie-Louise). Highlights of other salons include 17th-century tapestries, marble reliefs by Jacquet de Grenoble, and paintings and frescoes by the versatile Primaticcio.

The jewel of the interior, though, is the ceremonial ballroom, or **Salle de Bal,** nearly 100 feet long and dazzlingly decorated with 16th-century frescoes and gilding. It is luxuriantly wood-paneled, and a gleaming parquetry floor reflects the patterns in the ceiling. Like the château as a whole, the room exudes a sense of elegance and style—but on a more intimate, human scale than at Versailles: This is Renaissance, not Baroque. *Pl. du Gal-de-Gaulle, tel. 16/64–22–27–40. Admission: 30 frs adults, 19 frs ages 18–25 and senior citizens, under 18 free; 19 frs Sun. Open Wed.–Mon. 9:30–12:30 and 2–5; gardens open 9–dusk (admission free).*

On the western edge of the 62,000-acre Forest of Fontainebleau lies the village of **Barbizon,** home to a number of mid-19th-century landscape artists, whose innovative outdoor style paved the way for the Impressionists. Corot, Millet, Rousseau, Daubigny, and Diaz, among others, all painted here, repairing to **Père Ganne's Inn** after working hours to brush up on their social life. The inn still stands—though it's closed indefinitely for restoration—but you can soak up the arty mood at the houses of Millet and Rousseau farther along the single main street (rue Grande).

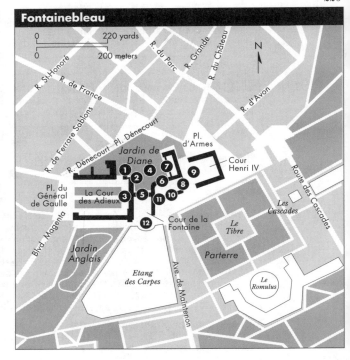

North of Fontainebleau stands the majestic château of **Vaux-le-Vicomte,** started in 1656 by court finance wizard Nicolas Fouquet. The construction process was monstrous: Villages were razed, then 18,000 workmen were called in to execute the plans of architect Louis Le Vau, decorator Charles Le Brun, and landscape architect Le Nôtre. The house-warming party was so lavish that star guest Louis XIV, tetchy at the best of times, threw a fit of jealousy. He hurled Fouquet in the slammer and promptly began building Versailles to prove just who was boss.

Entry to the high-roofed château is from the north. Decoration of the cupola, in the **salon,** was halted at Fouquet's arrest. Le Brun's major achievement is the ceiling of the **Chambre du Roi,** depicting *Time Bearing Truth Heavenwards.* The word "squirrel" in French is *écureuil,* but in local dialect they were known as *fouquets;* they appear here (along the frieze) and throughout the château, a sly visual tribute to Vaux's hapless owner. Le Brun's other masterwork here is the ceiling in the **Salon des Muses,** a brilliant allegorical composition painted in glowing, sensuous colors that surpasses anything Le Brun completed at Versailles.

A clever exhibition, complete with life-size wax figures, explains the rise and fall of Nicolas Fouquet. The version is, not surprisingly, favorable to the château's founder—accused by Louis XIV and subsequent historians of megalomania and shady financial dealings, but apparently condemned on little evidence by a court anxious to please the jealous, irascible monarch. The exhibition continues in the **basement,** whose cool, dim rooms were used to store food and wine and house the château's staff. The **kitchens,** a more cheerful sight with their gleaming copperwear and old menus, are also down here.

Le Nôtre's carefully restored **gardens** contain statues, waterfalls, and fountains, and provide fine views. There is also a **Musée des Equipages**—carriages, saddles, and smithy—on the grounds. *Admission: 48 frs adults, 38 frs students. Grounds only: 27 frs adults, 20 frs students. Château open daily 10–6; 11–5 Nov.–Mar. Closed Dec./mid-Feb. except Christmas/New Year's. Candlelight visits May–Oct., Sat. evenings 8:30–11 (65 frs adults, 52 frs students).*

Dining

Barbizon   **Le Relais de Barbizon.** Solid home-cooked meals are served alfresco. Among the offerings are duckling with cherries and lamb with parsley. Expect crowds in midsummer. The five-course, 135-franc weekday menu is excellent value. *2 av. Charles-de-Gaulle, Barbizon, tel. 16/60–66–40–28. Reservations advised. Dress: informal. MC, V. Closed Tues. evening and Wed. $–$$*

Fontainebleau   **Le Beauharnais.** Conveniently situated in the Aigle Noir hotel opposite Fontainebleau château, this recently restored restaurant offers classic French fare, including veal sweetbreads with prawns and duck with marjoram, in a grand setting. Set menus are priced at 220 and 300 francs, and there's a tranquil garden for alfresco dining in summer. *27 pl. Napoléon-Bonaparte, Fontainebleau, tel. 16/64–22–32–65. Reservations recommended. Jacket and tie required. AE, DC, MC, V. Closed last 2 weeks of Dec. $$$*

Giverny

This charming village in southern Normandy has become a place of pilgrimage for art lovers. It was here that Claude Monet lived for 43 years, until his death in 1926 at the age of 86. After decades of neglect, his pretty pink house with green shutters, his studios, and, above all, his garden with its famous lily pond have been lovingly restored—thanks to gifts from around the world and in particular from the United States. Late spring is perhaps the best time to visit, when the apple trees are in blossom and the garden is a riot of color; however, Giverny is worth a day trip from Paris at least into mid-autumn.

Monet was brought up in Normandy and, like many of the Impressionists, was attracted by the soft light of the Seine Valley, north of Paris. After several years at Argenteuil, just north of Paris, he moved downriver to Giverny in 1883 along with his two sons, his mistress Alice Hoschedé (whom he later married), and her six children. By 1890, a prospering Monet was able to buy the house outright. Three years later, he purchased another plot of land across the road to continue his gardening experiments, diverting the River Epte to make a pond.

The water lilies and Japanese bridges became special features of Monet's garden and now help to conjure up an image of the bearded brushman dabbing cheerfully at his canvases—capturing changes in light and weather in a way that was to have a major influence on 20th-century art. From Giverny, Monet enthusiasts may want to continue up the Seine Valley to the site of another of his celebrated painting series: Rouen cathedral.

Getting There

By Car Take expressway A13 from Paris to the Vernon exit (D181). Cross the Seine in Vernon and follow D5 to Giverny.

By Train Take the train from Gare St-Lazare to Vernon (50 min). Giverny is a 3½-mile walk, bus, or a taxi ride away.

Guided Tours

Guided excursions are organized by **American Express** (11 rue Scribe, tel. 47–77–77–37) and the **RATP Tourist Office** (pl. de la Madeleine, tel. 40–06–71–45), on either a half-day or full-day basis, combined with trips to Rouen.

Exploring

Monet's house has a warm family feeling that may come as a welcome break after visiting stately French châteaux. The rooms have been restored to Monet's original designs: the kitchen with its blue tiles, the buttercup-yellow dining room, and Monet's bedroom on the second floor. You will see the Japanese prints Monet collected so avidly and reproductions of his own works displayed around the house. His studios are also open for viewing. The garden, with flowers spilling out across the paths, is as cheerful and natural as the house—quite unlike formal French gardens. The enchanting water garden, with its lilies, bridges, and rhododendrons, is across the road. *84 rue Claude Monet. Admission: 30 frs; gardens only, 20 frs. Open Apr.–Oct., Tues–Sun. 10–6. Garden open 10–6.*

Close by is the newly opened **Musée Américain,** endowed by Chicago art patrons Daniel and Judith Terra. On view are works by American Impressionists influenced by Claude Monet. *99 rue Claude-Monet. Admission: 30 frs adults, 20 frs students and senior citizens. Open Apr.–Oct., Tues.–Sun. 10–6; closed Mon.*

Dining

Douains **Château de Brécourt.** This 17th-century brick château, set in extensive grounds, is a member of the stylish Relais & Châteaux chain and lies 7 miles west of Giverny (via D181 at Douains, near Pacy-sur-Eure). Creative dishes in an august setting make Brécourt a popular spot for people who drive to Giverny. The menu includes smoked salmon-and-crab cakes and turbot with caviar, as well as a dessert of pears in a flaky pastry roasted in honey. *Tel. 16/32–52–40–50. Reservations advised. Dress: informal. AE, DC, MC, V. $$$*

Giverny **Les Jardins de Giverny.** This commendable restaurant is close to Monet's house, and the old-fashioned dining room overlooks a rose garden. Tourists who lunch here are treated to inventive dishes such as foie gras laced with applejack or seafood terrine with a mild pepper sauce. *Chemin du Roy, tel. 16/32–21–60–80. Reservations advised in summer. Dress: casual. AE, V. Closed Sun. evening, Mon., and Feb. $$*

Reims and Laon

Champagne and cathedrals make a trip to the renowned city of Reims and the lesser-known town of Laon an ideal two-day break from the French capital. Reims is the capital of the champagne industry. Several major producers have their headquarters here, and you will not want to miss the chance to visit the chalky, labyrinthine champagne cellars that tunnel beneath the city. Reims cathedral, one of the most historic in France, was the setting for the coronations of French kings (Charles X was the last to be crowned here, back in 1825). Despite some indifferent 20th-century rebuilding, Reims is rich with attractions from Roman times to the modern era. Laon, which occupies a splendid hilltop site 25 miles northwest of Reims, is known as the "crowned mountain" on account of the many-towered silhouette of its venerable cathedral. This enchanting old town could easily be turned into one of France's leading tourist draws, were lethargic local authorities not firmly locked into the past: Laon was once, after all, the capital of France—almost 12 centuries ago.

Getting There

By Car   Expressway A4 goes via Reims on its way east from Paris to Strasbourg. The Belgium-bound N2 links Paris to Laon. The N44 highway links Laon and Reims—a 25-mile trip.

By Train   Scheduled trains cover the 110 miles from Paris (Gare de l'Est) to Reims in 90 minutes. The Paris–Laon route (from the Gare du Nord) takes up to two hours. Trains run daily between Laon and Reims.

Tourist Information

Office du Tourisme, 2 rue Guillaume-de-Machault, 51100 Reims, tel. 16/26–47–25–69; place du Parvis, 02000 Laon, tel. 16/23–20–28–62.

Exploring

The glory of Reims's **Cathédrale Notre Dame** is its facade. Its proportions are curiously deceptive, and the building is actually considerably larger than it appears. Above the north (left) door is the **Smiling Angel,** a delightful statue whose kindly expression threatens to turn into an acid-rain scowl—pollution has succeeded war as the ravager of the building. The postcard shops nearby have views of the cathedral after World War I, and on seeing the destruction, you'll understand why restoration here is an ongoing process. The high, solemn **nave** is at its best in the summer, when the lower walls are adorned with 16th-century tapestries relating the life of the Virgin. The east-end **windows** were designed by Marc Chagall.

With the exception of the 15th-century **towers,** most of the original building was constructed in the hundred years after 1211. A stroll around the outside will reinforce the impression of the harmony and discipline of its lines, which almost belie its decorative richness. The east end presents an idyllic vista across well-tended lawns. There are spectacular light shows both inside (40 frs) and outside (free) the cathedral in July and August. *Open daily 8–7. Guided tours in English available.*

The **Palais du Tau** next door is the former archbishop's palace and affords excellent views of the cathedral. It contains tapestries, coronation robes, and several outstanding statues removed for safekeeping from the cathedral's facade. *2 pl. du Cardinal-Luçon, tel. 16/26-47-74-39. Admission: 26 frs adults, 18 frs senior citizens, 6 frs children under 18. Open daily 10–noon and 2–6; 10–noon and 2–5 winter weekdays.*

The nearby **Musée des Beaux-Arts,** Reims's fine art museum, has an outstanding painting collection crowned by 27 Corots and David's celebrated portrait of Revolutionary leader Marat dead in his bath. Nine Boudins and Jongkinds are among the finer Impressionist works here. *8 rue Chanzy. Admission: 10 frs, under 18 free. Open Wed.–Mon. 10–noon and 2–6.*

As you leave the museum, turn right and continue along rue Chanzy/rue Gambetta to the 11th-century **Basilique St-Rémi,** devoted to the 5th-century saint who gave his name to the city. The building is nearly as long as the cathedral, and its interior seems to stretch away into the dim distance. The Gothic choir area has much original 12th-century stained glass. *Rue Simon.*

Several champagne producers run tours of their **champagne cellars,** combining video presentations with guided walks through their cavernous, chalk-hewn, underground warehouses. Few producers show much generosity when it comes to pouring out samples of bubbly, so we recommend you double back across town to **Mumm,** which does. *(34 rue du Champ-de-Mars, tel. 16/26-49-59-69. Open daily 9:30–noon and 2–5; closed weekends in winter).* If you don't mind paying for samples, however, the most spectacular cellars are those of Taittinger. *(9 pl. St-Nicaise. Admission: 15 frs. Guided 1-hour tours: weekdays 9:30–11:50 (last departure) and 2–4:20; weekends 9–10:50 and 2–4:50.*

Across from the Mumm Cellars is a modern **chapel** decorated by the Japanese artist Foujita, a member of the Montparnasse set in the '20s who converted and was baptized in Reims. Head down rue du Champ-de-Mars toward the railroad station, turn right onto avenue de Laon, then left onto rue Franklin D. Roosevelt. A short way along is the **Salle de Guerre,** where Eisenhower established Allied headquarters at the end of World War II. It was here, in a well-preserved, map-covered room, that the German surrender was signed in May 1945. *Admission: 10 frs adults, under 18 free. Open Apr.–Sept. Wed.–Mon. 10–noon and 2–6, Oct.–Mar. Wed.–Mon. 10–noon; closed Tues.*

The **Porte Mars** is an impressive Roman arch that looms up just across from the railroad station. It is adorned by faded bas-reliefs depicting Jupiter, Romulus, and Remus.

Visitors interested in the history of World War I may want to visit the **chemin des Dames,** a section of the road between Reims and Laon. The disastrous French offensive launched here by General Nivelle in April 1917 led to futile slaughter and mutiny. Take N44 from Reims to Corbény, then wind your way for some 17 miles along D18/D985 west, past Cerny-en-Laonnois, until it meets N2, which heads north to Laon, 12 miles away.

Laon's **Cathédrale Notre Dame** was constructed from 1160 to 1235 and is a superb example of early Gothic style. The light, recently cleaned interior gives the impression of immense length (120 yards in total). The flat ceiling at the east end—an English-inspired feature—is unusual in France. The second-floor galleries that run around the building are typical of early Gothic; you can visit them (and the towers) with a guide from the Tourist Office on the cathedral square. The airy elegance of the five remaining towers is audacious by any standard, and rare: French medieval architects preferred to concentrate on soaring interiors and usually allowed for just two towers at the west end. You don't have to be an architectural scholar to appreciate the sense of movement about Laon's west-end facade compared with the more placid, two-dimensional feel of Notre Dame in Paris. Also look for the stone bulls protruding from the towers, a tribute to the stalwart beasts who carted the blocks of stone from quarries far below.

The medieval **ramparts,** the old fortification walls, lie virtually undisturbed by passing traffic and provide a ready-made route for a tour of old Laon. Another notable and well-preserved survivor from medieval times is the **Chapelle des Templiers,** a small octagonal 12th-century chapel on the grounds of the town museum. *Admission to the museum: 10 frs. Open Apr.–Sept. Wed.–Mon. 10–noon and 2–6; Oct.–Mar. Wed.–Mon. 10–noon and 2–5; closed Tues.*

Dining

Laon **La Petite Auberge.** You can expect some imaginative nouvelle dishes from young chef Willy-Marc Zorn in this 18th-century-style restaurant close to the station in Laon's *ville basse* (lower town). Fillet of plaice with champagne vinegar, braised squab, and frozen nougat are among the choices. *45 blvd. Pierre-Brossolette, tel. 16/23–23–02–38. Reservations recommended. Dress: informal. AE, V. Closed Sat. lunch, Sun., and Aug. $$*

Reims **Boyer.** Gérard Boyer is one of the most highly rated chefs in France. Duck, foie gras in pastry, and truffles (served in a variety of ways) figure among his specialties. The setting, not far from the Basilique St-Rémi, is magnificent, too: a 19th-century château, built for the champagne firm Pommery, surrounded by an extensive, well-tended park. *Château des Crayères, 64 blvd. Henry-Vasnier, tel. 16/26–82–80–80. Reservations essential. Jacket and tie required. AE, DC, MC, V. Closed Mon., Tues. lunch, Christmas–mid-Jan. $$$$*
Florence. An old, high-ceilinged mansion is the setting for this elegant and well-run restaurant. Chef Laurent Helleu serves wonderfully light versions of classical French dishes—and at fair prices (especially the weekday lunch menu for 150 francs). *43 blvd. Foch, tel. 16/26–47–12–70. Reservations advised. Dress: informal. AE, DC, MC, V. Closed first 3 weeks in Aug. $$–$$$*

Lodging

Laon **Bannière de France.** This comfortable old hotel, just five minutes' walk from Laon cathedral, is favored by British travelers, perhaps because Madame Lefèvre speaks English well and offers a cheerful welcome. There is a venerable dining room where you can enjoy sturdy cuisine (trout, guinea fowl) at unbeatable value. *11 rue Franklin D. Roosevelt, tel. 16/23–23–21–44. 18 rooms, all with bath or shower. AE, DC, MC, V. Facilities: restaurant. Closed mid-Dec.–mid-Jan. $*
Les Chavaliers. Located in a quiet nook in the center of old Laon between the cathedral and Hôtel de Ville (town hall), Les Chavaliers is an ideal base for exploring the area and a good night's rest at a fair price. The family-run hotel isn't extravagant but offers all the comforts of home. The bar/tea room serves light fare. *3–5 rue Serurier, tel. 16/23–23–43–78, fax 16/23–23–40–71. 15 rooms, most with bath or shower. MC, V. Facilities: bar/tearoom. Closed in winter. $*

Reims **Gambetta.** This hotel near Reims cathedral has small, fairly basic
rooms and a decent restaurant, the Vonelly (closed Sun. evening,
Mon., and mid-Aug.), which serves a 180-franc menu featuring scallop salad with spinach and roast duck with cabbage. *9 rue Gambetta,
tel. 16/26–47–41–64, fax 16/26–47–22–43. 17 rooms with shower.
Facilities: restaurant. AE, MC, V. $*

Thoiry

Thoiry, 25 miles west of Paris, is an ideal day-trip destination, especially for families with children. It offers a splendid combination of
history and culture—chiefly in the form of a superbly furnished
16th-century château with its own archives and gastronomy museum—and outdoor adventure. Its safari park boasts over 800 animals
and is a great place to picnic; drinks and snacks can be bought here,
too.

Getting There

By Car Take highway A13 then highway A12 from Paris to Bois d'Arcy,
then take N12 toward Dreux. Just past Pontchartrain, D11 heads off
right toward Thoiry.

By Train From Gare Montparnasse to Montfort-L'Amaury (35 min), then a
10-minute taxi ride. A special shuttle bus operates to and from the
château on Sundays in summer.

Exploring

The **château** was built in 1564. Its handsome Renaissance facade is
set off by **gardens** landscaped in the disciplined French fashion by Le
Nôtre; there is a less formal Jardin à l'Anglaise (English Garden) for
contrast. Owners Vicomte de La Panouse and his American wife,
Annabelle, have restored the château and grounds to their former
glory and opened both to the public. Highlights of the **interior** include the grand staircase, the 18th-century Gobelins tapestries in
the dining room that were inspired by the adventures of Don
Quixote, and the Green and White Salon with its old harpsichord,
portraits, and tapestries.

The distinguished history of the Panouse family—one member,
Comte César, fought in the American Revolution—is retraced in the
Archive Museum, where papal bulls, Napoléonic letters, and Chopin
manuscripts (discovered in the attic in 1973) are displayed side by
side with missives from Thomas Jefferson and Benjamin Franklin.

Since 1984, the château pantries have housed a **Museum of Gastronomy,** whose *pièces montées* (banquet showpieces) re-create the designs of the premier 19th-century chef, Antoine Carême (his clients
included George IV of England and the emperors of Austria and
Russia). One is over 15 feet high and took eight months to confect.
Engravings, old copper pots, and early recipe books are also on
display.

You can stroll at leisure around the picturesque grounds, stopping
off at the Pré Angélique to watch a cricket match (summer weekends) and admiring giraffes, wolves, and—from the safety of a
raised footbridge—the world's first *ligrons*, crosses between a lion
and a tiger. There is an exploratory play area for children, featuring
giant burrows and cobwebs. For obvious reasons, pedestrians are
not allowed into the Bear Park or the African Reserve. Keep your

car windows closed if you want to remain on peaceful terms with ma-
rauding lions, rhinos, elephants, and mega-horned Watutsi cattle.
*Tel. 34–87–52–25. Château Admission: 23 frs adults, 20 frs chil-
dren. Château park and game reserve admission: 89 frs adults, 72
frs children. Open weekdays 10–6, weekends 10–6:30 in summer;
weekdays 10–5, weekends 10–5:30 in winter.*

Dining

The château's **self-service restaurant** in the converted 16th-century
stables (same hours as the safari park) offers a palatable choice
of fixed-price meals. Cold starters include salami, tomato salad,
and green salad; the main course may be roast chicken, veal with
mushrooms, steak and fries, or *andouillette* (small chitterling
sausage). *$*

Etoile. This restaurant, belonging to a three-star hotel, is situated
just 300 yards from the château along the main street. There are
special tourist and children's menus as well as a wide choice of à la
carte selections. Robust, traditional French dishes are served:
steak, chicken, fish, and pâté. *38 rue de la Porte St-Martin, tel. 16/
34–87–40–21. Reservations advised. Dress: informal. AE, DC,
MC, V. Closed Mon. $*

Versailles

Paris in the 17th century was a rowdy, rabble-ridden city. Louis
XIV hated it and set about in search of a new power base. He settled
on Versailles, 15 miles west of Paris, where his father had a small
château/hunting lodge.

Today, the château of Versailles seems monstrously big, but it
wasn't large enough for the army of 20,000 noblemen, servants, and
hangers-on who moved in with Louis. A new city—a new capital, in
fact—had to be constructed from scratch to accommodate them.
Vast mansions were built, along with broad avenues—all in an extravagant Baroque style.

It was hardly surprising that Louis XIV's successors rapidly felt un-
comfortable with their architectural inheritance. Indeed, as the
18th century wore on, and the taste for intimate, private apartments expanded at the expense of the public, would-be heroic
lifestyles of 17th-century monarchs, subsequent rulers built themselves small retreats on the grounds, where they could escape the
overpowering formality of court life. The two most famous of these
structures are the **Petit Trianon,** a model of classical harmony and
proportion built by Louis XV; and the simple, "rustic" **Hameau,** or
hamlet, that Marie Antoinette built so that she could play at being a
simple shepherdess.

The contrast between the majestic and the domesticated is an important part of Versailles's appeal, but pomp and bombast dominate the
mood here, and you won't need reminding that you're in the world's
grandest palace—or one of France's most popular tourist attractions. The park outside is the ideal place to get your breath back. Le
Nôtre's gardens represent formal landscaping at its most rigid and
sophisticated.

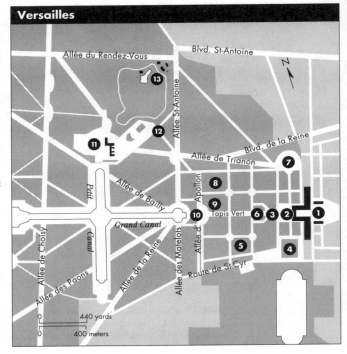

Getting There

By Car Take highway A13 from Porte d'Auteuil then follow the signs to Versailles.

By Train There are three train routes from Paris to Versailles (20–30 min). The RER-C to Versailles Rive-Gauche takes you closest to the château (just 600 yards away via avenue de Sceaux). The other trains run from Gare St-Lazare to Versailles Rive-Droite (⅔ mile via rue Foch and avenue de St-Cloud), and from Gare Montparnasse to Versailles-Chantiers (¾ mile via rue des Etats Généraux and avenue de Paris).

Guided Tours

Paris Vision and **Cityrama** (*see* Guided Tours in Chartres, *above*, for addresses) offer half- and full-day guided bus tours of Versailles, Fontainebleau, Barbizon, and Chartres. Trips cost from 190 francs (half day) to 435 francs (full day).

Tourist Information

Office de Tourisme, 7 rue des Réservoirs, tel. 16/39–50–36–22.

Exploring

The **château** was built under court architects Le Vau and Mansart between 1662 and 1690; entrance is through the gilt-and-iron gates from the huge place d'Armes. In the center of the building, across the sprawling cobbled forecourt, are the rooms that belonged to the king and queen. The two wings were occupied by the royal children and princes; attendants were housed in the attics.

The highlight of the tour, for many, is the **Galerie des Glaces** (Hall of Mirrors), now fully restored to its original dazzle. It was here that Bismarck proclaimed the unified German Empire in 1871, and here that the controversial Treaty of Versailles, asserting Germany's responsibility for World War I, was signed in 1919.

The royal bedchambers are formal; the **petits appartements,** where royal family and friends lived, are more on a human scale. The intimate **Opéra Royal,** the first oval hall in France, was designed for Louis XV. Touch the "marble" loges—they're actually painted wood. The chapel, built by Mansart, is a study in white-and-gold solemnity. *Admission to château: 40 frs; Sun. 20 frs. Open Tues.–Sun. 9–6:30 (5:30 in winter); Galerie des Glaces open 9:45–5; Opéra Royal open 9:45–3:30 (tours every 15 min). Closed Mon.*

The 250-acre **grounds** include woods, lawns, flower beds, statues, lakes, and fountains. They are at their best in the fall. The fountains play on several Sundays in summer, making a fabulous spectacle. *The grounds are open daily; Admission: 20 frs July–Sept., free Aug.–June.*

At one end of the Petit Canal, about a mile from the château, stands the **Grand Trianon,** built by Mansart in the 1680s. This pink-marble pleasure palace is now used to entertain visiting heads of state; at other times it is open to the public. *Admission: Grand Trianon: 20 frs adults, 13 frs children and senior citizens. Petit Trianon: 12 frs adults, 8 frs children and senior citizens. Open Oct.–Apr., Tues.–Fri. 10–5:30; May–Sept., Tues.–Sun. 10–6:30.*

The **Petit Trianon,** close by, is a sumptuously furnished neoclassical mansion erected in 1768 by architect Gabriel. Louis XV had a superb botanical garden planted here; some of the trees from that era survive today. Louis XVI presented the Petit Trianon to Marie Antoinette, who spent lavish sums creating an idealized world, the charming *hameau* (hamlet, a handful of thatched-roof cottages), complete with watermill, lake, and pigeon loft. *Hours same as for Grand Trianon.*

The town of Versailles tends to be underestimated. Visitors are usually exhausted from exploring the palace and park, but the town's broad, leafy boulevards are also agreeable places to stroll. The **Cathédrale St-Louis** is an austere edifice built from 1743 to 1754 by Mansart's grand-nephew, and it contains fine paintings and an organ loft. The **Eglise Notre Dame** is a sturdy Baroque monument, built from 1684 to 1686 by the elder Mansart as the parish church for the Sun King's new town, for which Louis XIV deigned to lay the foundation stone. The collection of the **Musée Lambinet,** housed nearby in an imposing 18th-century mansion, is wide-ranging, with a maze of cozy, finely furnished rooms full of paintings, weapons, fans, and porcelain. *54 blvd. de la Reine, tel. 16/39–50–30–32. Admission: 16 frs. Open Tues.–Sun. 2–6; closed Mon.*

Dining

Les Trois Marches. This is one of the best-known restaurants in the Paris area. It was recently relocated to the sumptuous Trianon Palace Hotel, near the château park. Chef Gérard Vié specializes in creative dishes such as duckling roasted with vinegar and honey. The great style that reigns here can be experienced less expensively by coming for the fixed-price (260 frs) weekday lunch. *1 blvd. de la Reine, tel. 16/39–50–13–21. Reservations essential. Jacket and tie required. AE, DC, MC, V. Closed Sun., Mon., and Aug.* $$$$

Quai No. 1. Barometers, sails, and model boats contribute to the nautical decor at this small, charming fish and seafood restaurant. During the warm summer months, you can relax on their open terrace. Home-smoked salmon is a specialty here, though any dish on the two set menus will prove to be a good value. *1 av. de St-Cloud, tel. 16/39–50–42–26. Reservations advised. Dress: casual. MC, V. Closed Sun. evening and Mon.* $$

La Grande Sirène. The addition of an appealing 148-franc lunch menu (wine included) served every day but Sunday makes this pretty spot near the château a popular noontime choice. Zesty simmered snails and well-prepared fish are good options here. *25 rue du Maréchal-Foch, tel. 16/39–53–08–08. Reservations advised. Dress: casual. AE, MC, V. Closed Mon.* $$

Conversion Tables

Distance

Kilometers/Miles To change kilometers to miles, multiply kilometers by .621.
To change miles to kilometers, multiply miles by 1.61.

Km to Mi	Mi to Km
1 = .62	1 = 1.6
2 = 1.2	2 = 3.2
3 = 1.9	3 = 4.8
4 = 2.5	4 = 6.4
5 = 3.1	5 = 8.1
6 = 3.7	6 = 9.7
7 = 4.3	7 = 11.3
8 = 5.0	8 = 12.9
9 = 5.6	9 = 14.5

Meters/Feet To change meters to feet, multiply meters by 3.28.
To change feet to meters, multiply feet by .305.

Meters to Feet	Feet to Meters
1 = 3.3	1 = .31
2 = 6.6	2 = .61
3 = 9.8	3 = .92
4 = 13.1	4 = 1.2
5 = 16.4	5 = 1.5
6 = 19.7	6 = 1.8
7 = 23.0	7 = 2.1
8 = 26.2	8 = 2.4
9 = 29.5	9 = 2.7

Weight

Kilograms/Pounds To change kilograms to pounds, multiply kilos by 2.20.
To change pounds to kilograms, multiply pounds by .453.

Kilo to Pound	Pound to Kilo
1 = 2.2	1 = .45
2 = 4.4	2 = .91
3 = 6.6	3 = 1.4
4 = 8.8	4 = 1.8
5 = 11.0	5 = 2.3

6 = 13.2		6 = 2.7	
7 = 15.4		7 = 3.2	
8 = 17.6		8 = 3.6	
9 = 19.8		9 = 4.1	

Grams/Ounces   To change grams to ounces, multiply grams by .035.
To change ounces to grams, multiply ounces by 28.4.

Grams to Ounces	Ounces to Grams
1 = .04	1 = 28
2 = .07	2 = 57
3 = .11	3 = 85
4 = .14	4 = 114
5 = .18	5 = 142
6 = .21	6 = 170
7 = .25	7 = 199
8 = .28	8 = 227
9 = .32	9 = 256

Liquid Volume

Liters/U.S. Gallons   To change liters to U.S. gallons, multiply liters by .264.
To change U.S. gallons to liters, multiply gallons by 3.79.

Liters to U.S. Gallons	U.S. Gallons to Liters
1 = .26	1 = 3.8
2 = .53	2 = 7.6
3 = .79	3 = 11.4
4 = 1.1	4 = 15.1
5 = 1.3	5 = 18.9
6 = 1.6	6 = 22.7
7 = 1.8	7 = 26.5
8 = 2.1	8 = 30.3
9 = 2.4	9 = 34.1

Clothing Sizes

Men   To change American suit sizes to French suit sizes, add 10 to
Suits   the American suit size.
To change French suit sizes to American suit sizes, subtract 10
from the French suit size.

U.S.	36	38	40	42	44	46	48
French	46	48	50	52	54	56	58

Shirts   To change American shirt sizes to French shirt sizes, multiply
the American shirt size by 2 and add 8.

To change French shirt sizes to American shirt sizes, subtract 8 from the French shirt size and divide by 2.

U.S.	14	14½	15	15½	16	16½	17	17½
French	36	37	38	39	40	41	42	43

Shoes French shoe sizes vary in their relation to American shoe sizes.

U.S.	6½	7	8	9	10	10½	11
French	39	40	41	42	43	44	45

Women
Dresses and Coats To change U.S. dress/coat sizes to French dress/coat sizes, add 28 to the U.S. dress/coat size.
To change French dress/coat sizes to U.S. dress/coat sizes, subtract 28 from the French dress/coat size.

U.S.	4	6	8	10	12	14	16
French	32	34	36	38	40	42	44

Blouses and Sweaters To change U.S. blouse/sweater sizes to French blouse/sweater sizes, add 8 to the U.S. blouse/sweater size.
To change French blouse/sweater sizes to U.S. blouse/sweater sizes, subtract 8 from the French blouse/sweater size.

U.S.	30	32	34	36	38	40	42
French	38	40	42	44	46	48	50

Shoes To change U.S. shoe sizes to French shoe sizes, add 32 to the U.S. shoe size.
To change French shoe sizes to U.S. shoe sizes, subtract 32 from the French shoe size.

U.S.	4	5	6	7	8	9	10
French	36	37	38	39	40	41	42

French Vocabulary

Words and Phrases

	English	*French*	*Pronunciation*
Basics	Yes/no	Oui/non	wee/no
	Please	S'il vous plaît	seel voo play
	Thank you	Merci	mare-**see**
	You're welcome	De rien	deh ree-**en**
	That's all right	Il n'y a pas de quoi	eel nee ah pah de kwa
	Excuse me, sorry	Pardon	pahr-**doan**
	Sorry!	Désolé(e)	day-zoh-**lay**
	Good morning/afternoon	Bonjour	bone-**joor**
	Good evening	Bonsoir	bone-**swar**
	Goodbye	Au revoir	o ruh-**vwar**
	Mr. (Sir)	Monsieur	mih-see-**oor**
	Mrs. (Ma'am)	Madame	ma-**dam**
	Miss	Mademoiselle	mad-mwa-**zel**
	Pleased to meet you	Enchanté(e)	on-shahn-**tay**
	How are you?	Comment allez-vous?	ko-mon-tahl-ay-**voo**
	Very well, thanks	Très bien, merci	tray bee-**en**, mare-**see**
	And you?	Et vous?	ay voo?
Numbers	one	un	un
	two	deux	deu
	three	trois	twa
	four	quatre	**cat**-ruh
	five	cinq	sank
	six	six	seess
	seven	sept	set
	eight	huit	wheat
	nine	neuf	nuf
	ten	dix	deess
	eleven	onze	owns
	twelve	douze	dooz
	thirteen	treize	trays
	fourteen	quatorze	ka-torz
	fifteen	quinze	cans
	sixteen	seize	sez
	seventeen	dix-sept	deess-**set**
	eighteen	dix-huit	deess-**wheat**
	nineteen	dix-neuf	deess-**nuf**
	twenty	vingt	vant
	twenty-one	vingt-et-un	vant-ay-**un**
	thirty	trente	trahnt
	forty	quarante	**ka**-rahnt
	fifty	cinquante	**sang**-kahnt
	sixty	soixante	**swa**-sahnt
	seventy	soixante-dix	swa-sahnt-**deess**
	eighty	quatre-vingts	cat-ruh-**vant**
	ninety	quatre-vingt-dix	cat-ruh-vant-**deess**

| | one-hundred | cent | sahnt |
| | one-thousand | mille | meel |

Colors	black	noir	nwar
	blue	bleu	blu
	brown	brun	brun
	green	vert	vair
	orange	orange	o-**ranj**
	pink	rose	rose
	red	rouge	rouge
	violet	violette	vee-o-**let**
	white	blanc	blahnk
	yellow	jaune	jone

Days of the Week	Sunday	dimanche	dee-**mahnsh**
	Monday	lundi	lan-**dee**
	Tuesday	mardi	mar-**dee**
	Wednesday	mercredi	mare-kruh-**dee**
	Thursday	jeudi	juh-**dee**
	Friday	vendredi	van-dra-**dee**
	Saturday	samedi	sam-**dee**

Months	January	janvier	jan-**vyay**
	February	février	feh-vree-**ay**
	March	mars	maars
	April	avril	a-**vreel**
	May	mai	meh
	June	juin	jwan
	July	juillet	jwee-**ay**
	August	août	oot
	September	septembre	sep-**tahm**-bruh
	October	octobre	ok-**toe**-bruh
	November	novembre	no-**vahm**-bruh
	December	décembre	day-**sahm**-bruh

Useful Phrases	Do you speak English?	Parlez-vous anglais?	par-lay vooz ahng-**glay**
	I don't speak French	Je ne parle pas français	jeh nuh parl pah fraun-**say**
	I don't understand	Je ne comprends pas	jeh nuh kohm-prahn **pah**
	I understand	Je comprends	jeh kohm-**prahn**
	I don't know	Je ne sais pas	jeh nuh say **pah**
	I'm American/British	Je suis américain/anglais	jeh sweez a-may-ree-**can**/ahng-**glay**
	What's your name?	Comment vous appelez-vous?	ko-mahn voo za-pel-ay-**voo**
	My name is . . .	Je m'appelle . . .	jeh ma-**pel** . . .
	What time is it?	Quelle heure est-il?	kel ur et-**il**
	How?	Comment?	ko-**mahn**
	When?	Quand?	kahn
	Yesterday	Hier	yair
	Today	Aujourd'hui	o-zhoor-**dwee**

Tomorrow	Demain	deh-**man**
This morning/ afternoon	Ce matin/cet après-midi	seh ma-**tanh**/set ah-pray-mee-**dee**
Tonight	Ce soir	seh **swar**
What?	Quoi?	kwa
What is it?	Qu'est-ce que c'est?	kess-kuh-**say**
Why?	Pourquoi?	poor-**kwa**
Who?	Qui?	kee
Where is . . .	Où est . . .	oo ay
the train station?	la gare?	la gar
the subway station?	la station de métro?	la sta-syon deh may-**tro**
the bus stop?	l'arrêt de bus?	la-ray deh **booss**
the terminal (airport)?	l'aérogare?	lay-ro-**gar**
the post office?	la poste?	la post
the bank?	la banque?	la bahnk
the . . . hotel?	l'hôtel . . .?	low-**tel**
the store?	le magasin?	luh ma-ga-**zan**
the cashier?	la caisse?	la **kess**
the . . . museum?	le musée . . .?	leh mew-**zay**
the hospital?	l'hôpital?	low-pee-**tal**
the elevator?	l'ascenseur?	la-sahn-**seur**
the telephone?	le téléphone?	leh te-le-**phone**
Where are the restrooms?	Où sont les toilettes?	oo son lay twah-**let**
Here/there	Ici/là	ee-**see**/la
Left/right	A gauche/à droite	a goash/a drwat
Straight ahead	Tout droit	too drwa
Is it near/far?	C'est près/loin?	say pray/lwan
I'd like . . .	Je voudrais . . .	jeh voo-**dray**
a room	une chambre	ewn **shahm**-bra
the key	la clé	la clay
a newspaper	un journal	un joor-**nahl**
a stamp	un timbre	un **tam**-bruh
I'd like to buy . . .	Je voudrais acheter . . .	jeh voo-**dray** ash-**tay**
a cigar	un cigare	un see-**gar**
cigarettes	des cigarettes	day see-ga-**ret**
matches	des allumettes	days a-loo-**met**
dictionary	un dictionnaire	un deek-see-oh-**nare**
soap	du savon	dew sa-vone
city plan	un plan de ville	un plahn de **veel**
road map	une carte routière	ewn cart roo-tee-**air**
magazine	une revue	ewn reh-**view**
envelopes	des enveloppes	dayz ahn-veh-**lope**
writing paper	du papier à lettres	dew pa-pee-ay a **let**-ruh

airmail writing paper	du papier avion	dew pa-pee-ay a-vee-**own**
postcard	une carte postale	ewn cart post-**al**
How much is it?	C'est combien?	say comb-bee-**en**
It's expensive/ cheap	C'est cher/pas cher	say sher/pa sher
A little/a lot	Un peu/beaucoup	un puh/bo-**koo**
More/less	Plus/moins	ploo/mwa
Enough/too (much)	Assez/trop	a-**say**/tro
I am ill/sick	Je suis malade	jeh swee ma-**lahd**
Call a doctor	Appelez un médecin	a-pe-lay un med-**san**
Help!	Au secours!	o say-**koor**
Stop!	Arrêtez!	a-reh-**tay**
Fire!	Au feu!	o fuw
Caution!/Look out!	Attention!	a-tahn-see-**own**

Dining Out	A bottle of . . .	une bouteille de . . .	ewn boo-**tay** deh
	A cup of . . .	une tasse de . . .	ewn tass deh
	A glass of . . .	un verre de . . .	un vair deh
	Ashtray	un cendrier	un sahn-dree-**ay**
	Bill/check	l'addition	la-dee-see-**own**
	Bread	du pain	dew pan
	Breakfast	le petit-déjeuner	leh pet-**ee** day-zhu-**nay**
	Butter	du beurre	dew bur
	Cheers!	A votre santé!	ah vo-truh sahn-**tay**
	Cocktail/aperitif	un apéritif	un ah-pay-ree-**teef**
	Dinner	le dîner	leh dee-**nay**
	Dish of the day	le plat du jour	leh pla do **zhoor**
	Enjoy!	Bon appétit!	bone a-pay-**tee**
	Fixed-price menu	le menu	leh may-**new**
	Fork	une fourchette	ewn four-**shet**
	I am diabetic	Je suis diabétique	jeh swee-dee-ah-bay-**teek**
	I am on a diet	Je suis au régime	jeh sweez o ray-**jeem**
	I am vegetarian	Je suis végétarien(ne)	jeh swee vay-jay-ta-ree-**en**
	I cannot eat . . .	Je ne peux pas manger de . . .	jeh nuh puh pah mahn-**jay** deh
	I'd like to order	Je voudrais commander	jeh voo-**dray** ko-mahn-**day**

I'd like . . .	Je voudrais . . .	jeh voo-**dray**
I'm hungry/thirsty	J'ai faim/soif	jay fam/swahf
Is service/the tip included?	Est-ce que le service est compris?	ess keh leh sair-veess ay comb-**pree**
It's good/bad	C'est bon/mauvais	say bon/mo-**vay**
It's hot/cold	C'est chaud/froid	say sho/frwah
Knife	un couteau	un koo-**toe**
Lunch	le déjeuner	leh day-juh-**nay**
Menu	la carte	la cart
Napkin	une serviette	ewn sair-vee-**et**
Pepper	du poivre	dew **pwah**-vruh
Plate	une assiette	ewn a-see-**et**
Please give me . . .	Donnez-moi . . .	doe-nay-**mwah**
Salt	du sel	dew sell
Spoon	une cuillère	ewn kwee-**air**
Sugar	du sucre	dew **sook**-ruh
Waiter!/Waitress!	Monsieur!/ Mademoiselle!	mih-see-**oor**/ mad-mwah-**zel**
Wine list	la carte des vins	la cart day **van**

Menu Guide

English	French
Set menu	Menu à prix fixe
Dish of the day	Plat du jour
Choice of vegetable accompaniment	Garniture au choix
Made to order	Sur commande
Extra charge	Supplément/En sus
When available	Selon arrivage

Breakfast

Jam	Confiture
Honey	Miel
Boiled egg	Oeuf à la coque
Bacon and eggs	Oeufs au bacon
Ham and eggs	Oeufs au jambon
Fried eggs	Oeufs sur le plat
Scrambled eggs	Oeufs brouillés
(Plain) omelet	Omelette (nature)
Rolls	Petits pains

Starters

Anchovies	Anchois
Chitterling sausage	Andouille(tte)
Assorted cold cuts	Assiette anglaise
Assorted pork products	Assiette de charcuterie
Mixed raw vegetable salad	Crudités
Snails	Escargots
Assorted appetizers	Hors-d'oeuvres variés
Ham (Bayonne)	Jambon (de Bayonne)
Cured pig's knuckle	Jambonneau
Bologna sausage	Mortadelle
Deviled eggs	Oeufs à la diable
Liver purée blended with other meat	Pâté
Light dumplings (fish, fowl, or meat)	Quenelles
Dried sausage	Saucisson
Pâté sliced and served from an earthenware pot	Terrine
Cured dried beef	Viande séchée

Salads

Diced vegetable salad	Salade russe
Endive salad	Salade d'endives
Green salad	Salade verte
Mixed salad	Salade panachée
Riviera combination salad	Salade niçoise
Tuna salad	Salade de thon

Soups

Cold leek and potato cream soup	Vichyssoise
Cream of . . .	Crême de . . .
Cream of . . .	Velouté de . . .

Hearty soup	Soupe
day's soup	*du jour*
French onion soup	*à l'oignon*
Provençal vegetable soup	*au pistou*
Light soup	Potage
shredded vegetables	*julienne*
potato	*parmentier*
Fish and seafood stew	Bouillabaisse
Seafood stew (chowder)	Bisque
Stew of meat and vegetables	Pot-au-feu

Fish and Seafood

Angler	Lotte de mer
Bass	Bar
Burbot	Lotte
Carp	Carpe
Catfish	Loup
Clams	Palourdes
Cod	Morue
Creamed salt cod	Brandade de morue
Fresh cod	Cabillaud
Crab	Crabe
Crayfish	Ecrevisses
Eel	Anguille
Fish stew from Marseilles	Bourride
Fish stew in wine	Matelote
Frogs' legs	Cuisses de grenouilles
Herring	Harengs
Lobster	Homard
Spiny lobster	Langouste
Mackerel	Maquereau
Mussels	Moules
Octopus	Poulpes
Oysters	Huîtres
Perch	Perche
Pike	Brochet
Prawns	Ecrevisses
Dublin bay prawns (scampi)	Langoustines
Red mullet	Rouget
Salmon	Saumon
Scallops in creamy sauce	Coquille St-Jacques
Sea bream	Daurade
Shrimp	Crevettes
Skate	Raie
Smelt	Eperlans
Sole	Sole
Squid	Calmar
Trout	Truite
Tuna	Thon
Whiting	Merlan
Fish used in bouillabaisse	Rascasse

Meat

Beef	Boeuf
Brains	Cervelle
Chops	Côtelettes
Cutlet	Escalope
Fillet steak	Filet

Double fillet steak	Chateaubriand
Kabob	Brochette
Kidneys	Rognons
Lamb	Agneau
Leg	Gigot
Liver	Foie
Loin strip steak	Contre-filet
Meatballs	Boulettes de viande
Pig's feet	Pieds de cochon
Pork	Porc
Rib	Côte
Rib or rib-eye steak	Entrecôte
Saddle	Selle
Sausages	Saucisses
Sausages and cured pork served with sauerkraut	Choucroute garnie
Shoulder	Epaule
Steak (always beef)	Steak/steack
Stew	Ragoût
T-bone steak	Côte de boeuf
Tenderloin steak	Médaillon
Tenderloin of T-bone steak	Tournedos
Tongue	Langue
Veal	Veau
Veal sweetbreads	Ris de veau
Casserole of white beans and meat	Cassoulet toulousain

Methods of Preparation

Very rare	Bleu
Rare	Saignant
Medium	A point
Well-done	Bien cuit
Baked	Au four
Boiled	Bouilli
Braised	Braisé
Fried	Frit
Grilled	Grillé
Roast	Rôti
Sautéed	Sauté
Stewed	A l'étouffée

Game and Poultry

Chicken	Poulet
Chicken breast	Suprême de volaille
Chicken stewed in red wine	Coq au vin
Chicken stewed with vegetables	Poule au pot
Spring chicken	Poussin
Duck/duckling	Canard/caneton
Fattened pullet	Poularde
Fowl	Volaille
Guinea fowl/young guinea fowl	Pintade/pintadeau
Goose	Oie
Partridge/young partridge	Perdrix/perdreau
Pheasant	Faisan
Pigeon/squab	Pigeon/pigeonneau
Quail	Caille

Rabbit	Lapin
Thrush	Grive
Turkey/young turkey	Dinde/dindonneau
Venison (red/roe)	Cerf/chevreuil
Wild boar/young wild boar	Sanglier/marcassin
Wild hare	Lièvre

Vegetables

Artichoke	Artichaut
Asparagus	Asperge
Broad beans	Fèves
Brussels sprouts	Choux de Bruxelles
Cabbage (red)	Chou (rouge)
Carrots	Carottes
Cauliflower	Chou-fleur
Chicory	Chicorée
Eggplant	Aubergine
Endive	Endive
Leeks	Poireaux
Lentils	Lentilles
Lettuce	Laitue
Mushrooms	Champignons
Onions	Oignons
Peas	Petits pois
Peppers	Poivrons
Potato	Pomme de terre
Radishes	Radis
Spinach	Epinard
Tomatoes	Tomates
Watercress	Cresson
Zucchini	Courgette
White kidney/French beans	Haricots blancs/verts

Potatoes, Rice, and Noodles

Noodles	Nouilles
Pasta	Pâtes
Potatoes	Pommes (de terre)
matchsticks	*allumettes*
mashed and deep-fried	*dauphine*
mashed with butter and egg yolks	*duchesse*
in their jackets	*en robe des champs*
french fries	*frites*
mashed	*mousseline*
boiled/steamed	*nature/vapeur*
Rice	Riz
boiled in bouillon with onions	*pilaf*

Sauces and Preparations

Brown butter, parsley, lemon juice	Meunière
Curry	Indienne
Egg yolks, butter, vinegar	Hollandaise
Hot pepper	Diable
Mayonnaise flavored with mustard and herbs	Tartare
Mushrooms	Forestière
Mushrooms, red wine, shallots, beef marrow	Bordelaise

Onions, tomatoes, garlic	Provençale
Pepper sauce	Poivrade
Red wine, herbs	Bourguignon
Vinegar, egg yolks, white wine, shallots, tarragon	Béarnaise
Vinegar dressing	Vinaigrette
White sauce	Béchamel
White wine, mussel broth, egg yolks	Marinière
Wine, mushrooms, onions, shallots	Chasseur
With goose or duck liver purée and truffles	Périgueux
With Madeira wine	Madère

Fruits and Nuts

Almonds	Amandes
Apple	Pomme
Apricot	Abricot
Banana	Banane
Blackberries	Mûres
Blackcurrants	Cassis
Blueberries	Myrtilles
Cherries	Cerises
Chestnuts	Marrons
Coconut	Noix de coco
Dates	Dattes
Dried fruit	Fruits secs
Figs	Figues
Grapefruit	Pamplemousse
Grapes green/blue	Raisins blancs/noirs
Hazelnuts	Noisettes
Lemon	Citron
Lime	Citron vert
Melon	Melon
Nectarine	Brugnon
Orange	Orange
Peach	Pêche
Peanuts	Cacahouètes
Pear	Poire
Pineapple	Ananas
Plums	Prunes
Prunes	Pruneaux
Raisins	Raisins secs
Raspberries	Framboises
Red currants	Groseilles
Strawberries	Fraises
Tangerine	Mandarine
Walnuts	Noix
Watermelon	Pastèque

Desserts

Apple pie	Tarte aux pommes
Caramel pudding	Crème caramel
Chocolate cake	Gâteau au chocolat
Chocolate pudding	Mousse au chocolat
Custard	Flan
Ice cream	Glace
Ice-cream cake	Vacherin glacé

Layer cake	Tourte
Sundae	Coupe (glacée)
Water ice	Sorbet
Whipped cream	Crème Chantilly
Thin pancakes simmered in orange juice and flambéed with orange liqueur	Crêpe suzette

Alcoholic Drinks

Straight	Sec
On the rocks	Avec des glaçons
With water	A l'eau
Apple brandy	Calvados
Beer	Bière
Light/dark	*Blonde/brune*
Brandy	Eau–de–vie
Cocktails	Apéritifs
Chilled white wine mixed with blackcurrant syrup	*Kir/blanc-cassis*
Cherry brandy	Kirsch
Cordial	Liqueur
Pear brandy	Poire William
Port	Porto
Wine	Vin
dry	*sec*
very dry	*brut*
light	*léger*
sweet	*doux*
red	*rouge*
rosé	*rosé*
sparkling	*mousseux*
white	*blanc*

Nonalcoholic Drinks

Coffee	Café
black	*noir*
cream	*crème*
with milk	*au lait*
caffein-free	*décaféiné*
espresso	*express*
Ginger ale	Limonade gazeuse
Herb tea	Tisane
Hot chocolate	Chocolat chaud
Lemonade	Limonade
Milk	Lait
Mineral water	Eau minérale
carbonated	*gazeuse*
still	*non gazeuse*
. . . juice (see fruit)	Jus de . . .
Tea	Thé
with milk/lemon	*crème/citron*
iced tea	*glacé*
Tonic water	Schweppes

Index

Personal Itinerary

Departure *Date*

Time

Transportation

Arrival *Date*   *Time*

Departure *Date*   *Time*

Transportation

Accommodations

Arrival *Date*   *Time*

Departure *Date*   *Time*

Transportation

Accommodations

Arrival *Date*   *Time*

Departure *Date*   *Time*

Transportation

Accommodations

At last — a guide for Americans with disabilities that makes traveling a delight

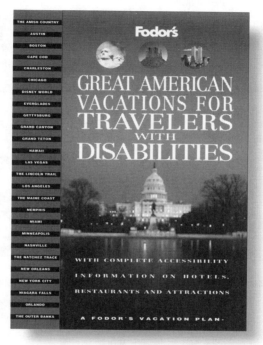

This is the first and only complete guide to great American vacations for the 35 million North Americans with disabilities, as well as for those who care for them or for aging parents and relatives. Provides:

- Essential trip-planning information for travelers with mobility, vision, and hearing impairments

- Specific details on a huge array of facilities, along with solid descriptions of attractions, hotels, restaurants, and other destinations

- Up-to-date information on ISA-designated parking, level entranceways, accessibility to pools, lounges, bathrooms

Fodor's Travel Guides

Available at bookstores everywhere, or call 1–800–533–6478, 24 hours a day.

U.S. Guides

Alaska

Arizona

Boston

California

Cape Cod, Martha's Vineyard, Nantucket

The Carolinas & the Georgia Coast

Chicago

Colorado

Florida

Hawaii

Las Vegas, Reno, Tahoe

Los Angeles

Maine, Vermont, New Hampshire

Maui

Miami & the Keys

New England

New Orleans

New York City

Pacific North Coast

Philadelphia & the Pennsylvania Dutch Country

The Rockies

San Diego

San Francisco

Santa Fe, Taos, Albuquerque

Seattle & Vancouver

The South

The U.S. & British Virgin Islands

USA

The Upper Great Lakes Region

Virginia & Maryland

Waikiki

Walt Disney World and the Orlando Area

Washington, D.C.

Foreign Guides

Acapulco, Ixtapa, Zihuatanejo

Australia & New Zealand

Austria

The Bahamas

Baja & Mexico's Pacific Coast Resorts

Barbados

Berlin

Bermuda

Brittany & Normandy

Budapest

Canada

Cancún, Cozumel, Yucatán Peninsula

Caribbean

China

Costa Rica, Belize, Guatemala

The Czech Republic & Slovakia

Eastern Europe

Egypt

Euro Disney

Europe

Florence, Tuscany & Umbria

France

Germany

Great Britain

Greece

Hong Kong

India

Ireland

Israel

Italy

Japan

Kenya & Tanzania

Korea

London

Madrid & Barcelona

Mexico

Montréal & Québec City

Morocco

Moscow & St. Petersburg

The Netherlands, Belgium & Luxembourg

New Zealand

Norway

Nova Scotia, Prince Edward Island & New Brunswick

Paris

Portugal

Provence & the Riviera

Rome

Russia & the Baltic Countries

Scandinavia

Scotland

Singapore

South America

Southeast Asia

Spain

Sweden

Switzerland

Thailand

Tokyo

Toronto

Turkey

Vienna & the Danube Valley

Special Series

The only guide to explore a Disney World you've never seen before:

The one for grown-ups.

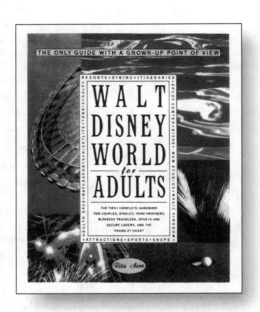

This is the only guide written specifically for the millions of adults who visit Walt Disney World each year <u>without</u> kids. Upscale, sophisticated, packed full of facts and maps, *Walt Disney World for Adults* provides up-to-date information on hotels, restaurants, sports facilities, and health clubs, as well as unique itineraries for adults. With *Walt Disney World for Adults* in hand, you'll get the most out of one of the world's most fascinating, most complex playgrounds.

At bookstores everywhere, or call **1-800-533-6478**.